Empowering Your Students for the 21ˢᵗ Century

Christian LeButt

LEBUTT PUBLISHING, LLC
HIGHLAND, MI

Printed in the United States of America

LeButt, Christian
Empowering Your Students for the 21st Century

Includes bibliographical references

Editing / Proofreading by Lynn DeGrande
Editing / Proofreading by Michelle Guthrie
Editing / Proofreading by Susan Dobson
Editing / Proofreading by Michael LeButt

ISBN 978-0-9882255-4-1

LeButt Publishing, LLC
PO Box 1268
Highland, MI 48357-1268

www.empoweringyourstudents.com

About the Author – Christian LeButt, M.Ed.

Christian LeButt is a teacher who grew up in rural schools and who has taught in an urban school. He now teaches in a suburban school. Early in his career, Christian was recognized as a finalist (top five) for the Michigan Teacher of the Year Award. Also, he served as President and as Assessment Chairman of the Michigan Future Problem Solving Program. He has led a variety of professional development activities for K-12 educators.

His passion, diverse experiences, creativity, and analytical skills have been directed toward the creation of this book, meant to empower educators with the tools to empower their students for the 21st century.

TABLE OF GOALS

1 | A New Challenge will Define Our Future

America and the world are at a turning point. Some people are quite familiar with the immense challenges that face us, while others are just learning about them. A global economy and new technologies are drastically shifting the work world. How American educators handle these issues will define the success of our profession and the lives of our students in the next century. We are about to play a central role in overcoming the challenges of our time. Before we look at what educators will need to do, let's look at the key challenges that lie ahead for our youth. You might want to strap on your seatbelt. The road is about to get bumpy!

Outsourcing and Offshoring

I recently had a global experience when troubleshooting a computer issue using Dell's customer service. When I called for assistance from Michigan, I was connected to a gentleman who told me that he was in India. In order to solve the issue that I was having, he used the Internet to take control of my computer (with my permission). I could see him remotely opening windows and performing functions on my computer desktop while I spoke with him. The experience of talking to someone who was simultaneously controlling my computer from halfway around the world was fascinating. However, the experience demonstrated that modern technology has enabled people from all parts of the world to have access to jobs that Americans have previously held. This transfer of work using the Internet and modern telecommunications is called **outsourcing**.

Many other jobs can be outsourced to foreign workers. In 2005, about 400,000 U.S. tax returns were prepared in India. How did this happen? The tax information was scanned in the U.S. and sent via the Internet to workers who calculated the tax returns and then returned them.[1] The number of U.S. tax returns prepared in India is estimated to grow to 1.6 million by 2011.[2]

What else can be outsourced using modern telecommunications? Workers in foreign countries like India can perform tasks such as selling credit cards, supporting customers with banking problems, helping American troops with computer glitches, and taking reservations for restaurants anywhere in the world. In India, these jobs bring prestige and what is considered to be good pay. From a financial standpoint, a company in the U.S. can offload work to a place

---

[1] (Friedman, 2005, pages 12-13)
[2] (Offshoring Tax Returns Preparation to India, ValueNotes, 2006, page 118)

on the other side of the globe where wages and rent are less than one-fifth of the cost in Western capitals.[3]

While one might think that only lower-skilled jobs are affected, there are examples of higher-skilled job outsourcing. Bill Brody, the president of Johns Hopkins University, reports that the reading of CAT scans from some medium and small American hospitals has been outsourced to physicians in India and Australia.[4] The airplane manufacturer Boeing has the technology to use engineers in Moscow, Russia in addition to its American engineers. Because it is daytime on the other side of the planet while we are sleeping, Russian and American engineers can design in continuous shifts as they share information via the Internet. With a shortage of American aeronautical engineers, this experiment became a necessity that has allowed Boeing to compete with the European airplane manufacturer, Airbus Industries.[5]

If you don't feel somewhat concerned yet, consider the issue of **offshoring**. In this practice, businesses move manual labor / manufacturing to other countries like China. The immensity of offshoring is rather easy to see. Just go to a store and read product labels to see the places where many of the goods are made. We have all encountered products made from all parts of the world, including China. With certain items, we may have difficulty finding any that are made in the U.S.A. Offshoring adds yet another example of displaced workers: *factory workers,* whose employment opportunities are affected by the global economy.

We have looked at some ways in which globalization can affect American physicians, engineers, accountants, service workers, and factory workers. Surely, you can imagine other examples. We are now living in a world where people from many different places can have a hand in the creation of a product or service.

If this new competition hasn't already made you at least a little uneasy, take note of the following: the combined populations of China and India are over eight times larger than that of the U.S.[6] If you consider what globalization has already done to the job market for Americans, imagine what it will be like when the immense populations of China, India, and other emerging economies develop the abilities to do even more of the jobs that our citizens are accustomed to doing. The Chinese and Indian people don't just want the outsourced and offshored work from American and European companies, they want to develop new companies that employ their own citizens in all aspects of creating, designing, producing, and selling a product or service.[7]

Any educator reading this information should be very concerned about the future of America's youth. I know I am. In order for our society to maintain and create American jobs into the future, educators must produce citizens who can compete for, and collaborate in, the creation and design of tomorrow's goods and services. The workforce of the future must be prepared to compete for the same jobs for which billions of people around the world are vying.

---

[3] (Friedman, 2005, pages 15, 18, 23, and 24)
[4] (Friedman, 2005, page 16)
[5] (Friedman, 2005, pages 227-228)
[6] (The World Factbook - Country Comparison: Population, 2012)
[7] (Friedman, 2005, pages 36 and 142)

Efficiency and Automation

Global competition is reshaping our future job market, but even if there were no competition from foreign countries, jobs in America have changed and will continue to change. One major force causing a significant transformation in the workplace is the increased use of **technology and automation to improve productivity**. A simple example is the development of self-checkout systems in retail stores. This technological tool allows customers to scan their own products and pay their bill without a cashier. Instead of hiring enough people to manually check

out all customers, the store owner can hire a small number of people to oversee the self-checkout area. This new type of work requires a slightly different skill set, because the job is to manage the functions of a network of checkout computers. The technology creates a situation where fewer people are needed and the work is more technical.

Automation has changed the face of the workplace, as people in modern factories can now be seen working in concert with machines. As automation technology advances, the role of humans as laborers decreases and changes.

After I finished my undergraduate degree, I had a summer job in a factory that produced aviation parts. Because of advances in technology and automation, I encountered an industrial environment very different from the one experienced by the previous generation. I observed and used many technological tools that created efficiency, but also reduced the number of people necessary to build a product. The skill set I needed to perform a task in the factory was very different from the skill set needed in the past.

New technologies and processes have changed and shifted the types of work and careers available throughout our history. Now, technologies are changing and advancing much more rapidly. Also, the new global economy has added the challenges of offshoring and outsourcing to the mix. Because of these factors, training our youth to work in the jobs of the 21st century becomes even more important.

Embrace the Challenge ... There is No Other Choice

I can imagine arguments both for and against globalization. Some arguments in favor of globalization include getting cheaper goods and services, growing the economies of poor countries, increasing efficiency, growing foreign markets for American goods, and promoting personal and economic freedom. Some arguments against globalization include the loss of jobs to outsourcing and offshoring, the loss of our country's independence in the production of its own goods, and the difficulty we face competing with poorer nations.

Personally, I am a realist. Regardless of how I might view globalization, I am a teacher, and I have no control over globalization. There *is* an Internet. People *do* want cheaper goods and services. People *do* work for lower wages in many other countries. The economies of the world *are* intertwined and will continue to grow even more so. All of these things contribute to the fact that there *is* a global economy whether anyone likes it or dislikes it. Additionally, there will continue to be new technologies and new forms of automation that further shift the job market. As educators, we cannot control these realities. *However, there is something that other educators and I can control… the education of our students.* The goal of this book is to deal with the realities of the world and to prepare our students for those actualities. As educators, we must not let our youth become victims of a global economy, technologies, and automation, but *empower* them to become citizens who thrive within that economy. As people who care so much for our youth, we have no other choice. Let's set out to build a brighter future for our students.

The Skills Our Kids Will Need

Many of the middle class jobs in the last century could be done by workers who could learn processes or tasks and then repeat them. Factory workers needed to replicate tasks in the production of goods. Clerical workers and secretaries needed to learn basic processes and then repeat those processes. Cashiers needed to repeatedly apply basic math skills when dealing with customers. Similar to workers in these jobs, many students have been taught in a manner in which they read or listen to a teacher talk, and then they regurgitate the information on a quiz or test; like the workers who repeat learned processes, students have been educated in a learn-and-repeat system in schools.

The problem in the new economy is that many of the learn-and-repeat jobs of the past are being lost to outsourcing, offshoring, technology, and automation. The types of occupations that are becoming available in the new century rely on a more advanced set of skills (even for those few people who will still work in factories or in such jobs as self-checkout monitors). The jobs that our students will perform require more advanced critical thinking, creativity, collaboration, and people skills. Therefore, we must help our students thrive in this new economy by empowering them with the right skills through the right kind of education. *This will be a new education for a new economy and a new world.*

What skills will our children require in order to successfully meet the needs of employers, customers, clients, and patients in the future? I recently read a collaborative study, performed by The Conference Board, Corporate Voices for Working Families, the Partnership for 21ˢᵗ Century Skills (www.p21.org), and the Society for Human Resource Management, which was titled "Are They Really Ready To Work? Employers' Perspectives on the Basic Knowledge and Applied Skills of New Entrants to the 21ˢᵗ Century Workforce." This study cited a survey of more than 400 employers in the United States. The survey showed that in order to have workplace success, new workers need to go beyond simply having a solid foundation of basic knowledge and skills in reading, writing, math, science, social studies, and language. They need "applied skills," which are the skills that allow a worker to apply his or her basic knowledge for practical purposes. Applied skills include such things as:[8]

---

[8] (Casner-Lotto, 2006, pages 9 and 16)

Job Skills, Attitudes, and Habits Needed

- **Critical Thinking/Problem Solving** - Use sound reasoning and analytical thinking; use information to solve challenges; apply math and science concepts to problem solving.
- **Creativity/Innovation** - Display originality and inventiveness; integrate knowledge.
- **Communications** - Articulate well through speaking and writing.
- **Teamwork/Collaboration** - Collaborate with coworkers and customers; use teamwork; manage conflicts.
- **Diversity** - Work with people of all backgrounds.
- **Leadership** - Promote the strengths of others; coach and develop others.
- **Professionalism/Work Ethic** - Maintain accountability and effective work habits.
- **Ethics/Social Responsibility** - Maintain integrity and ethical behavior; act in community-minded ways.
- **Lifelong Learning/Self-Direction** - Learn new things; monitor own needs; learn from mistakes.
- **Information Technology Application** - Use technology to accomplish tasks and to problem-solve.

Unfortunately, these employers also reported that many new workers do not have the skills they need to be successful.[9]

After researching the changing world and economy, Thomas Friedman describes the skills and attributes that he believes will lead to success in the future workforce in his well-known book, *The World is Flat*. In addition to reinforcing the skills above, he describes some other skills that will also be important for our students:[10]

Additional Job Skills, Attitudes, and Habits Needed

- **Passion and Curiosity** - With these intrinsic qualities, become self-educators and self-motivators.
- **Adaptability and Versatility** - Have a deep set of skills over a range of topics in order to keep a job and also to find new work in a quickly changing work world.
- **Efficiency** - Leverage skills and tools to quickly solve problems and create efficient processes in order to out-compete cheaper foreign workers or new machines.
- **Explaining Skills** - Explain the complexities of a product or process in simple terms to coworkers, customers, clients, or patients.
- **Personalizing Skills** - Add a personal, human touch that cheaper foreign labor or machines might not be able to add.
- **"Green" Skills and Habits** - With rapidly growing economies in India, China, and the former Soviet Republics, the demand for resources and environmental jobs will grow.

---

[9] (Casner-Lotto, 2006, page 10)
[10] (Friedman, 2005, pages 281-309)

Education Must be Updated for a New World

If you look at the list of skills our students will need for success in the new economy, it is obvious that educational techniques must change. The teacher-centered methods, in which children listen and regurgitate, will no longer work in a world where workers no longer learn basic processes and then endlessly repeat those processes. *A new 21ˢᵗ Century Education will require that we go beyond teaching basic core knowledge and skills to also developing the various social, personal, technical, and higher order thinking skills listed above.*

In addition, *a new education needs to address student engagement.* Children will need to be drawn into schools in such a way that they become passionate about learning. At the very least, our youth need to be engaged enough in school to stay in school. Currently, about one-third of students depart high school before they get a diploma![11] How can we possibly prepare them for such a challenging and complex new economy if they are not even in school? Clearly, our plan for a 21ˢᵗ Century Education must address this challenge of student engagement.

A logical question for teachers to ask is how they can teach all of these newly necessary skills in addition to their regular core subject curricula with no additional time to teach new skills. *The key is that educators will have to modify the ways in which student learning, skill practice, concept review, and assessments are performed in order to promote the skills of the 21ˢᵗ century. The development of such things as critical thinking, creativity, teamwork, explaining, adaptability, leadership, information technology, passion, and curiosity will have to be woven into the same activities that develop and assess math, reading, writing, science, social studies, language, health, and arts. Listen-and-regurgitate will no longer cut it.* This book is dedicated to the development of an education that engages all students and builds the skills and habits students need for the future while teaching the core curriculum.

---

[11] (Understanding High School Graduation Rates, 2009)

2 | A New 21st Century Education

As in the 20th century, we still need to get students connected to and engaged in an education that develops a set of core curricular knowledge and skills. However, this core understanding can be used for practical purposes in the 21st century only if it is accompanied by the social, personal, technical, and higher order thinking skills that are relevant to the new economy. In order to draw our students into an education that goes beyond the core curriculum to developing the skills required in the 21st century (discussed in the previous chapter), we will need to do three things very well: *1) Build meaningful connections between students and learning, 2) challenge our students in ways that are relevant to the 21st century, and 3) use a system of thoughtful teaching practices that empower students.* These are the major goals of this book. Let's look at each of them in more detail.

Goal #1

Build a Foundation of Connections (Ch. 3-10)

The first thing we need to do is draw our students into the learning environment and engage them in their education. If we do not create curiosity, a motivation and passion for learning, and a deep desire to be in school, effective learning will not occur. This means we must actively work to connect children to their curriculum, their teachers, their peers, their parents, the environment and spirit of their school, their community, their futures, and the world. Additionally, links must be made between parents and teachers. All of these various connections together will help draw students into learning and help them enjoy school (and at a very minimum, keep older kids from dropping out). *Connections are the foundation upon which a 21st Century Education must be built.* They provide the desire and motivation for students to learn.

For educators, our intuition and our experiences with students show us the importance of promoting student connections. In addition, University of Missouri researchers have shown the importance of connections. Their extensive survey of research titled "Attachment in School" shows that increased school attachment and relationships are associated with higher school achievement (including grades and standardized test scores), greater social and emotional success, improved behavior, and a greater willingness to work on challenging tasks.[12] Through connections, kids can be engaged in learning the core subject curricula and in developing 21st century skills.

The following are the connections upon which the first chapters of this book will focus.

---

[12] (Bergin, 2009, page 141)

Foundation of Connections

Student Connections with the Curriculum (Ch. 3)	Student Connections with Their Futures (Ch. 4)	Student Connections with Their Educators (Ch. 5)	Student Connections with the School Environment (Ch. 6)	Student Connections with Other Students (Ch. 7)	Student Connections with the Spirit of the School (Ch. 8)	Parent Connections (Ch. 9)	Student Connections with the Community and the World (Ch. 10)	Staff Connections with Other Staff (Ch. 10)

Goal #2

21ˢᵗ Century Challenge (Ch. 3 & Ch. 11-17)

Almost every educator hears the buzzwords "challenge" and "rigor" these days. I believe there is a problem with the ways in which these words are commonly used in schools and educational politics. Many people seem to think that there are only three major ways to increase the rigor and challenge of lessons, assessments, curriculum, and classes: 1) make learning activities *longer and more numerous,* 2) gear learning activities toward a *higher ability-level*, and 3) teach students *more information*. There are, however, limits to these methods. While some learning activities might be too short for us to teach or assess a concept or skill, simply doubling the size of the homework for a class does not necessarily mean that the homework will be doubly beneficial. While some young minds are not being challenged to meet their cognitive level, moving tenth grade math to the fifth grade is not age-appropriate for almost all students. While some lessons could be more challenging by adding more information, there is a limit to how many new ideas a brain can reasonably take in at one time and then retain. *In the 21ˢᵗ century, making our classes more challenging does not simply mean that we limit ourselves to the methods of increasing the amount of work, increasing the ability level of lessons, and teaching more information. We must expand our 20ᵗʰ century ideas about what "challenge" and "rigor" mean in order to meet the needs of a new world in the 21ˢᵗ century.* How can we do this? We need to stimulate our students by teaching the curriculum with a *"21ˢᵗ Century Challenge"* that develops the following skills, attitudes, and habits.

While Learning the Curriculum, Develop:				
Ability to Connect the Curriculum to the Real World	*Higher Order Thinking Skills* (includes Critical Thinking, Problem Solving, and Creativity)	*Social and Personal Skills, Attitudes, and Habits*	*Technological and Media Literacy*	*Ability to Learn* (includes Inquiry and Student-Centered Learning)

21ˢᵗ Century Challenge

Let's look at each of these methods of creating a 21st Century Challenge for students.

A) Develop the Ability to Connect the Curriculum to the Real World *(Ch. 3)*

In the new economy that is emerging in the 21st century, there will not be many jobs for people who simply know pieces of information, but there will be jobs for people who can apply and use their knowledge and skills to address real-world situations and problems. To prepare our students, educators should challenge them (through lessons and assessments) to develop an understanding of the real-world value and uses of curricular knowledge and skills (rather than simply learning information). This will allow our youth to be much more prepared to meet the needs of the 21st century work world when they grow into adulthood. Challenging students to develop connections between the real world and the curriculum provides the students with a 21st Century Challenge. Where in this book will this be addressed?

Ability to Connect the Curriculum to the Real World
Connecting the Curriculum to the Real World: *Ch. 3*
(Chapter 3 will serve double-duty, because it challenges students to make real-world connections with the curriculum while developing a motivating foundation of student connections to learning.)

B) Develop Higher Order Thinking Skills That Are Useful in the Future *(Ch. 11-13)*

Another idea for challenging students in 21st century schools is to shift students toward higher order thinking. These are essential skills in a global economy. To better understand higher order thinking skills, let's consider Bloom's taxonomy, a hierarchy of thinking skills. This taxonomy organizes cognitive skills from the lowest level of thinking complexity to the highest level. Originally developed in the 1950s, Bloom's taxonomy was recently revised. This revision was published in "A Taxonomy for Learning, Teaching, and Assessing: A Revision of Bloom's Taxonomy of Educational Objectives" and is shown below.[13]

Remember	Understand	Apply	Analyze	Evaluate	Create

Lowest Level Thinking   →   **Highest Level Thinking**

Students can build upon the lowest levels of skills, such as remembering and understanding, toward higher-level skills, such as analyzing, evaluating, and creating. Notice that many educational assessments reflect the lowest levels of understanding:

---

[13] (Anderson, 2001, pages 5 and 28)

remembering information and understanding a process. We have already seen, in the previous chapter, that in order for students to be prepared for the new economy, they must have skills in problem solving, creativity, and complex decision making. Rather than challenging our students by simply asking them to memorize and regurgitate infinite facts and processes, we need to challenge them by pushing them into higher levels of thinking as they learn the curriculum. By stimulating the development of higher order thinking skills within the teaching of our curricula, we provide students with a 21st Century Challenge.

> ### *Higher Order Thinking Skills*
> - **Critical Thinking and Analysis**: *Ch. 11*
> - **Real World Actions** such as Problem Solving: *Ch. 12*
> - **Creativity**: *Ch.13*

C) Develop 21st Century Social and Personal Skills, Attitudes, and Habits *(Ch. 14 & 15)*

In the new economy, adults need to be able to continuously learn, adapt, interact, explain, compete, use technology, self-motivate, and work in teams. We will clearly need to promote a variety of personal and social skills, attitudes, and habits that will allow our youth to be prepared. By weaving these skills within our core curriculum, we can further challenge students in a manner relevant to the 21st century. There will be some chapters that will look at how we can challenge our students in the development of these skills, attitudes, and habits. By embedding the development of these skills within our curricular lessons, we provide a 21st Century Challenge for our students.

> ### *Social and Personal Skills, Attitudes, and Habits*
> - **Understanding and Interacting with Others**: Understanding What Makes People Tick, Communication and Social Skills, Collaborating in Teamwork, Understanding Language and Culture, and Explaining: *Ch. 14*
> - **Personal Skills**: Proper Work Ethic, Ability to Adapt to Change, Ability to Compete, Stress Management Skills, and Organization and Efficiency: *Ch. 15*

D) Develop 21st Century Technological and Media Literacy *(Ch. 16)*

In the 21st century, students need to understand how to use technology for practical purposes in the workplace and personal life, recognize and avoid the potential dangers and pitfalls created by modern technology, and assess information that is found using the Internet. Adding technological elements to our teaching of the curriculum allows us to provide a 21st Century Challenge.

21st Century Technological and Media Literacy
- **Technological and Media Literacy:** *Ch. 16*

E) Develop the Ability to Learn (includes Inquiry and Student-Centered Learning) *(Ch. 17)*

    In an ever-changing global economy in which adults increasingly need to develop new skills over their lifetime, the ability to learn is amazingly important. To prepare our students for this world, we must guide them as they develop the ability to construct new understanding and skills, both independently and with others. They need to be ready for an adult life where there isn't always a teacher nearby with an answer to every question. Because of this reality, it is ideal for education to shift from teacher-centered to student-centered learning of the curriculum. We should not walk into classrooms and see youngsters staring at and listening to an exhausted teacher. Instead, students should reflect upon prior knowledge and use predictions in an attempt to build new curricular knowledge. With this strategy, kids will be inherently more challenged than if they simply sit still and soak up information as a teacher speaks. This type of 21st Century Challenge helps students learn how to learn.

Learning How to Learn
- **Learning How to Learn:** *Ch. 17*
- **Inquiry-Based and Student-Centered Learning:** *Common Theme in Many Chapters*

Summarizing Goal #2: 21st Century Challenge

    There are some things that we might teach in any given day that we know students will use repeatedly in their lives. There are also some things required by our curricula that we think students might not encounter very often in real life. Regardless of our perception of the real-life value of any given curricular idea, we should be sure of one thing each and every day ... the manner in which our students learn and the manner in which our classrooms function must work to promote real-life skills, regardless of what curricular idea is taught. I am in *no way* suggesting that we do not teach the curriculum or that we skimp on its content. Instead, we need to teach the curriculum in a more enriching way that promotes the development of real-life skills. The old way of thinking about rigor in education allows us to challenge our kids in only a few ways:

increasing the amount of work, increasing the ability level of lessons, and teaching more information. By adding a 21st Century Challenge to our idea of rigor, the possibilities for stimulating and growing the minds of our youth are limitless.

In sum, a modern day challenge for students should go beyond the methods of the past and stimulate kids to develop connections between the curriculum and the real world; develop higher order thinking skills; develop personal and social skills, attitudes, and habits; develop 21st century technology skills; and develop learning skills through inquiry and student-centered activities. These goals comprise an appropriate 21st century manner of challenging students while teaching the core curriculum.

While Learning the Curriculum, Develop:					21st Century Challenge
Ability to Connect the Curriculum to the Real World	*Higher Order Thinking Skills* (includes Critical Thinking, Problem Solving, and Creativity)	*Social and Personal Skills, Attitudes, and Habits*	*Technological and Media Literacy*	*Ability to Learn* (includes Inquiry and Student-Centered Learning)	

Putting Together Goals #1 and #2

Goal #1 of this book is to lay a foundation of connections in order to engage students in learning the curriculum. Goal #2 is to teach the curriculum using a 21st Century Challenge that will prepare our children with the skills and attitudes that will allow them to thrive in the new economy. On the following pages is a diagram that puts together the pieces of these goals.

Empowering Your Students for the 21st Century:
Building Blocks of a 21st Century Education

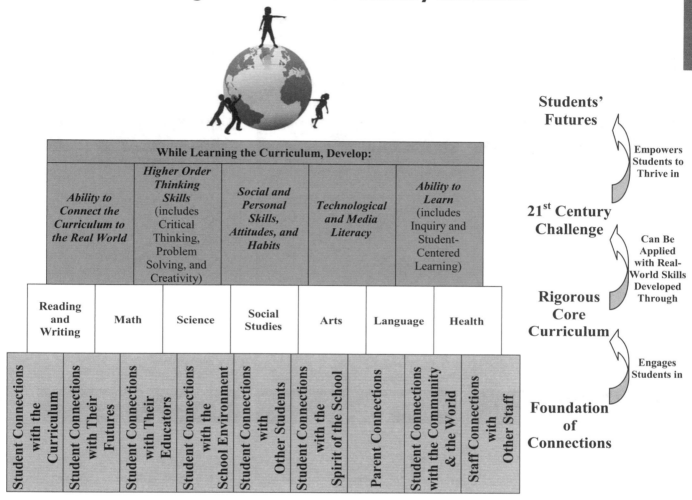

Reading from the foundation upward, we should see a 21st Century Education in which:

- **A foundation of connections engages students in a rigorous core curriculum.**
- **A rigorous core curriculum can be applied with real-world skills developed through a 21st Century Challenge.**
- **A 21st Century Challenge empowers students to thrive in their futures.**

The Building Blocks of a 21st Century Education that are shown above must drive what we do each and every day. If not, our youth will not be prepared for the world that awaits them. Therefore, we should always keep this diagram in mind when planning and educating. These will be our goals moving forward: to teach our curriculum in such a way that young minds not only learn facts and processes, but learn these things in a manner that will prepare and empower them for the future.

Empowering Your Students for the 21ˢᵗ Century:

Student Connections with the Curriculum *Ch. 3*	Student Connections with Their Futures *Ch. 4*	Student Connections with Their Educators *Ch. 5*	Student Connections with the School Environment *Ch. 6*	Student Connections with Other Students *Ch. 7*	Student Connections with the Spirit of the School *Ch. 8*	Parent Connections *Ch. 9*	Student Connections with the Community & the World *Ch. 10*	Staff Connections with Other Staff *Ch. 10*

Foundation of Connections

3 — Student Connections with the Curriculum

1. Looking for Answers (Engaging Through Inquiry)
2. Connecting the Curriculum to Everyday Life
3. Performing Real-Life (Authentic) Tasks that will be Useful in the Future
4. Developing Insights and Opinions about Real-World Issues
5. Imagining the Future World
6. Integrating New Learning with Prior Knowledge and Skills
7. Finding Cross-Curricular Connections
8. Creating Products and Models Related to the Content
9. Becoming the Content

4 — Student Connections with Their Futures

1. Learning About the New Economy
2. Learning which Skills, Attitudes, and Habits are Necessary for Future Success
3. Discovering Interests and Passions that Could Lead to Future Careers

5 — Student Connections with Their Educators

Educator-Focused Techniques
Showing Your …
1. Human Side
2. Passion and Excitement for Teaching
3. Fun Side
4. Positivity
5. Humility
6. Trustworthiness
   Student-Focused Techniques
Showing That You …
1. Care About Them
2. Notice Them
3. Respect Them
4. Like Them
5. Believe in Them
6. Appreciate Them
7. Are Helping Them
8. Support Them
9. Trust Them with Responsibility

6 — Student Connections with the School Environment

Creating an Environment that is …
1. Welcoming
2. Safe
3. Responsible
4. Successful
5. Distraction-Free
6. Goal-Oriented
7. Empowering
8. Team-Oriented
9. Fun and Exciting
10. Technological
11. Curious
12. Aesthetically Pleasing
13. Disciplined (through Proactivity, Respect, Communication, Follow-Through, Consistency, and Buy-in)

7 — Student Connections with Other Students

Creating Peer Connections
Inside the Classroom
1. Meeting New People
2. Developing Familiarity
3. Promoting Positive Student Interactions
   Creating Peer Connections
   Outside the Classroom
1. Getting Students Involved
2. Using Activities with the Specific Goal of Developing Connections

8 — Student Connections with the Spirit of the School

1. Creating a Team Feeling within the School
2. Promoting Participation in School Activities
3. Making School Successes a Big Deal
4. Creating Activities Specifically to Promote School Spirit
5. Showing Your (Teacher) Spirit
6. Encouraging Student Leaders to Promote Spirit
7. Creating a Physical Environment that Stimulates Spirit

9 — Parent Connections

Connecting Parents with …
1. The Teachers / School Staff
2. Their Children's Futures
3. The Curriculum
4. Their Children
5. Their Parent Peers
6. The Environment and Spirit of the School

10 — Other Important Connections

1. Student Connections with the Community
2. Student Connections to the World
3. Connections Among Staff Members

While Learning the Curriculum, Develop:				
Ability to Connect the Curriculum to the Real World *Ch. 3*	**Higher Order Thinking Skills** (includes Critical Thinking, Problem Solving, and Creativity) *Ch. 11-13*	**Social and Personal Skills, Attitudes, and Habits** *Ch. 14-15*	**Technological and Media Literacy** *Ch. 16*	**Ability to Learn** (includes Inquiry and Student-Centered Learning) *Ch. 17*

21st Century Challenge

3 Student Connections with the Curriculum

Developing the Ability to Use the Curriculum in the Real World
Chapter 3 not only serves to connect students with the curriculum, but also serves to challenge students to make connections with the information and skills they learn in school.

11 Critical Thinking: Analysis and Assessment

Specific Analytical Skills
1. Making Observations and Inferences
2. Comparing and Contrasting
3. Grouping and Categorizing
4. Understanding Cause and Effect
5. Understanding Sequence and Timing
6. Understanding the Big Picture
7. Identifying Patterns

Complex Assessment (Evaluating) Skills
1. Assessing Accuracy, Validity, or Logic (Informational Literacy)
2. Assessing the Workings of Processes, Events, Strategies, and Solutions
3. Self-Assessing
4. Identifying and Predicting Problems

12 Taking Action: Problem Solving and Other Actions

Basic Strategy for Taking Action (and Solving Problems)
1. Understanding the Task and Goals
2. Planning Your Action
3. Taking Action
4. Assessing Success

13 Creativity in Action

Promoting Creativity by …
1. Developing Creative Mental Pathways in Students (Training Creative Thinking)
2. Empowering Students to Determine and Utilize Their Best Creative Ideas (Training Wise Use of Creative Thoughts)
3. Providing Opportunities for Creativity in the Classroom (Providing Creative Outlets)

14 Understanding and Interacting with Others

1. Understanding What Makes People Tick (Recognizing the Wants, Needs, and Motivations of Others)
2. Communication / Social Skills (Speaking, Listening, Interpreting, Being Tactful, Having Positive Interactions, Developing Relationships, Self-Promoting / Interviewing, etc.)
3. Explaining and Presenting Ideas
4. Collaborating through Teamwork
5. Competing
6. Understanding Language and Culture

15 Personal Skills, Attitudes, and Habits

1. Setting Goals
2. Employing a Proper Work Ethic
3. Adapting, Changing, and being Versatile
4. Managing Stress
5. Being Organized and Efficient
6. Behaving in an Ethical Manner that Shows Integrity
7. Assessing Risks when Making Complex Decisions
8. Being Financially Literate

16 Technological and Media Literacy

1. Using Technology and Media in the Real World (for communication, presentation, organization, research / education, self and team promotion, design, and consumption)
2. Using Informational Literacy Skills to Assess the Accuracy of Content from the Internet and Other Forms of Media
3. Maintaining Safety and Privacy While Using the Internet
4. Recognizing the Future Implications of Internet Usage

17 Learning How to Learn

1. Learning Through Inquiry
2. Activating and Building on Prior Knowledge
3. Constructing the Learning of New Concepts Piece by Piece
4. Using New Learning for Real-World Tasks
5. Making Personal Connections with New Learning
6. Creating Depth of Understanding
7. Summarizing and Simplifying New Concepts
8. Comparing and Contrasting New Concepts
9. Using a Variety of Learning Methods
10. Taking the Time to Fully Process New Ideas
11. Breaking Down New Terminology
12. Learning New Ideas in an Easily Understood Context
13. Staying Focused and Alert when Learning
14. Retaining New Knowledge and Skills
15. Taking Personal Responsibility for Learning
16. Setting Goals and Monitoring One's Progress in Learning
17. Engaging in a Mindset that Leads to Success

Leadership and Motivating Others: A Great Side Effect

The skills developed through the 21st Century Challenge and making connections help students become effective leaders. Students learn higher order thinking, social, personal, technological, and learning skills that can be applied to leadership.

Goal #3

Putting Together the Building Blocks of a 21st Century Education Using a System of Thoughtful Teaching Practices (Ch. 18-21)

It might seem overwhelming to go beyond teaching the school curriculum, to weaving in connections and new 21ˢᵗ Century Challenges … all while looking out for the success of all students. To accomplish this, we will look at how to effectively and realistically meet the demands of a new 21st Century Education. This will include the development of a system of thoughtful teaching practices that include appropriate planning, assessment, remediation, and knowledge and skill retention. These four actions will allow us to successfully put together our building blocks of a modern education and empower our students.

> ### *Putting Together the Building Blocks of a 21ˢᵗ Century Education Using a System of Thoughtful Teaching Practices*
>
> - **Effectively Planning to Empower 21ˢᵗ Century Students:** Goal-oriented and long-term planning: *Ch. 18*
> - **Using Assessments to Empower 21ˢᵗ Century Students:** Using assessments (summative and formative) to promote learning: *Ch. 19*
> - **Using Interventions / Remediation to Empower 21ˢᵗ Century Students:** Systematic proactive, immediate, short-term, and long-term interventions: *Ch. 20*
> - **Promoting Knowledge and Skill Retention to Empower 21ˢᵗ Century Students:** Teaching to understand *and* remember: *Ch. 21*

By addressing the three major goals of this book, we will be able to develop student connections, promote a 21ˢᵗ Century Challenge, and use the thoughtful teaching practices above. We will be empowered to have the following daily thoughts and carry out those thoughts for the benefit of our students.

18	Effectively Planning to Empower 21st Century Students

1. Goal-Oriented Planning
2. Long-Term Planning

19	Using Assessments to Empower 21st Century Students

1. Using Assessments as Formative Tools (that provide feedback, identify misconceptions, guide interventions, stimulate student reflection, and drive further instruction)
2. Using Data from Assessments to Improve Future Teaching Strategies
3. Using Proficiency-Based Assessments
4. Using Assessments to Develop Student Awareness of Learning Progression
5. Using Assessments to Reinforce the Real-World Value of the Curriculum
6. Using Assessments as Learning Activities
7. Challenging Students at All Levels of Understanding in Assessments
8. Using Range-Line Rubrics to Provide Empowering Feedback

20	Using Interventions / Remediation to Empower 21st Century Students

1. Immediate Interventions (Performed as students learn)
2. Short-Term Interventions (Performed within the days and weeks following the intended learning)
3. Long-Term Interventions (Performed when students are months or more behind the intended pace of learning)
4. Proactive Interventions (Performed before the intended learning takes place)

21	Promoting Knowledge and Skill Retention to Empower 21st Century Students

<u>Promoting Lasting Long-Term Memory *In the Process of Learning*</u>
The concepts that improve the ability to "learn how to learn" from Ch. 17 also help students retain knowledge and skills *as they learn.*
<u>Promoting Lasting Long-Term Memory *After the Learning Occurs*</u>
Ch. 21 focuses on strategies for promoting knowledge and skill retention in the weeks and months after learning occurs:
1. Continuously Connecting Old Concepts to New Concepts
2. Continuously Using Review Activities Throughout a School Year
3. Using Proficiency-Based Long-Term Review Assessments
4. Using the Summer

Putting Together the Building Blocks of a 21st Century Education (Using a System of Thoughtful Teaching Practices)

Empowering Students for the 21ˢᵗ Century:

 ## Daily Thoughts for Educators

Before Teaching

Today, how can I promote <u>student connections</u> with:

- **The curriculum** (to engage students with passion and curiosity)?
- **Their futures?**
- **Me and other staff?**
- **The school environment?**

- **Other students?**
- **School spirit?**
- **Their parents?**
- **The community and the world?** (Ch. 3-10)

Today, how can I teach the curriculum so that my students experience a <u>21ˢᵗ Century Challenge</u> that develops:

- **The ability to connect the curriculum to the real world?**
- **Higher order thinking skills** (critical thinking, problem solving, and creativity)?
- **21ˢᵗ century social and personal skills, attitudes, and habits?**

- **21ˢᵗ century technological and media literacy?**
- **The ability to learn** (including inquiry and student-centered learning)? (Ch. 3 & 11-17)

Today, how can I empower students through <u>thoughtful teaching practices</u>, such as:

- **Planning in a goal-oriented manner?**
- **Using assessments to promote learning** (both summative and formative)?
- **Using systematic intervention and remediation?**

- **Promoting knowledge and skill retention in the short-term and long-term? (Ch. 18-21)**

After Teaching

- **How effective was I in reaching my goals above?**
- **What things worked today and in this unit, and what could I improve in the future?**
- **In what ways was it worthwhile to be a member of my class today?**
- **Did I teach students today, or did I empower students today?**
- **At the end of the day, I should be able to say to myself, "Today, my students learned the curriculum in such a way that it can be useful in their futures. But even if they never encounter that core subject material in real life, the students still got something valuable out of my class today, because the manner in which they learned deepened their connections to learning and improved their 21ˢᵗ century skills, attitudes, and habits. They had fun learning and are more empowered for the 21ˢᵗ century!"**

Valuable Extra in This Book

After addressing the three major goals of this book, there is an extra chapter that discusses how a staff can effectively identify and overcome challenges in working toward school improvement.

Making Things Happen
- **Avoiding and Overcoming Obstacles to Creating a New Education:** *Ch. 22*

Key Idea

Realistically Accomplishing the Goals of This Book

Before we begin to look at how we can accomplish the three major goals of this book, we need to consider that there are a couple of obstacles that often keep educators from consistently accomplishing new goals. Let's look at how we can overcome these obstacles.

1. The Challenge of Time and the Solution of "Meshing"

When attempting to work new ideas into our curriculum, we sometimes add these activities on top of what we have already done in the past. This can be frustrating as extra time is needed to do each unit. We might even give up the new cause or idea when it seems unworkable within the time constraints of the year.

We should not attempt to add new lessons and activities to the current workload. What educators should do is analyze the lessons that are already used to see how these lessons can be manipulated to promote student connections and the skills promoted with a 21st Century Challenge. Teachers need to look for ways to weave or *mesh* these things within our teaching of the curriculum, rather than adding completely new lessons on top of our current lessons. With this approach, the need for extra time is minimized. Sometimes we need to simply replace old methods, rather than tweaking those methods.

This book seeks to provide strategies for meshing the skills of the 21st century within the curriculum rather than simply asking you to add them on top of what you already have to do. With the right combination of modified lessons and replacement lessons, we can reasonably interweave the skills necessary for a new age into our classrooms. In addition, our lessons can become more engaging as they become more relevant.

2. The Challenge of Time and the Solution of "Flipping"

The solution of "meshing" described above will allow a teacher the time to *completely* implement the strategies of this book. I did, however, recently learn about an idea that could free up additional class time for even more 21st century classroom activities. The idea is called the "flipped classroom." In this practice, created by Colorado teachers Jonathan Bergmann and Aaron Sams, teachers create online video lessons for students to view. Because students can access the lessons on their own (even at home), teachers can spend class time coaching students who engage in assignments and activities related to the video lessons' content.[14] This freed-up class time would be perfect for promoting the

---

[14] (Bergmann, 2011)

Key Idea

connections and 21ˢᵗ Century Challenge outlined in this book. Thus, the flipped classroom concept and the concepts of "Empowering Your Students for the 21ˢᵗ Century" can work perfectly together, supporting each other. *It is important to note, however, that* **teachers do not need to flip their classrooms to implement the ideas in this book**. *The time-saving solution of "meshing" described above will allow anyone to weave the skills of the 21ˢᵗ century into his or her classroom. I am simply pointing out that the flipped classroom can provide even more time.*

3. The Challenge of Consistency and the Solution of the "Teacher Empowerment Menu" (Avoiding the "Kicks and Drops")

Across the country, one of the most common challenges for educators is that of consistency. As we take college courses and engage in various forms of professional development, we are continuously bombarded with new ideas to be used in the classroom.

This leads to what I call a cycle of "kicks and drops." For example, let's imagine a school where teachers would like to improve their students' reading comprehension. To do this, they do some research and bring in a professional development expert on the topic. They get really excited about implementing and succeeding with new strategies for reading across the curriculum. The staff is on a reading "kick." The next year, however, the school staff might find that their students did not do well on the writing portion of a standardized test. So, the staff gets fired up about a new topic, promoting writing across the curriculum. This is their new "kick" … for the second year. During the third year, the members of the school move on to a new focus of promoting parental involvement … another new "kick." Then, the fourth year brings yet another new "kick" dealing with yet another topic. Years later, the original focus and excitement on reading skills and writing skills has likely been dramatically reduced, if not forgotten. Over the course of these years, the staff members have gotten on a lot of "kicks" that were later "dropped" or diminished in importance. Thus, I like to call this a series of "kicks and drops."

There is a major problem with this cycle of events: each new major focus gets so much immediate attention that it couldn't possibly be sustained. Meanwhile, other important issues don't get the proper attention they need. This leads to a system in which schools repetitively overemphasize some things while underemphasizing others. Instead, schools need to have a clear view of all important issues and address those issues on a more reasonable and consistent basis. (It's not that the educators are doing something wrong. In fact, they are very passionate about taking on new practices for improvement. The difficulty is that it is challenging for educators to sustain consistency in all practices as we work to improve.)

This book will utilize a couple of strategies for promoting consistency. First, each topic throughout the book is organized so that you can easily recognize which key strategies need to be performed on a regular basis in 21ˢᵗ century classrooms and schools. Second, this book is accompanied by the "Teacher Empowerment Menu (for 21ˢᵗ Century Educators)." This flip chart has separate sections for each goal that teachers should consider while planning and teaching. Each topic has been broken down into its key ideas. With this "Teacher Empowerment Menu," educators have something they can continuously reference as they plan and teach so that they can be sure to meet all of their objectives with consistency … each and every year. The menu also has space for you to note your ideas for implementing the goals of this book in your particular teaching situation. Over the years, ideas can be added and referenced in one easy-to-use chart.

In addition to being a method for providing consistency, the chart can be used as an idea stimulator when planning lessons, assessments, and units. As teachers flip through the chart, they will run across potential teaching strategies and say things like, "Oh! My current curricular topic works well with developing critical thinking skills … and here are some ideas for implementation," "Great! The topic we are about to address will provide a great opportunity for my students to work on their explaining skills," or "I should relate this topic to their everyday lives. Here are some strategies in my Teacher Empowerment Menu!"

Side Note

Beyond Superficial
One of the strengths of this book is that it will go beyond simply letting you know *what* you need to accomplish. The book will also give strategies for *how* to accomplish your goals.

State Assessments, National Laws (such as No Child Left Behind), National Incentives (such as Race to the Top), and College Readiness

---

Today, schools experience various pressures, including high stakes tests for state assessments, No Child Left Behind, Race to the Top, and demonstrating the college readiness of students. Some readers might be concerned that focusing on the goals of this book could take away from teacher focus on these pressures.

While the goals of this book were not created with high stakes tests in mind, this book actually is a great plan for improving a school's success on high stakes tests. By adopting the goals of this book, educators will seek to connect children to learning in such a way that the students are engaged and creating lasting memories of concepts. Young minds will not simply learn concepts and skills that could be found on high stakes tests, but will engage in a 21st Century Challenge that stimulates kids to learn and use these ideas through critical thinking, problem solving, creative endeavors, technological activities, and inquiry-based lessons … deepening student understanding. Teachers will promote understanding through thoughtful assessment, careful curricular planning, intervention, remediation, and practices that promote a lasting long-term retention of knowledge and skills. In total, the goals of this book were not created to help students on high stakes testing, but to empower students for the 21st century. ***However, the plan and strategies that this book discusses are exactly what a school should do if that school needs higher test scores!***

Goal #1

Build a Foundation of Connections

(Ch. 3-10)

We want our students to learn a rigorous core curriculum in such a way that they are engaged in a 21st Century Challenge that empowers them with the relevant skills required by the new economy. This task is practically impossible if our students are not engaged, not curious, not inspired, not motivated, not willing to work hard, not buying into the educational processes, not feeling like they belong, not supported by parents, or not showing up at all (for some kids). For educators to even dream of unlocking the passion and curiosity within our students to prepare them for a new 21st century economy, we must overcome these obstacles. How can we do this?

It's all about the connections. As discussed in chapter 2, research shows that student attachment to parents, teachers, and schools is associated with greater school achievement (including grades and standardized test scores), greater social and emotional success, improved behavior, and a greater willingness to work on challenging tasks. In addition, these benefits are even stronger for higher-risk kids.[15] A variety of connections can create a learning environment that draws in students, motivates them, and supports them as they work to succeed:

<u>Foundation of Connections</u>

Student Connections with the Curriculum (Ch. 3)	Student Connections with Their Futures (Ch. 4)	Student Connections With Their Educators (Ch. 5)	Student Connections with the School Environment (Ch. 6)	Student Connections with Other Students (Ch. 7)	Student Connections with the Spirit of the School (Ch. 8)	Parent Connections (Ch. 9)	Student Connections with the Community and the World (Ch. 10)	Staff Connections with Other Staff (Ch. 10)

---

[15] (Bergin, 2009, page 141)

Working to create all these connections in your classroom and school is like adopting a multiple point 21ˢᵗ century plan for successfully drawing in, engaging, and empowering your students. Many educators probably see the two most important connections as those between the students and the curriculum and between the students and their teachers. This is reasonable considering the power that an inspiring teacher can have in unlocking the curiosity of students and engaging them in the curriculum. We must not, however, ignore the considerable power that the other connections can add. Each and every child is a different human being with different motivations. Some are motivated at school by a deep tie to their future and the goals that they wish to achieve. Others might be drawn to school through a camaraderie found in their bond to other students in classes, in a club, or on a competitive team. Still, the ties for others might be a deep passion, such as one for music or art, that draws them into the educational environment. Some students with difficult home lives might like school because it serves as a source of consistency and safety. *Because no two kids are the same, we must work to make as many connections for them as possible.*

In an ideal world, we could create all the connections possible for all students so that we are always lighting their fire and keeping them motivated … even when they are having a bad day. For some, though, the successful creation of *at least one connection* might be all that keeps them engaged and keeps them from dropping out altogether as they get older. Therefore, it can be beneficial for our students if we get to know them well enough to discover which types of connections they personally need and desire.

Think about the connections that drew you into the school environment when you were growing up. What were they? Did one type have an especially profound effect on you?

Schools that create connections are successful schools. If we can build various student links, we can overcome the potential roadblocks that might keep our kids from becoming passionate and curious people who like learning and like school. We must achieve this if we expect to be successful in creating a solid foundation of knowledge, coupled with the skills for success in a new economy. So, before focusing on the later chapters that create strategies for developing real world skills through a 21ˢᵗ Century Challenge, we must lay a solid foundation of connections that can draw students into the learning environment. This is the solid foundation on which a premier 21ˢᵗ century school is built.

This Section of the Book Goes Beyond Connections

While moving forward in the next few chapters to strengthen these connections, we will not only be doing something that is essential for motivating students, but we will also promote some 21ˢᵗ century skills at the same time. By helping students become connected to the school environment, we are giving them a framework in which they can develop their skills as collaborators. By connecting students to the curriculum, we help them develop the ability to apply the curriculum in the real world. Thus, connections not only pull kids into learning, but also serve to develop 21ˢᵗ century skills.

Ease of Implementation

As you move forward into the goal of creating connections, note that the strategies of each chapter are broken into categories that make the strategies easier to implement in a school. These categories also provide a framework for implementation that helps to minimize the over- and under-emphasis of various practices that come with the common "kicks and drops" of teaching. These categories and strategies are outlined in the "Teacher Empowerment Menu (for 21st Century Educators)" that accompanies this book. As you read and think about the strategies in the coming chapters, you can note your ideas in the "Teacher Empowerment Menu." Then, the "Teacher Empowerment Menu" can serve as an easy-to-use quick reference for implementing an empowering 21st Century Education in your particular educational setting.

In addition, there is a separate resource for students called the "Personal Empowerment Menu (for 21st Century Students)" which mirrors the content contained within this book. Unlike the book you are reading (that shows educators how to deliver a 21st Century Education), the "Personal Empowerment Menu" is designed to be used by students as a resource or text for developing 21st century skills, attitudes, habits, and connections. Check it out!

3 | Student Connections with the Curriculum

Arguably, the most important thing we can ever do for our students is help them develop connections with the curriculum. It is essential that our students enjoy learning, become curious, see the value of the curriculum, become inspired, be able to apply the curriculum in the real world, and become passionate about a career path. Surely, you can think of teachers from your past who very successfully created this kind of connection. These experiences probably left you with some of your most enjoyable experiences and memories of school (and maybe inspired you to become a teacher). What can someone do in order to be "that teacher"?

There are a variety of things that teachers can do to connect students to the curriculum. While these practices come in different forms for different age groups and subject areas, a general theme remains the same: *Students love to understand and be able to use what they learn in school in a **real world context**.* They like to know how everything around them works, how people and events shape the world in which they live, how to solve real world problems, how to use knowledge and skills to their advantage, or how to perform the tasks of future jobs. Kids want the things that they learn to spark their imagination and help them understand and do things in the real world. Adults are exactly the same. When we attend a college class or professional development course for educators, we want to learn things that we can use in the real world of teaching to help our students. How might we feel if this doesn't happen?

Let's look at some strategies for making real-world connections with the curriculum. These are the various types of real-world connections that engage students.

Connecting Students to the Curriculum

1. **Looking for Answers (Engaging Through Inquiry)**
2. **Connecting the Curriculum to Everyday Life**
3. **Performing Real-Life (Authentic) Tasks that will be Useful in the Future**
4. **Developing Insights and Opinions about Real-World Issues**
5. **Imagining the Future World**
6. **Integrating New Learning with Prior Knowledge and Skills**
7. **Finding Cross-Curricular Connections**
8. **Creating Products and Models Related to the Content**
9. **Becoming the Content**

Let's look more in-depth at each of these methods for connecting students to the curriculum.

Side Note

Application for Everyone

Because this is the first chapter containing educational strategies, we will look at more examples from varying age levels and content areas than in the following chapters. Here, it is important for each reader to see that this book has value and application regardless of each reader's educational role.

1   Looking for Answers (Engaging Through Inquiry)

Let's imagine that a group of students walks into a classroom and sees a question written on the board: "Why is it reasonable that the 2000 Summer Olympic Games in Sydney, Australia were held in the *fall of 2000*?" This question tickles the young minds of the students and catches their interest. The teacher uses this stimulus to engage the class in a series of inquiry activities related to the earth, the sun, and the seasons. In these activities, the students manipulate models, reflect upon prior knowledge, and slowly build new understanding piece by piece. As the kids learn the reasons that seasons change, they soon realize that when it is summer in America (Northern Hemisphere), it is winter in Australia (Southern Hemisphere). This allows the class to see that it wouldn't make sense for Australians to host the Summer Olympics during their winter season. So, when the Olympics were held in Sydney, Australia in 2000, the world waited until Australia (in the Southern Hemisphere) shifted from its winter to its warmer spring (and at the same time, our Northern Hemisphere shifted from its summer to its fall). Therefore, the Summer Olympics were held during our fall season.

In this example, students become engaged by the curricular subject matter through the use of an inquiry-based question or challenge. This is much more meaningful to students than if they walked into a classroom and were simply told what causes the different seasons. In addition, the inquiry approach can stimulate more questions in kids' minds, such as: "Could people go to Australia to ski during our summer?" or "Do the differences in seasons give some countries an advantage in the Olympics?" Stimulating young minds to generate these connections and questions deepens their understanding and retention of new information.

Our youth love to be presented with real-world questions, experiences, events, or phenomena for which they must seek and develop understanding. These situations create engagement that allows teachers to guide the students in developing new knowledge. Some examples include the following.

Examples - Science

Students can be asked questions or shown demonstrations that make them wonder about the world and why things happen. This technique is useful for Kindergarten to twelfth grade. In the younger grades, children can be engaged by questions about how bats can "see" in the dark or how fish breathe. In science, kids at all levels like to see demonstrations that are hard to explain and try to figure out the explanation.

Examples - Social Studies

In one of my college education classes, a group of aspiring educators presented a great Social Studies inquiry activity. The lesson, which was about the life of Cleopatra, was not simply a discussion of dates and events. Instead, we were asked, "What was Cleopatra; an Egyptian, a Greek, or a Roman?" Then, we were given a short reading piece that told us that Cleopatra was the ruler of Egypt, that her family came from Greece, and that she had children with a Roman. The question (along with the content knowledge) stimulated a discussion about the differences between the words "race," "ethnicity," and "culture." We were stimulated to care about Cleopatra's background and life. This was much more interesting than simply being told facts about Cleopatra and being told the definitions of the words "race," "ethnicity," and "culture." Instead, we became motivated to develop a better understanding of these ideas on our own through thought and discussion.

Examples - Language Arts

In language arts or English, teachers can also help students see the connections between the curriculum and the real world through inquiry. Before, during, and after the reading of stories, teachers can pose questions about the world that can be answered through the events, characters, or symbolism developed in a story: "What makes some people so persuasive?" (secondary age level) or "Why is it important to share?" (elementary age level). The answers to these questions come from the stories or history being read.

Regardless of the subject area, kids love to figure out and understand the functions and the circumstances of the real world in which they live. When they do this, their learning has meaning. When students take an active role in developing their understanding of the world, there is a sense of ownership that comes with the knowledge.

Looking for Answers (Engaging Through Inquiry)

We Should See Students Who ...	Personal Empowerment Questions (PEQs) for Students
👁 Reflect upon prior knowledge to learn new ideas	❓ Why?
👁 Ask questions	❓ How does _____ work?
👁 Build toward answers in learning activities	❓ How did _____ come to be?
👁 Piece together curricular concepts to get answers	❓ Why do we _____?
👁 Make predictions	❓ What are my predictions for _____?
👁 Are engaged	❓ What do I already know about this question, situation, problem, challenge, or phenomenon?
👁 Are curious	❓ What do I need to know to get an answer?

Students who ask and answer questions like these grow into adults who ask themselves similar questions in the workplace, developing a keen sense of how things function and how to make them better.

Key Idea

Tools For 21st Century Education Success

As this chapter and others move along, we will often stop to think about a few things.

1) **What We Should See** in a successful learning activity.

2) **Personal Empowerment Questions (PEQs)** that kids should ask themselves as they perform a task or exercise a skill. We want to help children develop into young adults who have the mental toolbox to solve their own challenges. This is critical. Thus, we will always look at what questions we should stimulate in the minds of our youth to get them to become more independent thinkers who are empowered for success in the real world. A well-crafted and successful lesson will require students to ask themselves questions that will make them independent thinkers. In the 21st century, educators must stimulate students to *"mind their PEQs."*

Teacher Empowerment Menu (for 21st Century Educators)

The Teacher Empowerment Menu that supports this book includes the educational tools described above in an organized and easy-to-use layout. For each educational goal, the menu has a section that includes "What We Should See," "Personal Empowerment Questions (PEQs)," and space to note ideas. It is an amazing tool for modern teachers. *As you read this book, make notes of your ideas about each topic in the Teacher Empowerment Menu.* When you are done, you will have a massive number of usable ideas that are tailored to *your* needs.

Personal Empowerment Menu (for 21st Century Students)

A student flip chart is available that contains the Personal Empowerment Questions (PEQs) that kids should ask themselves in order to empower themselves in the 21st century. In addition, it contains rubrics for assessing a student's 21st century skills, attitudes, habits, and connections. Beyond being useful for teachers, these rubrics allow students to self-assess and assess each other as they develop 21st century skills. Also, parents can use the rubrics to assess their kids and provide feedback.

In all, the Personal Empowerment Menu (for 21st Century Students) is very helpful for stimulating young minds to develop the skills, attitudes, habits, and connections within this book. You can use it as a valuable classroom resource and student reference during learning activities. It is an amazing tool for modern students.

Side Notes

Quick Idea

Create real-world questions and write them on the classroom board at the beginning of each unit to engage the students in the curriculum. Allow students to develop answers as they progress through inquiry-based activities that allow them to build understanding. These same questions, as well as derivatives, can be used as a writing assessment at the end of the unit.

Pitfall to Avoid

It is important that inquiry questions are interesting. Let's say that someone starts a lesson by asking, "What causes the seasons?" While this has elements of student inquiry, it is neither interesting nor engaging. Students need their attention grabbed with a better question, such as the previous Summer Olympics example. Then, the reason for the seasons becomes a part of the answer to an engaging question, rather than being a boring question in itself.

Inquiry and the Flipped Classroom

With the flipped classroom concept, teachers might have students view a video lecture

Side Notes

for homework and then practice concepts at school. The challenge with this is that students are not originally learning the concepts through inquiry activities that develop the brain's ability to seek answers and learn by constructing knowledge. There are two ways to deal with this.

First, the video lectures that summarize concepts could be given as homework *after* an inquiry lesson in class introduces the concept. In this way, the students learn using inquiry activities and then tie together and strengthen understanding by watching a teacher's summary lecture on the topic. Class time is saved as the teacher does not need to spend as much time tying together and summarizing in a lecture format. Also, kids are allowed to work at their own pace so teachers don't have to try to find an appropriate time to summarize with *everyone at once*.

Second, the video lectures could include points when students are required to pause and predict an answer to an inquiry question, predict how a process works or will unfold, predict what will happen next in a historical event, etc. While making these predictions, the students can be required to note their ideas.

Asking Their Own Questions

Stimulating children to look for answers to engaging questions or phenomena is great for engaging and connecting students. However, we can do one more thing that has a great deal of real world value. We should stimulate students to look at the world and *ask themselves* questions for which they can seek answers. When we accomplish this, we have given them a real world tool that will make them more successful and productive as they look for and develop their own understanding and connections.

Teachers can use formal lessons to ask kids to seek answers to their own questions. Also, I like to do a quick activity when I have five extra minutes. In this time, kids pose anonymous questions about the world around them that are relevant to my content area, such as, "Why is the sky blue?," and then we discuss possible answers as a group. This promotes curious thinking about the world.

2 Connecting the Curriculum to Everyday Life

In an addition to learning how things work, kids love to see how school learning connects to their everyday world. A variety of methods can help students see these relationships.

Examples - Various
Content Areas

Connecting content to children's lives begins at an early age. In preschool, students might enjoy thinking of all the things around them that begin with each letter that they learn. My niece loved show-and-tell days when each day was dedicated to a single letter. Students brought in or told about something that begins with that letter. The children connected what they were learning to their very favorite things and activities.

As students get older, there are other things that work well. In an English class in middle or high school, kids can read stories that connect with adolescent life. In Social Studies, they can develop an understanding of how current circumstances that influence everyday life are a direct result of historical events.

Stimulate the Students to Make the Connections

A teacher can and should take opportunities to share his or her knowledge of how the curriculum relates to everyday life. However, we should strive to get students thinking about and developing these connections on their own. The simplest technique can be used at any age level. When engaging students in a lesson, stop periodically and ask your students how the content relates to their lives or where they have previously encountered the content. Though simple, this is very effective. Even though a teacher generally knows more about the topic than the students, it is amazing to hear all of the types of connections that a roomful of students can make with the world around them. Often, they can think of things that did not occur to the teacher, because the teacher does not walk the same life path. One reason that this strategy works so well is that the connection is authored by the children and not simply given by the teacher. This gives the class more ownership of the information. Also, everyone benefits from the thoughts of others.

Promote the Development of Connections Outside of School

Seeing the relationships between the curriculum and everyday life cannot be something that is exercised only in school. Many more connections can be made if kids are looking for them outside of school on their own time. To stimulate this, students can be given homework that challenges them to find examples or relationships to the content in class from their everyday life. Notice how much more engaging this practice is … compared to writing definitions for homework. Instead, they can show their understanding of a concept by explaining it in the context of experiences in the real world. They still might end up writing down some definition, but the assignment is framed in a way that is more interesting and useful to the students. Giving an assignment like this can be done daily, weekly, or monthly and perhaps done in a journal. No matter how often they do it, kids are stimulated to get in the habit of looking for connections in the real world around them. Later in life, this can make them more effective, because they have learned to see the uses of knowledge and skills. Hence, they are able to more appropriately and effectively use the skills. To multiply the effects of this activity, the class can share the connections that they made on their own and benefit from each other's ideas. (This can also be done to provide an engaging review, rather than a review that simply asks students to regurgitate information.)

An additional way to enhance the development of connections outside of school is to involve parents in discussions with their children about the connections between school content and real life. By doing this, a wealth of life experiences can be passed on from the parents to further enhance the students' connections to the curriculum. I give students an assignment sheet called "Teach Your Parents," which has key curricular ideas listed on it. The task for the students is to teach these ideas to their parents and discuss the real world value of the concepts. There is a line for parents to sign to show that they have had a discussion with their children.

Connecting the Curriculum to Everyday Life

We Should See Students Who ...	PEQs for Students
👁 Describe curricular ideas in real-world context	❓ How does this relate to my life?
👁 Recognize why the curriculum is relevant	❓ Where have I encountered this before?
👁 Assess their everyday surroundings to see how the curriculum might relate	❓ Why does this matter to me?
👁 Are engaged	
👁 Are curious	

Students who ask and answer questions like these grow into adults who can determine the value of new knowledge and skills and use the skills and knowledge to their advantage.

When kids see that lessons from school have everyday relevance, they become more motivated and yearn for more learning.

Performing Real-Life (Authentic) Tasks that will be Useful in the Future

Not only do young people like to know how all the things from school affect their current everyday life, they like to know how school will help them in future jobs or important life situations. When knowledge can be applied to perform an authentic task or solve a problem, students are drawn into learning. They perceive the skills and knowledge as useful.

Examples - Life Tasks

Let's look at a few quick examples. In a Language Arts or English class, educators can challenge students to write a letter-to-the-editor that persuasively demonstrates their point of view on a topic. Students in a foreign language class can be challenged to imagine that they are in a dubious situation in another country and need their foreign language skills to succeed. A lower elementary math lesson can challenge students to determine which coins are necessary to buy a toy. An upper elementary math lesson can challenge children to figure out which choice is a better purchase in a store: "25% off" or "buy one, get 50% off the second item." A science class can work to determine how to reduce the risk of getting a cold by developing an understanding of related science concepts.

Examples - Professional Tasks

Educators can present their pupils with a challenge that involves a professional who is trying to do some aspect of his or her job. Students can work to determine what this person should do to complete the task. For instance, a math class could be asked to solve an engineering problem related to the design of a roller coaster. A science class could work toward understanding how a medical professional could diagnose and treat a disease. Students could be challenged to act as entrepreneurs and create business plans of their choice.

In the process of all these examples, students learn regular content benchmarks that would have been taught anyway, but are now framed in a meaningful way. When students learn how to do authentic tasks (or solve problems), they get a sense of empowerment that connects them to the curriculum. Particularly in professional authentic tasks, they also get exposure to the tasks that professionals perform. You never know when one of these activities will ignite a child's passion and help him see what he wants to spend his life doing.

Job shadows and career internships allow students to interact with professionals in real-world career settings. These opportunities can help students understand the ways in which school content is important for their future.

A Different Angle on Math

While growing up, I noticed a pattern in many of my math classes. Each day, we would come in to the class and learn a new math skill. Then, we were assigned some homework that would serve as a drill for the new skill. Sometimes (but not always), there would be a few story problems at the end of the homework assignment that *finally* showed how the skill could be used to solve real world problems. (At that point, students were less motivated and less inclined to dive into the story problem challenge.) This process seemed strange to me. Why didn't the teachers start by presenting a real world, authentic problem? Then, a new skill could be developed to solve the problem. Instead, the method was often to teach a new math skill without first engaging the students.

Teachers who focus on real-world problem solving capture the attention of their students, from the beginning of a lesson and beyond. The elementary and middle schools of my school district and others in our county use a math program that is based on problem solving and connecting math skills to the real world. In this program, young people develop math skills with the intention of using those skills to solve authentic problems that relate to everyday life. The students are very engaged, because they can see uses for the newly-learned math skills. Through informal conversations, teachers who use the program have told me that their students have more applicable math skills, as compared to previous skill and drill techniques that were light on application.

Performing Real Life (Authentic) Tasks

We Should See Students Who …	PEQs for Students
👁 Seek curricular understanding in order to accomplish an authentic task, solve a problem, or meet a goal	❓ What are my goals in doing _____?
	❓ How can I accomplish _____?
👁 Find real-world value in the curriculum	❓ What steps, information, and procedures will allow me to do _____?
👁 Engage in real, everyday life and career situations in lessons	❓ What can I do with this information or skill?
	❓ How do people commonly make use of this knowledge or skill?
👁 Are engaged	❓ How might I use this knowledge or skill in my future?
👁 Are curious	

Students who ask and answer questions like these grow into adults who can effectively and efficiently accomplish real world tasks.

4 | Developing Insights and Opinions about Real-World Issues

In our ongoing quest to make learning meaningful, one of our most valuable tools is stimulating our students to formulate their own ideas and opinions dealing with the content learned in school. When students are presented with a dilemma or issue, they can analyze and reflect in such a way that they produce independent thoughts. In the process of developing an opinion or idea, the students feel empowered. What the students might not realize is that the teacher has cleverly engaged them in a mental review of the content that they have learned.

Examples - Various Content Areas

When reading a story in an English class, a teacher may ask kids to develop an opinion about the characters' choices or actions. In Social Studies, a teacher may ask students to create an opinion about a certain type of policy or the way in which a historical figure took action. In science, students can talk about potentially controversial subjects, such as cloning. In all of these cases, teachers can ask children to write an essay or engage in a debate in order to express their ideas. Either way, they are given an engaging way to reflect upon the content that they have learned.

Grading

Grades for activities in which students express opinions should reflect their knowledge of the core content related to the opinion. Teachers can ask themselves what level of knowledge is being demonstrated through the presented opinion and if logical connections between the opinion and the curricular facts are being made. A rubric can help students see these expectations.

Side Note

Teacher Opinions

When students are developing their own opinions, they tend to be more open-minded when the teacher doesn't immediately tell them his or her opinion on the topic. The members of the class have a chance to think for themselves without the influence of the person they perceive to be the master of the topic: you.

Developing Insights and Opinions about Real-World Issues

We Should See Students Who ...	PEQs for Students
👁 Think independently	❓ What do I believe about _____?
👁 Gather relevant information	❓ How can I back up my opinion with facts?
👁 Develop opinions on topics that are relevant to the curriculum and real life	❓ How might my opinion differ from other people's opinions and why?
👁 Back up their opinions with facts	
👁 Are engaged	
👁 Are passionate	

Students who ask and answer questions like these grow into adults who can effectively find meaning and develop opinions that are relevant to success in their careers and lives.

⭐ 5 **Imagining the Future World**

Many people are fascinated by thoughts about what the world might be like in the future. Educators can take advantage of this curiosity when connecting their students to the lessons learned in class.

Examples - Various Content Areas

In Social Studies, when students learn how past events were created by certain circumstances, they can also be stimulated to think about how current circumstances might lead to future events. In Language Arts or English, stories about the future or unknown worlds can be stimulating to students. Additionally, writing creatively about the future can be engaging. In science and math, there are many opportunities to relate class curriculum to new technologies, as well as fascinating and sometimes strange new ideas.

Regardless of the class, whenever a teacher or student starts a sentence with, "Maybe someday, we can …," young minds are provoked to imagine new circumstances and new possibilities. Not only does this connect many students to the curriculum, but it also gets them thinking creatively about inventive new ideas. Thinking about the future sparks them to imagine things that they wish existed in the world. It is with thoughts like these that our youth will someday create the next big inventions and processes that carve out new jobs for Americans.

Imagining the Future World

We Should See Students Who …	PEQs for Students
👁 Dream	❓ How will things be similar or different in the future?
👁 Predict	
👁 Reflect upon current trends related to the curriculum	❓ What will my life be like in the future?
👁 Create logical inferences	❓ Given the current circumstances of _____, what could happen in the future?
👁 Are engaged	❓ What do I want to see in the future?
👁 Are curious	❓ Wouldn't it be neat if _____ happens someday?

Students who ask and answer questions like these grow into adults who look for future trends and anticipate what new skills and knowledge will be valuable.

6   Integrating New Learning with Prior Knowledge and Skills

When learning, students' minds are engaged when new knowledge and skills are connected to prior knowledge and skills. This connection activates brain cells that hold prior learning, thus "tickling" the brain. Human beings seem to enjoy making new ideas fit into the larger knowledgebase. In addition, relating new ideas to prior knowledge makes the process of understanding and remembering new concepts easier.

Examples - Various Content Areas

In all classes, students can discuss the ways in which new learning builds on their prior knowledge and skills. For example, when elementary students learn about multiplication, they can learn how the topic is an extension of addition.

Also, members of a class can compare the similarities and differences between new and prior learning. For example, a Social Studies class can compare the similarities and differences among various historical events in order to help students make connections. Students learning words can compare and contrast new words with words that are already a part of those students' vocabularies.

Another good exercise for young minds is reflection on how each new concept is important in their understanding of the big picture of a topic, unit, or subject. For example, students in a Biology class can think about how each new concept combines with others to affect the health of a person's body. In Social Studies, young minds can reflect on how each event was important in a large series of events that shaped the world.

Integrating New Learning with Prior Knowledge and Skills

We Should See Students Who ...	PEQs for Students
👁 Reflect upon prior knowledge and skills to connect them to new learning	❓ How does this new knowledge or skill relate to what I already know?
👁 Recognize how the smaller pieces of a topic fit together	❓ How does this new knowledge or skill deepen my understanding of ____?
👁 Look for similarities and differences between new learning and other concepts in their world	❓ Is this new concept similar to or different from other concepts I know?
👁 Use new learning to find new uses for prior knowledge and skills	❓ With my new understanding, how can I use prior knowledge or skills in new ways?

Students who ask and answer questions like these grow into adults who are able to recognize how knowledge, skills, systems, and tools relate to and can be used together to maximize productivity, efficiency, and creativity.

7 | Finding Cross-Curricular Connections

When skills and knowledge from two or more different content areas are woven together in a real-world learning activity, students can see that real-world challenges generally require multiple skill sets. When two subjects are required to do a task, the importance of both is reinforced in children's minds.

Examples - Larger Projects

Teachers from all levels can work independently or as teams to create activities that require students to integrate the various content skills. For example, kids might be asked to make a vacation plan using maps, researching the history of the destinations, looking at the science behind the environments of the destinations, calculating distances and costs, and writing a journal about their potential experiences.

Examples - Smaller Connections

Cross-curricular connections don't always have to be in the form of large projects. For just about any subject, teachers can reinforce proper language skills, use mathematical calculations, reference significant events, connect with arts, etc.

Regardless of the class, a teacher can generally find ways to bring in content from other subject areas to enrich their curriculum. I've encountered many people in my life who tell me that they learned a lot about English usage from learning a foreign language. Their foreign language teachers had discussed and reinforced tenses and the parts of speech in such a way that the understanding carried over and reinforced the skills of the native language, English.

Cross-Curricular Skills in the Real World

Emphasizing cross-curricular connections is very important for students. They need to recognize that in the real world, subject area skills don't exist in isolation. For instance, being an engineer doesn't mean that a person uses only math. Engineers must use quality writing and proper grammar to effectively communicate their ideas. A blending of skills is required in many careers. So, teachers outside of English classes should not let poor writing skills slide ... just because it is not English class.

Various connections between content areas help to connect students to the curriculum at large. Moreover, our youth develop the ability to relate and draw on a variety of skills when completing tasks and solving problems. This skill is very useful in a technical and global economy, where things are more complex and change at a much faster pace than at any other time in history. People who can connect different content areas are more likely to synthesize new and useful ideas in the future.

Finding Cross-Curricular Connections

We Should See Students Who …	PEQs for Students
☚ Integrate knowledge and skills from more than one subject area in the performance of classroom tasks	❓ How does this concept relate to other subjects?
☚ Look for connections among subject areas	❓ How do my knowledge and skills from one subject help me in another?
☚ Are engaged	

Students who ask and answer questions like these grow into adults who can integrate a variety of sources of information to create a larger view of a situation, challenge, or solution.

⭐ 8   Creating Products and Models Related to the Content

An awesome way to both teach and assess students is to have them create some sort of product that helps them connect to the curriculum.

Possible Product **Purposes**	Possible Product **Forms**	
• Assess Knowledge	• Presentations	• Cartoons
• Present Research	• Reports	• Business Plans
• Present New Ideas	• Journals	• Demonstrations
• Teach Other Students or Parents	• Persuasive Writings	• Stories
• Solve Problems	• Tools for Problem Solving	• Metaphors
	• Models of Objects or Processes	• Pamphlets
	• Videos	• Art
		• Websites, Blogs, Wikis, etc.

Examples - Various Content Areas

There is seemingly an infinite number of ways to use products in teaching.

- Some economics teachers at my school have the students prepare a budget project in which they have a make-believe job, home, and other responsibilities. Their task is to create a workable budget that demonstrates their understanding of economics.

- During a unit on ecology, students can be given the task of creating a pamphlet that can be used to educate the community about resource usage.

- When improving writing skills, students can assemble their works into a book.

- While learning about electricity and light, kids can be given the task of designing an electrical blueprint for a home, as though they were an engineer or an electrician.

- In Social Studies, students can take a stand on a current issue and back up their opinion by referencing historical events in a product, such as a persuasive essay.

- In artistic subjects, products are the norm. In these classes, students are often fulfilled by a sense of creativity and accomplishment. In core curricular classes, students can also make artistic products to demonstrate their knowledge.

- In elementary school, making products that relate to the content can make learning fun and real. A kindergarten class can learn how plants develop by growing seeds in clear plastic bags. As the children nurture the developing product with water, they get firsthand experience with the development of plants. A product is grown that kids can see and touch. When the plant finally develops, they can take it home and explain what they learned to their parents. This adds even more excitement to the product and deepens the bond with the curriculum.

- When younger students are first developing their motor skills and an understanding of shapes and letters, they can create a product in the form of a Mother's Day or Father's Day card. In addition to exercising their new skills, this type of creation has personal meaning for the students.

- Elementary school students can use toothpicks and marshmallows to create various geometric shapes. By making, seeing, and touching the product, the students can create deeper connections and understanding. Regardless of age level, many students seem to learn better when they can get their hands on something and manipulate it.

Side Notes

No Regurgitating, Please

It is important that students are not asked to make products that simply display facts. Instead, the products should force students to think, create, and demonstrate a deep understanding of skills and content. In the real world, students will need to actually manipulate facts and create products with the knowledge they possess. This is why the creation of products is so valuable, especially in a competitive new economy.

Pitfall to Avoid

There is a fine balance that teachers must achieve when developing product-based assignments. One doesn't want to structure the activity so that creativity is stifled, yet students must know what specific outcomes the teacher is going to measure. If not given goals to achieve, students can sometimes make very creative projects that do not reflect the curricular goals that the teacher had in mind. Thus, it is important for students to be given a grading rubric before the beginning of an activity that reflects both the desire for creativity on the part of the student and the standards that the student must address.

Creating Products and Models Related to the Content

We Should See Students Who ...	PEQs for Students
👁 Present curriculum in a creative way	❓ What am I trying to convey with my product?
👁 Do not simply regurgitate facts when creating products	❓ Who is my audience for this product?
👁 Demonstrate understanding through products	❓ How can I demonstrate my understanding of ____ through the creation of a product?
👁 Engage the audience of their products	❓ What can I produce with my understanding of ____?
👁 Are engaged	❓ How can I be creative when making my product?

Students who ask and answer questions like these grow into adults who can translate their knowledge and skills into usable products and services in any career. They can also model, demonstrate, persuade, or explain things to customers, clients, and patients.

9   Becoming the Content

A final (and a wonderful) way to bond our youth with the concepts that they learn is for the students to "become" the concepts. When kids actually take part in an event or process, they develop a deep understanding. There are many ways to accomplish this.

In Social Studies, students can re-create an important court trial from the past. In a foreign language class, they can imagine being in a foreign country and performing an interaction among people. In science, students can become the parts of a scientific process and act out that process (from an elementary water cycle to a secondary molecular bond).

One of the most valuable learning experiences I have ever had was in a Social Studies class. The teacher wanted the class to develop an understanding of the workings of a democracy. So, he asked the members of the class to write our own class constitution and form our own government, complete with legislators, a court, and law enforcement. Our class went through regular daily activities, but negative classroom issues were not directly handled by the teacher. We were graded on how well our society could function and behave during the activity. We had to create and tweak a system that maximized positive student participation, behavior, and interactions during normal lessons. Some students would find loopholes in the Constitution and attempted to exploit them. Learning how to deal with these situations was a great lesson in the development of a new country, the balance of power, and checks and balances. One of the best ways to learn about something is to live it.

3 - Student Connections with the Curriculum

Examples – Various Content Areas

Becoming the Content

We Should See Students Who …	PEQs for Students
👁 Actively "live out" curricular ideas 👁 Are engaged	❓ What would it be like if I were the object, person, place, or process from my new learning? ❓ What can I learn by imagining myself as this object, person, place, or process?

Students who ask and answer questions like these grow into adults who can imagine how things work and empathize with various situations.

Connecting Students to the Curriculum: Wrap-up

You can use the strategies in this chapter individually or in combination to create connections between students and the curriculum. It is important to note that not every strategy is ideal for teaching every skill or concept. Instead, the strategies make up a menu of possible techniques for engagement. Educators can choose from these options when teaching a particular curricular topic.

How Can Educators Think of Ideas for Connecting Kids to the Curriculum?

Sometimes, it might seem difficult to find ways to develop connections to certain parts of the curriculum. Teachers might ask themselves, "How will I connect students to this concept in math?," "How will I find a way to make a certain event in history interesting?," "How can I get students excited about a particular process in science?," or "How can I get kids to see the value in reading this story?" One important strategy is for teachers to ask themselves:
- *Why do we teach this?*
- *Why is this topic, concept, or skill important enough to be in our curriculum?*
- *How does this concept relate to interesting real-world facts, processes, events, etc.?*

The answers to these questions can unlock ideas for engagement.

A personal example of the usefulness of questions like these came in my first year of teaching Biology. Early in the year, I found that students were not very interested in learning about osmosis (water moving in and out of cells). So, I asked myself, "Why is this in the curriculum?" I realized that osmosis is important for a variety of reasons. We can get sick if we drink too much salty water, such as ocean water, because of osmosis. I realized that I could use the first technique described in this chapter, *Looking for Answers (Engaging Through Inquiry)*, to change the way that I taught.

The next time I taught about osmosis, I began by asking my class, "If a person is trapped in a lifeboat in the Atlantic, why would it be unsafe to drink lots of ocean water?" Additionally, I created some classroom and lab activities that helped my students figure out what salty water does to the cells in living things. This strategy changed everything. Students became highly engaged in inquiry-based activities and worked to develop their understanding of the real-world question I had posed. This engagement would not have been possible if I had not asked myself what real-world value the curricular concept of osmosis holds.

Teachers in all content areas can similarly ask themselves, "Why do I teach about World War II?," "What is the value of the theme of this story?," "What is the value of this math skill?," or "Why do we teach kids about the Constitution?"

Key Educational Strategies for Promoting the Student Connections in this Chapter

---

This chapter described various types of connections to the curriculum that students can develop. When setting out to promote these connections, teachers need some strategies for stimulating students to make these connections. *There are four strategies that will be used many times throughout this book in order to promote various 21ˢᵗ century skills, attitudes, and habits.*

Key Educational Strategies for 21ˢᵗ Century Skills, Attitudes, and Habits

- **Classroom Exercises -** Students are engaged in activities that help them develop 21ˢᵗ century skills, attitudes, and habits (preferably using inquiry).
- **Teacher Stories / Modeling -** Teachers model and tell stories that help their students develop 21ˢᵗ century skills, attitudes, and habits.
- **Assessment by Students -** Students make assessments of themselves, assessments of others, and assessments of their environment to develop 21ˢᵗ century skills, attitudes, and habits.
- **Curricular Examples -** Students are exposed to the ways that historical figures, scientists, characters from stories, etc. used 21ˢᵗ century skills, attitudes, and habits to their advantage.

We can promote the various types of connections to the curriculum described in this chapter by using these educational strategies. These techniques will also help us promote other goals found throughout this book.

The Value of Connections to the Curriculum

If we can challenge our students to make connections with their curriculum, then we ignite a passion for learning. When teachers use a variety of techniques for drawing connections, learning is exciting and stimulating. Members of a class might problem-solve one day, develop an opinion on another day, and create a product on yet another day. Our students will be able to see the value of their learning, become more curious, and, thus, enjoy learning. *Teachers are like salespeople whose job is to sell interest and passion for the subject matter through connections.*

In addition to connections helping our students become engaged, connections help our youth become much more prepared to apply what they learn in a real world context as an adult.

By learning to develop connections in their youth, future adults will be better able to make valuable real world connections between knowledge and its applications in careers. This will empower them to thrive in the new 21st century economy. In addition, students will be more likely to retain information and skills in the long term if they have deep connections with that learning.

One of the biggest benefits of connecting kids to the curriculum is that they will be more likely to discover a deep passion for a certain career path through their experiences with teachers who sparked their imagination. *Connections can stimulate young minds to dream.* All-in-all, connections to the curriculum are vital!

Thinking About It

- **Which of these types of connections made the biggest impact on you as a student?**
- **What are your strengths in creating connections to the curriculum?**
- **Which connections to the curriculum would you like to improve in your teaching?**

How Does This Chapter Support the Goals of This Book?

Let's take a moment to think about the ways in which the ideas of this chapter help us address the three main goals of this book by looking at the "Building Blocks of a 21st Century Education" on page 13 and our "Daily Thoughts for Educators" on page 18. We now have tools and strategies for empowering our youth by developing connections between students and the curriculum.

Make Note of Your Great Ideas!

If you haven't already, note your ideas for implementing the strategies in this chapter in your Teacher Empowerment Menu (for 21st Century Educators). In the future, you can easily reference usable ideas for your class.

In addition, consider the ways in which you can stimulate students to look for connections to the curriculum by using the Personal Empowerment Menu (for 21st Century Students), which contains the relevant PEQs and assessment rubric for this chapter.

4 | Student Connections with Their Futures

As described in Chapter 1, modern circumstances and technologies have changed the economic playing field. Now and increasingly in the future, Americans are competing head-to-head against foreign workers and machines for jobs that we have traditionally held. Modern jobs require a mixture of skills, habits, and attitudes that include problem solving skills, creativity, technology, personal skills, and interpersonal skills. There are no guarantees of lifetime employment at one job.

I think that helping our youth become aware of this situation is paramount in addressing it. (Friedman also makes this point in *The World is Flat.*[16]) What we need to develop is a "connection to the future" within all of our students. *Our youth need to understand the implications of global competition, new technologies, and automation and understand which skills, habits, and attitudes are required for success.* If our youth connect with and understand the future that awaits them, they will be more likely to value any learning activity that prepares them for that future.

Student Connections with Their Futures

1. **Learning About the New Economy**
2. **Learning which Skills, Attitudes, and Habits are Necessary for Future Success**
3. **Discovering Interests and Passions that Could Lead to Future Careers**

 Learning About the New Economy

It's not good enough to just make statements to our students like, "You need to learn what we teach you in school in order to get a job," and "Jobs are harder to come by these days." To truly motivate our students (and connect them to their futures), we need to get real and get specific. They need to know what makes the new economy different from the past. They need to know about automation. They need to know about the billions of people with whom they now compete for jobs. They need to know what types of work are more insulated from global competition and what types of work are not. **They need to know that this is serious and that they have the power to thrive**. Clearly, our approach to this will be different for different age levels. Certainly, at some point, each student needs to recognize what the new economy means

---

[16] (Friedman, 2005, page 385)

for his or her future. Kids need to understand the critical aspects of the new 21st century economy.

Learning About the New Economy

We Should See Students Who …	Personal Empowerment Questions (PEQs) for Students
☀ Understand how the economy of the world is changing ☀ Understand what factors are changing our modern economy ☀ Understand which careers are growing and which are shrinking ☀ Are motivated by their understanding of the modern economy	❓ What types of careers were common in the past and how have they changed? ❓ What careers will grow in the future, and what careers will likely shrink? ❓ What are automation, offshoring, and outsourcing? ❓ With whom are we competing for work in the modern economy? ❓ How do technology and automation affect the workplace? ❓ Which jobs are more insulated from global competition and automation and which are not? ❓ With which people and technologies will I likely work in the future? ❓ Against which people and technologies will I likely compete in the future? **Personal Empowerment Statements (PESs) for Students** • I understand how the past economy is different from the future economy. • I can achieve success in the future by developing knowledge and skills that are relevant to the modern economy and the careers in which I have an interest. • I will work hard for success!

Students who ask questions and make statements like these grow into adults who understand the 21st century economy and are motivated to thrive in it.

⭐ 2 — Learning which Skills, Attitudes, and Habits are Necessary for Future Success

We must go beyond simply teaching our youth about the new economy in which they will work. The next step is to help them understand which skills, habits, and attitudes will allow them to thrive in this new world. Without this critical lesson, students will be left feeling nervous and apprehensive about the future. With this lesson, they will feel empowered by their understanding of what skills are needed for success. They will become motivated and connected to their futures.

Learning which Skills, Attitudes, and Habits are Necessary for Future Success

We Should See Students Who ...	PEQs for Students
👁 Understand which skills, habits, and attitudes are relevant to their future (such as critical thinking, problem solving, creativity, communication, collaboration, understanding others, leadership, work ethic, personal management skills, ability to learn, technology skills, passion, curiosity, adaptability, versatility, efficiency, and explaining) 👁 Understand the real-world value of blending 21st century skills within their core curricular lessons 👁 Seek to develop their 21st century skills, attitudes, and habits	❓ Considering the rapid development of a global economy and technology, which skills will help me thrive in the 21st century? ❓ Which skills are especially important in my particular career field? ❓ In school, lessons teach me knowledge about various subjects. Why is it beneficial for these lessons to be taught in such a way that I develop critical thinking, problem solving, creativity, technological, or social skills? ❓ Beyond knowledge and skills, what personal attitudes and habits will help me succeed in the future? ❓ How and where can I learn more about the skills, habits, and attitudes I need for 21st century success? ❓ What are the strengths and weaknesses that I notice in the skills, attitudes, and habits of the people around me, and what can I learn from these people? **PESs for Students** • I understand which skills, habits, and attitudes will help me thrive in the future, and I will strive to develop these traits. • I will follow my interests with passion and curiosity.

Students who ask questions and make statements like these grow into adults who continuously seek to develop the skills, habits, and attitudes needed to thrive in the 21st century.

Personalizing the Future

Side Note

While a great motivator is to help students see the general skills required in the 21st century, it is also very important to get them thinking about the specific career paths in which they have an interest. In this way, kids can actually picture themselves using certain skills in a specific job, rather than simply imagining a general "future." This dramatically increases the already-large motivation that comes from reflecting upon the future, because thinking about specific career paths allows children to understand what knowledge and skills their own future will demand.

How Can Students Learn About the New Economy and the Skills, Habits, and Attitudes Required?

Now that we know *what* our youth need to learn about the new economy, we should focus on *how* to develop this awareness. In the last chapter, *four key educational strategies* were shown to be useful in developing connections to the curriculum: *Classroom Exercises, Teacher Stories / Modeling, Assessments by Students, and Curricular Examples*. Now, we can use these strategies to develop student understanding of the new economy.

Classroom Exercises

a) Activities Specifically Dedicated to Learning about the 21ˢᵗ Century Economy and the Skills, Habits, and Attitudes Required

Once I realized the seriousness of the world that awaits our students, I decided to create a lesson to educate my classes about this new world. The lesson involved student brainstorming, writing, discussing, and viewing of a PowerPoint® presentation. By the time we were done, the students understood the circumstances and implications of global economics, technology, and automation. They also discussed the types of work that are likely to be available in the future and the skills that are important in the new century. Throughout, we shared many examples with each other that highlighted the skills required in the 21ˢᵗ century. We discussed social, personal, technical, critical thinking, learning, and creative skills.

I was careful to frame the situation so that students viewed the world as a place where they could thrive if they obtained the correct skills, habits, and attitudes, rather than framing the situation as hopeless and grim. At the end of the activity, we focused on student ideas for developing these attributes, which left the students with a sense of what they can do to empower themselves. Part of my assessment for the lesson required that the students assess their own skills and brainstorm ideas for improvement. In addition, kids thought about possible career types in which they have an interest. Then, they looked at which 21ˢᵗ century skills were especially relevant to their own career pathway.

This activity turned out to be a great motivator. Throughout the year, I would explain how the lessons from class were helping the students gain the skills they would need in the future. This practice really helped get the young minds to buy into the things we did in class. (Although I did the lesson in a science class, it would be beneficial in all subject areas.) In addition, many students started looking differently at the world around them. One student told me that he had never realized how important certain abilities and skills would be for the career to which he aspired. He told me that he wanted to find ways to improve these abilities. For him, the activity was critical in allowing him to see the ways in which he needed to develop.

Beyond a single classroom activity, there can be a school-wide 21st century skills focus each week or month. In addition, various skills, habits, and attitudes can be posted around a school (along with PEQs for kids to ask themselves and PESs to assert).

> ## b) Develop a Connection to the Future through Classroom Activities that Reinforce 21st Century Skills, Habits, and Attitudes

Lessons can be designed to develop the skills of the 21st century while students are learning the curriculum. Strategies for accomplishing this goal will be shown throughout this book, especially in the unit that addresses the promotion of a 21st Century Challenge. For the goals of the current chapter, the key is that we *make kids aware* of the relevant 21st century skills that our learning activities promote. This helps create a connection to the future.

When doing any activity in class, why not take a tiny amount of time to rationalize the reason why that activity is useful to the students' futures? Rationalizing the value of lessons makes a world of difference in student motivation. If kids understand the reason that they are performing a task, they naturally become more motivated to do that task. I don't mean that we should make statements such as "You will need to know how to do this type of task in your next year of school." or "You will have to know this skill in college." Statements like these can frustrate kids, because the students are not learning why a new concept or skill is relevant *in their future lives.*

To rationalize our learning activities, we should instead say things such as "You are going to teach a concept to another student so that you have a better ability to explain things to a customer, patient, or client in the future," "You are going to do this inquiry-based activity so that you are better at learning things independently and more prepared for the future when teachers are not present," "We are going to analyze this problem so that you are empowered to overcome any type of challenge that you encounter in real life," or "We are going to write this opinion essay so that you are better able to develop your own opinions in the future, be persuasive, and express your ideas in writing."

When our youth believe that activities are beneficial, the youngsters will be more connected to their future and will be more motivated. (They will also be less likely to ask, "Why do I need to know this?")

Rationalizing Makes a Teacher Better

Side Note

A nice by-product of requiring oneself to rationalize classroom activities for students (and create buy-in) is that this practice forces a teacher to think deeply about why he or she is doing each lesson. If an educator realizes that he or she cannot explain why a lesson is important, he or she might want to rethink the lesson's methodology.

As a follow-up to lessons, I have asked students which 21st century skills were reinforced. I have asked kids to tell me how certain lessons could be delivered differently to reinforce other relevant skills for their futures. This not only generates ideas, but keeps students thinking about which skills are relevant to their lives. To help with this practice,

21ˢᵗ century skills, habits, and attitudes can be posted on the walls of a classroom to keep those goals present in students' minds.

In addition to creating lessons that exercise the actual skills of the new century, our learning activities and assessments can be constructed to model the functions of our 21ˢᵗ century workplace. Kids can do authentic math problems in which the youngsters imagine working for a multinational company that is engineering a product. In English, students can read and write about situations that involve the interconnected realities of the new economy. In Social Studies, kids can discuss the ways in which automation has and will change the world. These lessons develop an awareness of the new world in which we live.

Teacher Stories / Modeling

Educators can take opportunities during class time to tell stories that develop an understanding of the new economy. The stories can be about teacher's experiences or from current or recent real-world events. In addition to telling stories, teachers can model the ways in which people perform tasks that are useful in the 21ˢᵗ century economy. (Again, we will have many examples of this modeling throughout this book.)

Student Assessment

During class time, students can learn only so much about the demands of the 21ˢᵗ century. However, there is an infinite amount to be learned when they actively assess the world around them, rather than passively wander through their days. With a watchful eye, they can assess what new career opportunities are emerging and what skills are required. Wherever students go, they can look around to learn what skills, habits, and attitudes are required of various professionals, from hospitals to businesses. Young minds can also ponder what makes certain professionals successful and effective, while others are not. These thoughts help students think about what they need to thrive in the work world.

The challenge for teachers is to get kids thinking *independently* about the future and the skills they need. Stimulating young minds to assess the world around them can sound like a difficult task. What can we do to influence their minds in this way? We can plant the seeds of assessment. This means that we provide learning activities that include self-assessments and assessments of students and processes in classroom. We can also send home assignments that require young people to assess the world around them outside of school. If we plant these seeds of assessment, we can increase the likelihood that our youth will begin to look at their environment with a critical eye, asking themselves how things function, how things could be improved, and how the students could better themselves.

> ### Personal Empowerment Menu (for 21st Century Students)
> As mentioned in Chapter 3, a student flip chart is available that contains the Personal Empowerment Questions (PEQs) that kids should ask themselves and Personal Empowerment Statements (PESs) that kids should strive to affirm in order to empower themselves in the 21st century. In addition, this chart includes assessment rubrics that kids can use to assess themselves and others. This resource is great for helping kids learn to assess the world around them in order to develop their 21st century skills, attitudes, habits, and connections. The mental practice of reflecting on these traits will deepen students' connections to their futures.

Curricular Examples

Very often there are opportunities within the curriculum to highlight the various facets that create the new economy and the skills necessary to thrive in that new economy.

Examples - Various Content Areas

In a Social Studies class, historical work circumstances can be contrasted with those of the new economy to develop an awareness of the world around us and the skills that are required for thriving within it. Language Arts (English) content can involve a similar comparison when reading stories. The circumstances that face the characters can be contrasted with those that face our youth.

In science, students can assess how new knowledge and technologies are changing the work world and how they are shifting the skills that the kids need.

3   Discovering Interests and Passions that Could Lead to Future Careers

If children are able to imagine themselves working in future careers, they are more likely to be motivated in school and see it as a place of empowerment. Therefore, efforts must be made to help students discover and develop their interests and passions.

Examples - School-Wide

Schools should be ripe with opportunities for students to pursue their interests inside and outside of classes. Inside classes, the curriculum should be supported by connections to careers, and opportunities should exist for students to dig deeper into content that interests them. Outside classes, schools should offer a variety of extracurricular opportunities that allow students to pursue and develop their interests and passions.

To help students discover career interests, professionals can be invited to the school to speak with kids. For older students, job shadowing or career internship programs can be used. (To enrich what everyone learns, students can return to school and present what they've experienced to others.)

Discovering Interests and Passions that Could Lead to Future Careers

We Should See Students Who …	PEQs for Students
👁 Seek and pursue their interests in order to find enjoyment, accomplishment, fulfillment, and empowerment 👁 Explore their interests and possible career options with passion and curiosity	❓ What sparks my interest, curiosity, or passion? ❓ Which tasks do I really enjoy? ❓ Which tasks give me a sense of accomplishment, fulfillment, or empowerment? ❓ Considering my interests, what careers do I aspire to achieve? **PESs for Students** • I will follow my interests with passion and curiosity. • Through education, I can pursue my deepest interests.

Students who ask questions and make statements like these grow into adults who find fulfillment as they work with passion in a career of their highest interest.

Connecting Students to the Future: Wrap-up

Promoting a connection to the future is the second type of connection that we should promote within our students. Just like any of the other connections, this connection increases the chances that our youth will enjoy learning, find value in their education, become passionate about school, and want to be a part of the school community.

Thinking About It

- **How did you become aware of the new 21ˢᵗ century economy?**
- **Which strategies for developing an awareness of the new economy are appropriate for your age group, content area, and school?**
- **In order to help students understand the new economy, teachers have to understand it.**
- **What is the level of understanding of the new economy among your staff and how can you improve this understanding?**

How Does This Chapter Support the Goals of This Book?

Let's take a moment to think about the ways in which the ideas of this chapter help us address the three main goals of this book by looking at the "Building Blocks of a 21st Century Education" on page 13 and the "Daily Thoughts for Educators" on page 18. We now have tools and strategies for empowering our youth by developing connections between students and their future.

Make Note of Your Great Ideas!

If you haven't already, note your ideas for implementing the strategies in this chapter in your Teacher Empowerment Menu (for 21st Century Educators). In the future, you can easily reference usable ideas for your class.

In addition, consider the ways in which you can stimulate students to look for connections to their future by using the Personal Empowerment Menu (for 21st Century Students), which contains the relevant PEQs, PESs, and assessment rubric for this chapter.

5 | Student Connections with Their Educators

In our quest to bring out a passion for learning from within our students and connect them to the learning environment, we arrive at another very important type of connection … connections between students and their teachers. Educators who develop quality relationships within the learning environment can inspire, motivate, and get the best from their students. When we think back to our days in school, we can remember those teachers who did this most effectively. These teachers had a human quality beyond the lessons that they taught … a quality that made kids want to be in school and succeed for those teachers. A teacher like this might be the reason you were inspired to become an educator. So what is it that these teachers did and that all of us can do to develop great connections with our students? There are two major groups of techniques that teachers can use to achieve this goal. The first group focuses on teachers and the second focuses on kids.

Connecting Educators with Students: *Educator-Focused* Techniques	Connecting Educators with Students: *Student-Focused* Techniques
Showing Your … 1. Human Side 2. Passion and Excitement for Teaching and Learning 3. Fun Side 4. Positivity 5. Humility 6. Trustworthiness	Showing that You … 1. Care About Them 2. Notice Them 3. Respect Them 4. Like Them 5. Believe in Them 6. Appreciate Them 7. Are Helping Them 8. Support Them 9. Trust Them with Responsibility

Let's look at these techniques in depth so that we can use them to create connections between students and educators.

Educator-Focused Techniques for Connecting Students with Educators

 1   Showing Your Human Side

Students are often surprised to find out that their teachers are "real people" (the younger the child, the greater the surprise). When students figure out that teachers have a family, hobbies, a past, tastes, fears, dreams, and opinions, they realize that they can relate to these adults in both small and large ways. Teachers can do a variety of things to help students know them as individuals: Teachers can share short stories about their past and present, or display pictures of themselves doing hobbies. I find that simply talking with some of my teacher friends in front of students has a great humanizing effect. Kids will often ask, "Are you guys friends?" or "Do you hang out?" When I answer "yes" to these questions, it seems to blow their minds. Regardless of the technique, showing yourself as human can help connect you with your students.

 2   Showing Your Passion and Excitement for Teaching and Learning

There is something inherently motivating about passionate people. Kids are drawn in when they can see that we are having fun and are excited about what we are teaching. Is it really fun and inspiring to be around people who seem bored? Will people who appear to simply be collecting a paycheck spark a passion for learning in their students? Obviously, those teachers who show their love of the subject they teach will have a leg up in connecting with and inspiring their students.

 3   Showing Your Fun Side

A great way to connect with kids is to do things they might not expect. For example, teachers can sing (or perform some other talent), be spontaneous, use (appropriate) student-age slang, or wear a Halloween costume. I like to occasionally wear a child-sized backpack full of sidewalk chalk when teaching. Once in a while I break out a Darth Vader mask that changes my voice as I talk. Everyone has a different style and can find ways to show his or her own fun side.

 4   Showing Your Positivity

When teachers demonstrate positivity and confidence, they become a source of optimism. For example, educators can act positively when they encounter challenging tasks at school. They can also describe a difficult situation that they faced and then demonstrated a positive attitude toward success in that situation. People love to be inspired. Thus, our children connect with teachers who spread hope.

 Showing Your Humility

When teaching, educators might be afraid to admit to their students that they make mistakes, fearing that the students will not trust their knowledge of a topic. The truth is that a mistake here and there is not a big deal to students. They understand that their mentors are human. There is plenty of time in a year to demonstrate one's knowledge to the class. In reality, a bigger mistake is when teachers don't admit their errors. Students can lose respect for a teacher who has made an error but can't admit it. Instead, demonstrating humility can deepen an educator's connection with the members of a class.

I've shared with students instances in my life when I made mistakes. Not only did this make me seem more human, but it taught them lessons about life.

Teachers also seem more "real" to kids when teachers readily show that they are less than perfect. In addition, students can be inspired when they see how their teachers have worked to succeed and overcome personal challenges.

 Showing Your Trustworthiness

Students are more likely to connect with someone who is worthy of trust. Kids who truly need help are more likely to seek out someone who shows consistency and sincerity. We need to not only show these things, but we also need to avoid being judgmental. Instead, those students need to perceive their educators as trustworthy.

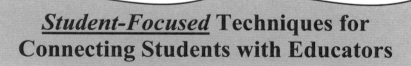

Student-Focused Techniques for Connecting Students with Educators

 Showing that You Care About Them

One of the best ways for educators to connect with students is to show that we care. If our youth do not have the perception that we care about them, we will have difficulty getting through to them. A variety of methods can be used to show that we care.

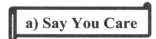 **a) Say You Care**

The simplest way to show our feelings is to come right out and tell students that we care. Although this is easy to do, we sometimes can get caught up in the business of teaching and let this important (yet simple) demonstration of caring slide.

b) Learn about Them

Sometimes the best way to let students know that we care is less overt. Our youth are very perceptive and will understand our sentiment when we *show* them that we care. When we take the time to get to know them, understand what their lives are like, and be familiar with their interests, we make a connection. We can quite easily find out these things through formal methods, such as questionnaires, or through informal methods, such as short conversations as you move around the room during a lesson. A few quick questions can lead to some surprising information. The teacher might find that one of his students is passionate about bodybuilding, another is a competitive figure skater, one child spends his spare time working on car engines with his grandpa, and a quiet student has a difficult home life due to certain circumstances. These pieces of information give educators topics for conversation as the year progresses. When I talk to students about their lives, I can see that they are truly happy to have someone taking an interest in them.

c) Refer to Their Names Early and Often

At the beginning of a school year, learn the students' names as quickly as possible and let them see that you know them by using their names. Kids love the effort. The use of names can go beyond classroom conversation. One of my former teachers used the names of the students in my class and their interests when he wrote test questions. This simple technique demonstrated to my class that he was paying attention to our lives and taking an interest in us.

d) Learn Student Motivations

A great by-product of getting to know students is that teachers find out what motivates them. Are they concerned with their grades, their future, their friends, their parents, their happiness, or their past? Students can really see that teachers care when those teachers go beyond a superficial understanding and get to know students' deep down motivations. In addition to showing that educators care, the practice of learning student motivations arms teachers with new tools for motivating kids and bringing out the best in them.

2   Showing that You Notice Them

When a student comes into the class and looks unusually sad, that student may be affected in a positive way if a teacher asks him about his feelings. The student might actually need help and be very grateful that someone noticed. Sometimes, he or she might not be interested in confiding in the teacher, but is nonetheless comforted in the fact the teacher showed concern for the student. At the very least, the child knows that the educator cares.

A teacher can demonstrate that he or she notices a student in simple ways … by complimenting the student on a new haircut or commenting on a new backpack or glasses.

Again, the simplest gestures can show students that their teachers notice them, thus, reinforcing connections.

Showing that You Respect Them

When a teacher is polite and civil to the members of his or her class, the students feel respected. Some of my teacher friends call this "treating a kid like a human." When our youth sense that their teachers respect them, they are more likely to reciprocate the sentiment. Mutual respect strengthens the teacher-student bond.

Even in situations in which a teacher must discipline a child, a respectful demeanor is the key. Yelling or using contemptuous language can provoke a kid to behave even worse. Some students (who might be trying to get under their teacher's skin) might feel as though their mission is accomplished if the teacher starts to raise his or her voice. A respectful and calm demeanor from an educator, coupled with rational and consistent consequences, can diffuse situations rather than erode the student-teacher relationship.

Showing that You Like Them

Time and time again, I have found that people simply like to be liked. It seems to be human nature to gravitate toward those who find us genial, interesting, and fun. I know that I feel a sense of satisfaction when people are fond of me and show it. I tend to want to return the sentiment. This can be seen in our students. They are human. They want to be liked, especially during their years of social development when they are looking for acceptance. A teacher who shows that he likes his students will be viewed by them as friendly and affable; by making those connections, he will be more likely to get his students to "buy into" his class.

Showing that You Believe in Them

Effective leaders must build self-confidence in others. Coaches must build self-assurance among their team members, and teachers must develop self-belief in their students. When educators act as the students' number one cheerleader ("You can do it!"), the kids gain the confidence to succeed and the student-teacher connection is deepened. Just like young people are drawn to those who like them, they are drawn to those who believe in them. Words of support and encouragement are crucial.

Showing that You Appreciate Them

When teachers are praised by their leaders, receive a thank you card from a student, or receive a compliment from a parent, we feel appreciated. These moments of appreciation are fulfilling and can get us through the tougher moments of the school year. For students, the need to feel appreciated is exactly the same. Like any other person, kids want to feel valued; they want to know that someone notices their contributions to the class. When an educator shows her appreciation for a child through a kind word, a short note to his parents, a phone call to his parents, or a pat on the back, she is deepening her connection with him by making him feel validated as a young person.

7   Showing that You are Helping Them

Showing our youth that teachers are there to help them can strengthen the teacher-student bond. Rather than simply doing a lesson, we should explain to kids what they will gain from it and rationalize the ways in which it will help them in their futures. In doing so, students are more likely to realize that we're not simply imposing work upon them for no reason. This can make them more likely to buy into class activities and work hard.

Occasionally, it is important for educators to discuss with students the effort that went into creating a lesson. In doing so, teachers should focus on how the lesson was developed to try to connect the activity to the students' lives. Even though they might not say it often, students do appreciate that we are working hard for them. They respect that we take the time to create valuable lessons. When students perceive that our hard work is helping them, the student-teacher connection deepens; the idea that the students and the teacher are a learning team is promoted.

8   Showing that You Support Them

Students like to know that their teachers champion what they do inside and outside of the classroom. When kids see the faces of their teachers and principals at school and non-school functions, they know that their educators support them and find their endeavors to be important. It can mean a great deal to a child when his or her teachers attend youth activities, such as a sporting event, a band concert, or a choir concert. Attending activities such as these requires a larger time commitment, but teachers can also show support in other ways. For instance, kids enjoy their teachers or principals volunteering to take a pie in the face at an assembly. They appreciate it when their teachers wear shirts with the name of the school on a game day. Students feel special when asked, "How did the dance recital go?" When kids see that we care about their interests, we develop a connection with them.

Connecting Students with Educators is a Team Endeavor

Side Note

Educators can work together to develop connections with their students. A great deal can be learned about students by talking with others who are familiar with them. We can quickly learn information about kids that took others months to discover and immediately take advantage of this information in developing connections.

A teacher's personality and hobbies will not perfectly match every student that he or she teaches, and that's fine. We can find other educators who can connect with our students. For instance, if "Teacher A" knows that one of his students likes to fish and knows that "Teacher B" also likes to fish, "Teacher A" can introduce the student to "Teacher B." A quick discussion in passing between a kid who likes fishing and a teacher who likes

Side Note

fishing can have a great impact on that student. The ultimate goal is to get students connected with the adult population of the school; the more, the better. A school can even create a mentoring program to promote this.

We don't have to know students to try to develop connections with them. When we see an athlete in the hallway wearing his football jersey on a Friday, we know he has a game that night. Why not say, "Good luck tonight"? Even though we might not personally know that student, we are still connecting him to the school's adult community. This goes for any kid who we recognize to be participating in an activity. Why not take these opportunities to connect?

★ 9 | Showing that You Trust Them with Responsibility

Many kids like to be given various forms of responsibility. When an adult trusts a student to do something, that student feels respected. Sometimes, an apathetic student can be "brought alive" when he or she is entrusted with an important task. Imagine a child who is good with computers. If he or she is asked by the teacher for help addressing a technological problem that could hinder the class, the child could feel empowered, feel important, and show new motivation. (Of course, doing this would require that the teacher previously learned about the student's interests.) In other examples, kids can be put in charge of feeding a class pet, watering a plant, passing out papers, leading a line of students down a hallway, or managing a team in class. Giving all students some form of responsibility at one point or another will strengthen student-teacher connections.

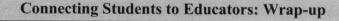

Connecting Students to Educators: Wrap-up

By connecting students to educators, we give them one more connection to the learning environment. We decrease the risk that they will drop out, and we increase the chance that they will buy into the school environment that will prepare them to thrive in the 21st century and find passion in learning. Additionally, the behaviors that educators demonstrate in developing connections can serve as models for how to appropriately function and communicate with others in the real world. As a youth, I know that I learned some of life's greatest lessons and received some of my greatest inspiration from teachers who worked to develop connections with the students in my schools. Did you?

Overall … It's the Little Things that Add Up

We need to remember that it is often the quick, little things (that don't take extra time) that make a huge difference. From all the categories above, there are so many things that can be done. There are so many times in a day when there is an opportunity to say a simple thing to a student to promote a connection. There are so many times to smile, be polite, and be positive. Each of these instances alone might seem insignificant. What we have to remember is that these moments build up over time to create a very, very powerful connection between educators and students.

Young people are always watching us. Every single time we do something to connect with a student, others notice it. Every child is affected positively when they see us do something constructive for a classmate.

Connections between Teachers and Students

We Should See Students Who ...	Personal Empowerment Question (PEQ) for Students
👁 Share mutual respect with their educators 👁 Benefit from the mentorship of educators 👁 Trust educators 👁 Feel understood and cared for by educators	❓ How do I promote mutual respect with my educators and mentors? ❓ How can I help my educators communicate with, connect with, understand, and mentor me? ❓ What connects me to my educators and mentors? **Personal Empowerment Statements (PESs) for Students** • I have quality relationships with my educators / mentors. • My educators and mentors are real people who are passionate, fun, positive, humble, and trustworthy. • My educators and mentors care about me, notice me, respect me, like me, believe in me, appreciate me, support me, trust me with responsibility, and help me.

Students who ask questions and make statements like these develop meaningful connections with educators and are drawn to the learning environment.

Thinking About It
- **Which student connection techniques have you seen in action that were effective?**
- **Will all students respond in the same ways to all techniques?**
- **Why is it important to work to become better at all of the techniques above?**
- **In what areas could you become more effective?**

How Does This Chapter Support the Goals of This Book?

Let's take a moment to think about the ways in which the ideas of this chapter help us address the three main goals of this book by looking at the "Building Blocks of a 21st Century Education" on page 13 and the "Daily Thoughts for Educators" on page 18. We now have tools and strategies for empowering our youth by developing connections between students and their educators.

Make Note of Your Great Ideas!

If you haven't already, note your ideas for implementing the strategies in this chapter in your Teacher Empowerment Menu (for 21ˢᵗ Century Educators). In the future, you can easily reference usable ideas for your class.

6 | Student Connections with the School Environment

In addition to the connections that we have already discussed, there is another that is very valuable. This connection deals with the environment of the school, both in a physical sense and in the impression of the attitudes the school staff generates. Our goal must be to create an environment that draws students in and supports their ability to thrive. The following is a series of conditions that should be met. Many go beyond simply drawing students into the school environment; they reinforce specific skills, habits, and attitudes that are necessary in the 21st century.

<u>Connecting Students with the School Environment</u>

Creating an Environment that is …
1. Welcoming
2. Safe
3. Responsible
4. Successful
5. Distraction-Free
6. Goal-Oriented
7. Empowering
8. Team-Oriented
9. Fun and Exciting
10. Technological
11. Curious
12. Aesthetically Pleasing
13. Disciplined

---

1 | **Creating a Welcoming Environment**

It is human nature to enjoy feeling wanted. Our youth want to feel welcome in the school in which they will spend a huge amount of their time. Whether it is with signs, words, or attitudes, educators must display a welcoming feeling to their students. For instance, I like to stand by my door and greet every student as he or she arrives. Teachers should also strive to make a welcoming classroom environment. Upon entering my room on the first day of class, students find that there is empty space on a wall (labeled "The Wall O' Pictures") on which they can post pictures of themselves. Through simple acts like these, teachers can convey the idea to their students that they are wanted and that the school is like a second home.

     Welcoming activities are not restricted simply to individual classrooms. Some schools have activities such as orientation days or student lock-ins. Of course, activities such as these should not be limited only to students. Receptions, such as school open houses to which parents are invited, are just as important in creating a welcoming school environment.

We Should See Students Who ...	Personal Empowerment Question (PEQ) for Students
👁 Are connected to visible, friendly, and helpful staff 👁 Are attracted to an aesthetically pleasing environment 👁 Participate in welcoming activities 👁 Welcome other students	❓ Why do I feel like I belong here? **Personal Empowerment Statements (PESs) for Students** • I feel welcome and important here. • I want to promote a welcome feeling among others.

Students who ask questions and make statements like these feel welcome and will tend to welcome others in school and as an adult.

⭐ 2   Creating a Safe Environment

     If students do not feel safe, teachers will have a difficult time connecting students to the school environment, making them want to be at school, and motivating them to learn. Therefore, it is essential that we promote safety. Physical or emotional threats from other students, teachers, or the structure of the school are unacceptable. Both inside and outside of the classroom, we should not tolerate threatening behaviors that detract from the learning goals of the educational institution.

We Should See Students Who ...	PEQ for Students
👁 Are stimulated to behave respectfully 👁 Trust their educators and peers 👁 Feel safe in the structure of the school 👁 Participate freely	❓ Why do I feel safe here? **PESs for Students** • I and others behave respectfully here. • I trust the people and physical structure around me.

Students who ask questions and make statements like these are free from feelings of fear and are emotionally prepared to engage in learning activities. They are more likely to respect others as young people and as adults.

⭐ 3   Creating a Responsible Environment

     When we promote responsibility in our students, we encourage them to take an active role in their education. This can give them a sense of ownership of their learning. While students can sometimes shy away from personal reliance, we don't do them any favors by minimizing or

6 · Student Connections with the School Environment

removing responsibility. Making students accountable actually sends the message that we believe they are capable. This message connects them to the learning environment, as they get a sense that they are trusted, respected, and considered competent.

Aside from connecting students to the learning environment, we have to promote responsibility among our students for other reasons. In an ever-changing 21st century where jobs are highly competitive and job skills are continuously changing, our future adults will need a dependable attitude. Gradually, during their years in school, our youth must develop a mind-set of personal reliance and dedication. These viewpoints are far superior to letting young adults go into the world thinking that life will just take care of itself. Of course, the approach to this process varies in different grade levels, and there are a multitude of mechanisms through which educators can promote accountability. Whether we stimulate young people to be prepared for class, complete assignments in a timely manner, or be organized, each action brings students one step closer to self-sufficiency. We cannot squander our opportunities to develop this real life skill.

We Should See Students Who ...	PEQs for Students
👁 Plan for success 👁 Behave proactively 👁 Accept responsibility	❓ What are my responsibilities as a learner? ❓ What do I need to do in order to be successful? **PES for Students** • I plan for success, behave proactively, accept responsibility, and work hard.

Students who ask questions and make statements like these are more successful in school and become responsible adults.

4 Creating a Successful Environment

Educators must create an environment where students feel like they can succeed. This does not mean that we make lessons less challenging. Rather, we must promote a positive attitude and demonstrate confidence that our students will succeed. The ways in which a teacher can work toward this goal range from what he says to how he structures his lessons.

First, speaking positively with students is a simple, yet powerful way to reinforce our conviction that students can succeed. Some students do not encounter role models outside of school who display confidence in them. We must be a source of positivity, because it is difficult for kids to believe in themselves if they perceive that educators do not have faith in them.

Second, we must consider how we structure our lessons and classroom activities. There are a few things we can do to promote confidence and build an attitude of success in our students. For instance, when a teacher has an activity that seems very challenging and potentially overwhelming, he or she can break it into smaller pieces that will seem more manageable to the students. By chunking the steps in an activity, the students feel more comfortable, because they are allowed to experience small successes along the way. When they finish, they can look back and see that a difficult task was actually manageable when compartmentalized into smaller pieces.

Another way to build student confidence is to allow students to have some choices in the method in which they will learn about a topic. When allowed to pick the process that works best for them, they can see the task as more manageable.

Whether we promote confidence through words or lesson structure, students respond well to an environment that promotes the idea that everyone can succeed.

We Should See Students Who ...	PEQs for Students
👁 Display a positive attitude 👁 Believe in their ability to succeed 👁 Are given tasks that are structured to be manageable	❓ In what ways am I prepared to handle challenges? ❓ Am I being positive and seeing my own great potential? ❓ In what ways am I building my success? ❓ What can I do to improve my performance? ❓ How can I perform this task so that it feels manageable? **PES for Students** • I will succeed!

Students who ask questions and make statements like these build confidence and are willing to take on bigger challenges.

5 Creating a Distraction-Free Environment

If learning is to be the focus of a classroom, then distractions must be limited. Students may have difficulties in learning if other students are talking at inappropriate times, moving around the room for no reason, coming into the room late, or playing games on their new micro-sized phone. An environment that is focused on learning has no place for these types of distractions. When teachers create a distraction free environment that allows for engaging activities, students appreciate that environment. If we are going to connect young minds with the learning environment and motivate them to learn, then we cannot allow other things to draw their attention away from lessons (especially because kids are a bit more impulsive than adults).

Having clear classroom behavior expectations is important. Students should agree on what constitutes a respectful, distraction-free environment. Having students help create a simple list of classroom expectations will give them ownership in the management of their classroom and will hold them accountable to one another.

We Should See Students Who ...	PEQs for Students
👁 Are focused 👁 Are good citizens 👁 Consider others and do not create distractions	❓ How can I positively affect the learning environment? ❓ How can I avoid creating distractions for others? **PES for Students** • I am a focused, good citizen who does not distract others.

Students who ask questions and make statements like these are more likely to support a focused learning environment and grow into focused adults.

6 Creating a Goal-Oriented Environment

I like to start off the year by asking my students to dream. I give them a questionnaire and ask them: What do you love to do and what would you like to do in the future? From these long-term dreams, I ask them to think about long-term educational goals that they would need to accomplish to achieve their vision. Then, I ask them to create short-term goals for the school year. These goals can include certain skills that they want to develop, certain activities in which they want to participate, grades that they want to achieve, habits they want to build, and attitudes they want to create in themselves. All of these targets are intended to help the students work toward their ultimate goals. Setting goals helps the students see the big picture of their lives and then break that into smaller, manageable pieces. Having aspirations provides students with direction, motivation, and a roadmap for their education. Periodically, kids should assess themselves so that their attention is drawn to their own objectives.

In addition to helping students connect with the learning environment, goal setting provides an invaluable life skill. In the 21st century, adults must have the ability to create short- and long-term, achievable goals that assist them in accomplishing their life's dreams and passions. Also, the process of setting and working toward goals will help adults to manage the complexities of an ever-changing business world. Adults who have practice in goal setting will be better equipped to modify what they are doing to adjust to changes in their personal and work environments.

We Should See Students Who ...	PEQs for Students
👁 Dream 👁 Set short- and long-term goals 👁 Self-assess regularly to monitor progress 👁 Develop strategies to attain goals	❓ What are my dreams for the future? ❓ What goals do I need to achieve in order to reach my dreams? ❓ To what degree am I meeting my goals? ❓ What things am I doing well? ❓ What do I need to improve? ❓ What steps can I take to better achieve my goals? **PES for Students** • I will accomplish my dreams, because I set goals and follow a plan for success.

Students who ask questions and make statements like these are more successful in school and also become adults who are goal-oriented in their careers.

7 Creating an Empowering Environment

Students need to know that school is a place where they will obtain the tools necessary to succeed in life. It is a place that empowers them to do and be whatever they want. Educators need to remind the students of the control that they have over their own lives. *They will get out of their education what they put into their education.* When students are persuaded to understand that school provides them with the power to create success in their lives, they become deeply connected to the learning environment; they see its value.

An empowering environment can also be created by allowing some choices in learning. Young minds love to be given options. If you think about it, kids are guided and told what to do on a regular basis. Choice is freedom. Classroom alternatives can come in many forms: selecting how to present something, picking how to learn something, choosing how to be assessed, or electing what extensions of a concept to learn. I have found classes to be satisfied by simply deciding the order in which we will do some activities. The power of choice liberates kids and puts them "in charge."

We Should See Students Who ...	PEQs for Students
👁 Work toward independence	❓ In what ways am I empowered to achieve my goals for the future and the present?
👁 Value their education	
👁 Recognize that they are empowered with control over their future	❓ In what ways are my school experiences preparing me for my future?
👁 Have some choices in the classroom	❓ How can I achieve self-reliance?
	❓ How would I like to demonstrate my understanding, learn a concept, or extend my knowledge of a concept?
	PES for Students
	• I will have future success, because I am empowering myself through positive educational choices.

Students who ask questions and make statements like these develop a sense of control and grow into empowered adults.

8 Creating a Team-Oriented Environment

To help connect students to the learning environment, it is valuable to promote a classroom atmosphere of teamwork. When kids feel as though they have an important role in a larger unit, they develop a sense of belonging. They can see themselves as valuable not only to their own learning, but to the learning of the whole class. By getting classmates to work as a unit, educators are not only helping to connect the students to the learning environment … they are actually increasing the chances of student success. A child's peers can be a source of motivation and a resource to enhance learning. A classroom full of students who ask each other questions and gain knowledge from one another will be much more successful than a classroom where the teacher is the sole resource for information. Not only can kids garner ideas from each other, but they can understand concepts better when they explain those concepts to their classmates. (To explain, you must clarify and order concepts in your own mind.) For all of these reasons, it is important to create a setting in which students think and act as a part of a team.

Working as a team is not limited only to the students. A successful classroom functions in such a way that the teacher and students are cooperative parts of a team working toward academic success. On the first day of school each year, I pass out a syllabus that describes what expectations I have of the students under a heading labeled "Student Responsibilities." The syllabus also describes what the students can expect from me as we work toward their success under a heading called "Teacher Responsibilities." Right from the start, it is important to develop the attitude that the teacher and student body are part of a unit, in which everyone is equally as important. This also helps to promote the idea that the adult is working hard for the students and that the teacher expects students to reciprocate by investing in their own success. Parents comprise another important part of the academic team. We will discuss their role in a later chapter.

We Should See Students Who ...	PEQs for Students
👁 Interact tactfully 👁 Are interdependent 👁 Are responsible to the group 👁 Build on each other's ideas	❓ How can we support one another in building success? ❓ How can I contribute to our success as a team? ❓ How can I promote positive group interactions? **PES for Students** • I am a supportive and positive member of the team.

Students who ask questions and make statements like these are more likely to support one another and grow into adults who function well in the work world of teams.

9   Creating a Fun and Exciting Environment

When attempting to create an environment that is safe, responsible, and free of distractions, the idea that a classroom can be fun is sometimes lost. We cannot afford to make this mistake. Creating an enjoyable and exciting classroom is one of the key facets of drawing students into learning. Promoting this type of atmosphere comes through both a teacher's attitude and actions and through the activities that the class will do.

First, let's look at teachers. When an educator demonstrates that he or she is passionate about classroom activities and the curricular content, the students feed off of that passion. Some teachers are afraid to smile for fear it will upset their ability to be disciplinarians. How will educators stimulate a passion for learning if it looks like they are bored or angry?

Teachers can take some very simple actions to create an enjoyable environment; for example, smile, crack jokes, or use nicknames. I like to wait until about a month into the school year and then walk into the classroom wearing a Darth Vader outfit, carrying a light saber, and playing Star Wars music. Sometimes, when my students seem tired and are slow to get their brains working early in the morning, I have them do the wave. These types of things are cheesy, but the kids enjoy the activities.

Second, aside from the behaviors and attitudes teachers exhibit, learning pursuits can be created to promote a pleasurable atmosphere. There are many activities that can be tweaked slightly to give them a "game feel." Certainly, the classroom should not be all games all the time. However, if it's possible to do a lesson that is modified in some small way in order to create excitement and fun, why not do it? Sometimes, the activity doesn't even have to be changed. Enthusiasm can be generated by simply allowing students to pick a name for their team in the activity. Little things add up to make a big difference.

Whether created through activities or through teachers' behaviors, a fun and exciting environment deepens students' connections to the classroom and school.

We Should See Students Who ...	PEQ for Students
👁 Are passionate 👁 Are having fun and laugh 👁 Engage in friendly competition 👁 Display spirit	❓ Why is school enjoyable, and how do I support this? **PES for Students** • School is fun, exciting, and interesting! I love it!

Students who ask questions and make statements like these will enjoy learning as a student and tend to seek out new learning as an adult. They will also tend to promote an enjoyable work environment as an adult.

10 ⭐ Creating a Technological Environment

Today's youth are growing up in a much different world than people in the past. The Internet, advanced computer programs, small audio players, smartphones, and other technological gadgets have created a generation of students that thinks and functions differently than those before it. If our classrooms are free of technology, how can we expect to connect with students who are used to a digital world? To draw technologically savvy children into learning, we need to use technology in the classroom. Students respond very well to activities that include the use of PowerPoint® presentations, the Internet, classroom response clickers, short video clips, or interactive whiteboards. The use of these technologies not only connects the students to the learning environment, but can help to prepare them for the 21ˢᵗ century. However, students cannot simply watch teachers use technology. Kids need to use classroom technology themselves in order to develop new understandings and creatively display new knowledge and skills. We will look more in depth at technology in a later chapter.

We Should See Students Who ...	PEQ for Students
👁 Use a variety of technologies in lessons and assessments 👁 Use technologies in a manner that mirrors their usefulness in the real world	❓ Why do I like these technological learning tools? **PESs for Students** • This technology suits the ways in which my generation thinks and creates. • This technology is useful for real-world purposes such as ____.

Students who ask questions and make statements like these have greater enjoyment for learning and grow into adults who leverage useful technological tools for accomplishing real world tasks.

11 ★ Creating a Curious Environment

In the world that awaits our students, they will need to have the ability to ask questions, probe for answers, and develop new knowledge on their own. Creating a setting that promotes curiosity and discovery not only prepares students for this new world, it also connects them to the learning environment. Whenever possible, students need to be stimulated to generate questions and make predictions about the curriculum. These opportunities can be formally built into class activities in which kids are required to ask probing questions. I also like to do something less formal in which students write down anonymous questions about anything related to science. I then answer the questions for the class by building on what they know. This rather simple act of asking questions promotes and allows an outlet for students' curiosity in science, and this activity can work in other subjects. (If I don't know an answer, I challenge the students to find the answer.) Sometimes, my students' favorite lessons are the result of their queries.

We Should See Students Who ...	PEQs for Students
👁 Generate questions	❓ Why?
👁 Think outside of the box	❓ How did that come to be?
👁 Engage in activities that prompt investigation	❓ How does that work?
	❓ How can I do _____?
	PES for Students
	• I want answers to interesting questions.

Students who ask questions and make statements like these have their imaginations sparked and grow into adults who are conscious consumers of the world around them.

12 ★ Creating an Aesthetically Pleasing Environment

We need to recognize that when the physical environment of both the classroom and the school at large are comfortable, students will be more engaged. A ton of money does not need to be tossed into making a school or classroom look like a royal palace. However, human nature dictates that we function better in a place that is generally clean, organized, and inviting. With a little care, classrooms, hallways, and other parts of the school can be attractive. Students who perceive their surroundings as being well maintained by adults and their peers are more likely to take care of their school by picking up trash, not writing on desks or walls, and keeping their general area clean and tidy. With a little artwork, some color, and some inspirational quotes on the walls, the physical environment can even be inspiring.

We Should See Students Who ...	PEQ for Students
👁 Are functioning comfortably in an inviting, clean, and organized environment	❓ Why am I comfortable here?
	PES for Students
	• I enjoy and support surroundings that are clean, well-maintained, attractive, and inspiring.

Students who ask questions and make statements like these feel comfortable in their learning environment and are more likely to promote and respect aesthetically pleasing work environments as an adult.

Side Note

6 - Student Connections with the School Environment

Getting Students to Help Create a Quality Environment

By meeting the previous twelve objectives, educators can create a learning environment that connects with the students. Above, some strategies were pointed out for meeting these objectives. In addition, it is important for students to see the big picture of the environment that an educator is trying to create. To do this, I like to start off the school year by asking students to think about their short-term goals for the year and longer-term education and career goals. Then, we have a discussion about the type of environment required for the students to meet their goals. I make sure that we touch on all of the objectives listed above for creating a positive and connected learning environment. (These objectives can be posted on the walls.) It is simple to get young people to buy into these objectives, because our youth generally want these things for themselves. By helping students create this big picture of what we expect our learning environment to look like, I increase the chances that the students will buy into my class and what we will do in it.

★ **13** ⟨ **Creating a Disciplined Environment** ⟩

As noted above, I have found it is very helpful to discuss the previous twelve objectives with my students very early in the year. Once the kids rationalize and understand my expectations dealing with these learning environment objectives, they realize that infractions against these objectives are infractions against a quality learning environment. So, if students are creating a distraction by chatting at an inappropriate time, I warn them that they are disrupting the learning environment for the class and that further infraction will require a consequence. This is much better received than if I were to simply tell the kids to quiet down for the sake of quieting down. Thus, I build my system of discipline around maintaining a quality learning environment where infractions against this environment are considered infractions against the learning goals of the class and all of its students.

Even though I have found this system minimizes disruptions, kids will inevitably be kids. So, consequences are needed. In situations dealing with consequences, I have found that there are keys to minimizing disrespectful reactions and to maximizing a positive change in future behavior.

<u>Keys to a Disciplined Environment</u>

- **Proactivity**
- **Respect**
- **Communication**
- **Follow-through**
- **Consistency**
- **Buy-in**

---

a) Proactivity

A proactive teacher addresses situations when they are minimal by smoothly redirecting the path of events or by using rational consequences that match the offense, rather than waiting for situations to escalate.

b) Respect

A respectful teacher is polite and never loses his or her cool when employing consequences with a student. By remaining calm, discipline can be more effective, because the teacher does not show that the student has gotten under his skin. This can occasionally be the goal of a student who wants to save face in front of peers when the kid is in trouble. With politeness, the educator does not embarrass the student or escalate the situation.

c) Communication

When communicating with a student, a teacher describes the infraction against the learning environment and explains that a consequence must be used to maintain a quality classroom environment. The educator should be clear that the choices of the student brought about the consequence.

d) Follow-through

When a warning is followed by continued negative student behavior, an educator must follow through and enact discipline. Without follow-through, students will not take warnings seriously in the future, disrupting a teacher's ability to diffuse small situations before situations escalate. (It is important that negative consequences are not academically-based so that students do not associate learning with something negative.) Another thing to consider is that when one student creates an infraction against the learning environment, everyone else is watching to see how the teacher will respond. Thus, follow-through is important not only in dealing with that one student, but in affecting the future behavior of all students.

e) Consistency

Teachers must consistently treat every single student equally. If kids perceive that a teacher has favorites, some might act out and situations might intensify.

f) Buy-in

Educators need to stimulate students to "buy in" to creating a positive learning environment. If students are disruptively chatting, the adult shouldn't simply tell them to be quiet for quiet's sake. Instead, he should say, "Let's create an environment that allows us to be focused and successful." It sounds cheesy, but that simple statement works, because the students see that the discipline is meant for their benefit.

Empower the Class to Make Positive Discipline Choices

Teachers can benefit from empowering students to make positive discipline choices. For example, a teacher can say, "When you are ready to start, we can do this fun activity. Otherwise, we won't have time for it." This statement shifts the classroom from being a place where the teacher is imposing discipline to a place where the kids *choose* to begin a lesson because they *want* to begin. Students will begin to "police" their peers when they see that they are empowered to affect the classroom activities.

Develop Respect Early

It is especially important that teachers stick tightly to these discipline guidelines early in the school year. If a teacher does not establish his or her role as the leader of a classroom at an early stage, that teacher will have difficulties later. Recovering from creating the perception of being a "pushover" can take weeks or months. When a teacher establishes his or her role as a respected leader in the beginning of the year, much less time will be spent dealing with discipline from that point on; it becomes a matter of maintenance. Also, a teacher who spends less time on discipline has much more time to focus on teaching and learning.

Stay Positive

Recognizing and telling students when they have done something wrong is easy, but sometimes we can forget to use positive reinforcement when youngsters are doing things right. Positive consequences for good behavior are just as effective as rational consequences for poor behavior. Telling students at the end of the day that they have worked very well on a task and that you are proud of them can be very powerful in creating a positive classroom environment. As stated earlier, though, these opportunities are easier to miss when we get caught up in all that we need to accomplish in a day.

We Should See Students Who ...	PEQ for Students
👁 Buy in to class objectives	❓ How do I view the system of discipline in this classroom?
👁 Respect their educators, their peers, the school, and the goals of their education	**PESs for Students**
👁 Understand, respect, and see the value of their teacher's discipline system	• I want a positive learning environment so that I can succeed, and my teacher's discipline system supports this goal.
👁 Demonstrate appropriate demeanor	• I see the value of my teacher's discipline system.
👁 Trust their teachers	• My educator is reasonable, fair, and trustworthy.
	• I feel respected here.

Students who ask questions and make statements like these become a positive part of the learning environment and are more likely to contribute positively to workplace situations as adults.

Connecting Students to the School Environment: Wrap-up

By connecting students to the learning environment, we further attract them to their school and increase the chances that they will develop relevant work skills and find passion in learning. Seemingly minor actions on the part of teachers add up to large connections between students and the school environment.

Side Note

Learn from Others; Recognize What Can Work For You

By observing and talking with other educators, teachers can gather great ideas for connecting kids to the learning environment. While we can learn a lot from one another, we must remember that teachers do have different personalities. A technique that works for one teacher in creating a fun classroom atmosphere might not work for another. For instance, if jumping up and down on the table (which you might have seen in a video about engaging teaching) is not your style, it does not mean that you are not an enjoyable or interesting teacher. We are all unique. As long as we can find personally suitable ways to meet the objectives above in our own settings, our students will connect with us and our classroom setting.

Thinking About It

- **What were the strengths of your school environment when you were a student?**
- **What could have been improved?**
- **What are the strengths of your classroom and school?**
- **What could be done to improve the environment in your classroom and school?**

How Does This Chapter Support the Goals of This Book?

Let's take a moment to think about the ways in which the ideas of this chapter help us address the three main goals of this book by looking at the "Building Blocks of a 21st Century Education" on page 13 and the "Daily Thoughts for Educators" on page 18. We now have tools and strategies for empowering our youth by developing connections between students and the school environment.

Make Note of Your Great Ideas!

If you haven't already, note your ideas for implementing the strategies in this chapter in your Teacher Empowerment Menu (for 21st Century Educators). In the future, you can easily reference usable ideas for your class.

In addition, consider the ways in which you can stimulate students to look for connections to their school environment by using the Personal Empowerment Menu (for 21st Century Students), which contains the relevant PEQs, PESs, and assessment rubric for this chapter.

7 | Student Connections with Other Students

In addition to the various connections already discussed, relationships among students can be very powerful in drawing our youth to school. When you think back to your own school days, think about the value that your peers had in connecting you to your school setting. Beyond drawing students into the learning environment, relationships among students also set the stage for them to develop a multitude of social and team-oriented skills that are important in the new economy. While we will look more closely at developing student social and interactive skills in later chapters, here we will think about ways in which we can develop connections among our students so that they can develop socially and more simply be drawn toward school.

Creating Peer Connections *Inside* the Classroom	Creating Peer Connections *Outside* the Classroom
1. Meeting New People 2. Developing Familiarity 3. Promoting Positive Student Interactions	1. Getting Students Involved 2. Using Activities with the Specific Goal of Developing Connections

Creating Peer Connections *Inside* The Classroom

1 Meeting New People

The first step in developing peer connections is simple, but essential. From kindergarten through twelfth grade, kids need to meet new people in school. From welcoming and getting-to-know-you activities to group pursuits dealing with the curriculum, there are numerous ways in which an educator is able to put students in situations that allow them to meet new people. For instance, teachers can structure teams for group activities so that kids make contact with someone new. These groupings should not be changed so often that relationships aren't allowed to develop past a superficial exchange of names. Relationships need time to grow, so a balance is required. But in total, it is important for educators to put the members of their class in contact with new peers. You never know when students might meet peers who eventually become their best friends, peers who become the reason that they don't drop out of school, peers who help them with their homework, or peers who help them when they are in great personal need.

Developing Familiarity with Others

Educators can promote connections among their students by helping kids develop a familiarity with each other within the school setting. Any little activity that can be woven into a lesson that allows classmates to learn each others' interests, hobbies, or personality traits can accomplish this goal. Some activities might focus directly on developing familiarity, such as show-and-tell in the younger grades. Other activities might work these goals into more curriculum-focused activities. For instance, math (or other) students might connect their understanding of a skill to the real world by creating story problems that include information about themselves. Not only does this strategy deepen the connection to the curriculum in a fun way and promote creativity, it gives the kids a chance to learn about one another when asked to solve the problems other students created.

Some of the same activities mentioned in Chapter 3 "Connecting Students to the Curriculum" can also help develop a familiarity among the students. For instance, if students create an engaging curricular product that they must present to the class, an opportunity is created for the learners to interact and develop a sense of each other's personalities. Similarly, when a class engages in a discussion dealing with the real-world application of the curriculum, they get a chance to develop an awareness of one another's opinions and identities.

Promoting Positive Student Interactions

We have already looked at stimulating students to meet new people and to develop a familiarity with their classmates. Rather than simply meeting peers and knowing about them through presentations or debates, it can be beneficial to go one step further. Connections among students can be much deeper if they have quality interactions with one another. This is where teamwork comes in. When classmates are required to develop knowledge together, collectively create a product, or jointly determine the best way to solve a problem, they have to go beyond simply knowing the names and basic interests of others. They have to cooperate with one another. Interactions require peers to present their ideas, respond to what they hear, explain concepts, and address disagreements. Not only does this interaction deepen their connection to and increase their understanding of their classmates, it also promotes the ability to work with others. This ability has always been important in life, but is even more important in the 21st century.

Creating Peer Connections *Outside* The Classroom

1 Getting Students Involved

Some of the most meaningful connections among students can be created outside of the traditional classroom. Extracurricular activities are crucial in developing student bonds. Through activities such as clubs, sports, field trips, retreats, or elementary recess, students are able to interact and grow closer. One reason these opportunities are so powerful is that they often bring together students with similar interests. For instance, kids who join a poetry club share a similar passion and likely will develop bonds with those who share that passion. Kids in a junior baseball or softball league are united by a common interest in their sport. Young students on the playground might find others with a similar fondness for a certain leisure activity. All sorts of pastimes serve to bring together students with common tastes. This increases the likelihood that students will become connected and satisfied with their learning environment. In addition, extracurricular activities provide students with opportunities to discover their passions and learn life lessons that will be important to them in the future.

2 Using Activities with the Specific Goal of Developing Connections

The high school where I work has used activities that are designed specifically to develop student connections. One activity with which I have been involved is a communications camp that we call "Camp Connections." For this activity, we take a group of students away from our school to a not-so-rustic camp for a couple of days. The students are selected so that participants come together from different school cliques. We choose leaders who can promote within the school those lessons that they learn at the camp.

During the camp, peers are divided into small and diverse groups of students with one male and one female teacher. The groups participate in communication sessions to discuss things about which they are passionate. They select a leader for each session and choose a discussion topic. Over the course of the camp, the students sometimes agree, sometimes disagree, sometimes laugh, and sometimes cry. Their participation and openness in the sessions generally grows as the camp progresses. The results are phenomenal. In my years of doing this, I have seen the students develop a greater understanding of one another and recognize that they are often very similar to people that they perceived to be "different." I've seen new friendships grow, while older ones were strengthened or repaired. Upon return to school, there is a noticeable and encouraging difference in the students. I cannot say enough about how this type of experience positively affects students.

Not only does a camp like this promote connections among the students, but it also serves to strengthen the bond between teachers and students. Students develop a familiarity and trust with adults, which is very positive in the school environment. Additionally, many of our teachers who have attended the camp find a much deeper connection with their peers within the staff.

Our staff was trained in the use of this communications camp model by Jerry Donnelly, an educational consultant who used the technique in other schools. (This communications camp model was originally developed by educational consultants Dan Hogan and Gayle Maudlin who adapted a communications model from the Focus Hope organization in Detroit, Michigan.) Over time, we tailored our administration of the camp to match the environment and climate of our school. With a positive attitude from our teachers, the camp continually improves.

While the camp described above is better suited for older students, a similar positive outcome can be generated for younger students. Elementary schools teachers can take children to places such as a nature camp. A middle school staff in my school district takes eighth graders to Washington, D.C. each year. While the overt focus of these activities is not for developing student connections, that very objective is accomplished (in addition to the wonderful way in which students connect to their classroom curriculum by seeing real-world examples of the curriculum).

There are various camps, school-wide activities, retreats, and festivals that a school can use to generate positive relationships among students and staff. These, along with extra-curricular activities and classroom activities, can be used to create connections among our students and further draw them into our learning community.

Connections Among Students: Wrap-up

We Should See Students Who ...	Personal Empowerment Questions (PEQs) for Students
👁 Meet new peers	❓ How am I connecting with those around me?
👁 Learn about their peers superficially at first and then make deeper connections	❓ How can I become more engaged with my peers?
👁 Interact in order to accomplish relevant curricular learning activities	❓ How can I meet new people?
👁 Are involved in activities outside of the classroom	❓ How can I develop relationships?
👁 Develop relationships	❓ What can I learn from others?
	❓ Which extracurricular activities grab my interest?
	Personal Empowerment Statements (PESs) for Students
	• I am meeting new people and developing deeper connections and relationships over time.
	• I am involved and connected with activities outside of the classroom.

Students who ask questions and make statements like these connect with their peers and grow into adults who are more likely to develop connections with others.

Thinking About It

- **What are some things that you will see when kids are well connected with one-another?**
- **What do you already do that promotes connections among students?**
- **What else could you weave into your learning activities to promote connections among students?**

How Does This Chapter Support the Goals of This Book?

Let's take a moment to think about the ways in which the ideas of this chapter help us address the three main goals of this book by looking at the "Building Blocks of a 21st Century Education" on page 13 and the "Daily Thoughts for Educators" on page 18. We now have tools and strategies for empowering our youth by developing connections between students and their peers.

Make Note of Your Great Ideas!

If you haven't already, note your ideas for implementing the strategies in this chapter in your Teacher Empowerment Menu (for 21st Century Educators). In the future, you can easily reference usable ideas for your class.

In addition, consider the ways in which you can stimulate students to look for connections with their peers by using the Personal Empowerment Menu (for 21st Century Students), which contains the relevant PEQs, PESs, and assessment rubric for this chapter.

8 Student Connections with the Spirit of the School

Yet another way to draw students into the learning environment is to connect them with the spirit of the school. It is human nature for people to be stimulated by feelings of belonging and pride. For our students, this stimulation can come in the form of feelings of pride and spirit for their educational institution. Tapping into this intrinsic aspect of humanity can be very powerful and motivating for our students.

School spirit is often associated with athletics, but pride can be found in many aspects of school life. Spirit can come from a club, a classroom activity, an art show, a music festival, a math competition, a successful graduation, a high test score, community service, or working on a yearbook. Spirit can also come from the simple feeling of belonging to a group larger than oneself. One might be tempted to assume that school spirit is reserved more for older students in middle school and high school, but school pride is just as valuable and effective in elementary school.

Let's look at some things that we can do to promote this connection.

> ### Connecting Students with the Spirit of the School
>
> 1. **Creating a Team Feeling within the School**
> 2. **Promoting Participation in School Activities**
> 3. **Making School Successes a Big Deal**
> 4. **Creating Activities Specifically to Promote School Spirit**
> 5. **Showing Your (Teacher) Spirit**
> 6. **Encouraging Student Leaders to Promote Spirit**
> 7. **Creating a Physical Environment that Stimulates Spirit**

1 Creating a Team Feeling within the School

If we're going to get our youth to take pride in their school, we need to make them feel like a part of the school community … or make them feel like a part of the team. In order to take pride in a school, students need to feel like they belong to it, have a role within it, and are a part of its successes. Some simple things can generate this feeling of belonging to the school. Schools can create signs such as "We are Springfield," make shirts, create songs, paint murals, or use a mascot in order to generate a feeling of unity and belonging. Seeing one's picture in a yearbook gives a student a sense that he or she belongs to the school at-large. When an elementary school student sees his or her painting at the "Springfield Elementary Art Show," he or she feels like an important part of the school.

We Should See Students Who ...	Personal Empowerment Question (PEQ) for Students
👁 Are unified 👁 Are mutually supportive 👁 Have spirit and pride 👁 Feel a sense of belonging	❓ What makes me proud of my school and my other teams? **Personal Empowerment Statement (PES) for Students** • I am a proud member of this amazing team.

Students who ask questions and make statements like these feel connected to their peers and grow into adults who take pride in their teams.

2 Promoting Participation in School Activities

Participation in various school activities, clubs, or teams should also be promoted, because those activities deepen the feeling of belonging to, and pride for, the school. Getting students to participate in spirited activities requires good communication within a school. There must be a system that allows students to find out about activities in which they can become engaged. This communication can be accomplished through announcements, newsletters, activity fairs, or classroom discussions. In addition to simply getting the word out, educators need to encourage students to get involved and participate. If a teacher recognizes that a kid is a good writer, that teacher can encourage participation in a writing club or writing contest. If an educator knows that a child is athletic, that teacher can encourage participation in a sport. (Notice how our previous chapter on connections between teachers and students supports an educator's ability to identify student interests and promote participation.) For the students who don't participate in a specific activity, teachers can make a point of talking about upcoming school events in order to get these students to attend and support their classmates. As stated above, attending an event and seeing your friends representing your school can promote a sense of pride and connection.

We Should See Students Who ...	PEQs for Students
👁 Are involved in school activities 👁 Join welcoming teams and clubs that seek new members 👁 Seek new members for their teams and clubs 👁 Find a variety of activities available at their school 👁 Attend the activities of peers 👁 Have school spirit and pride	❓ How can I become more involved in my school and other teams? ❓ How can I encourage peers to participate in activities? ❓ How can I support my peers in their activities? **PES for Students** • I am a supportive member of school and team activities, and I try to get other people involved.

Students who ask questions and make statements like these become involved in the school community and grow into adults who participate in, and encourage others to participate in, enriching activities.

3 Making School Successes a Big Deal

Once a sense of team and belonging is created in the school, students feel good when anyone in the school succeeds. If someone wins a competition, performs well at a band festival, or gets his or her picture in the news, educators should make a big deal out of the event. (A good system of communication is critical in spreading good news.) If something happens that promotes pride, everybody should know about it. Through announcements, web pages, or newsletters, the word should be spread about large and small accomplishments. Schools can have assemblies to honor successes. Special displays featuring clubs, teams, artwork, and trophies can be created. A success for one is a success for everyone in a well-unified school.

We Should See Students Who ...	PEQ for Students
👁 Take pride in the successes of everyone at their school 👁 Easily learn about the successes in their school through an effective communication system	❓ What gives me a sense of school and team spirit? ❓ What successes have my school and my team experienced? **PESs for Students** • I am proud of my school and my team. • This is a good school and team with successful students. • A success for any one of us is a success for our whole school and team community.

Students who ask questions and make statements like these take pride in their school and will grow into adults who take pride in the organizations and communities to which they belong.

4 Creating Activities Specifically to Promote School Spirit

From dances to assemblies, there are so many ways to get young people involved in, and enthusiastic about, their school. A homecoming week in high school is a prime example of connecting activities that can generate a great deal of spirit and pride within a school. In the younger grades, schools can create a similar week built around school pride with a different type of culminating activity. K-12 students will benefit from, and enjoy, a musical performance, a play, a talent show, a students-versus-teachers basketball game, or the creation of a school lip-dub video. (A school lip-dub involves a series of students who lip sync a song as a video camera travels through a school. Examples can be viewed online.)

We Should See Students Who ...	PEQ for Students
👁 Are involved in pride-generating	❓ What activities can I help develop that give

school activities 👁 Have spirit and pride	people a sense of school spirit? **PES for Students** • I enjoy participating in the creation of spirit-related activities.

Students who ask questions and make statements like these feel pride for their school and grow into adults who look for ways to develop and promote pride in their organizations and communities.

5   Showing Your (Teacher) Spirit

Getting students to become spirited is much easier if the staff is perceived as spirited. Teachers can do small things, such as wear a school shirt, occasionally play the school song as background music, or attend school events. For example, I like to use a foam #1 hand as a pointer in class. Teachers should show their excitement for school successes. The bottom line is that when teachers show spirit for the school, the students take that cue and do the same thing.

We Should See Students Who ...	**PEQ for Students**
👁 Take a cue from the example of teachers who show excitement, pride, and leadership in spirit	❓ How do my teachers and other leaders give me a sense of school and team spirit? **PESs for Students** • My teachers and leaders love this school. • My teachers and leaders care about us and support those things that are important to us. • My teachers and leaders are proud members of the team.

Students who ask questions and make statements like these see that their teachers care and then tend to emulate similar behaviors and grow into adults who recognize the value of positive leadership in promoting spirit.

6   Encouraging Student Leaders to Promote Spirit

When teachers get to know their students, they often find that there are some students who tend to be leaders. These kids are great for helping to promote school spirit. If student leaders can be encouraged to actively motivate their peers, the resulting spirit among the other students can be magnified. This encouragement also promotes the positive use of leadership skills in these students.

We Should See Students Who ...	**PEQs for Students**
👁 Display and promote school spirit among peers 👁 Step into leadership roles	❓ How can I promote school and team spirit and pride? ❓ How can I emulate the school and team

👁 Take positive behavioral cues from one another	spirit and pride of others? **PES for Students** • I am a leader in promoting school and team pride.

Students who ask questions and make statements like these promote school spirit, respond to the spirit of others, and grow into adults who lead in promoting spirit in the workplace.

7 Creating a Physical Environment that Stimulates Spirit

The physical environment surrounding our youth can have a large effect on their connection to the spirit of the school. If students walk past a large case full of trophies, a feeling of pride in their school can be generated. When arriving on campus, if kids see large banners and flags that promote their school, they can develop a sense of belonging. If they pass a display that shows a positive news article about their school, they know that they attend a quality school. If children see school colors and student artwork on the walls, they can feel connected.

Quick Idea

Recently, I collected information on every single success that occurred in our school for an entire year … whether it was athletic, academic, or extracurricular. With the information, our staff leaders created a banner (in school colors, of course) that listed all of these accomplishments. It was made to be roughly fifteen feet long and three feet high so that it could hang at the front entrance to our school. Banners like this can serve to remind students that they belong to a successful school of which they can be proud.

Side Note

We Should See Students Who ...	PEQ for Students
👁 Encounter examples of student work and achievement throughout their school 👁 Encounter school colors, banners, and other spirit-inducing images throughout their school	❓ How does the school and team environment increase my spirit? ❓ How can I contribute to a spirited physical environment? **PES for Students** • The things that I see as I walk around make me feel proud of my school and team, and fill me with spirit.

Students who ask questions and make statements like these feel connected to the physical environment of their school and grow into adults who understand the benefits of creating a spirited physical environment in the workplace.

◄ Connecting Students with the Spirit of the School: Wrap-up ►

We can do lots of big things to promote a connection to the "spirit of the school." It is important, though, to remember all of the small things that we can do on a regular basis. Small actions might seem insignificant, but these actions add up and have a very powerful effect.

Connecting students to the spirit of the school will draw them into the learning environment and make school more enjoyable. In addition, many of the activities suggested above support real-world skills, such as participating on a team, acting as a leader, or taking pride in and promoting an organization or community.

> **Thinking About It**
> - **What are the similarities and differences in techniques for promoting spirit among the schools you have attended, the school where you are an educator, and the other schools with which you are familiar?**
> - **What are some strengths of your classroom and school in promoting spirit?**
> - **What could be implemented that would work in your situation to promote spirit?**

How Does This Chapter Support the Goals of This Book?

Let's take a moment to think about the ways in which the ideas of this chapter help us address the three main goals of this book by looking at the "Building Blocks of a 21st Century Education" on page 13 and the "Daily Thoughts for Educators" on page 18. We now have tools and strategies for empowering our youth by developing connections with the spirit of the school.

Make Note of Your Great Ideas!

If you haven't already, note your ideas for implementing the strategies in this chapter in your Teacher Empowerment Menu (for 21ˢᵗ Century Educators). In the future, you can easily reference usable ideas for your class.

In addition, consider the ways in which you can stimulate students to look for connections with school spirit by using the Personal Empowerment Menu (for 21ˢᵗ Century Students), which contains the relevant PEQs, PESs, and assessment rubric for this chapter.

9 | Parent Connections

The types of connections in the previous chapters focus more on students and are critical to the success of a school. An educational institution, however, can never reach its full potential without the commitment and involvement of parents. I like to think of a child's education as a three-legged stool. The three "legs" represent the educational roles of a student, his or her educators, and his or her parents. On top of the stool are the hopes, dreams, and successes of the student. If one or more "legs" breaks (does not meet the educational responsibilities), the chances of holding up the young person's hopes, dreams, and successes are diminished. This chapter will focus on the parent "leg."

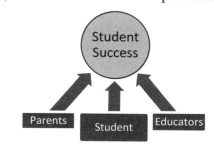

The easiest way to get parents connected to the learning environment is to create connections similar to those that we make for students. We can break down parental involvement into categories.

<u>**Parent Connections**</u>

Connecting Parents with ...
1. **The Teachers / School Staff**
2. **Their Children's Futures**
3. **The Curriculum**
4. **Their Children**
5. **Their Parent Peers**
6. **The Environment and Spirit of the School**

Communication is Essential

The ideas for connecting parents to their child's education hinge upon one important action that cannot be neglected ... *communication*. We must use every method at our disposal to set up quality lines of communication with parents. Phone calls, email messages, face-to-face meetings, conferences, Internet postings of grades and assignments, newsletters, teacher mailings, and parent organizations must all be used on a consistent basis for any of the strategies for parent involvement to work.

9 - Parent Connections

1 | Connecting Parents with the Teachers / School Staff

Because parents and teachers make up two "legs" of our stool of education, there must be a connection between them. The relationship can start with simple opportunities to meet and get to know one another through events such as a welcome night, an orientation event, phone calls, or a letter sent home with information about the teacher. Through these communication techniques, educators can establish a basic familiarity. They can also establish inroads for communication in the future.

Along with initially establishing a connection with parents, teachers should strive to build an image of commitment, trustworthiness, and excitement for teaching. By helping parents see that their children are in the capable, caring hands of educators who are intent upon student success, a relationship of mutual support and responsibility is developed. Every opportunity should be taken throughout the school year to take actions that will encourage support from parents.

We Should See Parents Who …	Personal Empowerment Questions (PEQs) for Parents
☜ Have a relationship with teachers / school staff that shows … • Communication • Mutual respect • A commitment to student success • Mutual responsibility	❓ What do I know about my child's teachers and school staff? ❓ How can I communicate with the school staff? ❓ In what ways can I work with the school staff to help my child succeed? ❓ What are my parental responsibilities in the success of my child? **Personal Empowerment Statements (PESs) for Parents** • Through various means of communication, I can work with my child's educators to support success. • I, my child, and my child's educators have a mutual responsibility to dedicate ourselves to educational success.

Parents who ask questions and make statements like these will take an active role in developing a working relationship with educators that leads to the educational success of their child.

2 | Connecting Parents with Their Children's Futures

In Chapter 4, we talked about how students must understand the world that awaits them and the skills required for success. In addition, parents must understand the realities of the workplace that awaits their children. Therefore, various modes of communication should be employed to educate parents about the new economy that is developing and what this new world means for their children. Parents can learn about this through various forms of communication, including school flyers, school websites, email messages, and parent nights. An understanding of these new realities not only motivates students, but also motivates parents. When empowered with an understanding of the modern economy, parents are more likely to take an active role in preparing their children for success.

There is another important reason to make this connection. If parents understand what lies ahead in the lives of their children and know that their children's educators are taking steps to prepare them for that future, the connection between parents and the school staff is strengthened.

We Should See Parents Who ...	PEQs for Parents
👁 Understand the 21st century economy and the skills, habits, and attitudes it requires 👁 Are motivated to reinforce relevant work skills 👁 Are enthusiastic about schools that focus on preparing children for the 21st century	❓ What awaits my child in the real world? ❓ What can I do to help my child be prepared? ❓ How can I support the 21st Century Education that my child's school is providing? **PES for Parents** • I am excited to support my child's school in promoting the skills, habits, and attitudes required for 21st century success.

Parents who ask questions and make statements like these understand the realities of the 21st century economy and support the development of relevant skills, habits, and attitudes.

⭐ 3 Connecting Parents with the Curriculum

We saw earlier that, possibly, the most important connection for students is a connection to the curriculum. We talked about the importance of students being engaged and seeing the real world value of those things that they learn in school. Why not get the parents involved in developing a connection between their students and the real world? Parents have a lifetime of real-world experiences that they can display to their children. There are informal and formal methods for tapping into these experiences.

a) Informally

First, we must encourage parents to talk to their children about the things that students learn in school each day. (I really promote this when I meet parents at an annual open house that kicks off the school year.) Through a simple conversation about what a student has studied at school, a parent might be able to think of a real-world example that can be shared with his child. Also, when a young person reflects upon and describes something that he or she has learned, a process of concept review and organization occurs in his or her mind. This process encourages understanding and long-term retention. Furthermore, when a student explains something, he or she is developing a career skill. Almost everyone will have to give an explanation of something to customers, patients, or clients in their jobs.

b) Formally

To connect parents to the curriculum, we can go beyond encouraging informal discussions between parents and their children and actually give assignments to students that require them to teach their parents concepts from class. Educators can require that each student obtain a signature from a parent that verifies that the child engaged his or her parent in learning. This activity not only connects parents to the curriculum, but the process of explaining increases the chances that students will understand ideas from class, because the act of teaching forces the explainer to think through the information … piece by piece. I know that, as a teacher, having to put something into plain words for my students helps me better understand my subject. Have you ever found that giving an explanation to others, for a topic that you are teaching, forces you to rationalize your knowledge in a way that deepens your own understanding?

The assignment can even come with a rubric that parents can use to give their children feedback on their "explaining skills." There is a section in Ch. 15 that focuses on improving students' "explaining skills" so that they are more effective in the 21ˢᵗ century.

c) Communication for Empowerment

Teachers can also help parents connect with the curriculum by sending out a newsletter to parents describing upcoming class concepts and skills. The newsletter can include ideas about how these lessons are valuable in the real world, so that parents can better reinforce the concepts at home. Schools can offer a curriculum night for parents to come and learn about those topics that will be taught in school. In this setting, parents can be involved in workshops that not only tell the parents what topics will be taught, but also give parents tips on how to support their kids' learning at home.

Newsletters, curriculum nights, and websites can be used to help parents who may not be familiar enough with the curriculum to help their children at home. Through these various sources of communication, parents can be given tips and lessons about how to help their children develop reading strategies, develop writing strategies, perform math techniques, etc. These tips are especially important given that many modern educational techniques might seem foreign to our parents. Even though parents learned about the same concepts when they were in school, they might have learned about them in a different way. Many parents are thirsty for educators to empower them with strategies to help their children. In addition to newsletters, meetings, or the Internet, some school districts have a public access television channel on which they can run programs about strategies for helping students. New Internet technologies, such as Ustream or YouTube, allow teachers to create their own educational channels through which they can teach parents about the concepts their students are learning in class, discuss upcoming curriculum, or report about fun things that kids are doing in class.

Another key area on which teachers should focus is giving parents tips on how they can help their children become more organized, develop study skills, or grow their communication skills; these are tips that are not necessarily related specifically to the curriculum itself. Overall, we need to remember that connecting parents to the curriculum doesn't just mean that we let them know what we're teaching. Connecting parents also means that we give them some tools for helping their children succeed.

We Should See Parents Who ...	PEQs for Parents
👁 Have an awareness of the curriculum 👁 Reinforce the curriculum and the skills of the 21st century with their children 👁 Have access to resources that help them reinforce the curriculum	? How can I help my child connect with and value his or her school curriculum? ? What can I do to reinforce the real-world value of the school curriculum? ? What can I do to help my child learn the curriculum? ? How can I learn more about the concepts that are being taught at school so that I can help my child learn? ? How are modern teaching methods similar to and different from those that I encountered in school? **PESs for Parents** • Because I understand the real-world applications of the curriculum, I can promote connections to the curriculum and uses of the curriculum at home. • I can and will try to find ways to help my child learn. If I don't understand a particular skill enough to help my child when he or she needs help, my child and I will communicate with the teacher to arrange for extra teacher help.

Parents who ask questions and make statements like these help connect their children to the curriculum and support the learning of that curriculum.

4 Connecting Parents with Their Children

Just as children respond well when they understand that their teachers are actively attempting to connect with them, they also respond positively to a connection with their parents. For this reason, educators should strive to provide opportunities to put parents in contact with their kids in the school environment. These opportunities can include chances to chaperone an event or become a mentor for a group within the school. Some educators are comfortable with parents coming into the classroom for tutoring or for talking about the parents' jobs. In elementary schools, parents can read a book during story time or play educational games. If a parent volunteers to work in the concession stand at an event in which his child is participating, the kid is aware that his parent is present and taking an interest in his life. Notice that all of the opportunities above for connecting parents to their children require communication and encouragement from educators about these opportunities.

Activities that connect parents to the school get parents connected with not only their own child, but with other children and parents. This networking allows for a community of people to become united. (I remember that when I was growing up other students learned a lot from my parents, and I learned a lot from their parents.) Thus, the positive effect of the connections between parents and students is multiplied.

Breaking Through

Parents can sometimes have a difficult time communicating with their children. This challenge can frustrate parents, because they are not sure what school assignments are due, if the students have homework, or if there are tests or projects coming. Teachers can help parents by posting assignments and schedules online, sending a mailing home to parents, and responding to email requests or phone calls from parents. Parents can then discuss these things with their kids. Educators can do a great deal to facilitate communication between parents and students. (Care needs to be taken so that the techniques used to empower the parents to communicate with their child do not remove all responsibility from the student and, thus, enable him or her to be disorganized or irresponsible.)

Help Students See the Value of Parent Connections

Teachers should take opportunities to help students see the ways in which parental involvement is valuable in educational success. Kids need to view parents as partners who can serve as mentors, motivators, and learning resources.

We Should See Parents Who ...	PEQs for Parents
👁 Are visible in their child's life 👁 Communicate with their child about school and life 👁 Are aware of their child's progress	❓ How can I become more involved in and connected to my child's life? ❓ How is my child progressing? ❓ How can I support my child? **PESs for Parents** • I am visible in my child's life, with awareness of his or her needs, his or her progress, and ways to help him or her. • My child and I communicate openly and regularly. **PEQs for Students** ❓ How is parental involvement helpful to my success? ❓ In what ways can I empower my parents as partners in my education?

Parents who ask questions and make statements like these make meaningful connections with their children and support their children's development.

 5 **Connecting Parents with Their Parent Peers**

Just as students are engaged by connections with their peers, parents enjoy a similar connection to other parents. Some of the volunteer activities described in the section above not only connect parents to students but connect parents to each other. These types of relationships are valuable for drawing parents into the learning environment and for providing opportunities

Side Note

9 - Parent Connections

for communication. Parents can share ideas with each other about dealing with the challenges of raising a child. Schools can offer opportunities to participate in or attend school activities (such as plays, athletic events, club events, fundraisers, or assemblies) in order to facilitate parent connections. Some activities can be specifically for parents, such as social mixers. Schools can also form parent organizations that foster communications among parents and simply help parents meet other parents. As always, communication is critical in helping parents find ways to become involved in school activities and to connect with other parents.

We Should See Parents Who ...	PEQs for Parents
👁 Communicate and connect with other parents 👁 Support one another in navigating the world of raising an empowered child 👁 Learn from one another	❓ How can I connect with other parents? ❓ What can I learn from other parents? ❓ How can I and other parents mutually support one another? **PES for Parents** • Through school activities, I meet, communicate with, learn from, and support other parents.

Parents who ask questions and make statements like these develop connections with other parents and support one another in raising their children.

Connecting Parents with the Environment and Spirit of the School

Developing a level of comfort and pride in the learning institution will draw parents into the learning environment just as this comfort draws in students. Parents should have the opportunity for a school orientation much like their children. This orientation can be coupled with an event that connects the parents with the staff of the school.

Getting parents comfortable at school is great, but that familiarity is not enough. Stimulating them to feel connected to the spirit of the school (in such a way that they take pride in the school) can also be very beneficial. Just like students can feed off the spirit of their teachers, they can feed off the spirit of their parents. Thus, any technique that can promote a parental awareness of the successes of a school is critical, because pride is developed. Any activity that can make a parent feel like he or she is part of the school community is critical, because a sense of belonging is developed. From shirts to bumper stickers to participation in school events, there are many ways to develop a connection between parents and the spirit of the school.

We Should See Parents Who ...	PEQs for Parents
👁 Participate in and attend school activities 👁 Are passionate about the school 👁 Feel like a part of the school community	❓ How can I become more involved in the school environment? ❓ How can I be a resource for the school community? **PES for Parents** • I am a proud member of the school

9 - Parent Connections

	family who promotes spirit through participation in school activities.

Parents who ask questions and make statements like these become connected to the school environment and spirit and contribute to promoting a positive school environment and spirit.

Give Connections a Chance

Some activities connect parents in a variety of ways. For instance, I ran an academic club called "Future Problem Solving." Each fall, we went on a bonding trip that parents attended as chaperones. During the trip, we did various activities to develop connections among the students. I found that the parents loved to be involved in these activities, developing connections with me (the educator), the students, and other parents. The students also enjoyed the participation of adults, because, deep down, they wanted to be connected with those adults. What these bonding trips taught me is that students and parents alike thirst for opportunities to connect. They just need to be given an opportunity.

Connecting Parents: Wrap-up

The ways in which parent connections can be created are similar to the ways in which student connections are developed. The bottom line is that they are critical. Without the parent "leg" of the educational stool, the chances of holding up the hopes, dreams, and successes of our students decrease.

Thinking About It

- **What are the roles you think parents should play in their children's education?**
- **What are the biggest challenges to creating parent connections and how can they be overcome?**
- **What strategies can you try in order to improve parental connections?**

How Does This Chapter Support the Goals of This Book?

Let's take a moment to think about the ways in which the ideas of this chapter help us address the three main goals of this book by looking at the "Building Blocks of a 21st Century Education" on page 13 and the "Daily Thoughts for Educators" on page 18. We now have tools and strategies for empowering our youth by developing parent connections.

Make Note of Your Great Ideas!

If you haven't already, note your ideas for implementing the strategies in this chapter in your Teacher Empowerment Menu (for 21st Century Educators). In the future, you can easily reference usable ideas.

10 Other Important Connections

- **Student Connections with the Community**
- **Student Connections to the World**
- **Connections Among Staff Members**

We will now look briefly at a few other connections that can be very beneficial for linking students to their school and for helping prepare them for the real world.

Student Connections with the Community

When schools are connected with the community, there are some very positive benefits. By linking students with community members and organizations, opportunities become available for students to make real-world connections with the curriculum, the community, and career examples.

There are also ways in which the community can benefit from a partnership with the school. Let's look at some of the key aspects of community connections.

Connections with the Community: *Student-Centered* Techniques	Connections with the Community: *Educator-Centered* Techniques
1. Community Members Volunteering as Mentors and Teachers 2. Students Serving the Community	1. Schools Partnering with Private Citizens / Businesses 2. Communicating with the Community

10 - Other Connections:
Community, World, and Staff

Student-Centered Techniques for Connecting Students with the Community

 1 **Community Members Volunteering as Mentors and Teachers**

As students grow and develop career interests, the community can be critical in educating youth about real-life work opportunities. Events such as career days (where professionals come to a school to discuss their vocations) and job-shadowing experiences (through which students experience various careers) are critical in helping students discover various job fields. On the flip side, career exposure can help a student realize that a certain line of work isn't what he or she really wants to do for the rest of his or her life, which can save a lot of headaches down the road.

There are a lot of intelligent and capable citizens who will volunteer as student mentors, tutors, or classroom helpers. Giving these volunteers opportunities to help educate our students and to connect with our schools is very valuable. With a large number of baby boomers beginning to retire, this resource will grow. We just need to tap into it.

We Should See Students Who ...	**Personal Empowerment Questions (PEQs) for Students**
👁 Learn from community members	❓ What can I learn from the members of my community?
👁 Are exposed to a variety of career options through interactions with professionals in the community	❓ How can my community serve as a source of inspiration and a tool for my personal development?
👁 Engage in activities involving the community	❓ How can I use community resources to learn about possible career options?
	Personal Empowerment Statements (PESs) for Students
	• Through community members and resources, I am learning a great deal about life and career options.
	• My community inspires me.

Students who ask questions and make statements like these learn valuable lessons from their community and develop connections that can support their learning. These students will also grow into adults who make positive and supportive community connections.

 2 **Students Serving the Community**

Whether through a club or actual classroom activities, experiences in community service can teach our youth many lessons that will be valuable to them in the future. When kids are given opportunities to serve others, those experiences give them a purpose greater than themselves and help them to see that they are part of a larger community. Young people can learn about the challenges that members of their community face and then have opportunities to help make a difference in the lives of others.

Service-learning experiences are especially valuable to students, because they are meaningfully tied to the curriculum. How is service-learning different than volunteering? According to the National Service-Learning Clearinghouse resource, "If school students collect trash out of an urban streambed, they are providing a valued service to the community as volunteers. If school students collect trash from an urban streambed, analyze their findings to determine the possible sources of pollution, and share the results with residents of the neighborhood, they are engaging in service-learning." This resource also states that, "Community members, students, and educators everywhere are discovering that service-learning offers all its participants a chance to take part in the active education of youth while simultaneously addressing the concerns, needs, and hopes of communities."[17] These types of experiences provide an educationally relevant way to develop connections with the community.

We Should See Students Who ...	PEQs for Students
👁 Help community members 👁 Develop an understanding of issues that face citizens	❓ How are the knowledge and skills I learn in school relevant to my community? ❓ What issues face the members of my community? ❓ How can I positively help, support, and work with the members of my community? ❓ How can I help or start a charitable organization? **PESs for Students** • School lessons and activities allow me to positively impact my community. • I can make a difference.

Students who ask questions and make statements like these can learn from and help the members of their community, and grow into adults who serve their communities.

Educator-Focused Techniques for Connecting Students with the Community

1   Schools Partnering with Private Citizens / Businesses

Citizens and businesses in a community can help school staff and educators facilitate educational activities. Businesses and citizens might donate funds, resources, or manpower that

---

[17] (ETR Associates, 2012)

help schools facilitate clubs, after-school activities, field trips, and sports. Community members are often willing to do this ... they just need to be asked. Citizens and businesses can also be important partners in developing school pride and spirit. Placing spirit placards in yards and business windows or putting bumper stickers on cars are simple examples of actions that generate school and community pride. Businesses will sometimes pay for the purchase of spirit gear (such as placards and pompoms) if they are allowed to print advertising information on the gear.

We Should See Educators Who ...	PEQ for Educators
👁 Partner with citizens and businesses to facilitate and/or fund school activities and stimulators of pride	❓ How can we involve citizens and businesses in facilitating and/or funding school activities?
	PES for Educators
	• We have a mutually beneficial relationship with the members of our community.

Educators who ask questions and make statements like these seek partnerships that will enhance the education of students.

Communicating with the Community

In order to connect with the community, quality communication from school administration and staff is crucial. Community members need to hear about the good things happening in their local schools, as well as learn about opportunities for becoming involved. Mentoring, teaching, service learning projects, and partnerships are nearly impossible if there is not a good system for communication. Thus, local newspapers, newsletters, television, and forums must not only tell the community about the local schools, but also must promote opportunities to become involved.

Former students are a great resource for connecting with the community. In addition, parents who were very involved during their children's participation in local schools are a good resource for future volunteer work and connection with the schools. A system that keeps a group of alumni students and alumni parents in touch with the schools can be very beneficial.

With the considerations above, we must connect our schools with the community for mutual benefit. Quality interactions can help students learn life lessons and better connect with their learning environment ... because it is community-wide.

We Should See Educators Who ...	PEQs for Educators
👁 Inform community members about school functions and successes	❓ What is happening at our school that would make our community proud?
👁 Promote community pride in the school	❓ How can we communicate our successes, needs, and general school information to the community?
	PES for Educators
	• Through effective communication, we are

	building community pride in the successes of our school.

Educators who ask questions and make statements like these communicate with the community in order to build connections and pride in the school.

Student Connections to the World

One of the basic premises that underlies Thomas Friedman's *The World Is Flat* is the idea that many of our children will someday interact on a regular basis with people from all over the world. In order for us to prepare our students for this reality, we need to help them understand and develop connections with the world outside their country. Our first instinct might be to have some kind of event at our schools or in a Social Studies class that helps students learn about the cultures of people from around the world. While this is a good idea, we have to go further.

Someday, many of our youth will have clients or customers who live in other parts of the world. They will sell goods to or purchase goods from other parts of the world. They might even manage employees in other countries or their manager might be in another country. In all of these situations, students need a deep understanding of other cultures. Therefore, modern workers need to understand the wants and needs of people in other countries, what makes those people similar and what makes them different, what makes those people proud, and their history. Students cannot learn all of this if educators hold only events in which kids sample foreign food, re-create authentic clothing, or sing songs from around the world. (Again, these activities are a step in the right direction, but they're just the beginning.)

Student Connections to the World

1. **Learning the Wants, Needs, Cultures, Histories, and Values of Others**
2. **Learning to Communicate Globally**

Learning the Wants, Needs, Cultures, Histories, and Values of Others

In a global economy, it is very useful to be able to understand the wants, needs, cultures, histories, and values of others. This knowledge allows people to create products and services for a worldwide pool of consumers. It also allows us to work effectively with people from all walks of life.

Depending on the class, the depth of understanding of another culture varies. In all classes, making connections between the curriculum and the wants, needs, cultures, histories, and values of another country can spice up a lesson and make it more engaging. When students understand that they live in a global economy, any lesson that teaches them about, and connects them to, the rest of the world is valuable.

Examples - Various Content Areas

In our history classes, we can tie historical events to current circumstances, ways of life, attitudes, and the needs of various peoples. In geography, we can look at how a country's location influences its wants and needs. When studying new theories and technologies of various countries in science, we can briefly ask ourselves, "What is it about the needs and wants of a particular country that promoted the development of a certain theory or technology?" Even in math, we can learn facts about other cultures through real-world problems simply by using details about a foreign country, such as in a currency exchange problem or in a problem dealing with the speed limit in Canada (where they use the metric system). In English classes, reading stories about other cultures can give us an even deeper understanding.

We Should See Students Who ...	PEQ for Students
👁 Learn about various countries and cultures 👁 Develop an understanding of how the wants, needs, and values of people affect their worldview and culture	❓ What are the values, religions, resources, needs, and wants of various people in countries around the world, and how are these things interrelated? **PES for Students** • With my understanding of people around the world, I can better work with others and generate products and services in a global economy.

Students who ask questions and make statements like these will grow into adults who understand people from other countries and cultures and are able to interact with them.

2   Learning to Communicate Globally

Foreign language classes are great venues for the development of a deep understanding of citizens of other countries. Along with learning a new language, we can learn about a new culture … and strive to develop an understanding of the wants, needs, values, and customs of that culture. As for teaching the foreign language itself, students should be taught in such a way that they become proficient in the *use* of the new language. Continuous rote memorization of new words is of little use without accompanying opportunities to exercise the use of those words. If students are required to engage in actual conversation, they will be more likely to think on their toes and be capable of speaking the new language in the real world. If they instead do a lot of sitting, listening, memorizing, and regurgitating of definitions for a written test, they will be more likely to struggle in a real-world context. Just as in any other class, the lessons of a foreign language class should be geared toward practical real-life use.

Side Note

Communicate Globally

Beyond the lessons about other cultures that we can work into our classroom curricula, our students can learn a great deal through direct communication with others from around the world. Becoming pen pals (or e-pals) is a great way for our young people to learn from, and connect with, others who live far away.

New technologies allow students from different parts of the world to do learning activities together. One example is using an online "wiki." A wiki is a website that can be modified by anyone who visits it. People can add, remove, and modify text, pictures, and videos. Kids in two different countries can collaborate on a project that they create in a wiki. They can build a wiki about a book, a scientific process, or a historical event.

Another technology that allows worldwide collaboration is the online blog where students have discussions by posting comments and questions on the website.

Both wikis and blogs can be created very easily. There are many websites that allow users to create them for free.

Connections to the World

We Should See Students Who ...	PEQs for Students
👁 Are able to *use* a foreign language 👁 Have an understanding of world cultures that goes beyond the superficial	❓ What can I do to effectively communicate with people from other countries and cultures? ❓ What are the similarities and differences among world cultures? **PES for Students** • With an understanding of language, social norms, and culture, I can communicate with people from other parts of the world.

Students who ask questions and make statements like these grow into adults who can interact with people from all over the world and thrive in a global economy.

The bottom line is that our kids will someday interact in real life circumstances with people from all over the world. We can affect the chances of their success if we help them explore the similarities and differences among cultures and understand how to better relate to different people from different parts of the world.

Connections Among Staff Members

For a school staff to function well as a team, they need to be well-connected and know each other beyond a superficial level. A great team knows each other's strengths and how to bring out the best in one another. Furthermore, they support one another, make each other laugh, and lend an ear after a frustrating day.

> ## Connections among Staff Members
>
> 1. **Creating and Taking Advantage of Opportunities to Get to Know Others**
> 2. **Supporting One Another**
> 3. **Working as a Team**
> 4. **Having Fun Together**

Creating and Taking Advantage of Opportunities to Get to Know Others

Staff meetings, newsletters, and email messages provide opportunities to learn basic information about other staff members in one's building. However, a deeper understanding of, and relationship with, our coworkers comes through more informal means. Relationships are built through interactions, such as the conversations we have in the hall, around the water cooler, at lunch, or at a holiday party. These conversations don't simply happen. We have to make an attempt to get to know one another. With the right attitude and some effort, we can find many occasions to develop meaningful relationships and connections.

Sometimes, these opportunities have to be created. To give her staff a comfortable place in which to socialize, my sister transformed the teachers' lounge at her school into an Italian café. With a bit of paint, some furniture and imitation trees purchased at garage sales, a nice coffee maker (donated by a student club), and an assortment of sweet and salty healthy snacks, she converted her staff lounge into a comfortable, fun place where teachers congregate to drink coffee, eat snacks, and talk about their day.

We Should See Educators Who ...	PEQ for Educators
🐚 Communicate regularly 🐚 Create opportunities to interact 🐚 Welcome newcomers	❓ What formal and informal opportunities exist or can be created in order to promote staff connections?
	PES for Educators
	• Our staff consistently interacts and develops meaningful connections that make our careers more fulfilling.

Educators who ask questions and make statements like these develop relationships that make the workplace more enjoyable and effective.

Supporting One Another

Educators understand best the challenges, stresses, and rewards of their jobs. Therefore, educators must support one another. We can lend an ear to someone after a stressful day and pat each other on the back after successes. When one of our colleagues puts in a substantial amount of time and does an excellent job with a club, a team, a lesson, or a difficult situation with a student, he or she might really enjoy finding a note in his or her mailbox or email inbox that simply says, "Nice job." Actions like these let educators know that someone appreciates what they're doing.

We Should See Educators Who ...	PEQs for Educators
👁 Empathize with one another 👁 Are proud of their colleagues 👁 Listen to one another 👁 Support one another	❓ What challenges face my colleagues? ❓ How can I be supportive of other staff members? **PES for Educators** • Our staff proudly supports one another.

Educators who ask questions and make statements like these create a supportive environment where staff members enjoy working.

 **Working as a Team**

When educators communicate about curriculum implementation, teaching techniques, or classroom situations, they greatly increase their chances of success. There is a massive base of knowledge to be tapped among a group of educators, as long as they are willing to work together. Communication among staff members is the most important facet of working as a team.

We Should See Educators Who ...	PEQs for Educators
👁 Are unified 👁 Communicate ideas and experiences with one another 👁 Seek opportunities to work as a team 👁 Share resources 👁 Mentor	❓ How can we share ideas, resources, and experiences? ❓ In what ways can we work together? **PES for Educators** • As a team, we are able to help each other become better than we could be if working alone, and our students reap the benefits.

Educators who ask questions and make statements like these use teamwork to increase the success of students.

 **Having Fun Together**

When people have fun, they tend not to see their job as work. While much of teaching happens inside the classroom, our perception of our job is greatly affected by our happiness outside the classroom. So … tell jokes, smile, challenge another school to a friendly competition, and go out together for dinner. Create and take advantage of opportunities to enjoy your coworkers and love your job.

We Should See Educators Who ...	PEQs for Educators
👁 Share their passion and excitement for	❓ In what ways can I be a positive force

education ❀ Laugh together ❀ Share friendship	within my staff? ❓ How can we make our days more fun and exciting? **PES for Educators** • We enjoy our work and time together!

Educators who ask questions and make statements like these enjoy their "jobs."

Community, World, and Staff Connections: Wrap-up

The three additional connections addressed in this chapter can further strengthen our foundation of connections. Connections to the community can provide students with mentorship and educational resources. Connections to the world help kids develop an understanding of people from other places in such a way that they can work in a new global economy. Staff connections not only make the workplace more satisfying, but also generate bonds that are mutually supportive in working toward student success.

Thinking About It

- **How can you seek out and engage community members in connections with your school?**
- **In what ways can you support connections to the world within your curriculum that are not simply superficial, but instead help students find a deeper understanding of the wants, needs, and motivations of people from other places?**
- **How can educators reach out to one another to make teaching a more positive and enjoyable experience?**

How Does This Chapter Support the Goals of This Book?

Let's take a moment to think about the ways in which the ideas of this chapter help us address the three main goals of this book by looking at the "Building Blocks of a 21st Century Education" on page 13 and the "Daily Thoughts for Educators" on page 18. We now have tools and strategies for empowering our youth by developing connections between students and the community, connections between students and the world, and connections among staff members.

Make Note of Your Great Ideas!

If you haven't already, note your ideas for implementing the strategies in this chapter in your Teacher Empowerment Menu (for 21st Century Educators). In the future, you can easily reference usable ideas for your class.

In addition, consider the ways in which you can stimulate students to look for connections by using the Personal Empowerment Menu (for 21st Century Students), which contains the relevant PEQs, PESs, and assessment rubric for this chapter.

Foundation of Connections (Ch. 3-10)
Final Thoughts

Connections are the Foundation … in All Schools … in All Classes

We must engage our youth in such a way that they see the value in their education, enjoy school, and become prepared for the real world. If we are going to do this, we must work to create and deepen every connection discussed in the previous chapters. The more connections we create for our students, the greater the chances of success. Whether we are trying to push an "all-As" student to his or her highest potential or are trying to keep an at-risk student in school, the connections we promote make a huge difference. Of course, the challenges that various schools face in creating connections are different, but the goals should be the same. There are educators in communities with every type of obstacle imaginable who succeed in engaging their students. I would argue that these educators are finding ways to develop relationships and make quality connections. If they encounter disinterested students or parents, they don't simply say, "Oh well, it's their fault." They ask themselves how to stimulate the parents and students to become connected to the learning community in such a way that they all share an equal role and responsibility in the child's education.

The categories of various connections we have discussed provide a good framework for educators to address these relationships both in their classrooms and school-wide. In a classroom, we can self-assess in order to see our connection strengths and those areas in which we could improve. A self-assessment might lead a teacher to find that he or she is effectively creating most types of relationships for students, but he or she might need to work on others. A school staff can use the categories of connections in order to assess the school at large for its strengths and to find areas in which they can improve connections. It is important for educators to remember that developing connections and the skills of the 21st century are not lessons to be tossed into one class, but lessons that need to be interwoven throughout the curriculum and the school environment. The prospect of making all these types of connections can be overwhelming, but we must remember that many creative activities, policies, and actions can promote and reinforce multiple connections at the same time.

A Vision can Help Educators Guide Improvement

If we are to succeed in generating the types of connections described in this book, we must be willing to continually improve our practices. This process requires consistent self-assessment and revision of strategies as needed. We must also be willing to work as a team and support one another in our classroom and school-wide endeavors. To encourage these types of habits, it is essential that schools develop a vision and purpose. I don't mean creating a vague vision, such as "student success." I mean that we need to develop a specific vision about what knowledge and skills we want for our students when they walk out of our doors. The first two chapters of this book described a purpose for empowering students (the new economy) and a vision about what knowledge, skills, and habits our students will need in the 21ˢᵗ century. From that point on, we've been discussing specific ways in which to implement that vision. One thing is for sure … both in a book and in a school, you must start with a vision or purpose and specific goals. Otherwise, you'll find yourself wandering.

Connections Fit with the Core Curriculum …
In Fact, Connections Allow the Curriculum to Be Taught

The development of connections described in the previous chapters, along with the promotion of real-world skills that will be described in the coming chapters, does not mean that we will de-emphasize the school's curriculum. Rather, we are working to engage students in learning and to deliver the curriculum in a more meaningful and useful manner. Not only do we want our youth to learn facts about the curriculum, but we want them to be able to do real things in life with their curricular knowledge.

Connections Promote Powerful Intrinsic Motivation
… but Don't Simply Dump the Other Motivators

This unit on connecting students to learning has presented a number of strategies for promoting an intrinsic desire to learn and be in school. As we attempt to promote these intrinsic motivators, we should realize that kids are human. Even the most intrinsically motivated kids will have days when they are tired, days when a social situation with friends distracts their focus, days when their impulsive side overruns their rational side, etc. At these times, extrinsic motivators can keep students on track.

For kids that are not yet fully, intrinsically motivated, extrinsic motivators can help them be successful while educators work to ignite their inner fire for learning. (Similarly, parents use some extrinsic motivators to help their kids do the right things before they have the maturity to understand why these things are right.)

In short … let's work vigorously toward intrinsic student motivation, but not forget about the other tools at our disposal ... like candy.

Whether motivation comes from connections, creative classroom strategies, or intrinsic and extrinsic motivators, motivating our kids comes down to doing the little things: a kind and connecting word from a teacher, a small challenge, a little reminder of the value of an activity, a quick activity to promote school spirit, or a silly moment in class. All these things seem small in the great scheme of things. However, when they are continuously used, they can add up to a monstrous sum of motivators that drive kids to work hard, succeed, enjoy school, and discover their passion.

Empowering Your Students for the 21st Century:
Building Blocks of a 21st Century Education

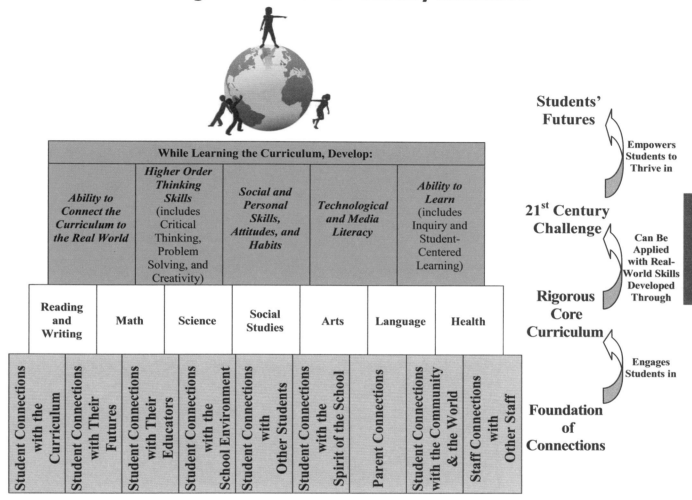

Reading from the foundation upward, we should see a 21st Century Education in which:

- **A foundation of connections engages students in a rigorous core curriculum.**
- **A rigorous core curriculum can be applied with real-world skills developed through a 21st Century Challenge.**
- **A 21st Century Challenge empowers students to thrive in their futures.**

The Building Blocks of a 21st Century Education that are shown above must drive what we do each and every day. If not, our youth will not be prepared for the world that awaits them. Therefore, we should always keep this diagram in mind when planning and educating. These are our goals: to teach our curriculum in such a way that young minds not only learn facts and processes, but learn these things in a manner that will prepare and empower them for the future.

Goal #2
21st Century Challenge
(Ch. 11-17)

Now that we have addressed the first goal of this book, building a foundation of connections, we will address the second goal of this book, promoting a "21st Century Challenge." Let's refresh our memory on the meaning of "21st Century Challenge."

In the 21st century, making our classes more challenging does not simply mean that we limit ourselves to the methods of increasing the amount of work, increasing the ability level of lessons, and teaching more information. We must expand our 20th century ideas about what "challenge" and "rigor" mean in order to meet the needs of a new world in the 21st century. How can we do this? We need to stimulate our students by teaching the curriculum in such a way that we promote the following 21st century skills, habits, and attitudes.

While Learning the Curriculum, Develop:				
Ability to Connect the Curriculum to the Real World Ch. 3	*Higher Order Thinking Skills* (includes Critical Thinking, Problem Solving, and Creativity) Ch. 11-13	*Social and Personal Skills, Attitudes, and Habits* Ch. 14-15	*Technological and Media Literacy* Ch. 16	*Ability to Learn* (includes Inquiry and Student-Centered Learning) Ch. 17

21st Century Challenge

By challenging our youth to develop these skills, attitudes, and habits while learning the curriculum, we empower our students for their futures.

Goal #2

21st Century Challenge – Part 1

Develop the Ability to Connect the Curriculum to the Real World

While Learning the Curriculum, Develop:				
Ability to Connect the Curriculum to the Real World Ch. 3	**Higher Order Thinking Skills** (includes Critical Thinking, Problem Solving, and Creativity) Ch. 11-13	**Social and Personal Skills, Attitudes, and Habits** Ch. 14-15	**Technological and Media Literacy** Ch. 16	**Ability to Learn** (includes Inquiry and Student-Centered Learning) Ch. 17

21st Century Challenge

Chapter 3 dealt with connecting students to the curriculum. The chapter was in the section of this book that dealt with connections, because connections to the curriculum help engage our youth in learning. These types of associations make learning interesting and fun. *We must also look at the development of connections to the curriculum as a method for challenging students*. Thus, Chapter 3 serves double duty. It not only provides ways for us to engage our students, but it also provides ways to challenge our students. Let's look at the types of connections to the curriculum found in Chapter 3. As you look at these connections, think about how they can serve to challenge students to make connections between the curriculum and the real world.

A Look Back at Chapter 3 - Connecting Students to the Curriculum

1. **Looking for Answers (Engaging Through Inquiry)**
2. **Connecting the Curriculum to Everyday Life**
3. **Performing Real-Life (Authentic) Tasks that will be Useful in the Future**
4. **Developing Insights and Opinions about Real-World Issues**
5. **Imagining the Future World**
6. **Integrating New Learning with Prior Knowledge and Skills**
7. **Finding Cross-Curricular Connections**
8. **Creating Products Related to the Content**
9. **Becoming the Content**

In order to turn Chapter 3 into a tool for challenging students, we cannot simply make the connections between the curriculum and the real world for the students. We must challenge our youth to make these connections in the process of learning. The Personal Empowerment Questions (PEQs) found in Chapter 3 can be very useful in stimulating our youth to look for connections to the real world. By stimulating our children to ask these questions, we challenge them to make connections. Let's look at some PEQ examples and think about how they can be used to challenge students to make connections.

1. Looking for Answers (Engaging Through Inquiry)

- Why?
- How does _____ work?
- How did _____ come to be?
- Why do we _____?
- What are my predictions for _____?
- What do I already know about this?
- What do I need to know to get an answer?

2. Connecting the Curriculum to Everyday Life

- How does this relate to my life?
- Where have I encountered this before?
- Why does this matter to me?

3. Performing Real-Life (Authentic) Tasks that will be Useful in the Future

- What are my goals in doing _____?
- How can I accomplish _____?
- What steps, information, and procedures will allow me to do _____?
- What can I do with this information or skill?
- How do people commonly make use of this knowledge or skill?
- How might I use this knowledge or skill in my future?

4. Developing Insights and Opinions about Real-World Issues

- ❓ What do I believe about _____?
- ❓ How can I back up my opinion with facts?
- ❓ How might my opinion differ from other peoples' opinions and why?

5. Imagining the Future World

- ❓ How will things be similar or different in the future?
- ❓ What will my life be like in the future?
- ❓ Given the current circumstances of _____, what would logically happen next?
- ❓ What do I want to see in the future?
- ❓ Wouldn't it be neat if ____ happens someday?

6. Integrating New Learning with Prior Knowledge and Skills

- ❓ How does this new knowledge or skill relate to what I already know?
- ❓ How does this new knowledge or skill deepen my understanding of _____?
- ❓ Is this new concept similar to or different from other concepts I know?
- ❓ With my new understanding, how can I use prior knowledge or skills in new ways?

7. Finding Cross-Curricular Connections

- ❓ How does this concept relate to other subjects?
- ❓ How do my knowledge and skills from one subject help me in another?

8. Creating Products and Models Related to the Content

- ❓ What am I trying to convey with my product?
- ❓ Who is my audience for this product?
- ❓ How can I demonstrate my understanding of _____ through the creation of a product?
- ❓ What can I produce with my understanding of _____?
- ❓ How can I be creative when making my product?

9. Becoming the Content

- ❓ What would it be like to actually be a working part of this curricular concept?
- ❓ What can I learn by imagining myself as this object, person, place, or process?

By stimulating our students to ask these types of questions, we move beyond connecting our kids to the curriculum. We *challenge them* to connect their learning to the real world. Developing this ability in our youth will empower them to apply the knowledge and skills they gain in school to real-life situations in the future.

In sum, Chapter 3 helps us challenge our children in a manner that is relevant to the 21st century. Thus, "Developing the Ability to Connect the Curriculum to the Real World" is the first method in our 21st Century Challenge.

Goal #2

21st Century Challenge – Part 2

Develop Higher Order Thinking Skills Unit (Ch. 11-13)

We will now look at the second method for providing a 21st Century Challenge for our students. The higher order thinking skills unit (Chapters 11-13) will focus on critical thinking (with analysis and assessment), authentic actions (such as problem solving), and creativity. The development of these skills will not only challenge our youth, but will empower them with skills relevant in the 21st century.

While Learning the Curriculum, Develop:				
Ability to Connect the Curriculum to the Real World Ch. 3	*Higher Order Thinking Skills* (includes Critical Thinking, Problem Solving, and Creativity) *Ch. 11-13*	*Social and Personal Skills, Attitudes, and Habits* Ch. 14-15	*Technological and Media Literacy* Ch. 16	*Ability to Learn* (includes Inquiry and Student-Centered Learning) Ch. 17

21st Century Challenge

- **Critical Thinking and Analysis**: *Ch. 11*
- **Taking Action:** Problem Solving and Other Real World Actions: *Ch. 12*
- **Creativity in Action**: *Ch.13*

A theme will run through these chapters. We need students to make various assessments. First, students need to develop an ability and habit for *self-assessment*. They need to be aware of their own thinking when they are solving problems and creating new ideas. They need to be aware of the ways in which they learn new things and how they are progressing in their education. We can think of this as a connection to oneself. Second, beyond this understanding of oneself, we also need students to *assess the world around them*, trying to understand new things around them and then integrating those things into their skill set. Whether understanding themselves or their environment, we must turn our youth into active thinkers and consumers rather than passive beings who sit, listen, and absorb.

What Do Higher Order Thinking Skills Allow a Worker to Do?

In the first couple chapters of this book, I presented an overview of the challenges posed by the 21st century. I also discussed abilities that will help our youth thrive in this world. *Regardless of their career choices, workers must be able to do the types of things listed on the next page. (These items are important in any career, including education, medicine, business, or skilled trades.)*

Part 2 - Higher Order Thinking Skills

Critical Thinking in the Real World ➡	**Extending Critical Thinking into Taking Action / Solving Problems in the Real World**
Assess how well systems or processes are working and meeting goals	Create better systems and improve methods to meet goals
Analyze all of the pieces of a process	Develop more efficient processes
Identify challenges and determine the root causes and symptoms of the challenges	Create and implement effective action plans to overcome challenges
Predict the outcomes and obstacles of various actions	Implement well-planned actions that are likely to succeed
Understand various types of relationships	Proactively plan to avoid problems
Determine accuracy of information, research, or opinions	Make educated plans that are likely to succeed
Assess the assets and strengths of a group	Lead and orchestrate tasks
Determine the needs and desires of clients, patients, and customers	Create and articulate a product or service that meets the needs of clients, patients, and customers
Understand what tools are available	Maximize the potential of tools
Understand coworkers	Collaborate with coworkers
Determine potential benefits and risks in situations	Take responsible risks
Assess and understand new circumstances	Adapt to new circumstances
Think logically	Act logically

The real-world skills listed above are separated into two lists for a very important reason. A person must first be able to think critically and analyze situations, processes, or problems before he can extend his critical thinking to solve problems or take other actions. Because of this reality, we will look first at developing critical thinking skills (Chapter 11). We will then see how these abilities provide the foundation that allows people to take effective actions and solve problems (Chapter 12). To follow that up, we will look at how to promote creativity in the actions we take (Chapter 13). Thus, the next three chapters build upon one another. After completing the three major topics of this unit, you will be able to provide students with the skills to accomplish anything in the two lists above, regardless of your students' future fields of work and regardless of the class and age you teach.

11 Critical Thinking Through Analysis and Assessment

Critical thinking, with the ability to analyze and assess, is necessary for effective performance in the 21st century. The real-world value of these abilities demonstrates why we need to challenge our students by pushing them toward higher levels of thinking ... rather than challenging them to simply memorize and regurgitate more information. Critical thinking skills are important not only on their own, but are an essential stepping stone for moving forward to take authentic actions and solve problems in school and life (discussed in the next chapter).

What is Critical Thinking, Really?

Critical Thinking   (We will use the following description of critical thinking as our guide.)

   1) **A person is *thinking critically* when exercising one of these <u>specific analytical skills</u>.**

> ### Specific Analytical Skills
> **(First Part of Chapter)**
> 1. **Making Observations and Inferences**
> 2. **Comparing and Contrasting**
> 3. **Grouping and Categorizing**
> 4. **Understanding Cause and Effect**
> 5. **Understanding Sequence and Timing**
> 6. **Understanding the Big Picture**
> 7. **Identifying Patterns**

   2) **A person is also *thinking critically* when he or she <u>combines two or more of the specific analytical skills</u> above to make a more <u>complex assessment</u>.**

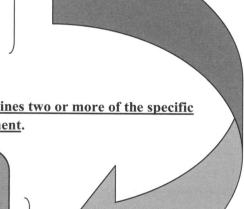

> ### Complex Assessment (Evaluating) Skills
> **(Second Part of Chapter)**
> 1. **Assessing Accuracy, Validity, or Logic (Informational Literacy)**
> 2. **Assessing the Workings of Processes, Events, Strategies, and Solutions**
> 3. **Self-Assessing**
> 4. **Identifying and Predicting Problems**

A Major Concern in Promoting Critical Thinking

When educators set out to promote critical thinking, most teachers are not likely to consider the various forms of specific analytical skills and general assessment skills. Because of this, students might not actually exercise all of the necessary critical thinking skills on a regular basis. Teachers are more likely to do thinking activities that reflect only some critical thinking skills. For example, an educator might do a critical thinking activity every day (which is great), but only exercise the specific analytical skills of comparing and contrasting along with categorizing and grouping (which is not as great). Another teacher might promote all of the specific analytical skills (from the first list) individually, but never ask students to combine them in activities that demand more complex assessment skills (from the second list). On the flip side, a teacher might do only critical thinking activities that involve complex assessments, but never help students improve the individual specific analytical skills that are required to soundly make complex assessments.

We have to move past a mindset in which we assume that any activity that requires any kind of thinking is an activity that meets the real-world demands of critical thinking. We must move into a mindset in which we recognize that there are different types of specific analytical skills and different types of complex assessment skills … and that we are determined to promote them all. So, we cannot simply look at the curriculum and ask ourselves how we can promote critical thinking within a particular topic. We must instead look at each topic and ask ourselves which one (or more) of the analytical and assessment skills we can promote (and also ask ourselves which of these skills we have not recently had a chance to promote in our classes).

How We Will Address Critical Thinking in this Chapter

This chapter will be broken into two major sections. <u>First</u>, we will independently address each of the <u>specific analytical skills</u> so that we can promote them in our classes. This is critical! We must exercise all of these skills in order to promote critical thinking. Our youth will not be prepared for the 21ˢᵗ century if they simply learn *some* aspects of analysis.

<u>Second,</u> we will look at how kids can use their analytical skills in concert in order to make <u>complex assessments (evaluations)</u>. Each of the assessment skills will be addressed independently so that we can learn how to promote all of them in our classes. Before we start …

Critical Thinkers Ask Questions and Find Answers

When an effective thinker uses specific analytical skills and complex assessment skills in the real world, she asks herself questions and determines answers. A critical thinker asks questions such as:

- What is going on in this situation?
- What factors are involved?

- What are the similarities and differences between different structures and processes?

- What is working well and what is not?
- Which factors and processes work well together and which do not?
- What is causing certain positive and negative outcomes to occur?
- What is the likely effect of certain structures and actions?

- How is the timing of this situation important?
- How do the small pieces of something affect the big picture?
- What patterns do I notice?
- What is likely to occur?

Then, this person answers these questions. When someone has the mental prowess to ask questions like these and is capable of answering them, that person is an effective thinker. *Thus, critical thinking is all about asking oneself critical questions and determining answers.*

So, what can we do when teaching each type of critical thinking in order to *1) promote the habit in students of asking themselves questions and then 2) promote the ability to find answers?* We can use our four key strategies when teaching each of the skills in this chapter.

Key Educational Strategies for 21st Century Skills, Attitudes, and Habits

- **Classroom Exercises** – Teachers engage students in activities that help them develop 21st century skills, attitudes, and habits (preferably using inquiry).
- **Teacher Stories / Modeling -** Teachers model and tell stories that help their students develop 21st century skills, attitudes, and habits.
- **Assessment by Students -** Students make assessments of themselves, assessments of others, and assessments of their environment to develop 21st century skills, attitudes, and habits.
- **Curricular Examples** – Teachers expose students to the ways that historical figures, scientists, characters from stories, etc. used 21st century skills, attitudes, and habits to their advantage.

To see how these techniques can be useful, let's move on to our first type of specific analytical skills, "Making Observations and Inferences."

Specific Analytical Skills

 Making Observations and Inferences

This analytical skill is extremely important. We are addressing this skill first because all of the other skills in the list rely on a student's ability to recognize who or what is involved in a situation, what is going on, and what it might mean. Above, we noted that the development of specific analytical skills such as this one requires us to 1) promote the habit in students of asking themselves analytical questions and then 2) promote the ability to find answers.

Classroom Exercises (Making Observations and Inferences)

Providing inquiry-based opportunities in classrooms for students to make observations and inferences (reasonable assumptions) is essential. This practice can be done in virtually any class at any age level. We can use activities that allow students to learn the curriculum in such a way that they must make observations and inferences. Some examples of questions that we might weave into activities that develop observing and inferring are given below. (We will use extra examples from a variety of subjects with this first analytical skill, so that we can get a good feel for how critical thinking can be promoted in all areas and ages.)

Observation and Inference Classroom Activities

We Should See Students Who ...	Personal Empowerment Questions (PEQs for Students)
👁 Make careful and rational observations 👁 Make reasonable assumptions and inferences	General PEQs ❓ What do I know about this object, challenge, situation, person, event, process, or action? ❓ What do I not know about this? ❓ What can I reasonably infer about this object, challenge, situation, person, event, process, or action? Math ❓ What information do I know about this problem? ❓ What objects or actions take place in this situation? ❓ What do I want to find out? ❓ What information is necessary and what is unnecessary? ❓ What mathematic skill will help me? ❓ What can I reasonably infer about the problem? English ❓ Who are the characters in the story? ❓ What is going on in the story? ❓ What part of speech is that? ❓ What sound does that letter make? ❓ What does that word mean? ❓ What is similar to that? ❓ What can I infer about the characters? English questions specific to older students ❓ What themes, symbolism, or archetypes do I recognize? ❓ What is this thesis and what is its supporting information? Social Studies ❓ Who was involved? ❓ What were the circumstances?

> **?** What did they do?
> **?** What went right or wrong?
> **?** What happened before or after that?
> **?** What seems to be the reason that it happened?
> **?** What can I infer about the people and situation?
> Science
> **?** What were the circumstances?
> **?** What happened?
> **?** What seems to be the reason that it happened?
> **?** What things are involved?
> **?** What can I infer about the experiment or data?
> Arts
> **?** What is the tempo or key?
> **?** What are the colors?
> **?** What patterns are there?
> **?** What is the style?
> **?** What can I assume?

Students who ask questions like these grow into adults who can make quality observations and reasonable inferences in a business, practice, hospital, or firm.

When we put students into learning situations that allow us to ask questions like those above, we promote the habit within their young minds of asking critical questions that develop the analytical skill of "making observations and inferences." ***As often as possible, we should design our learning activities so that they stimulate the students to ask questions like these in order to accomplish a task.*** Our lessons should also stimulate our students to ask questions that are relevant to other critical thinking skills that we will discuss throughout this chapter. (Notice that the sample questions above are not possible if the classroom lessons and activities are not designed to promote thinking, rather than listening and repeating.) Once we stimulate students to ask questions, we need to support them in their development of strategies for determining answers.

Teacher Stories / Modeling (Making Observations and Inferences)

First, a teacher can tell students what he or she is thinking during an analysis such as observing and inferring. This is very beneficial, as it gives young people an opportunity to hear how the teacher analyzes … *tell them and model how your thinking works* by thinking aloud. For example, teachers can describe their observations related to a story, a problem, an experiment, or a demonstration. They can then talk about how their minds develop inferences from the observations.

So, to promote the skill of "observing and inferring," we won't simply create lessons that allow us to pose analytical questions. We will also help young minds develop a mental toolbox by thinking aloud.

Observation and Inference Teacher Stories / Modeling

We Should See Students Who ...	PEQs for Students
👁 Are exposed to teachers who think aloud 👁 Get new ideas for critical thinking from their educators	❓ How does my teacher approach this type of critical thinking (observing and inferring), and will that critical thinking strategy work for me? ❓ How can I tweak the teacher's critical thinking strategy to work better for me?

Students who ask and answer questions like these grow into adults who can observe and infer in real life situations.

Assessment by Students (Making Observations and Inferences)

We can also stimulate students to develop their critical thinking skills toolbox by asking them to assess the thinking of other kids and assess their own thinking (meta-cognition). To help stimulate kids to observe and learn from others in the class, we can *ask students to describe to the class what happens in their minds* when they are doing a certain type of analysis. This process gives everyone a chance to hear a variety of strategies for a critical thinking skill, such as making observations and inferences, and adds to the critical thinking skills toolbox in their minds. In addition to looking outward in the development of critical thinking skills, kids can be encouraged to assess themselves and to *think about their own thinking*. We can promote this meta-cognition by stimulating students to think aloud, asking them to write down the steps they take when thinking, or asking them to create mind maps. When students think about their thinking, they develop an awareness of the steps they take to effectively analyze something. They need to understand what strategies are available to them and which strategies work best in their brains. (Forcing kids to show their work in a math class can develop this awareness. Similarly, creating outlines for reading and writing promotes meta-cognition. These tasks help young minds develop an awareness of the steps they take to accomplish a task.)

Observation and Inference Assessment by Students

We Should See Students Who ...	PEQs for Students
👁 Think aloud or explain their thinking while others listen 👁 Get new ideas for critical thinking from others 👁 Think about their own thinking and identify what techniques work best for them	❓ How do *I* perform this type of critical thinking? ❓ How do *you* perform this type of critical thinking? ❓ Which critical thinking strategies work best for me?

Students who ask and answer questions like these grow into adults who can observe and infer in real life situations.

Curricular Examples (Making Observations and Inferences)

Another way to help students develop analytical skills, such as "observing and inferring," involves the use of examples within the curriculum that demonstrate the skill. For example, a math teacher might teach students about the observations and inferences made by a famous mathematician when a new math concept was discovered. The same could be done in a science class in order to teach how observations and inferences have led to various discoveries. In a literature setting, a teacher can draw attention to the observations and inferences made by characters in a story (or how poor observations impacted a character). In all subjects, there are opportunities to demonstrate the use and misuse of critical thinking skills such as observation and inference.

Observation and Inference Curricular Examples

We Should See Students Who ...	PEQs for Students
👁 Develop observation and inference skills through examples from the curriculum	❓ How did _____ make _____ discovery? ❓ What observations and inferences did _____ make in a story, and were they correct?

Students who ask and answer questions like these grow into adults who can observe and infer in real-life situations.

The Key Educational Strategies Live On

The examples above show how Classroom Exercises, Teacher Stories / Modeling, Assessment by Students, and Curricular Examples can be used to promote the critical thinking skill of observing and inferring. These can also be used for developing all of the other types of critical thinking skills that are yet to be discussed in this chapter. To avoid being excessively tedious, we will not look at examples of how to use each of these four key educational strategies when discussing the other critical thinking skills throughout this chapter.

For the rest of this chapter, we will focus on developing your understanding of the critical thinking skills that you need to promote (using the key educational strategies).

Side Note

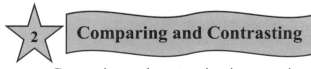

2 Comparing and Contrasting

Comparing and contrasting is a very important analytical skill that allows people in real-life situations to identify where the differences lie between processes, ideas, or solutions. Let's look at our goals.

Comparing and Contrasting

We Should See Students Who ...	PEQs for Students
👁 Consider the characteristics of objects, people, or events	General PEQs ❓ Considering the characteristics I observe,

👁 Seek and find similarities and differences	what similarities and differences do I notice in these objects, challenges, situations, people, events, processes, or actions? ❓ Are the differences I notice large or small? <u>Subject-Specific PEQs</u> ❓ How is this word similar to or different from that word? ❓ How are the actions of these characters similar or different? ❓ How is this math challenge similar to or different from that one? ❓ How is this animal similar to or different from that animal? ❓ How are protons, neutrons, and electrons similar and different? ❓ How is this situation in history similar to or different from that situation in history? ❓ How is this recipe similar to or different from that recipe? ❓ How is this athletic competition similar to or different from that athletic competition? ❓ How does this solution to a problem compare to that solution?

Students who ask and answer questions like these grow into adults who can compare and contrast resources, strategies, challenges, and solutions.

Organizational Tools

For activities in which students ask questions like those above, organizational tools can be very beneficial. Tools such as lists, graphic organizers, or Venn diagrams can be used.

The Extra Benefits of Comparing and Contrasting:
Understanding, Memory Retention, and Reading Comprehension

Beyond developing students' real-world analytical skills, comparing and contrasting exercises provide other benefits. First, developing a sense of the similarities and differences among curricular ideas promotes a better understanding of the content. Second, this practice promotes the mental connection of various curricular ideas, increasing the chances of retention and the perceived value to students.

In addition, I have found that unexpected benefits come from exercising this critical thinking skill. When I first started teaching, I wanted to promote reading comprehension. So, I assigned students to answer the two or three questions at the end of each section within a science textbook chapter. I soon found that many students would quickly skim the section to find the answers to these two or three questions. They had a tendency to neither read the whole chapter nor even attempt to comprehend the text. I decided to try an exercise in comparing and contrasting. I drafted my own questions for each section. First, students were asked to tell how each biological process is similar to something

Side Notes

from everyday life. Next, they were asked to compare and contrast key terms and ideas. The results were very pleasing. Students were not only forced to read the whole section to develop a deeper understanding of the new concepts, but they were also forced to think critically about what they were reading as they worked to compare and contrast ideas. The reading became something that helped comprehension and promoted connections to the real world. You never know when an analytical skill might have benefits beyond critical thinking.

3 Grouping and Categorizing (Organizing Information)

When dealing with complex real-world tasks, the ability to organize information is essential in planning, orchestrating systems, developing efficiency, writing, learning, and assessing quality. Let's look at some examples of how this skill of grouping and categorizing can be developed.

Examples - Various Content Areas

For the specific promotion of grouping and categorizing skills, we can ask students to organize information into categories by comparing and contrasting words, historical events, plots, shapes, theorems, foods, exercises, or even rocks. This can be done at all age levels in all subject areas. In kindergarten, young children can categorize the shapes of letters (round or straight, with "sticks" in them). In high school Social Studies, students can categorize and group the countries involved in an important world event. Whatever the activity, teachers need to pose questions to students to get them in the habit of asking analytical questions related to grouping and categorizing.

Grouping and Categorizing

We Should See Students Who ...	PEQs for Students
👁 Organize information 👁 Recognize various grouping possibilities and decide which one to use in light of the goals of the organizing activity	General PEQs ❓ What groupings make the most sense based on similarities and differences? ❓ Why does this item go into one particular group as opposed to another group? ❓ What types of groups would other people likely make? ❓ How does organizing these things help me accomplish my goals? ❓ Will this organization work better or worse if organized in a different way? Subject-Specific PEQs ❓ How can I categorize these animals? ❓ What categories can I create for the characters in this story? ❓ How can I categorize the types of math strategies we have learned? ❓ What groups formed during this time in history and why?

	❓ What type of exercise am I doing? ❓ To what genre of music does this song belong?

Students who ask and answer questions like these grow into adults who can organize the parts and processes of their work and life to maximize understanding, success, and efficiency.

Organizational Tools

In grouping and categorizing activities, students might be more engaged and find greater understanding if they make use of graphic organizers, Venn diagrams, or dichotomous keys. In these activities, kids need to go beyond simple grouping. They should write down their rationale for creating certain groupings and separations. This promotes meta-cognition … or thinking about one's own thinking.

Critical Thinking Activities Can be Great Student-Centered Activities

The promotion of critical thinking skills provides opportunities for student-centered learning. For instance, a teacher might want to develop his or her students' understanding of the biological kingdoms. So, he or she could simply tell the students about the characteristics of the living things in each kingdom. However, this is not student-centered; it does not promote higher-level thinking, and it does not connect the students to the curriculum. Instead, the teacher can present to the students examples of living things from the various kingdoms. (Pictures can be used for examples that are too small to see with the naked eye.) The students' task can be to *identify* the characteristics of each living thing, *compare and contrast* these characteristics, and predict how scientists *group* these living things into kingdoms. (Notice that these requirements match the first three types of specific analysis in this chapter.) After the activity, the students would compare their predictions to the real kingdoms used in biology. This lesson is more engaging, is connected to the real world, and stimulates higher-level thinking more than simply telling a class about the kingdoms. Similar activities for organizing information are possible in any class.

4   Understanding Cause and Effect

The previous three categories of critical thinking skills were very important. Observing and inferring, comparing and contrasting, and categorizing lay a foundation for more complicated thinking. To push our students to higher levels, we must improve their ability to understand cause-and-effect relationships. The complexity of these relationships varies depending on the number of details and relationships. Over the course of a child's education, he or she needs to build toward an understanding of very complex cause-and-effect relationships. Thus, this skill must be developed in age-appropriate ways from kindergarten to graduation. The ultimate goal is for young adults to be able to dissect and understand complicated situations that have many variables.

Let's look at some examples of how educators can promote an understanding of cause-and-effect relationships within the classroom. We will look at specific subject areas independently, because the techniques from one subject to the next vary widely.

Side Notes

11 - Critical Thinking Through Analysis and Assessment

Social Studies

Rather than simply learning facts about people, places, times, and events, students are likely to be more interested in developing an understanding of the intricate cause-and-effect relationships that shape the world and its people. In fact, the process of learning history is important, because we can learn what the causes and effects of various actions and events have been in the past, allowing us to make informed decisions in the future. To learn about cause-and-effect relationships in Social Studies classes, there are a number of possibilities.

Examples - Social Studies Classroom Exercises

Students can analyze historical circumstances and predict what happened next. In reverse, they can hypothesize the causes of certain events.

Learners can be asked what might have happened in history had events been different. In reverse, they can be challenged to hypothesize what would have needed to happen in order for certain events to have turned out differently than they did.

Young minds can be challenged to decide what they would have done under certain circumstances before they learn what real leaders and citizens actually did.

Students can be asked to make connections between past events and current conditions.

Cause and Effect in Social Studies

We Should See Students Who ...	PEQs for Students
👁 Reflect upon the causes and effects of events and circumstances	❓ What do I predict is the logical result of this situation?
👁 Understand chains of events in social studies	❓ What circumstances are likely to have led to this situation or event?
👁 Understand how the current world was shaped	❓ If _____ had done this, what might've happened?
👁 Predict	❓ If this leader or group of citizens had _____, what might have resulted?
	❓ What needed to happen for _____ to do _____?
	❓ If you were the leader of or citizen of _____ and these were the circumstances of a situation … _____, what would you have done?
	❓ What do we do today as a result of _____ event?
	❓ Which of the events that we have studied played the largest role in creating the current situation of _____?

Students who ask and answer questions like these grow into adults who can find the causes of problems, predict how effectively solutions will work, and recognize the importance of various details in a sequence of events.

Science

Again, our youth can exercise their critical thinking skills (and specifically, their ability to determine cause and effect) only if they are actively engaged in student-centered questions, activities, or experiments. Science is ripe with opportunities to present students with real-world questions or phenomena.

Students can make predictions (hypotheses) *before* observing a demonstration or experiment in order to develop the skills to determine "cause and effect." Conversely, they can be asked to rationalize why something happened *after* observing some interesting science phenomenon.

Students can predict what would happen in a scientific process or experiment if a variable was changed.

In total, science offers seemingly unlimited opportunities for young minds to assess the causes or effects of various processes. Thinking about why things work makes science much more interesting than simply learning facts; in the process, students develop real-world analytical skills.

Cause and Effect in Science

We Should See Students Who ...	PEQs for Students
☞ Reflect upon the causes and effects of real-world processes and phenomena ☞ Understand chains of events in scientific processes ☞ Make predictions	❓ Why does _____ happen? ❓ What would happen differently if I did _____? ❓ What do I predict would happen if ____ happened? ❓ What is my hypothesis? ❓ Was my hypothesis correct? ❓ Why did that happen? ❓ What scientific discovery allowed for the development of this new technology or process?

Students who ask and answer questions like these grow into adults who can determine how systems work, predict ways in which their practices can work better, and create completely new ideas and processes.

Math

In math, the sequence in which actions occur has a huge effect on the outcome. Any activity that illustrates this point is useful.

Examples - Math Classroom Exercises

Here is a quick activity that develops an understanding of cause and effect in math. Students can be given problems that are already solved, but the solutions were performed incorrectly. The challenge is for the students to figure out where the errors occurred.

Members of a class could also be challenged to create problems that are solved incorrectly so that other students can find the errors in the solutions.

Cause and Effect in Math

We Should See Students Who ...	PEQs for Students
👁 Recognize how problem-solving techniques work 👁 Understand how a series of mathematical steps affect one another	❓ How does this solution work? ❓ Considering what I know, how can I solve ____? ❓ In order to accomplish ____ in a math solution, what needs to be done? ❓ What is the result of performing this step in a math solution? ❓ If this solution strategy is performed incorrectly, what would be the likely result?

Students who ask and answer questions like these grow into adults who seek to understand the cause-and-effect relationships within various problem-solving strategies. They develop a deep understanding of processes that allow them to apply their skills in new ways.

English - Language Arts

There are many opportunities in an English language class to stimulate students to think about cause-and-effect relationships. Students can look at the connections between characters and events in stories and their effect on each other. They can also look at how grammar and writing style affect the ways in which their writing is perceived.

Cause and Effect in English - Language Arts

We Should See Students Who ...	PEQs for Students
👁 Seek the causes of events 👁 Make predictions about what could happen under various circumstances 👁 Think about the best ways to get through to an audience in speaking and writing 👁 Understand chains of events in stories and writing	When reading stories… ❓ What do I think will happen next in this story? ❓ Why did that character do what he or she did? ❓ What if ____ had happened in this story? ❓ What if ____ had not happened in this story? ❓ Why did the author use the word ____ there? ❓ What would I do if I were this character? ❓ How did I feel after I read ____? When reading articles or essays… ❓ What could be the real-world results of the information in this article or essay? When learning to read… ❓ How does this word change when ____ is

	added? **?** How does the sentence change when "!" is changed to "?"? <u>When writing…</u> **?** What could I include to create ____ mood? **?** What could I include to grab the reader's attention? **?** How will my writing be perceived if I say ____ ?

Students who ask and answer questions like these grow into adults who look at the world with an objective eye, analyze situations to find the root causes of challenges, and consciously think about the potential ramifications of solutions. They will think about the ways in which they say and write things in order to better achieve their goals.

Common Themes for the Various Content Areas

Although the techniques for the different subject areas vary when developing students' abilities to understand cause-and-effect relationships, there is a common theme. We need to get students to make *predictions* for what is yet to come and make *rationalizations* for what has already happened.

Cause and Effect

We Should See Students Who ...	PEQs for Students
👁 Make predictions and rationalizations 👁 Understand the causes and effects in a variety of situations 👁 Understand chains of events	**?** Why did that happen? **?** What is the root cause of this problem? **?** What do I expect to happen next? **?** If this happens, then what will occur? **?** What if this detail or relationship had been different? **?** What problems might arise as a result of this action or event? **?** Does this cause-and-effect relationship make sense? **?** Will this strategy or solution work?

Students who ask and answer questions like these grow into adults who can find the root causes of challenges, predict challenges, and create logical procedures that are likely to work.

5 Understanding Sequence and Timing

Understanding sequence and timing is an extension of the previous skill, understanding cause and effect. Once young minds develop an understanding of simpler cause-and-effect relationships, they can apply them to more complicated tasks, such as understanding the sequence and timing of various situations. In real-life careers, successful workers need an understanding of how the sequence and timing of steps and events affects the outcome of a situation. Let's look at how teachers can develop this skill in the classroom.

Examples - Various Content Areas

Students can be given out-of-order pieces of a story plot and be asked to determine the correct order. They can be given out-of-order steps of an experiment or scientific process and asked to determine the correct order. The same type of activity can be done in Social Studies, math, and arts. Also, students can do similar activities in which they analyze what would happen if portions of a story, experiment, or event were rearranged.

Learners can create directions to accomplish some task. Then, another student can perform the task and assess how well the sequence of the directions works.

As is generally the case, thinking about how to work this critical thinking skill into classroom studies is conducive to creating activities that are more student-centered, more connected, and more engaging.

Sequence and Timing

We Should See Students Who ...	PEQs for Students
👁 Seek to understand the proper order and timing for various events 👁 Recognize what can happen differently when the sequence and timing of events or processes are changed 👁 Develop ideas and processes that have rational sequence and timing	General PEQs ❓ What if ____ had happened before ____? ❓ What if ____ had happened a little sooner or a little later? ❓ What is or would have been the best order for the steps of ____ to occur? ❓ When would be the best time to do ____? Subject-Specific PEQs ❓ What if I do ____ before doing ____ in this math or science problem? ❓ What if this leader or citizen had done ____ a little sooner or little later? ❓ Considering the facts that you know, what would be the best order of presenting them in a persuasive essay? ❓ When writing a story, what should happen in the beginning, middle, and ending of the story?

Students who ask and answer questions like these grow into adults who can determine how the sequence and timing of actions and events affects the success of policies, plans, and organizations.

Side Note

Technology Has a Role in Developing Sequence and Timing Skills

A great way for students to develop an understanding of sequence is through technology. The best technological activity that I encountered in elementary school involved creating some very basic computer instructions to move a little turtle around a computer screen. During this process of trial, error, and revision, kids determined the best sequence of computer commands. The activity was fun and appropriately challenging for the youngsters' analytical skills. Later in my education, taking a computer programming class in high school was one of the best things I did to develop analysis and sequencing skills.

Today, our youth can get similar benefits from developing PowerPoint® presentations, building web pages, utilizing simple animation software for a presentation, using video editing software, etc. It's important for educators to be proficient in as many technological areas as possible, so that we can push students into these areas.

Some schools might elect to have technology classes to help students learn how to build web pages or design computer programs. Not only are these classes good for developing critical thinking skills, but they might lead to a future career.

6 Understanding the Big Picture

In the real world, adults are constantly faced with situations in which small details have a large effect on the big picture. People need to be able to comprehend how the small aspects of their work and personal lives add up to create a larger whole. With an understanding of the big picture and how finer details affect it, people can reflect on the best methods for doing various life tasks in order to attain larger goals.

Examples - Various Content Areas

There are opportunities in all classes for students to be challenged by the task of analyzing all of the details and relationships within a situation, problem, or event and then to develop an overall strategy or plan of action. The opposite is also true. Class-members can be challenged to look at an overall situation to determine why specific small details and relationships matter to the outcome.

Another activity that helps young minds understand how the little details affect the overall situation is to challenge them to predict what would happen if a small detail or relationship was modified or removed. The reverse can also be done. The students can be given a scenario with some small, crucial detail or piece of information absent and be challenged to find what is missing.

Other ideas … any activity that requires children to create a hierarchy of ideas, concepts, or facts forces them to rationalize how all of the small pieces fit together. (This type of activity can be done graphically.)

Sometimes, students can develop an understanding of curricular information while developing critical thinking skills for understanding the "big picture." They can be given disorganized or shuffled facts, circumstances, events, or drawings that make up a certain topic. The students can then attempt to organize these parts to determine the big picture.

Understanding the Big Picture

We Should See Students Who ...	PEQs for Students
☜ Look for themes	General PEQs
☜ Analyze situations and processes to find the roles of various small pieces that make up the big picture	❓ What is the overall meaning of these small details? ❓ What is the theme of these ideas or facts?

👁 Create solutions, processes, and hierarchies by considering the ways in which small details affect the big picture 👁 Recognize how larger situations can be manipulated by tweaking smaller details	❓ What role does ____ play in the big picture? ❓ Why is ____ important in solving this problem? ❓ What details should be addressed to improve the overall picture? ❓ How would the big picture be different if _____ were removed or changed? <u>Subject-Specific PEQs</u> ❓ What is the theme or general message of this story? ❓ What is the larger goal of solving this math challenge? ❓ How is this small concept important to our understanding of this science unit? ❓ What general mood are we trying to create with this music and how does each part of the song help?

Students who ask and answer questions like these grow into adults who can see how each small detail affects the overall success of a business or practice.

Side Note

Students Should Understand the "Big Picture" of the Curriculum

A great way to promote an understanding of the big picture is to develop student awareness of how each lesson fits into the bigger picture of a topic, a week, a unit, and the school year. They need to see how each lesson fits with what came before and what will come after the lesson. They need to see how each topic is important to the larger themes and goals of the course. Therefore, educators should review and tie together classroom activities during the day, at the end of the day, and at the end of the week to discuss why each was important. At the same time, we need to help our students understand where the class is headed as we begin each lesson, day, or unit. To accomplish these goals, we can ask specific curricular review questions or larger questions, such as:

PEQs for Students to See the Big Picture of the Curriculum
❓ What did we learn about yesterday and why was it important?
❓ Why are we doing this learning activity today?
❓ What do we predict we will learn next?
❓ What will/did our lessons today/this week accomplish?
❓ What are our learning goals and how do these activities help achieve them?

Notice that students will find it easier to understand a unit or class if they recognize the goals of the class. Therefore, we should develop these goals in our students' minds at the beginning of the year and continuously revisit them. By stimulating our students to think about the major goals of a class and how each lesson addresses those goals, we stimulate our youth to look for an understanding of the "big picture"; not just in school, but in everyday life. We need to train their brains to look at the "big picture" and see how all the little parts within it matter.

Not only should we tie together our classroom activities for the sake of developing an idea of the "big picture" for our students, but we should also do it for the simple reason that children will more easily understand what we teach. If a class is learning about a complex topic or idea, the kids can become confused if they lose sight of the overall point. This problem can happen within one lesson or over the course of a few lessons. Young minds need to be stimulated to rationalize how individual classroom activities fit together and work to achieve learning goals.

Critical thinking aside, tying lessons together helps students make connections within the curriculum. As we discussed in an earlier chapter, developing connections between students and the curriculum is essential. It motivates them, helps them see the value of what they are learning, deepens their understanding, and increases their long-term retention.

7   Identifying Patterns

In the real world, the ability to identify patterns that occur within a situation, workplace, or process is very beneficial. Recognizing patterns can help children create positive and efficient processes or solutions to problems. It can also help children identify what might be wrong in certain situations or problems.

Examples - Various Content Areas

Within some lessons, patterns exist that students can attempt to identify. For example, in a math class, students might recognize a pattern within certain types of problems. The identification of this pattern can help students understand how to recognize and solve that type of challenge.

In the language arts, as students read stories, they can learn to identify patterns that are common within a particular genre.

Children can also be stimulated to recognize the differences in patterns. Kids might recognize differing patterns in a variety of math problems or differing patterns in various types of writing.

Sometimes, patterns can emerge from topic to topic within a class. There can be patterns in music, historical events, plant survival techniques, animal body parts, sociology topics, values of various cultures, political structures, and so many more.

Identifying Patterns

We Should See Students Who ...	PEQs for Students
👁 Analyze processes and events in order to find patterns 👁 Compare various patterns encountered throughout a unit or school year 👁 Identify patterns that lead to the creation of effective processes, behaviors, and solutions	General PEQs ❓ What seems to be repeating itself here? ❓ How is this pattern different from others? ❓ What seems to be recurring among these _____? ❓ What patterns seem to work or not work when applied to various situations? Subject-Specific PEQs ❓ What patterns of development show up with each country that we study? ❓ How is the pattern of songs in this genre of music different from others?

| | ❓ What patterns do we see in the behaviors of characters in these stories? |
| | ❓ What pattern do the solutions to these math or science problems follow? |

Students who ask and answer questions like these grow into adults who can identify the best and worst ways in which tasks should be done.

Notice that identifying patterns is not simply useful for analytical purposes, but is also valuable for promoting the connection of different ideas, topics, and relationships within students' minds. Patterns can connect young minds to the curriculum, deepen their understanding, and improve retention.

Making Complex Assessments (Evaluations) by Putting Specific Analytical Skills Together

Up to this point, we've been looking at specific analytical skills. ***Now, we need to look at how all of these skills can be used simultaneously to make complex assessments or evaluations.*** Whether it is our youngest or oldest students, we can stimulate them with challenges that require them to use all of their specific analytical skills in concert. Let's look at some major categories of complex assessment.

1 ⭐ Assessing Accuracy, Validity, or Logic (by combining specific analytical skills) (Informational Literacy)

In any career, there are many instances when the worker will need to assess accuracy, validity, or logic. The same is true at home. In both cases, we need to determine if we will accept information and if we can make use of that information. Life is full of times in which we must make decisions about the information we obtain through various forms of media, friends, coworkers, research, politicians, etc.

We can promote this complex assessment skill within our classrooms. We must find opportunities within the curriculum for students to evaluate claims, proposed solutions to problems, arguments, theses, hypotheses, and opinions.

Examples - Various Content Areas

Teachers can improve student assessment skills by presenting children with something that is logically flawed … where the facts don't match a conclusion. Geometry teachers can give theorem proofs with logic flaws and ask kids to assess what is incorrect. The same can be done in science by presenting students with experiments which were set up illogically or experiments in which unsound conclusions were drawn from data. In any subject, students can be presented with a situation, process, or opinion and assess its validity, accuracy, or logic.

Students can also be asked to do research to find examples of media articles, video clips, or blog entries in which inaccurate, invalid, or illogical conclusions are drawn. The students can describe any potential sources of bias that they find. The students can also seek out and present examples in which the accuracy, validity, and logic are sound.

Teacher can also ask learners to develop opinions and debate relevant issues, processes, or points of view. During the debate, students can be asked to assess the logic and validity of statements made by others. The debates could deal with current and historical issues from Social Studies, the actions of characters in literature, current issues in science, and more.

Assessing Accuracy, Validity, and Logic (Informational Literacy)

We Should See Students Who ...	PEQs for Students
👁 Assess accuracy, validity, and logic of information, processes, solutions, and points of view 👁 Reflect upon prior knowledge 👁 Research relevant information 👁 Consider potential motives and biases when making assessments 👁 Consider all possibilities 👁 Use the seven specific analysis skills in concert when making assessments	❓ What background information do I need to make this assessment? ❓ What assumptions are being made? ❓ How do they know that? ❓ Do the steps of this solution, argument, or experiment follow a logical path? ❓ Are there possible biases in this claim or opinion? ❓ What background information and facts back up this information, assumption, theory, or opinion? ❓ What do I need to understand in order to make a quality assessment? ❓ Did this person or group follow the scientific method? ❓ Would this be the same in all situations? ❓ What is the truth?

Students who ask and answer questions like these grow into adults who can logically assess the accuracy and validity of something in order to determine the course of action that is best for them.

Lying

When I was in middle school, my dad gave me a book to read (that he read when he was younger) called *How to Lie with Statistics* by Darrell Huff. When I got to college, one of my professors assigned this same book as a reading, even though it is also appropriate for younger minds.

The word "statistics" in the title makes the book sound like it might be complicated, but it's not. It's a great little book that details various examples of how data, information, and the truth can be skewed in real life. I recommend this resource to teachers who want their students to become better at assessing what they see in the media, hear from politicians, encounter in the workplace, see in hypotheses, and encounter in everyday life. This book served as my inspiration for creating an assignment in which students find an article, movie clip, or television clip in which an invalid claim or inaccurate portrayal is made. The students then describe why it is illogical, doesn't follow the scientific method, or is biased. In all, determining accuracy, validity, and logic should be attacked in all subject areas. There is always an assessment to be made about the truth.

Assessing the Workings of Processes, Events, Strategies, and Solutions
(by combining specific analytical skills)

In the 21st century world that our youth will face, workers need to assess what's going on around them. They need to do this for various purposes, such as understanding how something works, determining if a process functions correctly and is efficient, understanding what's going on in their environment in order to learn from it, determining strengths and weaknesses, understanding logistics, or understanding social interactions. In schools, we can help students develop this habit through informal means or through assignments inside and outside of school.

Examples - Various Content Areas

In Social Studies, kids can be asked to determine how well certain governmental or political systems function. In science or math, students can figure out how a process functions. In language arts, kids can evaluate the strengths and weaknesses of characters in a book or seek to understand the style of various authors. In all classes, young minds can evaluate how well current and past practices work. They can also determine the most efficient and effective methods for doing tasks, such as solving problems, writing persuasively, or maintaining stability in a society. Children can assess one another's ideas, strategies, and writing.

Assessing the Workings of Processes, Events, Strategies, and Solutions

We Should See Students Who ...	PEQs for Students
👁 Assess how processes, events, strategies, and solutions work	❓ How does this process, event, strategy, or solution work?
👁 Look for the positives and negatives in these processes, events, strategies, and solutions	❓ Why is _____ happening?
	❓ Is this what is supposed to happen?
	❓ How does that person do _____ so well?
👁 Look for the most effective and efficient methods for doing various tasks	❓ Why is this process, event, strategy, or solution better than that one?
👁 Use the seven specific analysis skills in concert when making assessments	❓ What are the strengths and weaknesses of this process, event, strategy, or solution?
	❓ Is there something in this process, event, strategy, or solution that could be improved?
	❓ How would I prioritize these things?

Students who ask and answer questions like these grow into adults who can understand processes and structures in such a way that they can identify strengths and weaknesses and create effective ideas, processes, solutions, and products.

Creating a Habit of Assessment within Students

There are activities in all content areas in which students can make general and specific assessments, from evaluating a piece of writing to assessing the functions and sounds of an orchestra. In all cases, teachers can help students improve the quality of their assessments by providing them with a *goals sheet or rubric*. These tools focus attention on important objectives and provide criteria for making assessments. (As students progress in their education, they can begin to create their own goals sheets and rubrics.)

Once students get into the habit of making assessments based upon goals and criteria, *it will carry over into "non-school" thinking. Students can learn a great deal more than we have time to teach in school if they become conscious consumers of the world around them ... asking themselves how things work, what's going on, what's working and not working, and what could be better.* Assessing the world around oneself is also one of the greatest ways to develop improved social and team skills. Getting our youth to effectively analyze and evaluate their environment is a great habit to instill in them.

3 **Self-Assessing** (by combining specific analytical skills)

To compete in the 21st century, workers need the ability to assess their own knowledge, practices, skills, and roles within groups in order to work toward self-understanding and improvement. If students become good at self-assessment, then they can better work toward self-improvement.

The skill of self-assessment can be developed in school by giving students a chance to evaluate their own work with a goals sheet or rubric. This practice gives them an opportunity to self-assess and determine how effective they were in meeting certain objectives, such as writing, problem solving, working within a group, leading, or explaining. The Personal Empowerment Menu (for 21st Century Students) contains rubrics which students can use to self-assess as they develop the skills in this book.

When assessing themselves, **students need to know the goals** toward which they are working. During and after an activity, they can self-assess the manner in which they are meeting their goals so that they can work toward self-improvement. Children should also be involved in creating goals.

Opinion papers and debates are good activities for self-assessment. They force students to rationalize their own ideas and opinions in light of others. With a good rubric, these activities compel students to ask themselves what background knowledge and logic supports their ideas.

Self-Assessing

We Should See Students Who ...	PEQs for Students
👁 Set goals	❓ What are my goals?
👁 Self-assess their strengths, their weaknesses, and their roles in groups and processes	❓ Am I on track to meet my goals? ❓ What are my strengths and weaknesses? ❓ What is my role within this group or
👁 Have a passion for improvement	organization?

👁 Assess others in order to enhance self-assessment 👁 Use the seven specific analysis skills in concert when making assessments	❓ What can I do to be better? ❓ What new skills and knowledge would help me in ____? ❓ What did I just learn from that activity? ❓ How does my opinion or feeling differ from others? ❓ Why is this hard or easy for me to do? ❓ How can I improve? ❓ What can I learn about myself by observing others?

Students who ask and answer questions like these grow into adults who can set goals, track progress, improve, learn, and compete.

Side Note

Look Outside to Improve Assessment Inside

Note that self-assessment can actually be improved by assessing others. For instance, I found that when students review their own writing, they don't notice all of their mistakes. This seems to be because they skim quickly and know exactly what they meant to say. They might not realize that their intentions didn't translate into their writing. On the other hand, when the students assess the work of others, they have no idea what the other students meant to say. When the kids have to decipher what the others meant in their writings, they have an opportunity to assess closely … *"Did the ideas that the other person meant to convey end up in this paper?"* The students then become more likely to slow down when reading their own work and to ask themselves if the ideas they meant to convey actually translated to their writing.

In all, when our youth can assess themselves in any subject or in everyday life, they can become their own best advocate. They are better able to help themselves and to improve.

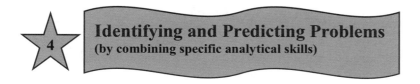

Identifying and Predicting Problems
(by combining specific analytical skills)

4

One of the great assessment skills for the real world is being able to figure out what went wrong or might go wrong in a complex situation. This analytical skill really is the first step of the problem-solving process that we will address in the next chapter. Before you can solve a problem, you must be able to find and understand the problem. Additionally, creating good solutions requires an ability to predict what might go wrong when certain strategies are implemented. Children can become better at problem identification and prediction in school.

Examples

There are problems to be found just about everywhere. In all of the subject areas, we can give students opportunities to identify what needs to be solved or predict what might go wrong within a process or situation.

Members of a class can identify what challenges lay before characters in stories and predict what might go awry. Learners can also discuss why circumstances are problematic and how those circumstances came to be.

In math and in science, students can be presented with a variety of situations in which a problem must be uncovered and identified. This is much more applicable to real life than if kids are always given problems where everything is spelled out for them. Young minds need plenty of experience looking for and determining the problem in a situation and what factors need to be addressed.

In Social Studies, students can look at various social and historical situations and determine what challenges exist or could potentially exist. They can seek core causes of problems. (When people determine the root causes of challenges, they can more effectively address them.)

Identifying and Predicting Problems

We Should See Students Who ...	PEQs for Students
👁 Thoroughly investigate situations and processes	❓ Based on everything I see here, what is the problem?
👁 Identify general problems and any related root causes	❓ What went wrong in this situation, event, procedure, solution, or action?
👁 Consider the goals of people, processes, and events in order to better understand challenges	❓ What is the root cause of this challenge or issue?
👁 Predict errors that can occur in situations and processes	❓ What are we trying to solve or fix? ❓ What problems might arise in this situation?
👁 Use the seven specific analysis skills in concert when making assessments	❓ What challenges could this solution create?

Students who ask and answer questions like these grow into adults who can find the root causes of problems, anticipate challenges, effectively prepare for the future, and predict the coming needs of their customers, patients, employees, and employers.

Critical Thinking Chapter: Wrap-up

Complex critical thinking is the combination of smaller analytical skills. These should be flexed individually and also together for the purpose of making larger assessments. To develop critical thinking skills, we cannot simply give students activities that require critical thinking. We must also help young minds develop the mental processes and tools required to accomplish complex critical thinking tasks.

The task of developing our students' analytical skills could seem overwhelming when we consider all that must be covered in a subject's curriculum. We must note that most critical thinking and assessment activities can be used as lessons to develop and assess *curricular* knowledge. Almost always, educators can find ways to create activities that serve the purpose of creating higher order thinking skills, as well as developing curricular knowledge. Promoting critical thinking skills does not need to be added on top of or replace the regular curriculum, but can be woven within it. This makes a class's content and skills more meaningful and promotes a connection between students and the curriculum. (Let's remember, though, that simply tossing in some critical thinking doesn't definitely make something engaging. When promoting critical thinking, we still must reflect upon the ideas in the connections to the curriculum chapter. We must find ways to make our activities interesting and engaging and relate those activities to the real world.)

Thinking About It

- **In what ways is it useful to separate the concept of critical thinking into specific analytical skills?**
- **How can critical thinking activities be meshed within your curriculum?**
- **What are the most difficult challenges that you see in developing students' critical thinking skills, and how can you overcome these challenges?**
- **In what ways do you and can you help your students develop new critical thinking strategies?**

How Does This Chapter Support the Goals of This Book?

Let's take a moment to think about the ways in which the ideas of this chapter help us address the three main goals of this book by looking at the "Building Blocks of a 21st Century Education" on page 13 and the "Daily Thoughts for Educators" on page 18. We now have tools and strategies for providing a 21st Century Challenge by developing critical thinking skills as we teach our curricula.

Make Note of Your Great Ideas!

If you haven't already, note your ideas for implementing the strategies in this chapter in your Teacher Empowerment Menu (for 21st Century Educators). In the future, you can easily reference usable ideas for your class.

In addition, consider the ways in which you can stimulate students to develop critical thinking skills by using the Personal Empowerment Menu (for 21st Century Students), which contains the relevant PEQs and assessment rubric for this chapter.

12 Taking Action: Problem Solving and Other Real-World Actions

Real-World Actions

In real life, assessments that are made through critical thinking are extended into action.

Critical Thinking in the Real World		Extend Critical Thinking into Taking Action / Solving Problems in the Real World
Assess a situation in order to determine what is going on, what problems exist, and what problems might occur.	→	*Follow up the assessment by creating and carrying out solutions / action plans.*
Analyze the circumstances and workings of processes within the workplace or home in order to identify inefficiencies and areas for improvement.	→	*Design improved or new processes and structures.*
Look at something with curiosity and seek to understand it.	→	*Develop a strategy for learning and put the strategy into action.*
Analyze a set of choices at work or home.	→	*Create an opinion, which might be promoted through conversation, speech, essay, or advertisement.*
A doctor assesses a patient, an engineer inspects the geography of an area where a bridge is to be built, or a teacher assesses the curriculum and skills that his or her students need.	→	*A doctor designs and carries out an action that will make someone healthier, an engineer designs a bridge to meet the geography, or a teacher creates and implements lessons and assessments that will meet the goals.*

It should be noted that Chapter 11 and this chapter are intrinsically intertwined … after developing and using analytical skills, the next logical step is to extend those skills forward to take some type of real-world action. It is nearly impossible to take a real-world action (such as

12 - Taking Action: Problem Solving and Other Actions

solving a problem) without effectively analyzing and assessing all of the details and relationships within a situation. Real-world actions (and problem solving) are an extension of critical thinking.

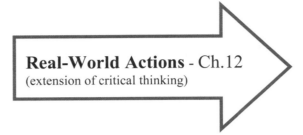

Critical Thinking Skills - Ch. 11

Real-World Actions - Ch.12
(extension of critical thinking)

A Variety of Real-World Actions are Possible

How can we extend critical thinking into taking real-world actions? In the classroom, teachers can provide opportunities to address the curriculum in a manner that develops the ability to perform real-world tasks.

Potential Real-World Actions in the Classroom

- Solving Problems
- Persuading Others by Various Means (Writing, Speech, Multimedia)
- Performing Real-World Professional and Life Tasks
- Designing a Process or Structure
- Generating New Knowledge

Science and math classes can allow students opportunities for all of these actions, but might focus more on problem solving and creating plans of action. English and Social Studies classes can do all of these actions, but might focus more on developing opinions and persuading others through writing or other means. All classes, obviously, should allow students to move from critical thinking into action. That will be the focus of this chapter. Notice that this supports a 21st Century Challenge for students.

It is very important that we imagine how real-world actions can be used in our own classrooms. Take a moment to think about possible real-world actions your students can perform.

At first, this chapter was going to be about problem solving only, but then I realized that there are many other ways in which people take real-world action after they have analyzed an issue or situation. A current buzzword is to promote "problem solving," but there is so much more.

Basic Strategy for Taking Action (and Solving Problems)

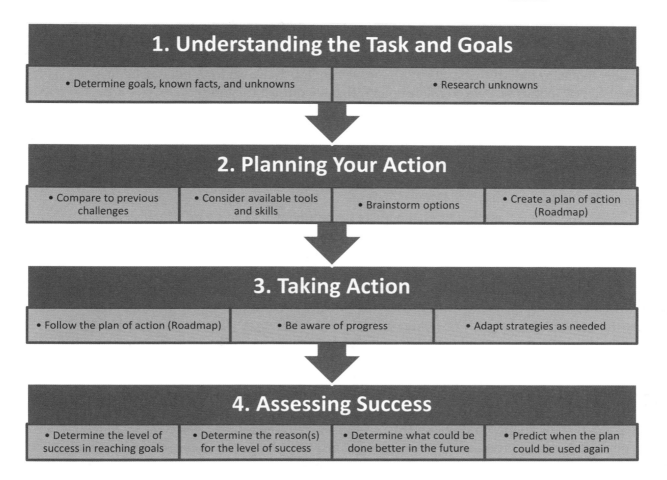

1. Understanding the Task and Goals

- Determine goals, known facts, and unknowns
- Research unknowns

2. Planning Your Action

- Compare to previous challenges
- Consider available tools and skills
- Brainstorm options
- Create a plan of action (Roadmap)

3. Taking Action

- Follow the plan of action (Roadmap)
- Be aware of progress
- Adapt strategies as needed

4. Assessing Success

- Determine the level of success in reaching goals
- Determine the reason(s) for the level of success
- Determine what could be done better in the future
- Predict when the plan could be used again

Clearly, we should help our students develop an understanding of this process and give them opportunities to use it. However, simply asking kids to perform real-world tasks using this process is not good enough. We must help them develop skills that will make them better at using the process above. As with earlier topics in this book, we can use four key educational strategies when teaching each of the real-world action skills in this chapter: Classroom Exercises (using inquiry when possible), Teacher Stories / Modeling, Assessment by Students, and Curricular Examples.

1 **Understanding the Task and Goals**

- Determine goals, known facts, and unknowns
- Research unknowns

In order to accomplish real-world tasks, people must understand the key elements and goals of the task. To solve a complex problem in math, students must first be able to make an overall assessment of the challenge. To create a reasonable experiment using the scientific method in a science class, students must first be able to analyze and assess a question or situation. To develop an opinion in a Social Studies class, students must first be able to assess a situation (using critical thinking skills, such as identifying key information, comparing and contrasting, understanding cause and effect, or seeing the big picture). To play music, children must be able to analyze all of the facets of a song. When you get down to it, good reading comprehension (an authentic action) relies upon reflective critical thinking.

If you popped open this book and turned right to this chapter, back up to Chapter 11. It's critical. The first step in successfully performing a real-world action is to successfully assess the situation or task using critical thinking skills. In my experience, students are more than halfway to solving a problem, designing a process, generating new knowledge, or developing and defending an opinion when they start by assessing the situation or topic with their critical thinking skills.

Once students have assessed a challenge to determine what known information is available and what unknown information is needed, they might need to do some research to find any unknown information that will be necessary for tackling the task.

Example - That Applies to Various Content Areas

When my students attempt to solve a problem in science, they are required to begin by assessing the problem. They must write down what information they know, what information they don't know (and need), and what they are trying to solve (their goal). Forcing them to make and record such an analysis makes a world of difference. It's much easier for kids to determine problem-solving strategies when they begin by rationalizing the available information and determining their goals.

Similarly, students can be more effective and find greater ease in doing tasks for other classes when they start by assessing their goals and the information at their disposal. This applies to problem solving, persuasive conversation and writing, opinion development and promotion, process design, and knowledge development. Students can be stimulated to assess real-world tasks in all subject areas in similar ways to the example above from my class.

12 - Taking Action: Problem Solving and Other Actions

Understanding the Task and Goals

We Should See Students Who ...	Personal Empowerment Questions PEQs for Students
👁 Identify goals	❓ What am I trying to figure out, prove, or develop?
👁 Identify given (or available) information	❓ What are my goals in this problem or task?
👁 Recognize what information they need, but do not have	❓ What information is given or is available?
👁 Research more information (if needed)	❓ What clues are relevant?
👁 Consider prior knowledge to improve their understanding of a task	❓ What information do I need, but do not have?
	❓ What do I need to find out in order to solve this problem or complete this task?
	❓ What do I already know about addressing this type of problem or task?

Students who ask and answer questions like these grow into adults who can understand all the facets of what needs to be done in any given situation and then set out to implement the proper strategy.

2   Planning Your Action (Creating a "Roadmap")

- Compare to previous challenges
- Consider available tools and skills
- Brainstorm options
- Create a plan of action (Roadmap)

Once students assess a problem, situation, or task (as in the section above), they are halfway to knowing how to accomplish their authentic task. Next, they need to create a plan of action (or roadmap) that will lead them to their goals. When creating a plan of action, students should compare their current task to previously performed tasks and consider the tools and skills they possess. With these things in mind, they can brainstorm possible methods for attacking the task at hand.

Examples - Various Content Areas

To stimulate kids to take these steps in creating a plan of action, teachers can require students to brainstorm ideas on paper. After deciding on a plan of action, the students can be required to outline the steps that they will take in order to accomplish their goals for a real-world task (thus creating a roadmap). If they are writing a persuasive paper, students should brainstorm and note possible arguments. Then, they should outline their final theses, key arguments, and supporting evidence. When writing a story, students can think about the general plot before beginning and take notes on their ideas. Then, the learners can outline the final plot of their story. If seeking understanding in science, children should brainstorm possible experiments and then outline their plan for an investigation. When solving math problems, students should plan the steps that they will take in order to perform the task. In art activities, young minds should generate a process that will best lead to a quality product.

Not Everyone will Necessarily Perform a Task in the Exact Same Way

For almost every real-world task, there are various ways in which people might accomplish it. We must recognize that not everyone's thinking works exactly the same. Some techniques for doing things might not "click" with certain students. Some kids are very capable of doing the task, but just need a different approach.

Educators in all subject areas should provide an array of strategies for tasks (when feasible) in order to provide differentiated options for various students' brains. Also, it is valuable when kids share with the class their ideas for how to do something. This allows students to hear about various methods that might work for them.

Even if everyone in the classroom understands how to accomplish a task in one manner, hearing about other options is helpful because it improves everyone's flexibility. Why not let students know about all of the tools at their disposal? In fact, I sometimes teach more than one method for problem solving in science and then require that students alternate among the methods as they work through a few problems. Once the class members have tried all the methods for a particular type of problem solving, I let them choose the one that works best for them on future tasks. This practice allows them to develop flexibility and then utilize what works best for them.

Teachers can also increase student flexibility by asking kids to describe another method to accomplish a task (other than the way they did it). In the real world, it is better if there is a diversity of styles that workers use in their tasks. It makes a company, firm, hospital, or any type of business more flexible and capable. With different styles, workers can complement one another's abilities instead of being clones.

Combining and Manipulating Strategies and Tools

In real-life situations, we often need to pull together a variety of techniques for accomplishing tasks. We encounter situations in which it is useful to tweak techniques in small or large ways to address challenges we have not yet encountered. Helping our learners bring together strategies and tools (as well as manipulate them) can give these young minds a competitive edge in the 21ˢᵗ century. This skill prepares our students to be much more flexible in the types of goals that they can accomplish in the real world.

In any class, pupils can engage in real-world actions that require them to blend together and/or manipulate strategies developed at different points during the year. Students can do a research / opinion project for which they simultaneously develop new knowledge through research, generate opinions on a topic, and create a persuasive paper. In this blending of skills, they can manipulate various action strategies as needed to make them work well together. In a math or science class, there are often opportunities to challenge students with problems that require a sequential combination of techniques. I like to give problems that are impossible to solve with one step or strategy. In these tasks, learners are required to determine a set of steps that can lead them from point A to point C. They need to rationalize that one technique can lead from point A to point B and another technique can lead from point B to point C. For problems like this, I emphasize 1) assessing which information we know and which we need to find out and 2) designing a roadmap of steps that can lead to the goal.

Planning Your Action (Creating a "Roadmap")

We Should See Students Who ...	PEQs for Students
✺ Consider their goals	❓ What are my goals in this task?
✺ Reflect on prior tasks, available tools, and personal skills	❓ Considering the goals and information I have, what do I need to do?
✺ Brainstorm and evaluate all possible strategies	❓ What tools do I have at my disposal?
✺ Combine and manipulate techniques when necessary	❓ Is this similar to another task I've done?
	❓ Do I already know a strategy for doing this task?
✺ Plan carefully	❓ Can I modify or combine strategies I've

👁 Understand how a plan will be carried out to meet their goals 👁 Are flexible	used for other tasks to do this one? ❓ Can I invent a new strategy to accomplish this task? ❓ Does someone else have another idea about how to do this? ❓ Considering my options, which strategy best accomplishes my goals? ❓ Considering my options, which strategy works best for my skill set? ❓ What is my plan (roadmap)?

Students who ask and answer questions like these grow into adults who understand the goals of any situation and logically develop plans of action for achieving those goals.

3   Taking Action

- Follow the plan of action (Roadmap)
- Be aware of progress
- Adapt strategies as needed

As students take action on a real-world task, they should monitor their plan of action to be aware of their progress and to efficiently stay on course. By monitoring their progress, students can see when their plan of action is not working and adapt their strategies.

Examples - Various Content Areas

To stimulate kids to take these steps in carrying out their plans of action, teachers can ask them to check off items on their roadmaps as they progress. (Teachers can monitor a student's progress to make sure that the steps of the plan match the actual product.) When a student is writing a persuasive essay, he or she can check off items on the roadmap as he or she writes a thesis statement and then moves on to defend that statement. In science, a student can check off the steps of a planned experiment as he or she completes them. In a math activity, a student can check off the steps of a plan to solve a problem as those steps are completed.

Taking Action

We Should See Students Who ...	PEQs for Students
👁 Follow their action plan as they progress through the process of completing a real-world task 👁 Monitor their progress as they follow their roadmap 👁 Adjust as needed when the action plan does not work perfectly	❓ What are my goals, and how does my action plan help me achieve these goals? ❓ Am I following my action plan (roadmap)? ❓ Where am I in my progression through this task? ❓ Do I need to adjust my plan in any way to better reach my goals?

Students who ask and answer questions like these grow into adults who work diligently to implement their plans of action and adjust as needed to achieve their goals.

Assessing Success

- Determine the level of success in reaching goals
- Determine the reason(s) for the level of success
- Determine what could be done better in the future
- Predict when the plan could be used again

It is critical that kids learn to assess their work after they have solved a problem or completed some other real-world task. By developing the ability to evaluate the success of a plan of action, the students learn to determine how well various strategies work. They can also use the assessment skills to look for better strategies and predict when similar plans of action could be used in the future.

To learn to assess success, students can be asked follow-up questions when performing a task. These questions can ask the students to reflect upon their goals, the methods they used, and the final results. If they are solving a problem, they can assess whether the answer makes sense. If they are writing a persuasive essay, they can assess the strengths and weaknesses of their arguments. Kids could also use an assessment rubric to assess their own work or the work of others.

Assessing Success

We Should See Students Who ...	PEQs for Students
👁 Assess how well their action plan worked in achieving their goals for a real-world task or problem	❓ What were my goals, and how well did my plan of action work?
👁 Look to understand why certain strategies work well and why others do not	❓ Why did certain strategies work well, and why did other strategies not work well?
👁 Seek methods for improving their future action plans	❓ How can I improve my action plans and methods in the future?
👁 Think about the potential future uses for the action plans they implement	❓ When might I be able to use these strategies again in the future?

Students who ask and answer questions like these grow into adults who assess their actions and seek improvement.

Helping Students Understand *Why* Various Action Plans Work

Let's imagine that a class develops a variety of skills over the course of a few months. With each new strategy, all of the young people understand what to do and do it well. But a challenge can arise after months of learning numerous skills that address a range of challenges. Sometimes, students can have difficulty recognizing which skill goes with which task or problem. This can be frustrating for the teacher, because he or she knows that the kids previously understood how to do each and every skill, but later have difficulty identifying which technique to use when given random tasks.

Why might young minds have this difficulty? I observed one possible reason when I was in school. (I will describe a math / science example, but a similar problem can arise in all subject areas.) Some of my teachers in math and science classes would show a type of problem and then describe exactly how to solve it … without talking much about *why* the solution works. This often led students to attempt to memorize equations and formulas that matched certain types of problems. Unfortunately, the members of the class were not gaining an understanding of why certain solutions effectively addressed certain challenges. As time passed, the students began to forget which equations worked with which problems. This made it very difficult for kids to be given a random challenge and to know which strategy to use. The frustrating thing is that the students had already learned how to do each type of challenge. This example from my past shows that educators cannot simply teach strategies for accomplishing tasks; we must also help students understand *why the strategies work.* This increases the chances of being able to remember and determine the proper methods of addressing tasks.

In sum, the four step process outlined above is a powerful tool for attacking all kinds of problems and real-world tasks. However, kids can sometimes get caught up in learning *how* to use action plan strategies for real-world tasks … without learning *why* those action plans work.

Side Note

This Difficulty can Emerge in *Any* Content Area or Grade Level

Student difficulties in identifying which strategies to use with different tasks can happen in other subjects. It can happen in writing when students are shown how to perform a specific type of writing but not shown why it is effective. For example, learning the steps of a five-paragraph essay does not mean that students understand the purpose and effectiveness of each paragraph. Kids need to understand why each part is important and how it supports the goals of a writing piece. Then, they will be capable of tweaking the writing technique to meet their needs in the future.

It can happen in any grade level. Let's look at math. This issue can occur in elementary school if children do not understand that multiplication is an extension of addition (3 x 4 is the same as 4 + 4 + 4) or in high school where students might not understand the reasons that the equation "force = mass x acceleration" works. If someone memorizes a simple skill or a complex equation without understanding why it works, he or she might be capable of only using that skill in very controlled situations where it is obvious what needs to be done.

Let's look at some ways to help students develop an understanding of *why* certain action plans work for accomplishing certain tasks. By understanding why an action plan works, students are more likely to know when it can be used and how it can be modified to achieve new challenges.

Helping Students Understand *Why* Various Action Plans Work
- Guiding Student Development of Strategies
- Rationalizing Solutions and Procedures
- "Figuring Out What is Wrong" Activity
- "Comparing Strategies" Activity
- "Creating Problems and Tasks" Activity

12 - Taking Action: Problem Solving and Other Actions

a) Guiding Student Development of Strategies

Example - Applies to ALL Content Areas and ALL ages

One of my physics teachers was so effective in helping us understand how complex equations worked in solving problems that some students did not need to memorize equations. (Memorizing or referencing equations is a very common occurrence in physics classes.) This teacher often used questions and prompts to get the class members to develop techniques for solving various types of problems. Because we developed the techniques and equations, we had a much better understanding of how these processes worked as opposed to simply being told the techniques or equations. At the very least, this teacher would explain how a scientist originally developed the idea so that we had an understanding of how the solution worked. In sum, these experiences showed me that it is not as effective in the long run for teachers to simply tell students the techniques and then ask them to plug in information like a robot. While my example discusses problem-solving in a science class, this premise holds for task strategies in all classes at all age levels. Young minds need to understand why a technique works for accomplishing a task. Otherwise, they are unlikely to remember the technique and recognize when to use it later.

b) Rationalizing Solutions and Procedures

Example - Various Content Areas

To help students understand why strategies for tasks work, when to use them, and how to modify them, we can ask the students to show their work on problems and to create outlines for writings, opinions, or processes. These practices force young minds to recognize the steps involved in accomplishing tasks and solving problems. While this is a good start, we can't stop there. It is important that students do not just recognize what steps they are taking to do something, but *rationalize the reasons* for each step. To accomplish this, children can be periodically asked to write a rationalization for each step in a process … describing how it works to accomplish the goal of the process.

c) "Figuring out What is Wrong" Activity

Example - Various Content Areas

We can show students examples of tasks or problems performed incorrectly and then ask the students to identify and describe what is not working. This practice will force the students to assess and rationalize the various steps and techniques being used. To go further, learners can be asked to consider what should be done differently. Again, this practice forces them to think about why each step in a process is important.

d) "Comparing Strategies" Activity

Example - Various Content Areas

We can show students a problem or task that has been done in two different ways. Then, the class members can be asked to assess which technique is better and explain why. By looking at the differences and thinking about how these differences affect the results, young minds think about how the process works to accomplish a goal.

e) "Creating Problems and Tasks" Activity

Example - Various Content Areas

Students can be challenged to create a problem or task that requires the use of a strategy that was just learned in class. This activity forces learners to reflect on how the strategy works to achieve real-world goals. When students create challenges, they can begin to imagine how different approaches can be used in different contexts or how strategies can be modified to accomplish new goals.

12 - Taking Action: Problem Solving and Other Actions

Helping Students Understand Why Various Action Plans Work

We Should See Students Who ...	PEQs for Students
👁 Actively develop strategies for accomplishing tasks (with the help of educators)	❓ What steps, techniques, and tools are necessary to accomplish the goals?
👁 Understand how each step, technique, and tool of a strategy helps to achieve the goals	❓ How does each step, technique, or tool in this process work to accomplish the goal?
	❓ How was this strategy or process developed?

Students who ask and answer questions like these grow into adults who can easily recognize which strategy or tool available to them is most effective in any given situation. They can understand, manipulate, and effectively create and choose tools and strategies in the workplace.

Taking Action: Wrap-up

In the real world, people make assessments and then take action. With the ideas above, we can provide authentic opportunities for our youth to extend their critical thinking into action by providing occasions and strategies for solving problems, generating plans of action, developing opinions, persuading others by using various means, designing a process or structure, and generating new knowledge. As in the last chapter, we must move beyond simply providing opportunities for kids to flex this skill. Students need their educators to help them develop new thinking skills to accomplish these tasks.

Side Note

Be a Supporter, not a Crutch

If we are to help students become truly independent in using real-world skills, then we have to be careful not to become a crutch. When kids get stuck or need help, we must not simply tell them how to do something or give them an answer. Instead, we should question, hint, and prompt in order to point them in the right direction, a direction in which they think for themselves.

Thinking About It

- **What real-world tasks are relevant to the subject area and age level at which you educate?**
- **What are the most difficult challenges that you see in developing students' skills in performing real life tasks?**
- **In what ways can you help students develop their skills for taking action?**

12 - Taking Action: Problem Solving and Other Actions

How Does This Chapter Support the Goals of This Book?

Let's take a moment to think about the ways in which the ideas of this chapter help us address the three main goals of this book by looking at the "Building Blocks of a 21st Century Education" on page 13 and the "Daily Thoughts for Educators" on page 18. We now have tools and strategies for providing a 21st Century Challenge by developing skills for solving problems and taking action as we teach our curricula.

Make Note of Your Great Ideas!

If you haven't already, note your ideas for implementing the strategies in this chapter in your Teacher Empowerment Menu (for 21st Century Educators). In the future, you can easily reference usable ideas for your class.

In addition, consider the ways in which you can stimulate students to develop skills in problem solving and taking action by using the Personal Empowerment Menu (for 21st Century Students), which contains the relevant PEQs and assessment rubric for this chapter.

13 | Creativity in Action

We will now extend the continuum we developed in Chapters 11 and 12. From critical thinking, we extended into problem solving and other real-world actions. Now, we will take another logical step by looking at ways by which we can promote creativity within these real-world actions. Creative skills have always been generally useful in the real world, but now their importance is skyrocketing. As we discussed early in this book, the job market is shifting away from basic skill jobs that can be outsourced and offshored. We are moving toward careers that require workers to design processes and solve problems in *new and creative* ways. In *The World is Flat*, Friedman states, "Even the Chinese will tell you that up to now they have been good at making the next new thing, and copying the next new thing, but not *imagining* the next new thing … China is now focusing on how to unleash more creative, innovative juices among its youth."[18] So, the challenge is this: America is already competing for jobs with foreign competition due to offshoring and outsourcing. Can we possibly afford to have this cheaper foreign competition (made up of billions of people) become more creative and innovative than we are? If we are not better at critical thinking and performing real-world tasks with *creativity and innovation*, what competitive edge will we have? To make things even more challenging, the number of "non-creative" jobs is being further decreased by advancements in technology and automation. So, let's set out to generate creativity within our youth.

When some people think of creativity, they might think mostly about artistic expressions. Actually, creativity can come in many useful forms.

Creative actions occur when …
- a physician thinks of new ways to help patients.
- a small business employee develops a new method for attracting customers to a store.
- a salesperson thinks of a new way to describe the uses of a product.
- an investigator brainstorms and develops new connections among pieces of evidence.
- a carpenter creates a system for being more efficient on the job.
- a teacher develops an engaging lesson plan.
- a journalist insightfully connects a set of facts to generate an opinion piece.
- an engineer creates a plan for building a car.
- a comic generates a humorous connection between ideas.
- anyone creates a new goal in their profession that people did not previously imagine achieving (like flying to the moon).

---

[18] (Friedman, 2005, page 352)

The possibilities for creative actions are endless. The bottom line is that *when Americans create in ways like those above, we are more effective, resourceful, and valuable to the economy. When we innovate better than any human or machine on Earth, our work is difficult to outsource, offshore, or automate. We are indispensable.* Let's look at some ideas for promoting creative student actions within our schools.

> **We want our students to be able to create and innovate by …**
> - **generating new ideas, processes, and tools.**
> - **finding new ways to use current ideas, processes, and tools.**
> - **making new connections among ideas, processes, and tools.**

In my experience, many people are unsure how to develop creativity in students. Some people even seem to perceive creativity to be a natural gift … you have or you don't. This is not the case! We can develop creative mental processes in students' minds. We have to recognize, however, that traditional listen-and-regurgitate learning does not achieve this goal. In this chapter, we will discuss ways to develop creative mental processes and discuss ways in which teachers can provide creative opportunities for children.

Promoting Creativity

1. **Developing Creative Mental Pathways in Students**
   (Training Creative Thinking)
2. **Empowering Students to Determine and Utilize Their Best Creative Ideas**
   (Training Wise Use of Creative Thoughts)
3. **Providing Opportunities for Creativity in the Classroom**
   (Providing Creative Outlets)

Developing Creative Mental Pathways in Students
(Training Creative Thinking)

Simply assigning an activity to students and saying, "Be creative!" is not good enough. We need to actively engage students in activities that develop creative mental pathways in their minds.

Creative Mental Pathways to Develop in Students

- **Making Connections** (among ideas, tools, objects, events, processes, skills, facts, strategies, and goals)
- **Shifting Perspectives**
- **With a Tool, Object, Process, or Skill in Mind …
  Imagining New Uses or Goals to Achieve**
- **With a Goal in Mind … Manipulating Current Tools, Objects, Processes, or Skills to Achieve the Goal** (using the SCAMPER techniques)
- **With a Goal in Mind … Imagining New and Unusual Tools, Objects, Processes, or Skills to Achieve the Goal**
- **Dreaming of New Circumstances, New Capabilities, and New Goals**

Educators can promote these creative thought patterns through the four key educational strategies discussed in earlier chapters. They include Classroom Exercises, Teacher Stories / Modeling, Assessment by Students, and Curricular Examples. Let's first look at how Classroom Exercises can be used to develop each creative mental pathway.

Classroom Exercises (to Develop Creative Mental Pathways in Students' Minds)

a) Making Connections (among ideas, tools, objects, events, processes, skills, facts, strategies, and goals)

Our earlier chapter on connecting students to the curriculum (Chapter 3) was important not only for engaging students in the curriculum, but also for developing creativity. When people make connections that others might not have seen, they can find new ways to use tools or strategies or uniquely interpret information. Thus, anything we do to help students connect what they learn to the real world or other concepts develops a skill that is essential for creativity… the skill of connecting seemingly unrelated ideas, tools, objects, events, processes, skills, facts, strategies, and goals.

Examples - Various Content Areas

Whenever possible, we should give students activities that stimulate them to find connections. A good exercise is to give kids two or more ideas, words, or objects (that seem unrelated). Then, students can figure out how these things could be used together to accomplish something or how one relates to the other. Or students can attempt to develop a story that relates seemingly unrelated objects. Another variation of this activity in a writing class is to present students with an object, idea, or character that must be worked into a creative writing piece. In science, kids can be given two scientific processes and be asked how they are related. In Social Studies, kids can look for ways that seemingly unrelated events are actually tied together.

We Should See Students Who ...	Personal Empowerment Questions (PEQs) for Students
👁 Connect new learning to prior knowledge 👁 Generate creative thoughts or ideas by connecting ideas, tools, objects, events, processes, skills, facts, strategies, and goals	❔ How are these things related? ❔ How does this relate to what I already know (my prior knowledge)? ❔ How can these things be connected to create useful new ideas, tools, objects, events, processes, skills, facts, strategies, and goals?

Students who ask and answer questions like these grow into adults who seek out and find connections that allow for the development of useful new ideas, tools, objects, events, processes, skills, facts, strategies, and goals.

b) Shifting Perspectives

With creativity, people often find new ways to look at something. In the classroom, students can exercise creativity to analyze a situation from various perspectives.

Examples - Various Content Areas

For example, they could be asked to analyze a story from various characters' perspectives. Or they can assess the value of a new technology from different people's perspectives. (How would a lawyer view this? How would a mother see this? How would a child see this? How will the government view this? How will the business world view this?) By developing the ability to shift perspectives, students become more likely to look at their resources in creative new ways.

We Should See Students Who ...	PEQs for Students
👁 Seek other points of view and perspectives (empathize)	❔ How would someone else interpret or view this _____? ❔ How does my perception of this _____ change by considering someone else's point of view?

Students who ask and answer questions like these grow into adults who can shift their frame of mind in order to see resources and situations in new ways.

c) With a Tool, Object, Process, or Skill in Mind ...   Imagining New Uses or Goals to Achieve

With creative thinking, people find new uses for tools, objects, processes, or skills that already exist.

To promote this ability, a teacher could present students with an object or a strategy from class. The teacher can then ask the class members to figure out new uses for what they are given. (The uses should be unlike the object or strategy's original intended purpose). "What else could we do with this math skill, this process for killing bacteria, this method for reducing waste, this art tool, this method of speaking, this method of writing, etc.?" "What else could a historical figure have done with a certain process, object, tool, or skill?"

We Should See Students Who ...	PEQs for Students
👁 Find new uses for tools, objects, processes, or skills	❓ What qualities does this tool, object, process, or skill possess? ❓ Does this tool, object, process, or skill remind me of something else? ❓ What else could I do with this tool, object, process, or skill?

Students who ask and answer questions like these grow into adults who create new uses for their resources.

d) With a Goal in Mind …
   Manipulating Current Tools, Objects, Processes, or Skills to Achieve the Goal (using the SCAMPER techniques)

   To be creative, people do not have to create completely new objects, tools, ideas, facts, skills, or processes. People can be creative by manipulating objects, tools, ideas, facts, skills, or processes that already exist in order to accomplish a task. To practice this creative mental pathway, students can "SCAMPER." SCAMPER is an acronym that represents a set of techniques that can be used to generate new ideas when attempting to achieve a goal or solve a problem.[19]

SCAMPER

Substitute	What could be removed and replaced in order to improve something, reach a goal, or solve a problem?
Combine	What tools, ideas, or strategies could be combined in order to improve something, reach a goal, or solve a problem?
Adapt	What part of a tool or strategy that already exists could be changed in order to improve something, reach a goal, or solve a problem?
Modify / **M**agnify / **M**inify	What could be magnified or minified in order to improve something, reach a goal, or solve a problem?
Put to Other Uses	What tool or strategy could be used in a different way in order to improve something, reach a goal, or solve a problem?
Eliminate	What could be taken away in order to improve something, reach a goal, or solve a problem?
Reverse / **R**earrange	What could be reordered in order to improve something, reach a goal, or solve a problem?

[19] (Eberle, 1996, page 6)

To exercise these SCAMPER tools, we can 1) give kids a goal or a problem and ask them to develop a strategy or tool using each of the techniques above or 2) give kids an object and ask them to improve the object using the techniques above.

We Should See Students Who ...	PEQs for Students
👁 Reflect on goals 👁 Consider the tools, objects, processes, or skills that already exist 👁 Manipulate and tweak conventional ideas into new, less conventional ideas	❓ What tools, objects, processes, or skills are already available? ❓ In order to achieve my goals, what can I … • Substitute? • Combine? • Adapt? • Modify / Magnify / Minify? • Put to other uses? • Eliminate? • Reverse / Rearrange?

Students who ask and answer questions like these grow into adults who can modify their resources in order to achieve their goals.

e) With a Goal in Mind …
Imagining New and Unusual Tools, Objects, Processes, or Skills to Achieve the Goal

Creativity sometimes comes in the form of generating completely new tools or strategies.

**Examples -
Various
Content Areas**

To promote this creative mental pathway, educators can provide students with goals to achieve and ask them to develop non-traditional ideas, tools, and strategies for achieving those goals. Learners could be asked for non-traditional ways for a character from a story to achieve a goal, for a historical figure to have better accomplished his or her goals, for people to play music, or for people to exercise.

We Should See Students Who ...	PEQs for Students
👁 Reflect on their goals 👁 Think "outside the box" 👁 Are not afraid to be unconventional	❓ What is my goal? ❓ What plan of action would seem "wacky" at first thought? ❓ What way of doing this would I create in order to sound funny? ❓ What is the last thing I would normally think of when trying to _____? ❓ If I ignore reality for a moment, how would I do this task? After I think of some outrageous ideas, can I create

	new objects, tools, skills, or processes to make it work?

Students who ask and answer questions like these grow into adults who break free from conventional thinking and generate ideas that spur unusual innovations.

f) Dreaming of New Circumstances, New Capabilities, and New Goals

As we saw above, creative thought often comes in the form of finding new ways to reach a goal or solve a problem. Another type of creativity is when people "dream up" completely new goals to reach or new problems to solve. At some point in history, someone looked at the moon and for the first time, thought that it would be neat for humans to go there. At some point, someone thought that maybe one day people would have their own computer at home. Dreams are the seeds that lead people to learn and create over time as they chase their visions.

Examples - Various Content Areas

In the classroom, we can take opportunities to get kids to imagine new goals and to dream. These dreams can vary from imagining computers without keyboards (in a computer class) to imagining the perfect day (in a creative writing class) to imagining what new technology the students would like to see (in a science class) to imagining what goals for the country and world students would like to see accomplished (in a Social Studies class).

Another good way to get students to imagine is to prompt them to think about their future … dreaming of themselves as a small business owner, a pilot, or a video game programmer. Anytime we get young minds to create goals for themselves and for the world, we are sending them down the path to achieving these new dreams (in addition to spurring creativity). Sometimes, children have a difficult time imagining themselves in the future because they are in a home environment that focuses less on the future and more on current survival. Sometimes, teachers need to stimulate dreams by putting their students into the roles of professionals during classroom activities.

We Should See Students Who ...	PEQs for Students
👁 Think of lofty ideas	❓ What would I love to see happen?
👁 Imagine unusual and exciting new processes, objects, and goals	❓ Wouldn't it be awesome if ____ happened?
👁 Imagine the world as he or she would like it to be	❓ What would I love to do or accomplish someday?

Students who ask and answer questions like these grow into adults who dream of new goals and visions of success and who set out to achieve those goals and visions.

By promoting creative mental pathways through the classroom activities above, we improve the ability of students to think creatively.

Teacher Stories / Modeling (to Develop Creative Mental Pathways in Students' Minds)

Not only should educators use classroom activities in order to develop creative mental pathways, we should also expand these pathways by modeling our own creative thinking.

Students learn a great deal about being creative when their teachers model their own creative thought processes. Educators can detail their own creative mental processes when introducing lessons that require creative thought. They can tell students about the mental steps they take when they are trying to generate creative ideas. This process can start with a statement like, "When I am trying to be creative, I ...." They can also tell stories of times in their lives when they did something creative and explain what inspired and drove the creativity.

Additionally, teachers can take advantage of unplanned opportunities to stimulate creative thinking. For example, a teacher might creatively say or do something funny, profound, or inspiring in class. This creates an unexpected moment when the teacher can explain the thoughts that made him or her generate the creative idea.

Developing Creative Mental Pathways with Teacher Stories / Modeling

We Should See Students Who ...	PEQs for Students
👁 Reflect on their teachers' creative thinking pathways and strategies 👁 Add new creative strategies (learned from their teachers) to their own mental toolboxes	❓ How does my teacher approach creative thinking? ❓ Will that creative thinking strategy work for me? ❓ How can my teacher's creative mental processes help me become more creative?

Students who ask and answer questions like these grow into adults who continuously add creative thinking strategies to their mental toolboxes. They also seek creative strategies and ideas as they look around them.

Assessment by Students (to Develop Creative Mental Pathways in Students' Minds)

Creativity can seem to come and go. People are sometimes unsure what helped them generate a creative idea. They might even think that they have stumbled upon creative ideas because they do not recognize what mental processes generated their new ideas. Students and adults need to realize that while creative thinking can *seem* to simply come from nowhere, there are actually many creative mental processes that the brain uses to generate new ideas.

Our challenge is to help students discover which thinking strategies will bring about creative ideas in their minds. To do this, we can stimulate students to assess their own creative thinking and assess the creativity of others. When kids think of a new idea, they should stop and ask themselves what thoughts led to the moment of creativity. When kids hear a creative idea from someone else, they can ask the author of the idea how he or she generated the thought. Assessing oneself and others can be very valuable in developing new thinking strategies.

An example in which a teacher can stimulate young minds to assess creativity comes from my childhood. I can remember writing an autobiography in an elementary school English class. One of the children in the class made a very creative autobiography title that used a pun related to his name. Our teacher showed the class how wonderfully creative he had been. For me, this was a good experience. First, it made me want to be creative, because I saw how it could make a product better (plus I wanted some praise like the teacher gave the other boy). In addition, the experience was valuable because it had not previously occurred to me that creativity was even possible in my autobiography title. At that point, I began to look for examples of creativity, look for opportunities to use creativity, and seek to understand what thought processes allowed me and others to be creative. Overall, the experience got me thinking about what makes something creative and how I could be creative. In addition to this particular classroom moment, the teacher in my English class took many opportunities to point out student creativity. In my experience, I've noticed that older students react similarly when they are exposed to examples of creativity. The examples make them more likely to attempt to be creative, allow them to see places where creativity might be possible, and get them thinking about how to be creative.

Assessing the ways in which other people develop creative thoughts will take a person only so far. One must look inward to unlock the workings of his or her own brain. Young people must stop when they generate a great idea and assess what sequence of thoughts and frames of mind led to their creative thoughts. This process of self-discovery will allow them to replicate creative thought processes on later tasks. When performing classroom activities that strengthen creative mental pathways, teachers can ask students to make a record of the thoughts the students had while generating new ideas.

Developing Creative Mental Pathways with Student Assessment

We Should See Students Who ...	PEQs for Students
👁 Reflect on the ways in which other people are creative 👁 Self-assess in order to unlock and replicate creative processes	❓ Where are opportunities to be creative? ❓ How did he or she come up with that idea? ❓ How did I think of that? ❓ How can I use similar thought processes in the future to be creative? ❓ What mood, thoughts, and strategies lead me to creativity?

Students who ask and answer questions like these grow into adults who assess, recognize, and utilize creative mental processes.

Curricular Examples (to Develop Creative Mental Pathways in Students' Minds)

Examples of creativity appear numerous times in the curricula of all subjects. Students encounter many things that were originally generated by a creative mind, such as a story, a piece of music, a piece of art, a recipe, a design, a sport, or a tool. Some people might not expect it, but there are also examples in math, science, and Social Studies. In these subjects, there were creative scientists and mathematicians who first imagined new theorems, processes, technologies, or theories. There were historians and archaeologists who pieced together clues to imagine how historical events probably occurred. When you get down to it, every class includes concepts that were first generated through creativity.

A good way to develop creative mental pathways within students is to get them "into creative minds." This means that we discuss the ways in which various creative thoughts were first generated by others. We can talk about what inspired an author to develop a story, what someone intended by creating certain rules for a sport, how someone pieced together historical clues, or what information and mental processes led to a new theory. From art to science, there are many opportunities to learn about creative thought processes.

When looking at examples of creativity that come from the curriculum, we should also make use of contemporary examples, including new theories, new pieces of art, new technologies, new designs for processes, and many more.

Developing Creative Mental Pathways with Curricular Examples

We Should See Students Who ...	PEQs for Students
👁 Reflect on the ways in which people from the curriculum are creative	❓ How did that person create that?
👁 Add to their creative toolbox as they reflect upon the creativity of others	❓ What was going on in their mind when they generated that thought?
👁 Recognize that creativity is everywhere, not just in the arts	❓ What information or other stimulus inspired them to create?
	❓ What were they trying to accomplish when they generated a creative idea?

Students who ask and answer questions like these learn new ideas for creativity from the world around them.

Empowering Students to Determine and Utilize Their Best Creative Ideas
(Training Wise Use of Creative Thoughts)

Not only do assessment skills help us when we analyze a situation or problem to understand it, they also help us when we generate creative ideas for taking actions or solving problems. During and after the process of idea and solution creation, students need to use their assessment skills to determine which creative ideas will work most effectively. *We want students to generate many and varied ideas about how to accomplish tasks or solve problems. This process will mean little if people cannot identify the best ideas to put into action.* Young minds need to get in the habit of asking themselves questions that will allow them to determine how effectively an idea might work when put into practice. In addition to assessing creative ideas to determine which should be used, assessment is important after ideas or solutions are put into action. People in the real world and our youth need to be able to determine how well their plans worked and if they need to be refined or replaced. (The same goes for teachers, too.)

There are some questions below that students can be stimulated to ask when they are generating creative ideas.

Determining and Utilizing the Best Creative Thoughts

We Should See Students Who ...	PEQs for Students
	Questions to use for assessing new ideas:
👁 Generate a variety of ideas from which they can choose	❓ Which idea or solution is most likely to achieve my goals?
👁 Reflect upon creative ideas to determine	

which ideas will be the most effective 👁 Reflect upon creative ideas that have been implemented in order to assess effectiveness 👁 Reflect upon goals and available tools	❓ Which criteria need to be considered in picking out my best ideas? ❓ What is likely to go right or wrong if I use any of my ideas? ***Questions to use after implementing new ideas:*** ❓ What did I hope my idea or solution would accomplish? ❓ Did I achieve my goals? ❓ What worked well? ❓ What didn't work well? ❓ What should I continue to do? ❓ What can I change?

Students who ask and answer questions like these grow into adults who can develop the best creative ideas, implement those ideas effectively, and adjust their plans as needed.

3 Providing Opportunities for Creativity in the Classroom (Providing Creative Outlets)

While the previous sections discussed training for creative thinking and idea assessment, this section will focus on providing classroom opportunities to be creative … giving students creative outlets.

Provide Opportunities for Creativity, such as …

- **Engaging in Activities that Stimulate Independent Thinking and Decision Making**
- **Engaging in Open-Ended Opportunities to Design**
- **Displaying Understanding and Skills Creatively through Assessments**
- **Brainstorming the Potential Uses for Curricular Knowledge and Skills**
- **Writing Fictional Stories Related to Curricular Knowledge and Skills**
- **Designing Challenges and Problems to Solve**
- **Creating Memory Strategies**
- **Imagining the Best and Worst Way to Do a Task**

a) Engaging In Activities that Stimulate Independent Thinking and Decision-Making

Examples - Various Content Areas

Rather than regurgitating curricular information, students can develop opinions based on facts and then defend their opinions in a debate or essay. The same curriculum is assessed, but students get to generate their own opinions. Students can develop opinions on the actions of historical figures,

13 - Creativity in Action

the actions of characters in a story, or the future implications of new scientific technologies.

b) Engaging in Open-Ended Opportunities to Design

Examples - Various Content Areas

Rather than asking students to follow "cookbook" directions for an experiment in science, allow them to create their own experiment. (Guidelines can help direct kids toward meaningful experiments.) Speaking of cooking … why not let kids design a recipe in a home economics class? Ask students to create their own piece of music in a music class. In a physical education setting, give students the task of creating a game with certain guidelines. Creative writing opportunities in English classes are perfect examples of this type of lesson. In all classes, open-ended opportunities to create provide opportunities for students to use creative technological presentation tools.

c) Displaying Understanding and Skills Creatively through Assessments

Examples - Various Content Areas

Allow students to demonstrate their understanding of knowledge and processes in creative, alternative ways. For instance, kids can write a creative story about the digestive system in which the function of each organ is demonstrated through characters in the story line. A similar creative activity can be done to demonstrate understanding of many curricular concepts. Class members can also demonstrate knowledge through role playing. A teacher can have students design a commercial to advertise a process, tool, or event. Students can be asked to generate similes and metaphors for curricular concepts. Learners can display understanding with role playing activities.

Notice that all of these examples allow teachers to assess curricular knowledge in a fun way. Creative assessments can also allow students to use engaging technological tools for displaying understanding. (So that students focus their creativity toward the goals of the curriculum, teachers should create rubrics outlining the intended outcomes of the activity. Otherwise, kids might get a little off-track.)

d) Brainstorming the Potential Uses for Curricular Knowledge and Skills

Examples - Various Content Areas

After students learn a skill, a tool, or information to be used for a particular purpose, educators can ask them to think of uses for these things … the sky's the limit. Elementary students can imagine ways to use a lever or pulley when learning about science. Middle school math students can imagine a way to use a math skill at home. Based on the knowledge that high school psychology students learn, they can imagine effective ways to interact with other people. In all subject areas at all ages, teachers can ask students to brainstorm the ways that new knowledge and skills can be used in the real world. This process serves to reinforce and deepen the value of the curricular content that the class is learning … and gets creative juices flowing.

e) Writing Fictional Stories Related to Curricular Knowledge and Skills

Examples - Various Content Areas

After reading a story, students can write an alternative ending. In Social Studies, the same can be done with a historical event. In music, young musicians can write a story that matches a song. In a physical education class, kids can write a story about someone engaging in a game. The process of creative thinking and design gives the members of a class more ownership of the material. In addition to writing, students can also use technologies that allow creative expression of ideas, such as videos or web pages.

f) Designing Challenges and Problems to Solve

Examples - Various Content Areas

After learning new knowledge or skills, students can generate their own questions, such as a story problem in math, for assessing the new knowledge or skills. Of course, it is better if kids create a real-world problem, so that the value of the curriculum is promoted. In addition to promoting creativity, I have found that this activity is a great study tool for children in my classes. (I ask students to imagine and write assessment questions related to a current classroom topic.)

g) Creating Memory Strategies

Examples - Various Content Areas

Students can generate strategies for remembering new knowledge and skills. They can make up word associations, acronyms, mental pictures, or other memory strategies. Not only does this activity flex the students' creative juices, it helps with retention of information. (Some specific examples are described in Chapter 21 – Promoting Knowledge and Skill Retention.)

h) Imagining the Best and Worst Way to Do a Task

Examples - Various Content Areas

A fun way to spur creativity is to ask students to imagine the best and worst applications of a tool or process. They can think of the most and least logical opinion that could be derived from some facts, the best and worst way to go about solving a problem, or the best and worst simile or metaphor for a word or concept. Activities like these generally stimulate humor. Imagining the worst application sounds counterproductive. However, while imagining the worst application of a tool or knowledge, a child's brain is actually reflecting upon whether various possible applications are good.

When using the many classroom opportunities that allow for creativity, rubrics or guidelines can help direct the students' creative thoughts toward ideas that are relevant to the curriculum. (Sometimes youngsters can get a little off-task with creativity. With the right activity parameters, this can be avoided.)

13 - Creativity in Action

Creativity in Action: Wrap-up

When a real-world worker completes a task or produces a product, creativity can make the difference between a mediocre and a wonderful product. As with the last two chapters on higher order thinking skills, we must note that it will not be good enough to simply give our youngsters tasks that require creativity. We must also help these young minds develop new creative thinking pathways.

Don't Neglect the Fundamentals in the Name of Creativity

How can an architect generate a creative building design without understanding the principles of sound structures, materials, and building logistics? How can a researcher design a new medicine if he or she does not understand the principles of the human body and biology? How can an entrepreneur put a creative idea for a business into action without an understanding of finance, business laws, or sales? How can a teacher generate innovative history lessons if he or she does not know the history? In *The World is Flat*, Friedman quotes Bill Gates (co-founder of Microsoft): "I have never met a guy who doesn't know how to multiply who created software (…) You need to understand things in order to invent beyond them."[20] It is important that we do not neglect fundamental skills and knowledge when promoting creativity. We should weave them together. *In fact, lessons that promote creativity tend to make the curriculum more engaging and valuable.*

All Ideas are Welcome in a Creative Classroom

Certain environmental conditions make creative thinking possible. Students need to feel comfortable voicing new ideas. I have seen instances where one student offered an incomplete idea (that might not work perfectly or be perfectly logical) that triggered another student to think of a way to complete or improve the idea. By piggybacking on one another, their ideas grew and evolved into something workable. This exchanging process is unlikely to occur if students have a fear of tossing out possibilities … they need to feel that "anything goes."

Similarly, when students generate new ideas, it is better if teachers don't immediately dismiss incorrect ones. Instead, teachers can think of ways to prompt and direct students toward more workable ideas. In this way, members of a class are more likely to offer their thoughts. The teacher can also encourage students to listen to one another and build on each other's contributions. This classroom climate is also more likely to occur if educators ask open-ended questions as springboards to discussion, rather than always asking questions with exact right and wrong answers.

Another good environmental aspect for creativity is giving students time to think and reflect, rather than rushing through activities.

---

[20] (Friedman, 2005, page 351)

Teaching Style Affects Student Creativity

In this chapter, we looked in-depth at how to promote creativity in young minds. We must recognize that creative thoughts are unlikely to be stimulated in a teacher-centered learning environment where information is spoon-fed and students passively absorb information like a sponge. Instead, a student-centered environment that challenges our children to generate tools, ideas, solutions, or opinions is the ideal.

Side Note

Creativity for All

Creativity is not limited to "creative subjects," such as the arts. We must also promote imaginative thought processes in non-artistic content areas. Students should create their own real-world story problems in math, design an original experiment or useful application for a concept in science, create a piece of music in band or choir, design a game in gym class, write stories in English, write creative alternative endings for events in history, etc. ALL classes can promote creativity.

Thinking About It

- **What is creativity?**
- **How can activities that promote creativity be meshed within your curriculum?**
- **What are the most difficult challenges that you see in developing students' creativity?**
- **In what ways do you and can you help your kids develop creativity?**

13 - Creativity in Action

How Does This Chapter Support the Goals of This Book?

Let's take a moment to think about the ways in which the ideas of this chapter help us address the three main goals of this book by looking at the "Building Blocks of a 21st Century Education" on page 13 and the "Daily Thoughts for Educators" on page 18. We now have tools and strategies for providing a 21st Century Challenge by developing creative skills as we teach our curricula.

Make Note of Your Great Ideas!

If you haven't already, note your ideas for implementing the strategies in this chapter in your Teacher Empowerment Menu (for 21st Century Educators). In the future, you can easily reference usable ideas for your class.

In addition, consider the ways in which you can stimulate students to develop skills in innovation and creativity by using the Personal Empowerment Menu (for 21st Century Students), which contains the relevant PEQs and assessment rubric for this chapter.

Higher Order Thinking Skills Unit
Final Thoughts on Themes, Literacy, and Activities that Support Higher Order Thinking

Themes

In the last three chapters, some themes emerged as we moved from analyzing to taking actions to developing creativity.

a) Break Skills into Pieces

We can do specific things to improve our students' abilities in all three areas of higher level thinking. By systematically breaking these three topics into smaller pieces, we are more likely to provide our children with all of the tools that they need without underemphasizing some or overemphasizing others. (The Teacher Empowerment Menu that accompanies this book can help teachers quickly implement and meet all these higher order thinking goals.)

b) Kids Need to Ask Questions

Another theme that emerged is the idea that young minds must assess and ask questions about the world around them. The PEQs provided throughout the unit help us get our students thinking. The Personal Empowerment Menu (for 21st Century Students) can help you stimulate students to ask these questions and become empowered thinkers.

c) Skills Build upon Each Other

An interesting thing to note about the three topics of this unit is that they rely upon one another. Critical thinking helps creativity and creativity helps critical thinking. Critical thinking can happen in a music class and creativity can happen in a math class. ***All the higher level thinking skills can be supported in every content area at every age level.***

Literacy

I am not a secondary language arts teacher, nor am I an elementary teacher who teaches students to read and write. However, I do recognize that the role of every teacher in every subject area and grade level is to promote reading and writing skills. For our youth to be truly literate, they need to develop their abilities in all forms of reading comprehension and writing, from science and math to art. Our youth need to be able to apply their literacy skills in all realms of life. This is what the real world demands.

So, why do I bring up literacy at this point? Because the promotion of quality reading and writing skills relies on the promotion of the higher order thinking skills developed in the last few chapters. For instance, when we want to improve reading comprehension for almost any age group in any subject, we promote the ideas from our chapter on critical thinking (Ch. 11): making observations and inferences, comparing and contrasting, categorizing and grouping, understanding cause and effect, understanding sequence and timing, seeing the big picture, and recognizing patterns. If we want to improve writing skills, we use many of the strategies found in the chapter on extending critical thinking into action (Ch. 12): understanding the task and goals of writing, creating roadmaps, and recognizing which strategies work best and when to use them. Promoting creativity (Ch. 13) also has a great effect on the development of writing skills. In total, promoting reading and writing in all subject areas requires the higher order thinking skills of this unit.

Higher Order Thinking
Themes, Literacy, and Activities

Examples - Using Higher Order Thinking Skills to Promote Literacy

I recently wanted to improve my students' science reading comprehension. I noticed that if kids are given a few reading questions, they simply skim for answers without slowing down to read for comprehension. So, I created a guide for reading a section of their textbook, which asked students to use the analytical skills from our previous chapter in their reading. The guide asked them to:

- summarize new ideas
- compare and contrast terms and ideas
- predict what will come next
- assess the meaning of figures and diagrams
- relate figures and diagrams to the reading
- draw picture representations of what they were reading
- assess how small details affect the big picture of the concept
- reflect upon what was difficult to understand
- use context clues to decipher meaning
- connect new ideas to prior knowledge

By thinking about their reading in this way, the children in my class had a much easier time developing meaning and comprehension. They also gained skills that they can apply in the future by learning to ask themselves similar critical thinking questions while reading. Furthermore, the application of analytical skills to reading reinforced and promoted general critical thinking skills in all situations. Regardless of the grade level or subject area, getting young minds to use meta-cognition (or thinking about thought processes) is critical in developing sound literacy.

We all should work to improve our learners' reading and writing skills. Chapters 11-13 provide some tools for teachers in any subject area, especially those who are not comfortable promoting reading and writing skills.

> ## Activities that Support Higher Order Thinking Skills:
> ## Future Problem Solving

There are activities that support and develop higher order thinking skills in students. One such activity with which I have been involved is Future Problem Solving (FPS). I have always loved the critical thinking, problem solving, and creativity benefits that this competitive program provides to students. As I was writing the last three chapters, I gained an even better appreciation of FPS. It supports so many facets of higher level thinking that I am compelled to talk about it, hoping that others might try it. The Future Problem Solving Program was created by Dr. E. Paul Torrance and has participants from most American states and also from some other countries.[21]

> ### a) What do Students do in FPS Competitions?

In FPS, students work in teams of four. Before competing, each team learns about issues that might be important in the future, such as genetic engineering, nutrition, health care access, depletion of oceanic species, media impact, body enhancement, and artificial intelligence.

At competition time, a team receives a one-page, fictional story based on the topic they researched. This story is set in the future and is called the "future scene." The task for the students is to do the following steps in a two-hour period without any adult help.

1. Identify sixteen challenges that the people in the future scene face.
2. Identify one underlying problem or important challenge that the team would like to solve.
3. Create sixteen solutions for the underlying problem that the team chose to address.
4. Create five criteria that can be used to determine which solution is best.
5. Rank the solutions using the criteria and determine the best solution.
6. Develop an action plan for implementing the best solution.

The team writes ideas for the six steps above into a competition packet.

> ### b) Assessment in FPS Competitions

Evaluators read each team's competition packet. The team gets points for identifying reasonable problems, picking an important problem to solve, and creating solutions that are effective in solving that problem. Extra points are awarded for creating a diverse range of ideas. Also, extra points are given for originality.

---

[21] (Future Problem Solving Program International, Inc. - Home)

Higher Order Thinking
Themes, Literacy, and Activities

c) How are FPS Competitions Organized?

There are four different competitions each year, based on four different topics. The first three competitions are done at school and mailed into the state FPS organization for assessment and feedback. The fourth is the state championship.

Teams compete with students from around their state in three age divisions (fourth-sixth, seventh-ninth, and tenth-twelfth grades). A school can enter as many teams in an FPS competition as it wishes.

For teams that have great success at their state championships, there is an international competition each year.

d) Real-Life Skills are Promoted

In what ways does FPS promote real-world skills?

1. Students learn about topics that are likely to affect the world in the future.
2. Students develop analyzing and assessing skills as they look for challenges in the "future scene."
3. The teams assess the whole future scene and its challenges to determine what major problem should be solved.
4. Creative thinking is reinforced in generating solution ideas.
5. Students assess their solutions to determine the best plan of action.
6. A realistic plan of action must be outlined and detailed.
7. Students develop skills in working as a team. They learn to motivate each other, assess and integrate each other's ideas, work tactfully, etc.
8. Students must effectively explain their ideas to their teammates.
9. Varied and original thinking is rewarded.
10. Students quickly learn that effectively conveying their ideas in writing can convince an evaluator to give them points. This stimulates them to be more reflective as they write. (They are also stimulated to assess and help their teammates improve their writing.)
11. The spice of competition and the reward of working with real-world topics motivate students to learn and become passionate about higher level thinking activities.
12. The assessment and feedback that the state FPS organization returns stimulates students to reflect upon their strategies and how to improve.

Almost every aspect of higher order thinking is addressed in FPS … and that's just the beginning of the benefits.

A great part of the FPS process is that it provides students with a logical and sequential set of steps for addressing an issue. Young minds learn to determine the heart of a problem and then to effectively attack the problem. Sometimes, people can be observed in real world settings attempting to solve problems in a haphazard manner. In FPS, students develop an understanding of an organized way to deal with challenges.

e) Who can Coach Students in FPS?

Anyone can coach FPS. I was first exposed to the program in my fifth-grade English class. I later took part in an after-school club in middle school. Later, I coached FPS students in an extracurricular high school club. Some English and Social Studies teachers include FPS in their classes. Some writing teachers use FPS within the writing curriculum, because it supports many writing skills. Some educators use FPS as a gifted and talented activity. I have also seen the FPS process used as a special education activity. In all, this program can be used with a variety of age levels and in a variety of ways within a school.

f) Using the FPS Process in the Classroom

The FPS process can be used in a regular classroom without any connection to the actual FPS program. Students can use the same problem-solving steps to address a curricular issue. I have given students in a science class an issue related to the curriculum and asked them to do a mini version of FPS as follows:

1. Identify three to four challenges dealing with the issue.
2. Pick a challenge to solve.
3. Create three to four solutions.
4. Generate criteria and pick the best solution.
5. Create a detailed action plan.

The same mini process can be used in many classes for different reasons, such as addressing a social issue, promoting writing skills, or solving a problem.

Higher Order Thinking
Themes, Literacy, and Activities

Goal #2

21st Century Challenge – Part 3

Develop Social and Personal Skills, Attitudes, and Habits Unit (Ch. 14 and 15)

We will now continue our promotion of a 21st Century Challenge by addressing the development of social and personal skills, attitudes, and habits. These are skills, attitudes, and habits that might get lost in the modern-day demands of education. They are, however, crucial to our youths' success in the 21st century. We can challenge our students to develop these skills within the teaching of our curricula.

While Learning the Curriculum, Develop:				
Ability to Connect the Curriculum to the Real World Ch. 3	*Higher Order Thinking Skills* (includes Critical Thinking, Problem Solving, and Creativity) Ch. 11-13	*Social and Personal Skills, Attitudes, and Habits* Ch. 14-15	*Technological and Media Literacy* Ch. 16	*Ability to Learn* (includes Inquiry and Student-Centered Learning) Ch. 17

21st Century Challenge

- **Understanding and Interacting with Others:** *Ch. 14*
- **Personal Skills, Attitudes, and Habits:** *Ch.15*

14 | Understanding and Interacting with Others

Whether our students work in a global or local career, they will need to interact well with other people. With offshoring, outsourcing, and automation, many of the jobs that remain for our future adults require abilities in communication, collaboration, understanding other people, and explaining. Whether you work for a global corporation and deal with people from all over the world or you work in a local business or practice, the ability to interact with others is crucial, especially as lower-skilled jobs fade away.

Let's set out to prepare young minds to thrive in the future job market. There are some major categories of interactive skills that they will need.

Understanding and Interacting with Others

1. **Understanding What Makes People Tick**
   (Recognizing the Wants, Needs, and Motivations of Others)
2. **Communication / Social Skills**
   (Speaking, Listening, Interpreting, Tact, Positive Interactions, Relationships, Self-Promotion / Interviewing, etc.)
3. **Explaining and Presenting Ideas**
4. **Collaborating Through Teamwork**
5. **Competing**
6. **Understanding Language and Culture**

Let's look at each of these categories to determine the ways in which we can promote these skills within our schools. As always, our goal should be to weave the development of these skills into the learning of the required curriculum.

1 Understanding What Makes People Tick

Understanding what makes people "tick" can facilitate many tasks in the workplace and in life. With this knowledge, we can help a customer better understand a product, meet the needs of the client, work with teammates on the job, motivate others, lead a group, interpret others' ideas, empathize, and predict what people will want from us. We can generally add a personal touch (to our social interactions) that appeals to customers, clients, patients, coworkers, friends, and family members. (Besides all the benefits we can gain in interacting with other people, understanding what makes people "tick" can also help someone develop a product or service that customers will demand.) So, what is necessary for "understanding what makes people tick"?

Critical Aspects of "Understanding What Makes People Tick"

- Recognizing the Wants, Needs, and Motivations of Others

When interacting with others in the real world, our students will need to understand and make use of these critical aspects: *recognizing the wants, needs, and motivations of others*. How can we develop this ability in school? As with earlier topics in this book, we can use the four key educational strategies: Classroom Exercises, Teacher Stories / Modeling, Assessment by Students, and Curricular Examples. Let's look at some examples to see how these strategies can work for this topic and others in this chapter.

Classroom Exercises (Understanding What Makes People Tick)

There are various classroom activities for promoting an understanding of other peoples' points of view and an understanding of what motivates them. The following is just one idea out of many possibilities.

Periodically, I have students debate the social or political aspects of a scientific topic. Before the debate, I place two stacks of paper in the front of the room. One stack is for people who support a certain position and the other stack is for people who do not support that position. Each student takes one of these papers and finds questions written on it. These questions ask the students to support and defend their opinion. The twist in the activity comes after the students have finished their writing. At this point, they take the opposing viewpoint's paper. They must imagine why people would hold the opposing opinion and how they would defend it. They fill out the paper for the opposing opinion as they attempt to empathize with it. After the students have supported their own opinion and empathized with the other, they engage in a classroom debate. I have found that class members are much more understanding and tactful when debating their ideas after performing this activity, because they have a better understanding of other students' points of view. The activity is not intended to change the students' minds, but to stimulate them to seek rational understanding of how other people think. This is just one example of a classroom exercise to meet the goal of empathy.

Teacher Stories / Modeling (Understanding What Makes People Tick)

When teachers talk with students in everyday interactions (developing connections), there are sometimes opportunities to share a quick story or experience with students. These times allow children to hear examples that might teach them something about how others think and how others are motivated. Educators can highlight their own motivations and tell stories that give insight into themselves. Teachers can share real-life examples where their perceptions of other people were helpful. Conversely, they can share examples of how a lack of understanding or empathy caused a problem.

Assessment by Students (Understanding What Makes People Tick)

The skills in analysis and critical thinking that we covered in an earlier chapter allow students to make complex assessments about situations, systems, or problems. These assessment skills can be exercised in developing an understanding of what makes other people tick. We need to get learners to make observations of human interactions and to analyze the ways in which people's needs and wants affect those people's behaviors. To get kids to make assessments in order to develop their interactive skills (such as understanding what makes people tick), we can promote the Personal Empowerment Questions listed throughout this chapter. (The Personal Empowerment Menu for 21st Century Students is a very valuable tool for promoting interactive skills, because it allows students to easily access the PEQs and assessment rubric for this chapter.)

We can also stimulate kids to assess the ways in which their *own* needs and wants are related to their own actions. Because people have many similarities (despite their differences), self-assessment can sometimes give insight into other people.

Curricular Examples (Understanding What Makes People Tick)

In just about every subject, we can get young minds to think about how people's needs, wants, and motivations affect people's actions and decisions. A nice by-product of this approach is that it makes learning more interesting and engaging.

Examples - Various Content Areas

When learning about a historical event, we can ask our students to think about what needs, wants, and motivations led people to take certain actions. In science, we can ask what needs and desires drove the development of new technologies and theories. When reading literature, we can analyze what motivated characters to act in particular ways. In math, we can assess how people can use or misuse numbers or statistics to motivate other people or affect their opinions.

Promoting Student Understanding of What Makes People Tick

We Should See Students Who ...	Personal Empowerment Questions (PEQs) for Students
👁 Seek an understanding of other people's wants, needs, and motivations	❓ What does that person need or want?
	❓ What need or want led that person to do ____?
👁 Assess the values of others	
👁 Self-assess to compare and contrast with others	❓ Why is that important to them?
	❓ What makes them happy / unhappy?
👁 Use their understanding of others in	❓ What do I need or want?

order to improve communication, collaboration, motivation, and leadership 👁 Add a personal touch (to social interactions) that appeals to others	❓ Why do I do certain things or see things in a certain way? ❓ Why is that important to me? ❓ What makes me happy / unhappy? ❓ Why might that person have a differing view? ❓ Where is our common ground? ❓ How can I use my understanding of others to improve communication, collaboration, motivation, and leadership? ❓ How can I add a personal touch to my interactions with others in order to appeal to their wants, needs, and motivations? **Personal Empowerment Statements (PESs) for Students** • I am developing a better understanding of my own and other peoples' wants, needs, motivations, and values. • By better understanding what makes people tick, I have better interactions with others.

Students who ask questions and make statements like these grow into adults who can effectively understand, interact, compromise, and persuade.

In this section, I gave an in-depth explanation for how to use the four key educational strategies to stimulate an "understanding of what makes people tick." For the other abilities below, I will assume that the reader understands how to use these techniques.

2   Communication / Social Skills

The abilities to communicate effectively and to display social skills are critical for effective interactions with people in the work world (and in personal life).

Critical Aspects of Communication / Social Skills

- Speaking Skills
- Assessing How Others Perceive and Interpret You
- Listening Skills
- Interpreting Nonverbal Communication
- Building Positive Interactions and Relationships - *Developing positive impressions; resolving and thwarting conflict; exhibiting appropriate behavior for a setting; and showing general tact, honesty, integrity, respect, courtesy, consistency, loyalty, follow-through, and dedication*
- Self-Promotion / Interviewing

a) Speaking Skills

Children (and adults) should be aware of volume, eye contact, "fillers," body language, posture, confidence, intonation, articulation, and using people's names. In order to be effective and engaging, they need to consider the audience to whom they are speaking (their expectations, needs, and desires), the use of key words that evoke intended audience emotions, what to say in order to meet the goals of their speech, and what is appropriate for the situation.

We Should See Students Who ...	PEQs for Students
👁 Consider their goals when communicating	❓ What is my goal in speaking?
👁 Consider the expectations, needs, and desires of their audience and speak appropriately	❓ What are the expectations of my audience?
👁 Use words that evoke desired emotions	❓ What do I need to say to make my point?
👁 Correctly use volume, eye contact, body language, posture, confidence, intonation, articulation, and names	❓ How can I engage and connect with my audience?
👁 Avoid using "fillers," such as "like," "uh," and "um"	❓ Am I audible and articulate?
👁 Engage the audience	❓ What is my body language saying?
	PES for Students
	• With thoughtful words and an appropriate demeanor, I can engage my audience.

Students who ask questions and make statements like these grow into adults who can effectively communicate and articulate their ideas.

b) Assessing How Others Perceive and Interpret You

People need to assess how well they are being interpreted, followed, and understood. They also need to consider how their actions affect others. This self-assessment allows people to adjust as they speak in order to communicate more effectively.

We Should See Students Who ...	PEQs for Students
👁 Assess their audience through the audience's body language, facial expressions, reactions, and questions 👁 Pause to find out if the audience has questions	❓ Based on the reactions of my audience, am I being understood? ❓ Am I being interpreted in the manner in which I intend? ❓ What misconceptions might my audience have? ❓ How do my actions and speech make others feel? ❓ Do you (audience member) have any questions or is there something that I can clarify? **PES for Students** • By carefully assessing my audience, I can determine how well I am understood and what steps to take to improve the audience's experience.

Students who ask questions and make statements like these grow into adults who can assess how well they are being understood and adjust their communication accordingly.

c) Listening Skills

When listening, people should assess what the speaker is trying to say, assess the speaker's goals, think about what questions they might have for the speaker, and determine what they need the speaker to clarify. Listeners should show that they are paying attention and are interested by asking questions, making eye contact, responding thoughtfully to questions, and exhibiting interested body language and posture.

We Should See Students Who ...	PEQs for Students
👁 Engage with a speaker through eye contact, body language, posture, questions, and responses 👁 Assess the speaker's ideas 👁 Tactfully ask questions for clarification	❓ Do I look engaged and interested? ❓ Are my actions putting the speaker at ease? ❓ Am I using proper eye contact, body language, posture, questions, and responses? ❓ What idea is this person trying to express? ❓ What do I need clarified? **PES for Students** • I strive to understand and show interest in the things other people say.

Students who ask questions and make statements like these grow into adults who effectively listen and who put a speaker at ease.

d) Interpreting Nonverbal Communication

     Students should learn to recognize what other people are trying to convey with certain types of body language and actions. This requires people to become skilled at assessing and understanding personalities, humor, sarcasm, and societal differences.

We Should See Students Who ...	PEQs for Students
👁 Make careful observations and assessments of body posture, movements, and patterns	❓ What does that person's body language suggest about their feelings or intentions?
	❓ What patterns of behavior do I observe from that person?
	❓ Is that the normal body language of this person?
	❓ What cues allow me to know when a person is being sarcastic or is using humor?
	PES for Students
	• By assessing nonverbal cues, I can develop a deeper understanding of others when communicating.

Students who ask questions and make statements like these grow into adults who can interpret subtle forms of body communication to understand other people's intentions, reactions, and feelings.

e) Building Positive Interactions and Relationships - *Developing positive impressions; resolving and thwarting conflict; exhibiting appropriate behavior for a setting; and showing general tact, honesty, integrity, respect, courtesy, consistency, loyalty, follow-through, and dedication*

     In order to develop relationships, students should work to make good impressions, behave tactfully, show respect to others, show interest in others, be "real" (and not fake), be courteous to others, etc. Kids can build trust by following through, being honest, being consistent, being loyal, and showing dedication to others.

     Our youth need to get in the habit of thinking about how to positively resolve conflicts and react to less than desirable communication from others; they should also get in the habit of predicting challenges to positive communication, recognizing possibilities for misinterpretation, and finding ways to avoid these things.

We Should See Students Who ...	PEQs for Students
👁 Develop relationships	❓ What impression of myself am I creating?
👁 Make positive impressions	❓ What is appropriate behavior for this situation?
👁 Recognize social norms	❓ Am I exhibiting tact, integrity, respect, courtesy, humility, and a real sense of who I am?
👁 Show integrity, tact, honesty, respect, courtesy, consistency, loyalty, follow-through, humility, and dedication	❓ Am I being consistent, honest, loyal, and dedicated?
👁 Behave in a manner that is worthy of respect from others	❓ Am I following through with my commitments and promises?
👁 React well in difficult circumstances	❓ What can I say or do to make this interaction run smoothly?
👁 Predict communication challenges and potential misconceptions	❓ How should I behave when things don't go well?
👁 Contribute to a positive society	❓ What communication challenges might I encounter, and how can I proactively diminish potential conflict?
	❓ How can I positively overcome any differences in opinion?
	❓ How should people generally treat each other in a positive society, and am I treating others this way?
	PES for Students
	• With thoughtful and positive behaviors, I build meaningful interactions and relationships.

Students who ask questions and make statements like these grow into adults who have very positive and fruitful interactions and relationships with others.

f) Self-Promotion / Interviewing

By developing all of the communication and social skills in this section, students develop the ability to promote themselves as a worker. They are better able to interview with potential employers. They are also more socially prepared to network and promote their services in the 21ˢᵗ century economy.

We Should See Students Who ...	PEQs for Students
👁 Can apply quality communication skills and social skills to promote themselves in an interview with potential employers	❓ In an interview, how should I dress, carry myself, and communicate in order to make a great impression?
👁 Can network and promote	❓ How can I enhance my networking skills by building positive relationships?
	❓ How do my social behaviors and

themselves in the 21st century economy	communication skills affect my ability to promote myself in the workplace? ❷ What are the social expectations in an interview or workplace social interaction? **PES for Students** • I show my strengths and qualities and appropriately present myself in order to make a great impression and positively promote myself.

Students who ask questions and make statements like these grow into adults who can use effective social and communication skills to acquire employment and to promote themselves.

For building overall communication skills, student assessment is very important. Students can assess one another during public speaking activities or they might videotape themselves performing and then complete self-assessments using a rubric. (Remember that the PEQs and assessment rubrics for this book are contained in the Personal Empowerment Menu for 21st Century Students.) Students can use a similar rubric during class discussions to assess speaking, listening, body language, and broader themes for interaction. Outside of class, the habit of assessment can make youngsters more socially aware and make them more likely to learn from their observations.

3 Explaining and Presenting Ideas

Professionals in global and local careers all need to have effective explaining skills. Plumbers describe plumbing needs to customers. Doctors clarify diagnoses or procedures to patients and coworkers; business people give details about how products or services work and why customers need those products and services. My grandfather was an engineer and often told me that he was constantly explaining tasks, processes, and tools to coworkers and customers during his career. With offshoring, outsourcing, and automation, many available careers will require skills in explaining. Everyone is now a teacher.

Technically, explaining skills are part of communication skills (which were addressed in the previous section). We will look more in depth at explaining skills here, because there are a number of fine details involved in explaining that go beyond basic communication skills. Let's look at the critical aspects of explaining.

Critical Aspects of Explaining and Presenting Ideas

- Determining the Goals of an Explanation
- Creating an Understandable Sequence and Flow of Information
- Predicting Challenges and Potential Misconceptions
- Assessing Prior Knowledge of the Audience
- Capturing Attention, Engaging, and Inspiring Confidence
- Explaining with Clarity, Focus, and Conciseness
- Using Aids for Understanding
- Assessing Understanding
- Shifting Strategies
- Promoting Information Retention and Reinforcement in the Audience Members

Through the following ideas, we can help our students become proficient in the finer skills of explaining.

a) Determining the Goals of an Explanation (before beginning)

Developing a consciousness of one's goals can make it easier to develop a strategy and a path for an explanation.

We Should See Students Who ...	PEQs for Students
👁 Consider their goals in order to prepare the key ideas of an explanation	❓ What do I want my listener(s) to get out of this explanation?
	❓ Which key ideas will I need to convey in my explanation?
	PES for Students
	• I know what I want others to understand.

Students who ask questions and make statements like these grow into adults who speak concisely and directly in creating an understanding of their goals among audience members.

b) Creating an Understandable Sequence and Flow (before beginning)

The order in which ideas are presented and the transitions between those ideas can greatly affect how well a listener understands.

We Should See Students Who ...	PEQs for Students
👁 Present information in a logical and understandable order	❓ What does the listener need to know first, and how can I build his or her understanding from this starting point?
👁 Use effective transitions when	

speaking	❓ In what order should I make my points so that I maximize understanding? ❓ What transitions will make my explanation flow well? **PES for Students** • My speaking sequence and flow allow people to easily understand me.

Students who ask questions and make statements like these grow into adults who speak using a pattern of ideas that flow well and are easy to understand.

c) Predicting Challenges and Potential Misconceptions (before beginning)

Before beginning, a speaker should assess the topic to determine what details might be difficult to understand. Then, he or she can include information within the explanation to address potential misconceptions.

We Should See Students Who ...	**PEQs for Students**
👁 Assess the topic to predict misconceptions 👁 Reflect upon any prior explanation attempt to enhance current explanation techniques 👁 Use any necessary strategies to avoid potential misconceptions	❓ What are the most difficult aspects of this topic to understand? ❓ What challenges did I encounter when I tried to explain this before? ❓ What did I have trouble understanding when I first learned about this topic? ❓ What can I say or do to avoid these potential challenges? **PES for Students** • I make it easier to understand my explanations by predicting those things that could be misunderstood and working to avoid these misconceptions.

Students who ask questions and make statements like these grow into adults who predict and avoid potential misconceptions in their audiences. They are clearer in making points as explainers.

d) Assessing Prior Knowledge of the Audience (early in explanation)

Asking questions in order to determine the listener's prior knowledge allows the explainer to begin in an appropriate place.

We Should See Students Who ...	**PEQs for Students**
👁 Probe their audience for prior knowledge 👁 Make adjustments in consideration of the prior knowledge of the audience	❓ What does the audience already know? ❓ Considering what the audience already knows, do I need to add or subtract

	any information from my explanation?
	PES for Students
	• By determining what the audience already knows, I can make my explanations better suit their needs.

Students who ask questions and make statements like these grow into adults who can adjust their explanations as needed to meet the knowledge and needs of their audience.

e) Capturing Attention, Engaging, and Inspiring Confidence (throughout explanation)

A listener is much more likely to pay attention to and understand the speaker if the listener is drawn into what the speaker is saying. Therefore, the listener needs to be engaged through techniques such as humor, storytelling, inspirational ideas, "deep ideas," or connections between the audience and the information. The speaker's demeanor should be energetic, passionate, and inspire confidence from the audience. It is also important that the speaker does not appear to be a "know it all."

We Should See Students Who ...	PEQs for Students
👁 Help the audience connect with the information that is being explained	❓ How can I engage my audience?
👁 Are energetic and passionate	❓ Why might my listener(s) care about or be excited about the topic that I am explaining and how can I tap into this?
👁 Engage audience members with questions, "deep ideas," inspiring ideas, or stories	❓ How can I convey the real-world value of my topic?
👁 Give the audience confidence in the speaker's knowledge	❓ What techniques for engagement are appropriate for this setting?
👁 Make eye contact	❓ How should I carry myself and speak so that I inspire confidence and portray myself as knowledgeable?
👁 Use appropriate gestures	❓ Am I making eye contact with a variety of people?
👁 Engage the audience using body language	❓ Will the use of appropriate and non-repetitive gestures help capture attention?
	❓ What does my body language convey to my audience about my energy and passion for this topic?
	PES for Students
	• My energy, passion, and engaging approach draw people into listening to my words.

Students who ask questions and make statements like these grow into adults who engage their audience in such a way that the audience is drawn in and wants to listen.

f) Explaining with Clarity, Focus, and Conciseness (throughout explanation)

Explaining with clarity, focus, and conciseness is crucial. Speakers who are not clear and focused can confuse, distract, and turn off listeners.

We Should See Students Who ...	PEQs for Students
👁 Enunciate	❓ Am I speaking clearly / enunciating?
👁 Use an appropriate and even speaking pace	❓ Is my speaking volume appropriate for clear communication?
👁 Avoid the use of "fillers"	❓ Am I moving at a reasonable pace through my explanation?
👁 Stay on topic in order to avoid confusion	❓ Am I avoiding the use of "fillers" that are distracting?
👁 Use appropriate language and slang for the desired audience	❓ Do I stay focused as I speak so that I do not drift off-topic?
	❓ What type of language and slang is appropriate for this audience?
	PES for Students
	• My use of language is soothing and easy to understand.

Students who ask questions and make statements like these grow into adults who make it easy for others to listen.

g) Using Aids for Understanding (throughout explanation)

A speaker should consider the possibility of using visual, auditory, and technical aids in order to enhance an explanation.

We Should See Students Who ...	PEQs for Students
👁 Assess the tools available in order to determine if visual, auditory, or tactile aids could engage the audience or help them understand challenging concepts	❓ Would this be easier to understand with a visual, auditory, or tactile aid for understanding?
👁 Use visual, auditory, or tactile aids that grab attention and enhance the explanation	❓ What aids are available to me and in what ways could I make use of them?
👁 Avoid the use of aids that add nothing to the explanation or confuse the explanation	❓ What aids would make this more interesting?
	❓ What aids will actually help me achieve the goals of my explanation, rather than confuse my listeners?
	PES for Students
	• When helpful, I use props to grab attention and make myself easier to understand.

Students who ask questions and make statements like these grow into adults who make use of appropriate aids to help listeners understand the students' points.

h) Assessing Understanding (throughout explanation)

Rather than waiting until the end of an explanation, a speaker can intersperse questions to assess how well their audience understands. This can help squash misunderstandings before they grow. In addition, an explainer should assess the facial expressions and body language of listeners to look for cues that listeners understand or that they need clarification.

We Should See Students Who ...	PEQs for Students
👁 Probe the understanding of listeners with questions 👁 Use a tactful manner of assessing so as not to insult the audience 👁 Assess the facial expressions and body language of listeners to see if they understand	❓ Do you have any questions for me? ❓ What can I clarify for you? ❓ Can you summarize what I said so far? (This question is good for student explainers to ask during a classroom activity, but not for adults to ask customers.) ❓ Do the facial expressions and body language of my audience suggest that they understand me? **PES for Students** • I monitor how well people understand me in order to improve further discussion.

Students who ask questions and make statements like these grow into adults who recognize how well others understand them and can adjust accordingly.

i) Shifting Strategies (throughout explanation)

An explainer needs to be prepared and willing to show things in a different light if he or she finds that his or her explanation is not working as planned.

We Should See Students Who ...	PEQs for Students
👁 Recognize the need for a shift in strategies when an explanation is not working as planned 👁 Are willing to shift strategies 👁 Assess the potential causes for misconceptions among listeners 👁 Brainstorm other explaining strategies when needed and use the best option	❓ Is this explanation really working as planned, or should I shift my strategy? ❓ Which part of this is the listener not understanding? ❓ Is there an example that I can give to clarify what I am saying? ❓ Should I try to explain these ideas again in a different order? ❓ In what other creative way can I present this information to my audience? **PES for Students** • I am flexible and shift the way I am

	explaining when it is clear that my first approach is not working.

Students who ask questions and make statements like these grow into adults who are flexible and can adapt when needed during explanations.

j) Promoting Information Retention and Reinforcement in the Audience Members (throughout and after explanation)

A speaker can consider what he or she can do during and after an explanation to help listeners remember the information.

We Should See Students Who ...	PEQs for Students
👁 Create connections between new ideas and the prior knowledge of the audience	❓ How can I draw connections between this information and something else that the audience already understands?
👁 Review periodically when explaining	❓ What can I do to help the listener(s) remember the things that I explain?
👁 Wrap up and summarize at the end of an explanation	❓ What are the key ideas of my explanation and how can I summarize them?
	PES for Students
	• By reviewing and wrapping up what I say, my audience remembers the objectives of my speech.

Students who ask questions and make statements like these grow into adults who create lasting understanding of their ideas, products, or services among others.

Explaining Skills in the Classroom

In the classroom, activities that exercise explaining skills can be small or large. Class members can explain something to the whole class or less formally to a partner or team. As with the other interactive skills above, these opportunities are much more valuable when students assess others, as well as self-assess (with a rubric or goals sheet). In this way, they develop a consciousness and habit of thinking about their own skills and looking for good practices in other people (to incorporate into their own endeavors). PEQs and assessment rubrics can be easily referenced by students using the Personal Empowerment Menu (for 21st Century Students).

Explaining at Home

In the chapter that discussed connections with parents (Ch. 9), an idea was addressed that dealt with students explaining new knowledge from class to their parents. This activity can be assigned to kids by giving them a list of questions (preferably those that reflect real-world connections to the curriculum). Their assignment would be to teach their parents the concepts related to the questions and get a parent signature to verify that the task is complete. This will 1) deepen parent-student connections, 2) deepen student understanding through explanation, and 3) reinforce the real-world explaining skills of this section. In

Side Notes

fact, the assignment can include a rubric that reflects explaining skills. Parents can give their child feedback on his or her skills. This increases the parents' awareness of the skills that their child needs … so they can further reinforce them.

Challenge *All* Kids to Explain

There is a concern when promoting quality explaining skills within the classroom. It can be beneficial to have certain students, who easily master concepts, help other students by explaining. This can be a good strategy for deepening the understanding of both the higher-achieving and the struggling students, but there is a hidden difficulty. If the same students always explain things to the struggling students, those struggling students never get a chance to develop *their* explaining skills. Because of this, it is also good to have differentiated learning opportunities in which certain students tackle a more basic understanding of the concept, while others tackle a higher level understanding. In this type of situation, struggling students get a chance to explain things to *each other* as they develop their understanding. Higher-achieving students are challenged to explain more difficult concepts to *each other*. I am not saying that it isn't beneficial to have higher-achieving students explain things to struggling learners. I am simply saying that balance is needed in order to allow *all students* a chance to develop their explaining skills.

Collaborating Through Teamwork

Another essential ability in the workplace and in life is the capacity to function well within a team. We can promote this skill within the activities of our classrooms.

Critical Aspects of Collaborating Through Teamwork

- Creating a Team Attitude (with respect for and dedication to the team)
- Using Positive Communication
- Demonstrating Mutual Responsibility and Support
- Building Upon and Respecting Each Other's Ideas
- Motivating Each Other
- Relying on Each Other Before Seeking Outside Help
- Finding Common Ground

Especially important are classroom exercises in which students function together as a team to achieve learning goals. It is not enough, however, for students to simply participate on teams. They need to work to understand and improve team dynamics through observations and assessments. This goal can be accomplished by having students perform team and self-evaluations using a rubric (available in the Personal Empowerment Menu for 21ˢᵗ Century Students). Assessments of this type allow everyone to get feedback. (Do you think that this should factor into their grade for an activity?)

a) Creating a Team Attitude (with respect for and dedication to the team)

We can promote student attitudes that are conducive to team success. Our youth should have a sense of respect for and dedication to a team's goals. Teammates support one another.

We Should See Students Who ...	PEQs for Students
👁 Respect the team member's goals 👁 Demonstrate dedication to the team 👁 Demonstrate loyalty to the team 👁 Support the other team members 👁 Show that they are happy to be on the team	❓ What is important to my teammates? ❓ Am I contributing to and supporting a positive team attitude? ❓ In what ways do I demonstrate that I am dedicated to and loyal to the team? ❓ In what ways do I demonstrate that I am a happy team player? **PES for Students** • My presence improves the team atmosphere. • I enjoy being on the team and my teammates can see that.

Students who ask questions and make statements like these grow into adults who thrive in a positive team atmosphere.

b) Using Positive Communication

Within teamwork, quality communication is a must. The skills in the section above (creating a team attitude) are not possible without positive communication. Team activities provide an opportunity to build communication skills.

We Should See Students Who ...	PEQs for Students
👁 Use effective and tactful speech 👁 Carefully listen to teammates 👁 Show interest in what teammates have to say	❓ Am I effectively expressing myself to my team? ❓ Am I communicating politely and tactfully? ❓ Am I carefully listening to my teammates and showing interest? ❓ Do I understand or have questions for my teammates? **PES for Students** • I add to the positive communication of this team.

Students who ask questions and make statements like these grow into adults who communicate in a fruitful manner that helps a team achieve its goals.

c) Demonstrating Mutual Responsibility and Support

Teammates need to share in the responsibility and workload for achieving a goal. In a classroom, activities can have built-in consequences for minimal participation. Good teammates find ways to encourage one another to participate. A strategy that might work with certain activities is for members of the team to assume particular roles that are relevant to the task at hand. The teacher can assign the roles or the members can determine their roles.

We Should See Students Who ...	PEQs for Students
👁 Share responsibility 👁 Encourage each other 👁 Support each other 👁 Meet the expectations of the group 👁 Are willing to shift their role to maximize the team's potential 👁 Do not selfishly avoid the work and responsibilities of the team	❓ How do I support the success of my teammates? ❓ What are my responsibilities as a team member? ❓ Am I doing my share of the team's work? ❓ What more can I do to help the team succeed? ❓ In what role can I best support the success of the team? **PESs for Students** • We work as a team and succeed as a team. • If we don't meet our goals, we figure out how to find success ... together. • We are responsible to the team.

Students who ask questions and make statements like these grow into adults who support their teams and amplify the success of their teams.

d) Building Upon and Respecting Each Other's Ideas

A good team welcomes new ideas from everyone and assesses how they can be used. They also look for ways to tweak one another's ideas for improvement.

We Should See Students Who ...	PEQs for Students
👁 Welcome all ideas 👁 Piggyback on each other's ideas 👁 Demonstrate tact when discussing each other's ideas 👁 Feel comfortable sharing ideas and don't worry whether the team will use those ideas 👁 Seek the ideas that will best serve the goals of the team	❓ How can I encourage my teammates to share their ideas? ❓ How can I add to or tweak my teammates' ideas? ❓ How can I be tactful in giving my feedback on my teammates' ideas? ❓ What ideas can I offer the team? ❓ What idea(s) will give our team the best chance of success? **PES for Students**

	• We respectfully work together to develop our best ideas.

Students who ask questions and make statements like these grow into adults whose teams generate better ideas than they could generate as individuals.

e) Motivating Each Other

An effective group finds ways to motivate each other and to stay on task. Quality teams effectively assess which team members are best suited for and motivated to do various tasks, so that they can maximize output.

We Should See Students Who ...	PEQs for Students
👁 Show excitement for their task(s)	❓ How can I show my own excitement?
👁 Assess what makes their teammates tick	❓ What makes my teammates tick? (What are their wants, needs, and desires?)
👁 Motivate others through actions and words	❓ What actions and words can I use to motivate my teammates?
👁 Assess each other's skills and passions	❓ What roles would bring out the best in each of our team members?
👁 Find appropriate roles for team members	❓ How can I "spice up" the work environment to make team members have more fun?
👁 Devise ways to increase the enjoyment of working on a task	**PES for Students**
	• We bring out the best in each other.

Students who ask questions and make statements like these grow into adults who find ways to bring out the best in teammates and make team members enjoy tasks.

f) Relying on Each Other Before Seeking Outside Help

In some instances when children are having difficulty with a classroom task, they immediately ask the teacher for help. Instead, they should try to work through the issue by using all of the resources of their team. The challenge in the real world is that there isn't necessarily a teacher-like figure who has all the answers. Thus, any guideline or structure that is built into a team activity to encourage self-reliance first (before seeking out the teacher) would be positive.

We Should See Students Who ...	PEQs for Students
👁 Trust teammates	❓ What skills, tools, and resources can we use or access in order to accomplish this task on our own?
👁 Display self-reliance as a team	
👁 Are helpful to teammates	❓ Now that we have made every effort to be independent, with what tasks or tools do we need help?
👁 Have a determined attitude as a team	
	PESs for Students
	• I trust my teammates.

14 - Understanding and Interacting with Others

	• We can do this!

Students who ask questions and make statements like these grow into adults who create successful, confident, and independent teams.

g) Finding Common Ground

In the team activities of school and life, disagreements are bound to occur. The key is for students to find common ground and find ways to work through their differences.

We Should See Students Who ...	PEQs for Students
👁 Consider the goals of the team	❓ What are our goals?
👁 Listen to teammates	❓ What suggestions are my teammates offering?
👁 Tactfully persuade teammates	❓ What are my ideas for the team?
👁 Are willing to compromise and yield when teammates' ideas might work better	❓ Which ideas will work the best for our team's goals?
	❓ What criteria can we use to make tough choices as a team?
	❓ Can we integrate each other's ideas together?
	PES for Students
	• We don't always agree, but we seek and find a shared vision for our team that will lead to success.

Students who ask questions and make statements like these grow into adults who contribute to and work effectively in a group setting.

5 Competing

The world is filled with competitive situations. When people job hunt, they compete with other prospective employees. When entrepreneurs start businesses, they vie with other businesses for customers. Lawyers contend for clients. Teenagers compete for admission into colleges. Politicians battle for votes. Global competition, along with new forms of automation and new technologies, add new forms of competition to our lives. Life presents us with many opportunities to succeed and get what we want ... or not succeed. If we don't do our part to help our youth prepare for this reality, we are doing them a disservice.

The nice thing about teaching competitive lessons is that students compete in classes, games, and clubs where the stakes are relatively low. In these situations, we can control the competitive environment. With our mentorship, our students can learn how to succeed and how to handle setbacks and disappointment. We can promote teamwork, integrity, and dedication. The alternative to teaching these lessons is to allow our youth to go through their developmental years without learning how to handle life's realities. If our young people are never in competitive situations and never learn how to handle wins and losses, what will they do when they need to

21st Century Challenge – Part 3: *Social and Personal Skills*
(Understanding and Interacting with Others)
203

compete for a job? What will they do if they are unsuccessful in finding a job, starting a business, or getting into a particular school … and have never experienced any sort of setback in their lives?

I, for one, am glad that I had opportunities in school to learn lessons from coaches and mentors about what it takes to win and how to overcome losses in *track races…* rather than having to learn these lessons for the first time as an adult in the *real world*, where the stakes are very high. While success in a school competition, such as track, was important to me, losing didn't keep me from having an income. I was able to learn important life lessons without losses ruining my life.

Putting students into competitive situations doesn't just teach them a future skill. For many students, competitive situations can be great motivators that stimulate them to learn and grow. Furthermore, competition can promote the interactive and team skills from the previous chapter.

We should note that the type of competition that younger and older students are ready to handle is different. Clearly, our youth need to gradually build into competitive situations from elementary school to high school. We must not forget that the ultimate goal for students is to graduate with the ability to deal with the world's competitive realities.

Let's help our youth prepare for competitive situations, so that they are ready for the inevitable situations when there are opportunities for success, risks of disappointment, and times to overcome setbacks. There are two major categories that need to be addressed: knowing how to succeed in competitive situations and learning from wins and losses.

Critical Aspects of the Ability to Compete

Knowing How to Prepare for and Succeed in Competitive Situations

- **Having a Proper Work Ethic in Preparation for Competition**
- **Considering the Competitors**
- **Having a Proper State of Mind in Competition**
- **Displaying Proper Demeanor** (Sportsmanship)

Learning from Wins and Losses After a Competition

- **Assessing and Learning from the Performance of Yourself and the Team**
- **Assessing and Learning from the Performance of Your Competitors**
- **Learning the "Ins And Outs" of the Competition**
- **Developing New Strategies Over Time**
- **Finding Positives in and Motivation from Competition**

Knowing How to Prepare for and Succeed in Competitive Situations

a) Having a Proper Work Ethic in Preparation for Competition

The aspects of a positive work ethic from the section above are essential to competitive abilities: *Having Vision and Dreams, Developing a Path to Success, Developing an Empowered and Positive Attitude, Sacrificing, Staying the Course, Acting Proactively, Behaving with Personal Responsibility, and Displaying Responsibility to Others.* To have a competitive edge, young people who play games and adults who "play" life need all of these abilities, attitudes, and habits for competitive situations. We must periodically promote these critical aspects of proper work ethic <u>within competitive situations</u>. Also, competition can often be a motivating factor for kids to improve their work ethic. Competition and motivation can go hand-in-hand.

We Should See Students Who ...	PEQs for Students
👁 Have vision, dreams, and goals 👁 Develop a path to success 👁 Develop an empowering and positive attitude 👁 Make sacrifices 👁 Stay the course 👁 Act proactively 👁 Behave with personal responsibility 👁 Display responsibility to others	❓ What are my (our) goals and dreams in this competition? ❓ How will I (we) succeed in this competition? ❓ Why should I (we) be confident in this competition? ❓ What might I (we) have to sacrifice in order to win? ❓ What obstacles will I (we) have to overcome to win? ❓ In what ways am I responsible for my own and my teammates' successes? **PES for Students** • I know my competitive goals and am prepared to succeed.

Students who ask questions and make statements like these grow into adults who are more likely to win due to a proper work ethic.

b) Considering the Competitors

When preparing for a competition, participants must take their competitors into consideration, because the actions of opponents can clearly have an effect on the outcome. This will also be true in the competitions of adult life (such as a competition between two businesses or competition to get a job).

We Should See Students Who ...	PEQs for Students
👁 Assess the possible plans, possible strategies, and strengths of the competition 👁 Proactively plan for overcoming the actions of the competition 👁 Determine the best strategies for winning in consideration of the	❓ What are my (our) competitors doing or planning to do in order to win? ❓ How will I (we) prepare for and react to the competition's actions? ❓ What preparations, skills, or plans will most likely help us beat another team? ❓ What might my (our) competitors do to

competition	satisfy the needs and wants of customers, clients, or patients, and what do I (we) need to do to better satisfy them? (PEQ for adults)
	PES for Students
	• I (We) understand my (our) competitors and will meet the challenges they pose.

Students who ask questions and make statements like these grow into adults who anticipate and prepare for the actions of their competition in order to maximize success.

c) Having a Proper State of Mind in Competition

Competing successfully requires a certain state of mind. Mentors can help our youth develop the right mental approach to competition. Competition requires the ability to focus on tasks, react positively, and appropriately direct one's attention.

We Should See Students Who ...	**PEQs for Students**
👁 Are focused, determined, and confident	❓ Where should my (our) focus lie in order to be successful?
👁 Embrace competition	❓ What is a positive, appropriate, and determined way for me (us) to react when competitors do well or get an edge?
👁 Do not get discouraged during competition	
👁 Balance their focus between their competition and themselves (paying attention to, but not obsessing on, the competition)	❓ When is it in my (our) best interest to focus more on my (our) own actions, rather than on the competitor's actions?
	PESs for Students
	• I (we) can do this!
	• I am (we are) looking forward to the challenge.
	• I (we) can overcome any obstacles.

Students who ask questions and make statements like these will grow into adults who approach competitive situations with a state of mind that allows them to succeed.

d) Displaying Proper Demeanor (Sportsmanship)

During a competition, people should display appropriate demeanor. People have an opportunity to develop respect from others in competitive situations, but they can also lose respect with inappropriate behavior. Whether winning or losing, students should be humble, polite, and respectful. (Poor behavioral displays by those who win can further motivate their opponents to beat them in the future.)

We Should See Students Who ...	**PEQs for Students**
👁 Display integrity	❓ How does my (our) behavior affect the

	integrity of this competition or situation?
👁 Display respect 👁 Display humility 👁 Display maturity	❓ How should I (we) behave in order to show respect, humility, maturity, and integrity? ❓ What will be the consequences of immature behavior on my (our) part? **PES for Students** • I am a good sport, showing integrity, respect, humility, and maturity.

Students who ask questions and make statements like these grow into adults who behave gracefully and maturely in their lives.

Learning from Wins and Losses after a Competition

When people are exposed to competitive wins and losses, they get a chance to assess their competitive qualities and deficiencies. Then, they can work to improve, so that they are more successful in the future. One of the most important reasons to expose our youth to competitive situations is that kids can learn from wins and losses in childhood games rather than in adult situations. A soccer team will have wins and losses. A coach can guide, teach, motivate, and inspire a group of youngsters to work hard to improve after they lose a game. This allows them to grow into adults who, when confronted with competitive situations, are better able to self-assess and improve, bounce back after disappointments, and understand that hard work puts them in control of their future. So, let's promote the following behaviors.

e) Assessing and Learning from the Performance of Yourself and the Team

Wins and losses provide opportunities, motivation, and data for assessing what we can improve in order to do better in the future. Developing the habit of self and team assessment should carry into adulthood.

We Should See Students Who ...	PEQs for Students
👁 Assess their personal and team's performance after a competition (regardless of winning or losing) in order to improve	❓ Which strategies worked well and which did not? ❓ In which areas was I (were we) well prepared and not well prepared? ❓ What should I (we) do the same and what should I (we) do differently in the next competition? ❓ Which team roles did and did not work? **PES for Students** • Based on my (our) performance, I (we) know what can be done to improve

	future performances.

Students who ask questions and make statements like these grow into adults who self-assess in order to constantly improve themselves.

f) Assessing and Learning from the Performance of Your Competitors

Our youth can also learn how to assess their competitors. This allows them to learn from their competitions' strengths and practices. It also allows them to evaluate the ways in which the competition might try to improve in the future.

We Should See Students Who ...	PEQs for Students
👁 Assess their opponents in order to learn from them 👁 Are willing to accept that their opponents might have an edge in some areas and work to surpass them 👁 Evaluate the ways in which their opponents might react and change in light of previous competitions	❓ What did my (our) competitors do well and what did they not do well? ❓ What can I (we) learn from my (our) competitors to help me (us) improve? ❓ What did my (our) competitors probably learn from my (our) performance and their own performance? ❓ In what ways will my (our) competitors probably react and change in light of this competition? **PES for Students** • Based my (our) competitors' performance, I (we) know what can be done to improve future success.

Students who ask questions and make statements like these grow into adults who assess their competitors in order to learn from them and predict their next moves.

g) Learning the "Ins And Outs" of the Competition

Students can learn to assess how the environment and the rules of a game affect their ability to succeed. They can use this knowledge to shift their strategies and use the environment of the competition to their advantage. For example, a sports team might consider the rules of a competition and determine that the rules allow for a few different strategies. Then, the team can use this understanding to their advantage by utilizing strategies (within the bounds of the rules) that support their strengths.

We Should See Students Who ...	PEQs for Students
👁 Assess and understand the rules and environment of a competition 👁 Recognize common practices and etiquette that are found in certain competitions 👁 Recognize what can be controlled	❓ What are the rules, common practices, etiquette, and environmental factors associated with this type of competition? ❓ In previous competitions, what was and what was not in my (our) control?

and what cannot be controlled in a competition 👁 Create strategies that will maximize their performance by considering the rules, environment, and common practices of a competition	❓ In previous competitions, what happened that I (we) did not expect, but should expect in the future? ❓ Considering the rules, common practices, etiquette, and environmental factors associated with this type of activity, which strategies will allow me (us) to maximize my (our) performance in the future? **PES for Students** • I am (We are) developing a better understanding of the "ins" and "outs" of this competition, and it will help in the future.

Students who ask questions and make statements like these grow into adults who assess the circumstances of their environment in order to create strategies that will maximize their potential.

h) Developing New Strategies Over Time

Young minds need to get in the habit of using their assessments of situations in order to decide if, when, and what new strategies are necessary. Then, they need to apply their skills in taking creative actions in order to improve their strategies. This practice is important because the opponents and circumstances of competitive endeavors shift over time, and require new strategies.

We Should See Students Who ...	**PEQs for Students**
👁 Assess circumstances in order to determine if and when new strategies are needed 👁 Are willing to recognize that change might be needed 👁 Are creative in developing new strategies for competition when needed	❓ What is working well in my (our) competitive endeavors? ❓ What competitive strategies need to change? ❓ What new strategies are necessary for continued success in competitive situations? **PES for Students** • I am (We are) finding new ways to be successful in competition.

Students who ask questions and make statements like these grow into adults who adapt to changing situations in order to maintain success.

i) Finding Positives in and Motivation from Competition

Students need to use competition to see what positive things they do and use competition as a motivator for future improvement.

We Should See Students Who ...	PEQs for Students
👁 Recognize what positive things happen during competition (whether they win or lose) 👁 Use competition as motivation for further success (whether they win or lose) 👁 Show personal and team pride in competitive activities (whether they win or lose)	❓ What did I (we) do well in this competition? ❓ How can I (we) turn this success into more successes and more motivation? ❓ How can I (we) use this disappointment for motivation? ❓ Why should I (we) be proud? **PES for Students** • My (Our) experiences are giving me (us) motivation for future competition.

Students who ask questions and make statements like these grow into adults who use competition as a source of pride and motivation for improvement (whether or not they succeed).

Let's consider some final thoughts about competition and competitive situations.

Side Notes

Promoting Teamwork in Competition

Some people might say that the promotion of competitive skills goes against the promotion of teamwork. To the contrary, competitive situations can be set up so that they require teamwork and promote motivation. I know that, as a youth, my best lessons in teamwork came from competitive situations.

Competing Against Oneself

To teach kids about competition, they don't always have to compete against one another. Activities can be created that challenge students to compete against *themselves*. For instance, I have created games in which a classroom of students is challenged to raise its class average score from one assessment to the next by five percent. This puts the control of the students' success squarely on their own shoulders, because they are simply competing against their own prior performances. It also promotes a team atmosphere in the classroom in which students are motivated to help each other learn and grow.

6 | Understanding Language and Culture

In *The World is Flat*, Friedman states that "HP (Hewlett Packard) today has well over 150,000 employees in at least 170 countries. It is not only the largest consumer technology company in the world; it is the largest IT (information technology) company in Europe, the largest IT company in Russia, the largest IT company in the Middle East, and the largest IT company in South Africa."[22] Considering the global nature of many modern businesses, we must prepare our students to interact, work, and compete with people from around the world. We should help our youth learn the critical aspects of "understanding language and culture."

---

[22] (Friedman, 2005, page 243)

Critical Aspects of Understanding Language and Culture

- Learning the Wants, Needs, Cultures, Values, and Histories of Others
- Learning to Communicate with People from Other Cultures

a) Learning the Wants, Needs, Cultures, Values, and Histories of Others

In Chapter 10, we talked about the need to do more than have an occasional cultural day at school. While this is beneficial, lessons about the wants, needs, values, cultures, and histories of different people from around the world need to be woven within the curriculum of various content areas.

Core Content Matters

Students cannot compare the similarities and differences between American culture and the cultures of others if the students do not have a deep understanding of the core beliefs and values that are common to Americans. Thus, we should not neglect the teaching of our own core democratic values when teaching about other societies. Learning about other cultures should go hand-in-hand with learning about our own culture.

Side Note

Students need to understand that even though Americans share many core beliefs, there might be some differences in values, needs, and desires among the citizens of different regions, religions, sexes, or ages. Thus, our youth need to not only understand the differences outside our country, but also those within it.

We Should See Students Who ...	PEQs for Students
👁 Empathize 👁 Consider the differences and similarities between their own needs, wants, and values and those of others 👁 Recognize what other people consider important 👁 Understand the circumstances that shape the values and desires of others	❓ What core beliefs and values are common among most Americans? ❓ How are the values, needs, and wants of people from around the world similar and different? ❓ How does a country's history affect its current culture? ❓ What circumstances affect the needs and values of various groups of people? ❓ What motivates and inspires people of various cultures? **PESs for Students** • I continue to learn about other cultures so that I can better understand them. • My understanding of various cultures helps me to better interact with people from around the world.

14 - Understanding and Interacting with Others

Students who ask questions and make statements like these grow into adults who can better understand the similarities and differences in cultures and countries, and better motivate, communicate, and compete with others.

b) Learning to Communicate with People from Other Cultures

Students need to develop proficiency in communication with people from other cultures and places. This means that children must learn to *use* foreign languages (as opposed to only memorizing vocabulary and regurgitating it on a written test). In addition, they should understand the social expectations of communication in other cultures.

We Should See Students Who ...	PEQs for Students
👁 Can *use* another language 👁 Recognize the expectations of communication in other cultures	❓ How can I become more proficient in speaking another language? ❓ What expectations do people in other cultures have in communication? ❓ What do I need to know in order to communicate effectively and appropriately with people in other cultures? **PES for Students** • I am empowered by my ability to communicate using a foreign language.

Students who ask questions and make statements like these grow into adults who are empowered to communicate effectively with people from other countries.

Side Note

Travel if Possible

Opportunities to travel to different countries are invaluable. High school trips and student exchanges that embed young people in another culture and language are great experiences.

My brother-in-law attended a college that requires foreign study. Making this a requirement at schools is a bit much, but at the very least, foreign study can be encouraged in high school and college.

Another option is to host a foreign exchange student. This experience allows students to learn about the culture and values of those in other countries.

Understanding and Interacting with Others: Wrap-up

Interactive skills are priceless in the real world. A person can be brilliant, but if he or she does not have good interactive skills, his or her potential for success in a variety of career paths is vastly decreased. We must find ways to shape learning activities so that our youth are provided with interactive skill growth. This is an important skill in the 21st century in which we want our students to thrive.

Students Must Look at the World with Reflective Eyes

At first glance, promoting interactive skills might seem simple; we can just have students work with others or explain things to each other. However, as we can see from the details above, we must go much deeper. Each of the topics above has a variety of factors that are important. Our students need to be aware of all the factors that go into having good communication skills. They need to assess themselves and other people to look for ways to improve themselves. When young minds begin to look inside and outside themselves with a reflective eye, they learn so much more about human interactions than we can teach in structured lessons. Therefore, a good goal for educators is to help students understand the facets of good interactions (as broken down above) and then to stimulate them to inspect (or assess) the world around them. Classroom activities and lessons that help kids learn the facets of good interactions seem relatively easy to implement. However, stimulating young minds to look reflectively at the world around them seems a little more challenging. How can we do that?

With many possible activities geared toward the major skills above, students are explaining, working together toward a common goal, discussing, or debating. With any of these skills, we can provide kids with the relevant PEQs in order to stimulate assessment of their own and others' skills. In addition, kids can assess themselves and others using assessment rubrics that are relevant to the skills we want them to develop. To help students make these assessments, the Personal Empowerment Menu (for 21ˢᵗ Century Students) contains both the relevant PEQs and assessment rubrics for the skills of this book. For instance, if students work on a team during an activity, they can follow-up the activity by assessing their teamwork using the PEQs and rubric found in the Personal Empowerment Menu. In this way, they can see what they did well and see what they could improve. (In addition to using the rubrics to follow-up activities, students can look at the rubrics before activities. In this way, the person who will be assessed understands what he or she is trying to achieve and those who will assess him or her will understand the important facets of the skill ahead of time.)

In addition to being assessed by others, a pupil can self-assess (using the appropriate rubric) in order to see how his or her perception compares to the others' perceptions.

In yet another example, students might present information to the class or speak during a discussion or debate. Along with an assessment of the students' content knowledge, the teacher can break down and give feedback about the students' speaking skills using a rubric from the Personal Empowerment Menu.

The broader point is that there are constant opportunities to get students to reflect upon themselves and others. This reflection gets them in the habit of looking for ways to improve themselves and of looking at others to get ideas for improvement. These opportunities can be woven into the regular classroom activities so that the teacher is not required to add extra activities (that take from what little time is available). Because there are many ways to exercise and reflect upon interactive skills, activities can be done in almost any class at any age. Developing speaking skills is not just for a speech class. Understanding culture is not just for Social Studies. Learning how to explain is not just something for teachers to master.

When we do the little things that get young minds to reflect upon interactions in school, those minds are more likely to carry this habit into their everyday life … where they can "learn a TON" by observing and assessing everyday life. This same premise applies to our previous unit about analysis, actions, and creativity. The little things and big things that we do in schools to get students to look at the world with a reflective eye carry over into their lives outside of school, where they can learn even more.

Journaling to Improve Real-World Skills

Another activity that can get our youth to reflect upon themselves and the world around them is journaling. Kids can be asked to reflect upon their own skills in a journal using the PEQs of this book. They can also take note of quality 21st century skills demonstrated by others. Maybe they notice that someone was good at being tactful, explaining, or leading. Then, they write down what that person did well. Maybe they realize something that they could have done better in a social situation, and they make a note about it. In addition to getting children to assess various situations, a journal can become a resource for reflection in the future.

A journal of this kind wouldn't have to be geared toward only interaction skills, but can be geared toward all of the 21st century skills, attitudes, and habits we have discussed. Young minds can reflect upon how a lesson in school connects to the real world, a new critical thinking skill that they learned, an example of someone effectively solving a problem, or a realization of what brings out their own creativity.

Extra Opportunities for Interaction

Before we move to the next chapter, we must note an additional opportunity for developing interactive skills. Extracurricular clubs, activities, and sports are great opportunities for our youth. As mentioned in an earlier chapter, these activities help connect students to their advisors/coaches, their peers, their communities, and more. Beyond this connection that motivates kids, these extracurricular activities provide *great* opportunities for students to develop their interactive skills. Bringing students with common interests together is a recipe for fun, comfort, and bonding. I have known many people who attribute "coming out of their shell" to their participation in after-school activities.

Thinking About It

- **What are the biggest challenges for students in developing interactive skills?**
- **What social skills do you believe students lack today?**
- **What strategies have you seen that work well for developing student social skills?**
- **How can you promote the various interactive skills described within this chapter?**

How Does This Chapter Support the Goals of This Book?

Let's take a moment to think about the ways in which the ideas of this chapter help us address the three main goals of this book by looking at the "Building Blocks of a 21st Century Education" on page 13 and the "Daily Thoughts for Educators" on page 18. We now have tools

14 - Understanding and Interacting with Others

and strategies for empowering our youth by developing their understanding and skills in interacting with others.

Make Note of Your Great Ideas!

If you haven't already, note your ideas for implementing the strategies in this chapter in your Teacher Empowerment Menu (for 21st Century Educators). In the future, you can easily reference usable ideas for your class.

In addition, consider the ways in which you can stimulate students to develop their skills in understanding and interacting with others by using the Personal Empowerment Menu (for 21st Century Students), which contains the relevant PEQs, PESs, and assessment rubrics for this chapter.

15 | Personal Skills, Attitudes, and Habits

We will now continue our promotion of a 21st Century Challenge by addressing the development of 21st century personal skills, attitudes, and habits. These are concepts that might get lost in the modern day demands of education. They are, however, critical to our youths' future success.

To help our students in the 21st century, we must challenge them within the regular curriculum to develop the following attributes.

Personal Skills, Attitudes, and Habits

1. **Setting Goals**
2. **Employing a Proper Work Ethic to Achieve Goals**
3. **Adapting, Changing, and Being Versatile**
4. **Managing Stress**
5. **Being Organized and Efficient**
6. **Behaving in an Ethical Manner that Shows Integrity**
7. **Assessing Risks when Making Complex Decisions**
8. **Being Financially Literate in Personal and Professional Life**

The new economic challenges that we face require our pupils to have the skills, attitudes, and habits listed above. As usual, we should not view these goals as "extras" that will require more time that we don't have available. We must view them as *essentials* that should be seamlessly interwoven into our curriculum in such a way that our classrooms are more engaging and valuable to students.

1 Setting Goals

For a person to find success in achieving the personal skills, attitudes and habits above, he or she must start with setting goals. Goals provide the motivation and vision for someone to create a pathway to personal success and to diligently follow that path. The critical aspects of setting goals are as follows.

15 - Personal Skills, Attitudes, and Habits

Critical Aspects of Setting Goals

- **Developing a Vision and Dreaming** (Intrinsic Motivation)
- **Developing Short- and Long-Term Goals** (Creating a Pathway to Success)
- **Assessing Progress and Modifying Pathways as Needed**

As with earlier topics in this book, we can help our students to understand and make use of the critical aspects of "setting goals" by using four key educational strategies: Classroom Exercises, Teacher Stories / Modeling, Assessment by Students, and Curricular Examples. Let's look at some examples to see how these techniques can work.

Classroom Exercises (Setting Goals)

Many times, a teacher can provide classroom opportunities for students to perform a task that involves the creation of goals. This could involve creating goals for a project, a school activity, a fundraiser, or grades. In the process, teachers can help students develop a vision and dream, create short-term and long-term goals, and assess and modify goals as needed.

Teacher Stories / Modeling (Setting Goals)

It is not enough to provide classroom exercises in goal setting alone. Teachers should model the ways in which goals can be set. We can model goal setting in a formal way when giving kids the task of creating goals as described in the "classroom exercises" above. Informally, we can tell some of our personal stories about setting and working toward goals in our own lives. Teacher anecdotes can be very valuable if teachers describe situations from their lives that highlight proper goal setting and success. In addition, our learners can benefit when a teacher is comfortable enough to tell them about mistakes that he or she has made in working toward goals. Beyond stories, the simple everyday actions of educators send constant and important signals to students. What do we show them about goal setting, dreaming, and working toward goals? We must model the behavior we want to instill in our students. It's not enough to just tell stories; we have to show successful behavior, too.

Assessment by Students (Setting Goals)

The skills of analysis and critical thinking from Chapter 11 allow students to make complex assessments about situations, systems, and problems. Students can use and exercise these evaluation skills to develop an understanding of setting goals. If we can get young minds to make observations about themselves and others, students can deepen their understanding of the value of goal setting. They can assess what dreams and goals drive disciplined, dedicated, and determined people, as well as assess what steps these people take to be successful. As mentioned earlier in the book, getting kids to critically analyze and assess the world around them, as well as themselves, might be the best thing we can do for them. Any method that educators can use to stimulate this awareness and assessment of the world will be highly valuable.

Curricular Examples (Setting Goals)

There are many opportunities within a regular curriculum to highlight examples of average and famous people who have exercised proper goal setting. Whether we use a story, a history lesson, or a sport, there are many examples that highlight and show the value of the critical aspects of dreaming and goal setting to students. These examples show the positive results that come from the discipline, dedication, and determination created by goals. Students can be inspired by what people have done to achieve their dreams and visions. Telling students that someone worked hard is not enough. Our youth need to be exposed to stories that highlight hard work, setbacks, and sacrifices in the pursuit of goals. Conversely, they need exposure to examples that show how a break down in goal setting kept someone from an ultimate success. As usual, when we work to weave a relevant life skill into the curriculum, we should engage and connect our students to what they learn.

Critical Aspects of Setting Goals

Through the four methods above, educators can help students understand and make use of the critical aspects of "setting goals." Let's look at these aspects.

a) Developing a Vision and Dreaming (Intrinsic Motivation)

Having an ultimate, important vision or dream for one's work makes success much easier. Dreams motivate people and help them persevere.

We Should See Students Who ...	Personal Empowerment Questions PEQs for Students
👁 Dream 👁 Display forward thinking 👁 Have the attitude that great things can be accomplished 👁 Imagine themselves succeeding	❓ What is my vision or dream? ❓ Why is this vision or dream important to me? ❓ What do I have to gain? ❓ What will my future look like when I succeed? ❓ Why should I be intrinsically motivated to work hard? ❓ I want to be realistic, but am I selling myself short ... I know that I can accomplish great things! **Personal Empowerment Statement**

	PES for Students
	• I can see myself achieving my vision and dreams.

Students who ask questions and make statements like these grow into adults who seek and achieve their highest potential.

---

b) Developing Short-Term and Long-Term Goals (Creating a Pathway to Success)

When faced with a task that requires a great deal of work, dedication, and discipline, a person should outline a pathway for achievement. He or she needs to know what short-term and long-term goals he or she needs to achieve and how to achieve those goals.

We Should See Students Who ...	**PEQs for Students**
👁 Display forward thinking	❓ What do I need to accomplish to meet my dreams and vision?
👁 Break larger tasks into manageable pieces	❓ What short- and long-term goals will lead me to ultimate success?
👁 Create short- and long-term goals for accomplishing the pieces of larger tasks	❓ What steps do I need to take to achieve these goals?
👁 Create measurable goals so that success can be monitored	❓ How can I compartmentalize the steps of this task in order to make it feel less overwhelming?
👁 Consider what resources are available to help them accomplish goals	❓ How will I know if my goals are being met … how will I measure success?
	❓ What resources can I use to accomplish my goals?
	❓ How do others accomplish similar goals?
	PES for Students
	• By working toward the short-term and long-term goals I have created, I will achieve my dreams.

Students who ask questions and make statements like these grow into adults who systematically work to create goals and accomplish those goals.

---

c) Assessing Progress and Modifying Pathways as Needed

As people work toward their goals, they must assess their progress in order to find motivation when results are positive, to stimulate action or a new approach when results are not positive, and to modify or shift goals when necessary to stay on track toward achieving larger goals and dreams.

We Should See Students Who ...	PEQs for Students
👁 Assess their progress in achieving short-term and long-term goals	❓ How am I progressing toward my short-term and long-term goals?
👁 Find motivation to push forward when successful	❓ In which successes can I take pride?
👁 Take action to improve their progress when goals are not being met	❓ In what ways do I need to improve my actions in order to better achieve my goals?
👁 Determine when short-term goals need to be modified to better achieve long-term goals	❓ Are my short-term goals helping me achieve my long-term goals? If not, what modifications should I make?

PES for Students

- I am monitoring my progress and actively working to meet my goals.

Students who ask questions and make statements like these grow into adults who continuously monitor their success and modify their paths as needed.

2 Employing a Proper Work Ethic to Achieve Goals

We must promote a proper work ethic in our student population, so that they can carry it into adulthood. This might be a larger challenge than it was for previous generations. In *The World is Flat*, Friedman points out that "… we were the only economy standing after World War II, and we had no serious competition for forty years. That gave us a huge head of steam but also gradually bred a sense of entitlement and a cultural complacency. That is, a pronounced tendency in recent years to extol consumption over hard work and investment, immediate gratification over long-term thinking and sacrifice."[23] With this attitude and a lack of insulation from foreign competition, our youth could find it difficult to compete with workers from poorer countries who are desperate to have what we have enjoyed. This alone would be a sufficient reason for us to help our youth develop a proper work ethic, but recent domestic economic troubles make this even more critical. Our students will need to understand and make use of the critical aspects of a proper work ethic.

---

[23] (Friedman, 2005, page 325)

15 - Personal Skills, Attitudes, and Habits

Critical Aspects of Proper Work Ethic

- **Having an Empowering and Positive Attitude**
- **Sacrificing**
- **Staying the Course / Persisting**
- **Acting Proactively**
- **Behaving with Personal Responsibility / Accountability**
- **Taking Initiative with Self-Direction and Independence**
- **Showing Responsibility to Others**
  (Family, Team, School, Community, and Country)
- **Giving Quality Performance … Not Just Being Present**

a) Having an Empowering and Positive Attitude

    If people are going to dedicate themselves to tasks, they must feel capable of achieving their goals. They must see that they control their destiny and take pride in their successes.

We Should See Students Who ...	PEQs for Students
👁 Have a positive attitude	❓ What skills and habits do I have that will allow me to succeed?
👁 Take control of their own destiny	❓ What empowering resources can I use to accomplish my goals?
👁 Feel empowered	❓ Who can help me achieve my goals?
👁 Understand their own potential	❓ What things did I do when I experienced success in the past?
👁 Consider and use the available resources that can help them achieve their goals	❓ In what ways am I in control of the outcome of my journey to succeed?
👁 Take pride in their successes	❓ How can I have fun while working toward my goals?
	PESs for Students
	• I am prepared and capable … I can do this!
	• If I don't already know how to do something, I can learn how.
	• I am proud of my successes.

Students who ask questions and make statements like these grow into adults who take on challenging tasks because they feel empowered to succeed.

b) Sacrificing

A person must understand that sometimes he or she might have to sacrifice immediate gratification in order to achieve long-term success ... and be willing to make that sacrifice.

We Should See Students Who ...	PEQs for Students
👁 Recognize when sacrifices must be made 👁 Are willing to make sacrifices for success	❓ What sacrifices might be necessary to achieve my vision? ❓ When might sacrifices need to be made? ❓ How will my sacrifices help me achieve my goals? ❓ Why are the sacrifices worth it? ❓ How will I persuade myself to make sacrifices? **PES for Students** • I make sacrifices that will pay off in the future.

Students who ask questions and make statements like these grow into adults who make difficult choices that result in the achievement of their goals.

c) Staying the Course / Persisting

Worthwhile ventures often come with obstacles and moments when a person can get sidetracked from his or her path. Developing the ability to stay the course is crucial.

We Should See Students Who ...	PEQs for Students
👁 Have their eyes on the "prize" (their dreams and goals) 👁 Recognize obstacles 👁 Predict obstacles 👁 Determine ways to move past obstacles 👁 Are motivated to persist 👁 Consider the available resources that can help them overcome obstacles 👁 Find opportunities in challenges	❓ What dreams and goals do I want to achieve? ❓ How will I know if I have encountered an obstacle or am off course? ❓ What obstacles can I expect to encounter? ❓ What will I do if I get sidetracked from achieving my goals by predictable or unpredictable obstacles? ❓ What do I stand to lose if I don't stay the course? ❓ Who is counting on me to succeed? ❓ Who or what can help me stay on course to achieve my goals? ❓ How is this obstacle an opportunity? **PESs for Students** • I will fight through challenges and

	achieve my goals. • I will stay the course.

Students who ask questions and make statements like these grow into adults who work through difficult challenges and maintain their path toward success.

d) Acting Proactively

In the real world, the success of a person in his or her professional (and personal) life can be greatly enhanced with the ability to act proactively. Rather than waiting for problems to arise or for situations to develop, a person can take reasonable actions to prepare himself or herself for future tasks and situations. Then, he or she will have fewer challenges that take him or her off course.

We Should See Students Who ...	PEQs for Students
👁 Assess current circumstances and trends to make predictions of possible challenges 👁 Take actions that will make future success more likely (without immediate gratification) 👁 Take steps to avoid, diminish, or overcome potential future challenges	❓ What might I have to overcome to achieve my goals? ❓ How might I get sidetracked? ❓ What will I likely need in the future to accomplish my goals? ❓ What can I do now that will make me more prepared later? ❓ What support structure can I put in place to deal with unexpected problems? **PES for Students** • I am readying myself for the challenges I will or might face.

Students who ask questions and make statements like these grow into adults who take steps to avoid potential challenges. Thus, they are better able to avoid and overcome obstacles.

e) Behaving with Personal Responsibility / Accountability

When a student or adult takes personal responsibility for his or her work and actions, he or she is much more likely to succeed.

We Should See Students Who ...	PEQs for Students
👁 Recognize the positive and negative consequences of various actions 👁 Look inward for solutions rather than outward for blame 👁 Display a responsible attitude	❓ What are the consequences of my actions or inaction? ❓ In what ways am I in control of my own destiny? ❓ Why is my own hard work the most important factor in my success? ❓ What are my responsibilities? **PESs for Students**

	• I am responsible for my success. • The actions I take have consequences. I plan to create positive consequences.

Students who ask questions and make statements like these grow into adults who find success through personal responsibility.

f) Taking Initiative with Self-Direction and Independence

In order to have a proper work ethic, students have to display the habit of self-direction in which they take initiative and independently work toward their goals. This does not mean that students do not get help from or give help to others. This means that they set goals, create paths for success, and work hard without having to be forced or stimulated to do so. Obviously, students vary in their degree of self-direction. Our job as teachers is to create structures that stimulate kids to work hard, but to also coax those students toward independence by slowly removing the "training wheels" throughout their educational career.

We Should See Students Who ...	PEQs for Students
👁 Take initiative with self-direction and independence 👁 Set goals, create plans for success, and work hard by their own will	❓ Without waiting for someone to tell me what I should do, what goals can I set out to accomplish? ❓ What plans can I create for myself? ❓ How can I take control of my own success? ❓ How can I become more independent? ❓ Why is it crucial for my long-term success that I behave in a self-directed manner? **PES for Students** • I can direct myself to succeed.

Students who ask questions and make statements like these grow into adults who take action to achieve their goals.

g) Showing Responsibility to Others
(Family, Team, School, Community, and Country)

Loyalty to others creates relationships that are mutually beneficial for youth and adults alike. Proper work ethic is also promoted when a person feels and understands his or her responsibility to those around him or her.

We Should See Students Who ...	PEQs for Students
👁 Recognize their role within a group 👁 Recognize the value of the group 👁 Exhibit mutually beneficial behaviors	❓ What is my role in this group, and what do I need to do to meet my responsibilities?

15 – Personal Skills, Attitudes, and Habits

in a group 👁 Are loyal 👁 Respect others 👁 Have a personal drive to help others and be charitable	❓ Why does my participation and hard work matter to the group? ❓ What do we have at stake? ❓ Who is counting on me in this family, team, school, community, or country? ❓ How can I use what I'm learning in class to benefit my family, team, school, community, or country? ❓ How can I demonstrate respect for others? ❓ How can I be charitable and helpful? **PES for Students** • My team needs me, and I will do my part to help us succeed.

Students who ask questions and make statements like these grow into adults who are responsible, charitable, and helpful to their family, teams, schools, community, and country.

h) Giving Quality Performance … Not Just Being Present

To be successful in life, our youth need to learn that simply showing up at school or work and performing with mediocre effort is not good enough. Students need to understand that school success and career advancement requires that they work at their maximum potential, not just be present. We cannot afford to have young minds develop the notion that being present and going through the motions is good enough. (Teachers should avoid regularly giving students credit for simply completing tasks without assessing the quality of the students' work.)

We Should See Students Who …	PEQs for Students
👁 Perform in a way that reflects their potential, not mediocrity and simple presence	❓ Is this the best that I can do? ❓ In what ways can I maximize my potential? ❓ In what ways is simply being present not good enough for success? **PES for Students** • It's not good enough to just show up. I will work to meet my potential.

Students who ask questions and make statements like these grow into adults who give their best effort when working to accomplish tasks.

	What Should Grading Reflect?
Your Opinion	Should grading reflect: • Completion of learning activities? • Proficiency on learning activities? • Performance on authentic assessments for each topic? • Performance on assessments for a unit? • Performance on assessments at the end of the year that reflect the knowledge and skills obtained and retained? • Some combination of these?

If educators help students use the critical aspects of work ethic discussed above in the pursuit of educational successes, students can later translate these work ethic skills into real-world successes. With these work ethic skills, attitudes, and habits, kids will grow into adults who are more self-motivated and successful. (Notice that the abilities addressed in earlier chapters that dealt with critical thinking and problem solving enhance a person's ability to address the various aspects of proper work ethic. The various skills addressed in this book are highly interconnected.)

3   Adapting, Changing, and Being Versatile

In the 21st century, change is constant. There are always new technologies, new types of jobs, new circumstances in the workplace, and new circumstances in society. Thus, our youth will need to be prepared to adapt to the world around them. Workers need to quickly learn new things and then must be comfortable using them. This will allow them to be more versatile and valuable.

Critical Aspects of the Ability to Adapt to Change and be Versatile

- **Identifying New Circumstances and Expectations**
- **Acquiring the Resources and Skills Needed**
- **Finding Comfort and Confidence in Change**
- **Expecting Change**

In the previous section, we looked in-depth at how to use the four key educational strategies of Classroom Exercises, Teacher Stories / Modeling, Assessment by Students, and Curricular Examples in order to help students understand and make use of the critical aspects of "proper work ethic." Now, I will assume that readers understand how we can generally employ these strategies to promote any personal skills found in this chapter. Thus, we will not go into depth on each one. Instead, let's focus on the critical aspects of "adapting and changing" that our youth need to learn.

a) Identifying New Circumstances and Expectations

Change can be difficult, because it generally comes with new circumstances and expectations. It can happen as children change teachers and when adults change jobs. A change can occur smoothly when a person is capable of quickly identifying his or her role and expectations in a new situation. One also needs to be able to relate his or her previous encounters with change (and how he or she handled that change) to each new experience.

We Should See Students Who ...	PEQs for Students
👁 Assess the expectations of new environments and new roles 👁 Prepare for future change by learning from previous change	❓ What are the expectations in this new situation or place? ❓ What is my role in this new situation or place? ❓ What do I expect when changes occur (based on my previous experiences with changes)? **PES for Students** • I know what it takes to be successful here.

Students who ask questions and make statements like these grow into adults who recognize the expectations of their environment and adapt accordingly.

b) Acquiring the Resources and Skills Needed

Once a person understands the expectations of his or her new circumstances, he or she must acquire the resources or skills necessary for success in the new environment. These resources and skills can be found through family members, friends, the community, the internet, books, or relevant classes. Later, there will be an entire chapter (Chapter 17) on "learning how to learn."

We Should See Students Who ...	PEQs for Students
👁 Recognize which resources and skills they need 👁 Determine the best methods for obtaining needed resources and skills 👁 Take responsibility for acquiring necessary resources and skills	❓ What resources and skills do I already have? ❓ What new resources and skills do I need to be successful under these new circumstances? ❓ How and where can I acquire these new resources and skills? **PES for Students** • I have and will acquire those things that I need to be successful.

Students who ask questions and make statements like these grow into adults who assess new circumstances and set out to empower themselves for success.

c) Finding Comfort and Confidence in Change

Change can sometimes lead to anxiety. People need tools and resources for developing familiarity and confidence in change. In addition, they can find comfort in support from friends, family, educators, and community members. It is valuable for our youth to develop connections that can serve as a support system. As adults (especially in new places), it can be helpful to actively build connections that can serve as mutually supportive relationships when needed.

We Should See Students Who ...	PEQs for Students
👁 Understand their sources of anxiety	❓ What might I fear in this change?
👁 Work to gain familiarity and consistency after a change	❓ What is unfamiliar?
👁 Identify methods to handle the sources of anxiety	❓ What can I do to overcome any anxiety or unfamiliarity?
👁 Identify the reasons to be confident in change	❓ How can I get some consistency in my life?
	❓ What reasons do I have to be confident during this change?
	PESs for Students
	• I know the potential sources of anxiety and am addressing them.
	• I will make it through this change to a place of higher familiarity, consistency, and peace of mind.

Students who ask questions and make statements like these grow into adults who can work through and find confidence in change (which is ever-present in adult life).

d) Expecting Change

Even if someone does not know when or what change might come, it makes a great deal of difference to simply understand and expect that change is likely. With *proactivity*, a person can be even more prepared for both expected and unexpected change. This proactivity could take the form of constantly learning about new trends and skills in one's field of work, so that new changes are easier to handle.

We Should See Students Who ...	PEQs for Students
👁 Understand that change is common	❓ Considering the current trends, what changes are likely to occur?
👁 Expect change	❓ What changes are not likely, but could happen?
👁 Predict potential changes	❓ What do I need to do to prepare myself for potential changes?
👁 Proactively prepare for possible changes	❓ What new work and technical skills will make me more adaptable, versatile, and prepared for future circumstances?

	PES for Students
	• I know that change will come, and I am continuously preparing myself.

Students who ask questions and make statements like these grow into adults who are not surprised by change, as they view change as a regular part of life and are prepared.

By helping our students understand these critical aspects to "Adapting to Change," we are empowering them to handle change and be versatile.

Adapting to Change in a Classroom

Our youth need the ability to find comfort and ease in change. An obvious approach in the classroom to help students adapt to change is to use varying learning activities that have different styles and flex different thinking strategies. Promoting the ability to change does not mean, however, that we should have little or no structure in a classroom. A teacher must balance consistency that develops connections between students and the learning environment with activities that help students learn how to adapt to new situations. I like to keep a set of consistent routines and expectations within the classroom and then shift and tweak learning activities to keep things fresh and "changing." This helps students to both develop a sense of familiarity with the classroom environment and simultaneously develop the ability to perform tasks and learn in different ways.

Adapting to Change in a School

In order to create an environment of super consistency, administrators may be tempted to ask all teachers to generate procedures for their classrooms that are exactly the same. Under these circumstances, students would have a difficult time developing the ability to adapt to change, because every teacher would have identical classroom expectations. While it is good for schools to have general consistency in rules and policies, it is not necessarily bad for kids to find slightly different expectations from one teacher to the next. (The older the children, the better they can adapt. High school students need the most practice, because they are about to enter the real world.) As with anything, balance is necessary. In this case, the need for consistency to develop student connections to the learning environment needs to be balanced appropriately with the development of students' abilities to adapt to change.

4 Managing Stress

Domestic competition, global competition, automation due to technology, continuously shifting job needs, and generally challenging economic times will demand a great deal from our youth. They will clearly need to manage the potential stresses that can come with such challenges. We should help our children understand and make use of the critical aspects of stress management.

Critical Aspects of Stress Management

- **Addressing the Source of Stress**
- **Diffusing Stress**
- **Picking Your Battles**

a) Addressing the Source of Stress

If possible, negative stress (that affects well-being) can be reduced by dealing with the source of that stress. Students should recognize, though, that some minor forms of stress could be motivating and improve thinking. By recognizing which stresses are negative in nature, kids can learn to address their root causes. For some students, addressing sources of stress could be as simple as getting more sleep, setting a test reminder alarm on a smartphone, or using a planner. For others, stress sources could be much more complex and require the help of parents, teachers, and counselors.

We Should See Students Who ...	PEQs for Students
👁 Identify their sources of stress 👁 Minimize or compartmentalize their sources of negative stress 👁 Recognize beneficial minor stresses and channel them into sources of positive performance	❓ What is causing this stress? ❓ Can I reduce or eliminate the sources of stress? ❓ Can I compartmentalize the sources of stress in order to keep them from affecting other parts of my life? ❓ Can I use some stresses to perform better? **PESs for Students** • I am finding ways to reduce sources of negative stress. • I am using certain minor stresses to my advantage.

Students who ask questions and make statements like these grow into adults who can identify and minimize the stresses that can inhibit their performance and happiness in life and who use minor stresses to their advantage.

b) Diffusing Stress

Sometimes, sources of stress cannot be reduced. Then, people must be armed with the ability to diffuse their stress by doing relaxing activities, creating relaxing environments, or shifting attention away from the sources of stress.

We Should See Students Who ...	PEQs for Students
👁 Engage in relaxing activities 👁 Create a relaxing environment 👁 Shift their attention away from	❓ What activities make me happy / relaxed? ❓ What environment and people reduce my stress?

15 - Personal Skills, Attitudes, and Habits

sources of stress	What can I do to shift my attention away from this stress?
	PES for Students
	• I know how to let things go and find relaxation.

Students who ask questions and make statements like these grow into adults who can relax and decompress when they are stressed.

c) Picking Your Battles

Sometimes, people become stressed over circumstances that are not too important in the larger picture of their lives. Thus, students should learn to determine the validity of various sources of stress so that they can learn to worry less about "problems" that are not as important as others or worry less about circumstances that are out of their control. Students need to learn to pick their battles.

We Should See Students Who ...	PEQs for Students
👁 Assess the importance of stress sources in the bigger picture of their lives	❓ How important to me is this problem?
	❓ Is this issue worth worrying about?
👁 Recognize what they can and cannot control	❓ What is or is not in my control?
	❓ Is worrying about this issue helping me or changing anything? If not, should I let it go?
	PES for Students
	• I know which things are not truly worthy of creating stress. I let them go.

Students who ask questions and make statements like these grow into adults who focus their attention on problems and circumstances that are important and can be changed rather than becoming stressed over small concerns or unchangeable circumstances.

If educators help their students learn the skills above to deal with the stresses the students might encounter, then the youngsters will be more prepared to deal with the stresses of a very complex and challenging world.

 ## 5 | Being Organized and Efficient

Organization and efficiency are skills that can help students succeed. Also, these skills are very valuable in the work world. Doctors, engineers, store owners, store workers, and teachers are all more likely to be successful if they are organized and efficient. They can make the best use of their time and resources to maximize the quality of their products and services. Let's promote these skills and habits in our classrooms.

Critical Aspects of Organization and Efficiency

- **Focusing on Goals and Making Plans**
- **Managing Time**
- **Managing Resources for Organization and Efficiency**

a) Focusing on Goals and Making Plans

People generally have a difficult time being organized and efficient when performing tasks if they are not focused on goals. Focus allows us to make appropriate plans for success rather than doing frivolous things that may not help us attain our goals. With goals, we can create and follow an organized plan of action.

We Should See Students Who ...	PEQs for Students
👁 Focus on goals	❓ What do I want to achieve?
👁 Create manageable plans for attaining goals	❓ What actions must I take to achieve my goals?
👁 Avoid actions that detract from or are unimportant in achieving goals	❓ What actions tend to lead me away from following my plans of action and away from achieving my goals?
	PES for Students
	• I make plans and take actions that actually lead to my goals.

Students who ask questions and make statements like these grow into adults who identify goals and make plans that will allow them to work in an organized and efficient manner.

b) Managing Time

To maximize the results of their work, people must be able to make the best use of the time available. This requires them to proactively look forward to determine what and when things need to be done. For example, a simple, effective time management strategy one can employ is the use of a planner to set goals for completing tasks. Teachers can also encourage students to use the alarm notification and calendar/list functions on their mobile devices to help them prioritize tasks and alert themselves to important events.

We Should See Students Who ...	PEQs for Students
👁 Proactively plan time for the tasks that will lead to success, so they don't wait and hope things fall into place	❓ What tasks do I need to accomplish and when can I do them?
👁 Prioritize their tasks	❓ What are my priorities?
👁 Make time to finish important tasks	❓ How can I create the necessary time for my tasks?
👁 Efficiently use their time	❓ How can I most efficiently use the time

👁 Use tools for time management (planner, electronic device) 👁 Monitor their progress and modify plans as needed	available? ❓ Should I multitask to get more than one thing done at a time? ❓ What tools can I use to help manage my time? ❓ How will I know that I am on track to achieve my goals? ❓ Considering my current progress, do my plans need to be modified? **PES for Students** • Due to my organized and efficient use of time, I can accomplish all of my goals.

Students who ask questions and make statements like these grow into adults who use their time wisely and work efficiently toward their goals.

c) Managing Resources for Organization and Efficiency

To maximize potential results, people must be able to assess what resources (such as tools, strategies, or helpers) are available and how to use them wisely. Teachers can discuss and model the use of resources in an efficient manner.

We Should See Students Who ...	PEQs for Students
👁 Seek available resources for accomplishing tasks 👁 Assess which resources are best for accomplishing their goals 👁 Gain organization and efficiency through the use of available resources 👁 Assess the effectiveness of the resources they use	❓ What tasks do I need to accomplish? ❓ What resources are available, and what resources will best help me perform my tasks? ❓ Who can help me in accomplishing my goals? ❓ What will be the most efficient use of my resources? ❓ Is there an easier way to do this task? ❓ What resources are actually helping, and what resources can I do without? **PES for Students** • With the proper strategies and tools, I can efficiently manage tasks as I work toward my goals.

Students who ask questions and make statements like these grow into adults who seek out and use the best resources for maximizing their organization and efficiency.

> ## Go Beyond Telling about Organization and Efficiency ... Build Kids Toward These Goals

When promoting the various aspects of organization and efficiency in the classroom, it can be helpful to use schedules and planners, while stimulating students to think about the ways in which these tools are used to manage time and resources. We have to go one step further, though. Some kids might understand the various facets of organization and efficiency, but not take the time to put this understanding into action. Kids might have a planner, but not use it. They also might know that time management is important, but not practice it.

For these reasons, educators can provide various forms of motivation and stimulus that encourage students to be proactive and responsible. We can give them tasks during class time that require them to write information in a planner, organize classroom work into a folder, or use their class time wisely. The use of rewards and consequences to motivate these actions can be useful.

Over time, students should build toward more independence in their organization. The goal is for them to eventually self-organize. They just might need a little stimulus to get there.

> ## Careers in Efficiency

Before moving on, we should take note of the fact that while resource management is a great skill for anyone in any career, there are likely to be new jobs that specifically deal with resource management. In *The World is Flat*, Friedman points out that "When three billion people from China, India, and the former Soviet Empire walk onto the flat-world platform in a very short period of time, and every one of them wants a house, a car, a microwave, and a refrigerator, if we don't learn how to do more things with less energy and fewer emissions, we are going to create an environmental disaster and make our planet unlivable for our children. So there are going to be a lot of jobs involving the words 'sustainable' and 'renewable' ..."[24] The more the economies of the world grow, the greater will be the demands on our resources. Teaching our kids about resource management can go far beyond teaching them about wise use of time and resources in class. We can teach them about the efficient use of the Earth's natural resources and the future jobs that could develop that deal with resource usage. This would provide a real-world and engaging method of teaching about efficiency.

Organization and Efficiency Help with Other Skills, Attitudes, and Habits

Side Note

To wrap things up, let's take note of the fact that improved organization and efficiency skills within our students' everyday activities help students with other skills, such as stress management, competition, work ethic, and adapting to change. Again, many of the skills that our youth need are interrelated.

---

[24] (Friedman, 2005, page 293)

15 - Personal Skills, Attitudes, and Habits

6   Behaving in an Ethical Manner that Shows Integrity

To empower our youth and our society for the 21ˢᵗ century, we can promote ethical and principled behaviors that show integrity. If our youth behave with integrity, they will enjoy meaningful lives in their careers and with their families and friends.

We Should See Students Who ...	PEQs for Students
👁 Behave ethically and show integrity	❓ What is ethical behavior?
👁 Have principles for behavior to which they adhere	❓ What are my principles for behavior?
👁 Consider the effects of their actions on others	❓ How do my actions affect other people?
👁 Do not cheat	❓ Why will cheating hurt me in the long run?
👁 Work hard without taking unethical shortcuts	❓ Why would it be unfair to my peers if I were to cheat?
	❓ Why is it important to work hard for the things I would like to achieve, rather than taking unethical shortcuts?
	PES for Students
	• Because of my ethical behavior and integrity, I can be proud of my actions, and I can earn peoples' trust.

Students who ask questions and make statements like these grow into adults who behave with integrity and who can feel proud of their achievements and positive relationships.

7   Assessing Risks when Making Complex Decisions

In life, there will be various situations in which our youth will have to weigh the pros and cons of potential decisions in order to assess the risks involved. In these situations, our students will need to make challenging decisions with rational thinking. There are opportunities in all classes to challenge students to make complex decisions. Students can develop ideas about what should (or should have been) done by politicians, historical figures, scientists, characters in stories, etc. Case studies provide students opportunities to consider a situation from various angles and develop a plan or point of view.

We Should See Students Who ...	PEQs for Students
👁 Carefully consider the pros and cons of potential decisions	❓ What are the potential positive and negative outcomes that could result from my potential decisions?
👁 Weigh the risks of their choices	
👁 Think rationally when making complex and consequential decisions	❓ What do I want to accomplish, and is it likely that some courses of action are too risky?
👁 Do not make hasty choices	❓ Am I thinking carefully about this important decision?
👁 Make responsible decisions and take responsible risks	❓ Who might have experiences with this type of choice, and can he or she give me advice?

	❓ Am I rushing into this decision, or am I carefully weighing my options?
	❓ Who could be affected by my decision?
	❓ Considering my goals and the potential consequences of my actions, am I making a responsible decision?
	PESs for Students
	• I carefully and rationally consider the potential risks along with the potential rewards when making complex decisions.
	• I make responsible decisions and take responsible risks.

Students who ask questions and make statements like these grow into adults who carefully think before acting, make responsible decisions, and take responsible risks.

8   Being Financially Literate in Personal and Professional Life

In the real world, there are numerous financial decisions that adults must make. Unfortunately, there are a large number of financial concepts that are not generally taught in schools, but have important implications for the life of citizens. To empower our students, these ideas should be taught. (Most of these concepts are more appropriate for secondary students, but the foundation for them can be laid in earlier schooling.) These could be blended into various classes with a focus on math and social studies.

We Should See Students Who ...	PEQs for Students
👁 Work toward financial security throughout life	❓ How can I responsibly save or invest my money throughout life?
👁 Prepare to be financially secure in retirement	❓ How do I save for retirement? What is a 401(k)? What are stocks, mutual funds, bonds, and property investments? How does Social Security work? What is a pension?
👁 Understand how to avoid unnecessary debt	
👁 Understand what insurance options are available and can decide which options best suit their needs	❓ How can I avoid unnecessary debt?
	❓ What types of insurance are available, and what do I need? What is life insurance? What is disability insurance?
👁 Understand the tax system	
👁 Understand basically how to create a business and employ others	❓ How do I pay my taxes? What are property taxes, and who assesses them? How do I pay federal tax? What is an exemption or a deduction?
👁 Understand the options available for acquiring mortgages and loans	
👁 Can determine the best options for transportation and housing	❓ How can I start my own business? What licenses are involved? What laws must I consider? How do I go about employing people?
👁 Can see the big picture of their finances and relate it to their financial goals	
👁 Shift their financial strategies as their	❓ What is a mortgage, and how do I get a

lives change	mortgage? What is a thirty-year fixed mortgage versus a five-year ARM mortgage? **?** Should I buy a home or rent a home? **?** Should I buy a car, lease a car, or use public transportation? **?** What are my overall financial goals, and where do I stand in attaining those goals? **?** What should I be doing right now to achieve my goals for financial security? **PESs for Students** • I understand how to manage my financial resources in a responsible manner. • I know the ways in which I can work toward financial growth and stability.

Students who ask questions and make statements like these grow into adults who create financial goals, work toward those goals, and become financially secure?

Example

Topics such as those above can sound intimidating and complex … maybe too complex for our youth. The truth is that there are interesting ways in which these skills can be woven into our current curricula. My algebra teacher in high school asked us to solve a problem in which a person was not sure whether to save money and then buy a home or to get a mortgage and immediately purchase the home. We did a cost-benefit analysis using the appropriate algebra skills. Not only did this problem fit smoothly into the curriculum, it also made class more interesting, engaging, and "real world." Our youth will definitely deal with these topics someday. If we prepare them, they will be empowered.

Personal Skills: Wrap-up

The personal skills addressed in this chapter do not generally appear in an official school curriculum, but are critical for students to function in the 21st century. By helping our students obtain these abilities, we are giving them the tools to thrive in a quickly-changing world where dedicated and effective individuals are in demand.

Goals are Essential in Personal Skills

After discussing the various types of "personal skills," it becomes obvious that there are some common themes running through all of them. To be successful in each, students and adults need to consider their goals in various situations. Then, they need to ask themselves what steps they must take in order to achieve their goals. Because of this, we can see the value of promoting goal-oriented behaviors in schools. In this practice, children set goals for themselves and determine reasonable paths for achieving these goals. Along the way, they develop the ability to self-assess, manage challenges, and modify their course.

Thinking About It

- What are the biggest challenges for students in developing personal skills?
- Which personal skills do you believe are most lacking among students?
- What strategies have you seen that work well in developing students' personal skills?
- How can you promote the various personal skills described within this chapter?

How Does This Chapter Support the Goals of This Book?

Let's take a moment to think about the ways in which the ideas of this chapter help us address the three main goals of this book by looking at the "Building Blocks of a 21st Century Education" on page 13 and the "Daily Thoughts for Educators" on page 18. We now have tools and strategies for empowering our youth by developing their personal skills, attitudes, and habits.

Make Note of Your Great Ideas!

If you haven't already, note your ideas for implementing the strategies in this chapter in your Teacher Empowerment Menu (for 21st Century Educators). In the future, you can easily reference usable ideas for your class.

In addition, consider the ways in which you can stimulate students to develop their personal skills, attitudes, and habits by using the Personal Empowerment Menu (for 21st Century Students), which contains the relevant PEQs, PESs, and assessment rubrics for this chapter.

Goal #2

21st Century Challenge – Part 4

Develop Technological and Media Literacy (Ch. 16)

Technological and informational literacy will allow our students to thrive in a new world rather than become a victim in it. This chapter will continue our promotion of a 21st Century Challenge by addressing the development of 21st century technical and media literacy skills while learning the curriculum.

While Learning the Curriculum, Develop:				
Ability to Connect the Curriculum to the Real World Ch. 3	*Higher Order Thinking Skills* (includes Critical Thinking, Problem Solving, and Creativity) Ch. 11-13	*Social and Personal Skills, Attitudes, and Habits* Ch. 14-15	*Technological and Media Literacy* Ch. 16	*Ability to Learn* (includes Inquiry and Student-Centered Learning) Ch. 17

21st Century Challenge

16 | Technological and Media Literacy

Clearly, new technologies have shifted the job market. They put us into closer contact and into greater competition with people from all over our country and our world. We also have greater contact and competition with automated machines than ever before. Technology has drastically changed the ways in which we do business, communicate, learn and study, collect data, and so much more. New and rapidly changing technological tools are deeply interwoven within our workplace and personal lives. A grocery clerk monitors and controls self-checkout machines. A doctor uses a handheld PC to update medical records stored electronically. A mother uses a cell phone to order an airline ticket to visit her daughter. A small business owner uses a website to attract, retain, and sell his or her product or service to customers. A company uses new software to teleconference with and integrate the work of people around the world. Our youth must become technologically literate by learning to effectively, efficiently, and securely use many amazing tools.

In addition, students need to develop the ability to assess the accuracy of content on the Internet, maintain privacy online, and assess the potential social safety hazards of the Internet.

To help our youth in the 21st century, we must challenge them in the regular curriculum to develop the following skills.

Technological and Media Literacy

1. **Using Technology and Media in the Real World**
   (for communication, presentation, organization, research / education, self and team promotion, design, and consumption)
2. **Using Informational Literacy Skills to Assess the Accuracy of Content from the Internet and Other Forms of Media**
3. **Maintaining Safety and Privacy While Using the Internet**
4. **Recognizing the Future Implications of Internet Usage**

As with other educational goals, we must help our students become technologically literate by using the four key educational strategies of Classroom Exercises, Teacher Stories / Modeling, Assessment by Students, and Curricular Examples.

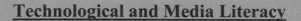 **Using Technology and Media in the Real World**

16 · Technological and Media Literacy

A variety of technological tools can be used for practical purposes in the real world. These tools can be broken into categories based on their use.

<u>Types of Technological and Media Tools</u>

- **Communicating and Collaborating**
- **Presenting and Modeling**
- **Being Organized and Efficient**
- **Researching and Learning**
- **Promoting Oneself** (Resumes, Portfolios, and Networking)
- **Promoting an Organization** (Networking, Advertising, and Selling)
- **Consuming Goods and Services**
- **Designing Programs, Objects, Tools, and Processes**

Our youth need to learn why and how the tools in each of these categories are used in real life (and also discover how fun the tools can be).

a) Communicating and Collaborating

In the world that our children face, people are and will be using advanced communication tools such as email, text messages, blogs, wikis, teleconferencing, and social networking websites and apps. Without literacy in the use of these tools, our youth will be at a great disadvantage to those who can use the tools more quickly and more efficiently. Thus, any experiences using these technologies would be beneficial for our pupils.

Students need to develop an understanding of how they can use these communication tools in the real world to enhance processes, rather than simply seeing the tools as useful for talking with friends.

Beyond learning how to use technological tools for communication and collaboration, our youth need to learn to use these tools *appropriately*. A growing concern for communication tools is that children are developing habits that do not reflect proper communication etiquette for formal situations. While communicating with friends, many youngsters use acronyms and abbreviations in text messages and in email messages, while others completely ignore grammatical rules. While this does not seem like a big deal among friends, the misuse of proper grammar and professional etiquette can carry over into more formal technological communications. Children need to develop an understanding of what is proper etiquette when using technology on the job, in search of a job, or in other formal situations. They must be taught that the manner in which they communicate shapes other people's perceptions. (Our youth also need to understand that it is not appropriate in some situations to have beeping cell phones or to answer them.) Again, their behavior can shape other people's perceptions.

16 - Technological and Media Literacy

We Should See Students Who ...	Personal Empowerment Questions PEQs for Students
👁 Use technological tools to communicate and collaborate 👁 Recognize the efficiency and value of technological tools for communicating ideas and collaborating as a team 👁 Recognize and use an appropriate level of formality and etiquette in communication	❓ What goals am I trying to accomplish, and what communication and collaboration tools can help me achieve my goals quicker, more efficiently, and with higher quality? ❓ How can tools (email, text messages, blogs, wikis, social networks, and teleconferences) be used to enhance learning (as a student) or enhance products or services (as an adult)? ❓ How would professionals use this technological tool? ❓ Who is my audience in this communication? ❓ What are the social expectations in this situation, and how should I communicate and behave? ❓ What does my style of communication suggest about me? **Personal Empowerment Statements PESs for Students** • I use technology to efficiently and effectively communicate and collaborate. • I understand and use the proper communication style and etiquette to suit my digital audience.

Students who ask questions and make statements like these grow into adults who properly use technological tools to improve communication of ideas and to collaborate.

b) Presenting and Modeling

In virtually all professions, people present information for a purpose, such as advertising, selling, teaching, modeling a product or process, or persuading. Our students surely need literacy in technological tools for accomplishing such tasks in effective, efficient, and sensory-pleasing ways. It can be very helpful to understand how to use presentation tools, such as slideshow presentation programs, word processing programs, basic Internet webpage design tools, podcasting tools, video design programs, newsletter publishing programs, and social-networking internet pages. These tools are used in the real world to create displays in stores, present information to clients, or build business websites.

To help our youth develop these real-world skills, we can ask them to make presentations in school using these technological tools. We must go a little further, though, to help them understand which technological tools are best for each job.

We Should See Students Who ...	PEQs for Students
👁 Use presentation tools to communicate information, present ideas, model processes, and describe products 👁 Recognize which tools work best in various situations 👁 Engage their audience with technological tools	❓ What are my goals in this presentation? ❓ Who is my audience? ❓ What key pieces of information do I want to convey? ❓ What technological tool will best accomplish my goals? ❓ How will I grab attention and keep it using technological tools? **PES for Students** • My technological presentations both engage and inform my audience.

Students who ask questions and make statements like these grow into adults who make use of appropriate and engaging tools to communicate information and ideas.

c) Being Organized and Efficient

Technological tools can be very useful for organization and efficiency. A medical researcher can organize and easily access data using a spreadsheet program. A small business owner can keep track of transactions with an accounting program. Anyone with a computer can prepare his or her taxes using a tax preparation program. A teacher can track student progress using an educational data program or grade book program. Children can be better prepared for the adult world if they understand how to use basic organizational programs.

We Should See Students Who ...	PEQs for Students
👁 Determine what objects or information need to be organized or what processes need to be more efficient 👁 Pick the best technological tool for the job 👁 Consistently use their tools for organization and efficiency	❓ What information or process do I need to organize? ❓ In what areas can I become more efficient? ❓ What technological tool(s) can help me achieve my organizational and efficiency goals? ❓ How will I stimulate myself to consistently use the technology? **PES for Students** • My use of technology allows me to be more efficient and productive.

Students who ask questions and make statements like these grow into adults who maximize their speed and organization through the use of technological tools.

d) Researching and Learning

Today, technology can be used in research, learning, and forming new opinions. The Internet and various computer programs open many opportunities for gathering information in ways never before imagined. We can create technological and informational literacy by using these learning tools in our classrooms. Such technologies are perfect for inquiry-based learning in which students seek out and find useful information, such as through web quests. (There are pitfalls to Internet research, which we will address later.) Furthermore, we can help our students find and access learning tutorials.

We Should See Students Who ...	PEQs for Students
👁 Learn using technology 👁 Research using technology 👁 Ask questions and seek answers with the help of technology	❓ What technological tool will help me access the correct information and learn what I want or need to know? ❓ What shortcuts or tricks can help me more efficiently use this learning tool? ❓ What can I learn using this tool? **PES for Students** • With technology, I am able to unlock the answers to a seemingly infinite number of questions.

Students who ask questions and make statements like these grow into adults who easily and independently learn new skills and information using technological tools.

e) Promoting Oneself (Resumes, Portfolios, and Networking)

Many technological tools can be very valuable in self-promotion. When people are seeking jobs, they can create resumes, websites, electronic portfolios, videos, etc. Students will benefit from learning how to use technologies to create these job-seeking tools.

There are also many online tools for networking. Rather than simply seeing all of these technological tools as "neat technologies for interacting," students need to develop an understanding of how these tools can be used for self-promotion in attaining jobs, customers, or clients. Without using modern technological tools in self-promotion, our youth will be at a disadvantage.

To develop students' skills in technologically-based self-promotion, they can develop a digital portfolio of their work and assessments. This could be a website, wiki, blog, etc. that allows students to digitally display the work (such as writings, digital presentations, or video productions) they produced for their classes. The students could include descriptions of the concepts and skills they learned from each digital activity. (If each student in a school was asked to create a digital portfolio of their digital assignments from all classes, it might encourage teachers to assign such beneficial assignments.)

We Should See Students Who ...	PEQs for Students
👁 Use technological tools in self-promotion to acquire jobs, clients, and customers	❓ What technological tools are available for self-promotion? ❓ How can I use technological tools to create a great resume, portfolio, website, and/or video in order to impress potential employers? ❓ How can I use technological tools to network in order to acquire a job, clients, and customers? **PES for Students** • Technology empowers me to network and promote myself in many ways.

Students who ask questions and make statements like these grow into adults who advocate for themselves with the help of technological tools and resources.

f) Promoting an Organization (Networking, Advertising, and Selling)

Organizations, such as businesses, clubs, charities, and political organizations, can use technological tools to promote themselves. A group can use the Internet to find and attract customers, clients, organization members, and voters. Being on the cutting edge of new technological tools can be the key to success for an organization.

Schools can model this organizational promotion for students by using technological tools, such as school or teacher Facebook® pages, websites, or blogs, to promote school activities and successes.

We Should See Students Who ...	PEQs for Students
👁 Use technological tools in organizational promotion to network, advertise, and sell products and services	❓ What technological tools are available for promoting our organization, networking, advertising, or selling our products and services? ❓ How can we use these technological tools to acquire and maintain customers, clients, members, or voters? **PES for Students** • With technology, we can reach a wider audience for our organization.

Students who ask questions and make statements like these grow into adults who advocate for organizations with the help of technological tools and resources.

g) Consuming Goods and Services

Modern technology allows people to quickly access a variety of services and products from around our country and around the world. If students understand how to access these services and products in their future private and professional lives, they will be able to function in an efficient, cost-effective, and satisfying manner. In their lives, our youth will benefit from being able to use the Internet to locate products, compare quality, make purchases, and plan travel.

We Should See Students Who ...	PEQs for Students
👁 Use technology to identify, compare, evaluate, and purchase products and services 👁 Use technological tools for efficient consumption	❓ What technological tools can I use to find and purchase the products and services I need or want? ❓ How can I evaluate the quality of various products that I find? ❓ Which technological tools will save me money and time? **PES for Students** • With technology, I am an empowered consumer.

Students who ask questions and make statements like these grow into adults who are efficient and informed consumers of goods and services.

h) Designing Programs, Objects, Tools, and Processes

With lessons in basic programming tools, students can design their own computer programs. With lessons in the use of CAD (computer aided design) programs, students can design and model objects. With lessons in animation programs, students can design and model processes. All of these designing skills will have great value in the future job market.

Realistically, not all students will be able to fit programming, animation design, and CAD classes into their educational career. However, students who learn all the technological uses in the categories above will have many opportunities to design through the use of presentation, communication, and organizational tools, such as basic web page, presentation, and spreadsheet design.

We Should See Students Who ...	PEQs for Students
👁 Create useful programs or websites that can be used as tools for accomplishing tasks 👁 Design and model objects and processes using technological tools	❓ How can I achieve my goals with the design of a program or website? ❓ How can I use technology to design objects and processes? ❓ How can I use technology to represent (or model) my objects and processes? **PES for Students** • I can use technology to design.

Students who ask questions and make statements like these grow into adults who use technology to design programs, objects, tools, and processes.

Students who become proficient in the uses of technology described in the categories above will be very competitive, efficient, productive, and successful in the current and future economy.

The Real-World Value of Technology

Students need to develop an understanding of how they can use technological tools in the real world. When giving an assignment that requires members of a class to present information using a technological tool, an educator should help them see the real-world value of the tool. Beyond helping them in their future, this strategy can help students see the value of their classroom activities and increase motivation.

Speaking of motivation, the weaving of technology into everyday classroom activities should be a welcome prospect for educators. Children are naturally drawn to technological tools. The use of these tools can instantly increase focus and classroom engagement.

Don't Fear Technology and Don't Assume Everyone Can Already Use It

Even if a teacher does not feel comfortable with all of these technological tools, he or she can still promote the use of these tools within the classroom. Often, there will be a number of students who understand how to use various technological tools and who can serve as mentors to others. Groups can be formed around technological "mentors."

Because there are youngsters who know how to use technology, it can be a common mistake to assume that all of the students know how to use the various technologies available (leading a teacher to not worry about using the technology in the classroom). While some might know more than many adults, others might not have had any exposure to various technologies. Educators should keep this in mind and provide opportunities to use technological tools whenever appropriate.

Money

When some educators set out to use technological tools with students, there is an obvious roadblock … money. These educators need to get creative. They can apply for grants to get technology. They can also seek donated computers from local businesses. (Even if the technological tools are not top-of-the-line, they are better than nothing.) Considering the world in which our youth will have to thrive, we might have to get creative in order to prepare our students.

Whether a school has a bounty or a minimum of technology, the goal should be the same … students need to develop technological literacy that they can apply in the future. This will allow them to learn and adapt to new technologies that arise over time.

Using Informational Literacy Skills to Assess the Accuracy of Content from the Internet and Other Forms of Media

The seemingly infinite amount of information that comes from the Internet and other media sources has great potential for empowering our children and adults. It also creates some challenges. One challenge is assessing the accuracy of information found in various media sources. There are blogs on which people portray opinions as facts. There are websites that

Side Notes

16 - Technological and Media Literacy

promote conspiracy theories based on partial truths and sometimes ignorant perceptions of history and science. There are even seemingly reputable web pages that give "facts" that are not true. There are television shows that promote particular points of view. To be a healthy consumer of the vast information available on the Internet and from other media sources, our youth need to be able to assess the accuracy of the information that they find. They need to be able to recognize when something is biased, pushing an agenda, lacking in all of the facts, or presenting an opinion as a fact.

In any content area, this skill can be simply interwoven within research activities. Teachers can give students the task of assessing the validity of certain sources that they or educators find online.

We Should See Students Who ...	PEQs for Students
👁 Look for bias 👁 Verify "facts" 👁 Discern opinion from fact 👁 Seek opposing opinions 👁 Have critical eyes when consuming information	❓ What are the goals of the people who publish this information? ❓ Do the authors have a potential bias or agenda? ❓ What proof or research is presented? ❓ Is there an opinion or a fact being presented? ❓ Where can I learn about an opposing opinion? ❓ What are some clues that might make me think that this is or is not a reputable web page? ❓ What sources can I use to check the accuracy of this information? **PESs for Students** • I know how to assess the accuracy of things I encounter in various forms of media (Internet, news, TV, etc.). • I do not simply accept everything I see or hear from various media sources, and I attempt to seek the truth.

Students who ask questions and make statements like these grow into adults who are critical and logical consumers of information.

3 ⭐ Maintaining Safety and Privacy While Using the Internet

Another challenge when using the Internet is social safety and privacy. The vast connectivity of the web provides an avenue for stealing personal information, predatory acts, scams, and privacy invasion. Our students need to understand how to safeguard their privacy and avoid technological assaults against them.

We Should See Students Who ...	PEQs for Students
👁 Are aware of the potential techniques used by those who scam, invade privacy, and steal personal information (identity fraud) 👁 Protect their private information through careful technology use and defensive technological tools	❓ Who has access to my personal information, and can I trust them? ❓ What signals indicate that I am encountering a scam? ❓ How can I identify a "sketchy" website? ❓ What technologies are available to aid me in online protection (such as identity theft protection or Internet security software)? ❓ What actions should I take when using technology to keep myself safe? ❓ What information do I find if I perform an Internet search of my own name? **PES for Students** • I am very careful to keep my identity and privacy safe when using technology.

Students who ask questions and make statements like these grow into adults who assess situations to find potential technological safety and privacy risks.

4 Recognizing the Future Implications of Internet Usage

The past follows one on the Internet. There are many instances when employers might enter a potential employee's name into an Internet search engine. This can bring up all kinds of information about that person's life. The potential employer can be led to a Facebook® page, a news article, or any number of online information resources. Our youth need to be aware of how each action that they take (on and off the Internet) and the people with whom they associate online can affect them in the future.

We Should See Students Who ...	PEQs for Students
👁 Consider the future implications of their actions 👁 Give careful thought to what is appropriate and wise to post on the Internet	❓ How will this action potentially affect me and others in the future? ❓ Who might someday use technology to gain access to this information? ❓ Will this information help me or harm me? ❓ Will this information help others or harm others? **PESs for Students** • What I place on the Internet today can affect me and others for many years to come. • I am very careful to use technological tools in such a way that I leave a trail of information of which I can be proud.

Students who ask questions and make statements like these grow into adults who hopefully have not taken actions on and off the Internet that are damaging to themselves and others.

Technology and Media Literacy: Wrap-up

In a world like ours, technology is becoming essential for many tasks. Without high-level technological skills, our youth will be ill-equipped for the world that awaits them. We must set out to help them develop the technological literacy described above. There are some additional considerations with this topic.

Managing Student Technology Use

While it is essential for our students to develop technological literacy, there are some challenges that educators need to manage. Youngsters sometimes misuse technology. If a teacher assigns an Internet activity, students may be tempted to get off-task and visit web pages that are not related to the assignment. Luckily, educators can stay one step ahead of students by employing the proper technology. My school acquired a program that allows teachers to use a teacher computer in order to monitor all of the students' computer screens in a computer lab. The program also allows teachers to enable only specific programs and web pages on the student computers. This can keep children from straying off-task.

Unfortunately, teachers recognize that new technological tools provide new possibilities for dishonest behavior. Text messaging phones, camera phones, and MP3 players make it easier to transmit information about tests from one student to another. Educators need to be aware of these possibilities and implement guidelines to deal with them.

Teacher Use of Technology

Just like their students, educators should model the use of technological tools for *communication, presentation, organization, research / education, self-promotion, and design*.

Class web pages and email can enhance communication with parents. To further promote communication, teachers can use an online grading system so parents and students can access their grades and assessment information.

Presentation software, such as PowerPoint®, can allow an educator to engage the class during a lesson or activity. These presentations can include pictures, animations, and video clips.

Another engaging technology is a class blog on which students post comments online. Blogs can promote quality communication, explaining, tact, analysis, and assessment skills. There are free and easy-to-use blog services available online.

The Internet also allows members of a class to collaborate with each other. A great way to accomplish this is with the use of wikis, which are web pages on which anyone can add content. Additionally, the members of a wiki can modify and delete previously added content. This format allows children to collaborate on a project in cyberspace. There are free wiki resources online that allow participants to add text, pictures, video clips, and other files.

To aid in assessment, educators can use classroom response technology (wireless response "clicker" devices that allow students to answer questions from their seats). Even without a set of classroom response "clickers," students can be surveyed using text-messaging. Using free online resources, teachers can ask questions that students answer with text messages. The results of the responses can be displayed in real time. With both classroom response clickers and text-message surveying, data analysis tools allow educators to collect formative assessment data on individual students and classes.

Today, personal digital devices allow students access to a great variety of useful content. They can download e-books from public libraries (for free) to be read on e-book readers, tablet PCs, or smartphones. By showing kids that they can use technology to access e-books, we overcome the challenge that kids might perceive paper books to be "old-fashioned." In addition, students can use their digital devices to access apps that can enhance their development of science, math, health, art, and social studies knowledge and skills. These resources can serve to differentiate instruction to help learners who are either advanced or struggling.

In order to maximize their teaching effectiveness, educators need to keep up with the newest technologies. This requires that teachers engage in professional development in order to keep up to speed … just like anybody else who wants to stay on top in the 21ˢᵗ century. Teachers might feel out of their comfort zone as they continuously use new and useful educational technologies. Surely this unease can be overcome if educators stay on top of new trends and also when new technologies actually free up class time as tasks are done more efficiently and effectively.

Who knows … maybe someday teachers will have paperless classrooms in which students work on electronic writing tablets and information is transferred wirelessly. Just like our students, we have to be literate in the use of the technologies of today in order to be ready for the technologies of tomorrow. As technologies advance, we have to be ready to take advantage of the potential benefits created by new learning tools.

Thinking About It

- **How comfortable are you in using technology in your personal life and teaching?**
- **What new technological skills would you like to obtain?**
- **What technological resources are available in your educational setting and what resources would you like to obtain?**
- **In what ways can you empower your students with technological literacy?**

How Does This Chapter Support the Goals of This Book?

Let's take a moment to think about the ways in which the ideas of this chapter help us address the three main goals of this book by looking at the "Building Blocks of a 21st Century Education" on page 13 and the "Daily Thoughts for Educators" on page 18. We now have tools and strategies for empowering our youth by developing their technological and media literacy.

Make Note of Your Great Ideas!

If you haven't already, note your ideas for implementing the strategies in this chapter in your Teacher Empowerment Menu (for 21st Century Educators). In the future, you can easily reference usable ideas for your class.

In addition, consider the ways in which you can stimulate students to develop their technological and media literacy by using the Personal Empowerment Menu (for 21st Century Students), which contains the relevant PEQs, PESs, and assessment rubric for this chapter.

Goal #2

21st Century Challenge – Part 5

Develop the Ability to Learn (Ch. 17)

We will now finish our dissection of the 21st Century Challenge by addressing the development of students' ability to learn. Our goal is to engage students in student-centered learning activities that teach the curriculum and develop students' learning skills. By developing our youth's ability to learn, we challenge them in a manner that is relevant to the 21st century.

While Learning the Curriculum, Develop:				
Ability to Connect the Curriculum to the Real World Ch. 3	*Higher Order Thinking Skills* (includes Critical Thinking, Problem Solving, and Creativity) Ch. 11-13	*Social and Personal Skills, Attitudes, and Habits* Ch. 14-15	*Technological and Media Literacy* Ch. 16	*Ability to Learn* (includes Inquiry and Student-Centered Learning) Ch. 17

21st Century Challenge

17 Learning How to Learn

As educators, we must help our students learn how to learn new information and skills by developing their independence as learners. In *The World is Flat*, Friedman goes so far as to say, "The first, and most important, ability you can develop in a flat world is the ability to 'learn how to learn' - to constantly absorb, and teach yourself, new ways of doing old things or new ways of doing new things. This is an ability every worker should cultivate in an age when parts or all of many jobs are constantly going to be exposed to digitization, automation, and outsourcing, and where new jobs, and whole new industries, will be churned up faster and faster. In such a world, it is not only what you know but how you learn that will set you apart."[25]

We cannot assume that simply because students are in our classrooms and learning new information that they are learning how to learn … at least in a way that will help them in their futures. We must remember that in the real world, there will be no teachers to provide new information or strategies for accomplishing tasks on a daily basis. Sometimes, there might be a mentor, but not always. Our youth will be ill-prepared if their only ability to learn centers around sitting in front of a teacher, listening, and regurgitating information. In the real world, people often need the ability to develop an understanding of new concepts *on their own*. They need to both connect new understanding to prior knowledge and to use it in new ways for practical purposes.

To provide a 21st Century Challenge for our students, we must teach our curriculum in a way that promotes the following important aspects of learning how to learn.

Developing the Ability to Learn

Students need to develop the skills, habits, and attitudes of …

1. **Learning Through Inquiry**
2. **Activating and Building on Prior Knowledge**
3. **Constructing the Learning of New Concepts Piece by Piece**
4. **Using New Learning for Real-World Tasks**
5. **Making Personal Connections with New Learning**
6. **Creating Depth of Understanding**
7. **Summarizing and Mentally Simplifying New Concepts**

Continued on next page …

---

[25] (Friedman, 2005, page 302)

8. **Comparing and Contrasting New Concepts**
9. **Using a Variety of Learning Methods**
10. **Taking the Time to Fully Process New Ideas**
11. **Breaking Down New Terminology**
12. **Learning New Ideas in an Easily Understood Context**
13. **Staying Focused and Alert when Learning**
14. **Retaining New Knowledge and Skills**
15. **Taking Personal Responsibility for Learning**
16. **Setting Goals and Monitoring One's Progress in Learning**
17. **Engaging in a Mindset that Leads to Success**

Not only do the skills, attitudes, and habits listed above help students learn effectively, they also help kids remember new concepts. We can help students develop these learning skills, attitudes, and habits by using the same four key educational strategies used throughout this book: Classroom Exercises, Teacher Stories / Modeling, Assessment by Students, and Curricular Examples.

1   Learning Through Inquiry

Student-centered, inquiry-based learning activities are critical in helping students learn how to learn. They challenge kids to seek answers to engaging questions. For the sake of their futures, kids *must* engage in learning activities that require them to learn and discover new skills and information with a teacher's *guidance*. If youngsters instead learn by sitting, listening, and regurgitating, they will not be prepared for a world in which they have to be able to independently learn and generate new ideas. We cannot simply tell our youth that they will need to be able to gain new knowledge and skills in their future field of work. We must give our youth experiences in which they seek answers and build their own understanding of new information. Here are some goals for inquiry-based activities.

Inquiry Activities Should …

- **Challenge Students to Answer Interesting Questions by Building New Understanding**
- **Be Student-Centered**

a) Inquiry Activities Should Challenge Students to Answer Interesting Questions by Building New Understanding

In inquiry activities, students should seek to answer interesting questions, understand processes, or understand phenomena. There were some examples of this type of learning activity given early in Chapter 3 as ways to connect students with the curriculum. These examples showed how students can be engaged by a "hook" (like a question) that entices them to seek to build understanding. The teacher can then guide students through the process of building new knowledge or skills.

Side Note

Break Larger Inquiry Topics into Smaller Concepts to Help Students Piece Together an Understanding of the Big Picture

When working through a series of learning activities in order to answer an interesting question, young minds can lose sight of the ultimate goal of those activities (which is to answer the big question). A helpful practice is the introduction of additional interesting questions that guide students through and engage them in the smaller steps of building understanding of the big question. For example, when teaching about the food chain, a teacher might ask the big question:

How is your body powered by energy from the Sun?

To answer this question, the class will need to engage in smaller learning activities that help students understand the steps of the food chain. To draw the students into each learning activity, questions that address smaller topics can be used, such as:

- *How hot is the Sun?* (to help kids understand that the Sun produces an enormous amount of energy)
- *How does the Earth stay warm?* (to help students understand that the Sun shoots energy through space toward Earth)
- *How do plants get their food?* (to help students understand that plants use energy from the Sun to build their own sugar)
- *If they make sugars, why don't all plants taste sweet?* (to help kids understand that plants can modify their sugars into different forms of carbohydrates that don't all taste sweet)
- *How do we get energy by eating plants?* (to help kids see that the Sun's energy trapped by plants in sweet and un-sweet carbohydrates is transferred to us)
- *How does eating other animals provide us with energy?* (to help kids see that the energy transferred from plants to animals can be transferred to us)
- *How is your body powered by energy from the Sun?* (to bring kids back to the original question and challenge them to piece together all of the smaller lessons and questions)

b) Inquiry Activities Should be Student-Centered

As much as possible, an inquiry-based activity should require students to build and develop their own understanding with a teacher's *guidance*. This helps the students gain the ability to build knowledge on their own. This is crucial, because they will often be on their own to learn new knowledge and skills as adults. By challenging students to think rather than simply listen when developing new understanding, teachers provide young minds with a 21st Century Challenge.

Overall Inquiry

We Should See Students Who ...	PEQs for Students
👁 Are engaged by interesting questions, processes, and phenomena 👁 Are curious and want answers 👁 Think of new questions to ask 👁 Seek new learning in order to answer questions 👁 Build understanding through activities, discussions, and investigations 👁 Strive to learn independently or with a group, rather than waiting for a teacher to simply explain things 👁 Use teachers as guides to learning	❓ Why is ____ the way it is? ❓ How does ____ work? ❓ What will happen if ____? ❓ What new questions do I have that I want to answer? ❓ How will I learn the answers to my questions? ❓ How can I / we figure this out? ❓ What steps will I need to take to find answers? ❓ How do the discussions, activities, and investigations that we are doing relate to the question(s) I am trying to answer? ❓ How can I use the new pieces of information that I am building to answer the question, understand the process, or understand the phenomenon? **PESs for Students** • I am curious about the world around me. • I ask questions and seek answers. • I piece together the things I learn in discussions, learning activities, and investigations to build understanding. • I strive to think through and independently discover new learning. • My teachers are guides in my learning and do not simply "spoon-feed" me information … and this empowers me.

Students who ask questions and make statements like these grow into adults who ask questions and are capable of independently building new understanding. They are more effective and independent learners.

What Misconception Keeps Some Teachers from Using Inquiry and Student-Centered Learning?

Some new concepts are highly complicated. In these cases, kids might not simply be able to figure them out or discover them on their own. This does not mean that we should "throw out" inquiry-based learning on these occasions; it simply means that we will have to blend more structure and teacher involvement with the inquiry.

A teacher can lead a class through learning a complex concept by asking questions and assigning activities that will help students build toward the development of new understanding. This will not appear at first to be as student-centered as when individual students or groups develop simpler concepts, but it is still student-centered, because the teacher is not simply lecturing and telling students about a new idea. Instead, the teacher is guiding student minds in the construction of new knowledge and skills by stimulating the class members with questions and activities. *A possible misconception for educators is to assume that inquiry-based, student-centered learning means that a teacher can never be leading a learning activity. In actuality, student-centered learning activities range greatly in their level of teacher participation.* The master teacher must assess the concepts that students will learn in order to determine the appropriate type of student-centered learning that should take place. (The key is that the teacher should not simply "tell" the class information, but should create activities and discussions that guide students in constructing new knowledge.)

Our first instinct must not be to assume that a concept or skill is too difficult for students to develop on their own. With effort, I find that many things I previously thought students could not reasonably "discover" actually can be … given the proper activity and structure.

Inquiry and the Flipped Classroom (as noted in Ch. 3)

With the flipped classroom concept, teachers might have students view a video lecture for homework and then practice concepts at school. The challenge with this is that students are not originally learning the concepts through inquiry activities that develop the brain's ability to seek answers and learn by constructing knowledge. There are two ways to deal with this.

First, the video lectures that summarize concepts could be given as homework *after* an inquiry lesson in class introduces the concept. In this way, the students learn using inquiry activities and then tie together and strengthen understanding by watching a teacher's summary lecture on the topic. Class time is saved as the teacher does not need to spend as much time tying together and summarizing in a lecture format. Also, kids are allowed to work at their own pace, so teachers don't have to try to find an appropriate time to summarize with *everyone at once.*

Second, the video lectures could include points when students are required to pause and predict an answer to an inquiry question, predict how a process works or will unfold, predict what will happen next in a historical event, etc. While making these predictions, the students can be required to note their ideas.

2   Activating and Building on Prior Knowledge

When learning new concepts, students should be stimulated to look for and understand the relationships between new and prior knowledge. This will influence young minds to activate their prior knowledge base when they learn new things in the future … a process that will help them understand and retain new concepts.

We Should See Students Who …	PEQs for Students
👁 Use prior knowledge as a tool for developing new understanding	❓ How does this relate to what I already know?
	❓ Can I use my prior knowledge to help me understand this new concept?
	PES for Students
	• I build new understanding by reflecting on

Side Notes

	and building upon what I already know.

Students who ask questions and make statements like these grow into adults who use their prior knowledge in order to build understanding of new concepts.

3 Constructing the Learning of New Concepts Piece by Piece

Mentally processing and retaining a series of ideas that seem disjointed is a challenge for many people. Instead, people need to have the ability to assess how each new concept builds upon the previous concepts learned and how each new concept will allow for further learning. In other words, humans need to see how each detail fits into the big picture of a topic.

In classrooms, special care must be taken to arrange the parts of a lesson or series of lessons so that each new idea builds on the last in a way that is reasonable to understand. Teachers should continuously stimulate students to assess how each new concept builds on previous concepts, how new knowledge allows for further learning, and how each concept is important to a whole topic. By creating this habit of assessing the pieces of new concepts, we make classroom learning easier and establish a mental routine in students' minds. This routine stimulates young people to build understanding by constructing new ideas piece by piece in a rational order. As adults, their minds will be more likely to build understanding by assessing how new concepts build on each other to create a big picture and how those concepts allow further learning.

We Should See Students Who ...	PEQs for Students
👁 Assess new concepts to see how those concepts build on other learning	❓ How does this piece of knowledge build on other new concepts that I am learning?
👁 Assess how each new concept will allow for further learning	❓ Now that I know this, what else can I learn?
👁 Seek to understand how concepts fit into the big picture of a topic	❓ How does this idea fit into the big picture of this topic?
	PESs for Students
	• I construct understanding of larger ideas by building them piece by piece.
	• I seek to understand how the smaller pieces of a concept fit together to create the big picture.

Students who ask questions and make statements like these grow into adults who mentally scaffold their learning so that each new idea builds on other ideas and leads to further learning.

4 Using New Learning for Real-World Tasks

In the real world, people need to understand how new knowledge and skills are useful and applicable to their work and everyday lives. Students should be challenged to use new knowledge and skills for an authentic purpose. This practice will help students develop the ability to apply new learning to real-world tasks.

17 - Learning
How to Learn

We Should See Students Who ...	PEQs for Students
👁 Apply knowledge and skills to applicable tasks or actions 👁 Think about the ways in which they could use new knowledge and skills	❓ How can I use this new knowledge or skill to accomplish a task? ❓ In what ways does my new understanding empower me?
	PES for Students
	• I can perform real-world tasks with the knowledge and skills I learn.

Students who ask questions and make statements like these grow into adults who are empowered to make valuable use of their new knowledge and skills.

 5 Making Personal Connections with New Learning

Chapter 3, which dealt with connecting students to the curriculum, was important for motivating, inspiring, and connecting students to new learning. But that's not all. When students connect to new concepts, they can better understand those concepts. Learners can make these important connections by looking for the ways that new ideas relate to everyday life, their futures, the past, other topics, opinions, challenges, and solutions. These connections allow people to fit new learning into their understanding of the world.

We Should See Students Who ...	PEQs for Students

👁 Connect new concepts to:
    • Everyday life
    • The future
    • The past
    • Other topics
    • Opinions
    • Challenges
    • Solutions
	❓ How does this new learning relate to me and the world in which I live?
	❓ How does this relate to the future?
	❓ How does this affect my opinions?
	❓ How does this create challenges?
	❓ How can this be used for good?

	PES for Students
	• The knowledge and skills I learn have everyday relevance to my life.

Students who ask questions and make statements like these grow into adults who assess new information to see how it relates to their understanding and view of the world.

 6 Creating Depth of Understanding

When students only "scratch the surface" of a concept, they will have a more difficult time remembering it, because connections and repetition are not created in their brains. Instead, we should help young minds understand how processes, systems, and organizations work. This is superior to getting only a superficial understanding.

When learning about a writing technique, kids should develop an understanding of why it is useful and beneficial as opposed to simply being told to "do it this way." When learning about a process or problem-solving technique in math or science, students should develop an understanding of why the process or technique works, rather than being instructed to simply "do it this way; memorize this formula." When learning about historical events, kids will understand events better if they understand what brought about the events and why the events matter … rather than just memorizing superficial facts. When learning facts in a health class, pupils should learn why certain behaviors are healthier.

In all situations, when young people understand how things work, how things are organized, or how things came to be, they are more likely to understand and remember that knowledge. Even if they eventually forget the official names of processes or can't recite the names of various parts of something, they will still be able to generally apply concepts and processes.

We need to stimulate kids to habitually ask "why" and "how" and then seek answers. This is one of the reasons that inquiry-based learning is so beneficial. When kids are actively involved in developing new knowledge, they naturally gain a better understanding for how concepts and processes work and relate.

We Should See Students Who ...	PEQs for Students
👁 Seek a deep and non-superficial understanding of new concepts	❓ What is the deeper meaning of this concept? ❓ Why does this process work so well or so poorly? ❓ How did this come to be? **PES for Students** • I work to develop a deep understanding when I learn rather than simply scratching the surface.

Students who ask questions and make statements like these grow into adults who go beyond superficial understanding and seek a deeper understanding.

7   Summarizing and Mentally Simplifying New Concepts

Workers regularly encounter new concepts. As human knowledge, business practices, and technologies progress in the 21ˢᵗ century, the concepts that workers encounter will become more complex. Therefore, the ability to mentally summarize and simplify these new ideas is a valuable skill for workers. Teachers can help students develop this learning skill by regularly requiring kids to summarize and outline the key ideas of new learning. This practice develops the mental habit and skill of identifying and mentally organizing the key elements of new concepts. Teachers can stimulate learners to summarize and simplify new knowledge and skills through informal discussions and formal assignments.

We Should See Students Who ...	PEQs for Students
👁 Identify the key words, ideas, and processes that make up new concepts 👁 Summarize the basic ideas that make up concepts 👁 Take complex knowledge and skills and mentally simplify them	❓ What are the key words, ideas, and processes that make up this new concept? ❓ How can I make this complex idea simpler? ❓ What are the most important ideas and skills I should get out of learning this concept? ❓ If I had to summarize this new concept or skill in a sentence or two, what would I say? **PES for Students** • When I learn new concepts, I summarize them and look for ways to make complex ideas simpler to understand.

Students who ask questions and make statements like these grow into adults who are able to mentally organize complex new concepts so that those concepts are simpler to understand.

 8   Comparing and Contrasting New Concepts

Students should engage in the process of comparing and contrasting new concepts in order to deepen understanding and improve memory retention.

Example – Various Content Areas

Elementary level kids can tell how "addition" and "subtraction" are similar and different. This process of analyzing new ideas to see how they compare helps students understand, use, and retain concepts. Children at various ages can compare and contrast: triangle versus square, noun versus verb, simile versus metaphor, city versus village, monarchy versus democracy, electron versus proton, aerobic versus anaerobic, derivative versus integral, and so many more.

We Should See Students Who ...	PEQs for Students
👁 Compare and contrast new concepts in order to develop deeper understanding	❓ In what ways is this new concept similar to others? ❓ In what ways is this new concept different from others? **PES for Students** • I can see the ways in which this concept relates to others ... I see how it is similar and how it is different.

Students who ask questions and make statements like these grow into adults who recognize the small and large similarities and differences that exist among knowledge and skills, which create a better understanding of new learning.

17 - Learning
How to Learn

9 Using a Variety of Learning Methods

As adults, our youth will have a variety of methods available for learning new concepts, including seeking mentors for explanations, using published resources to read about new ideas, taking classes, building understanding through trial and error, using interactive computer programs and Internet websites, and watching instructional videos online. Because our students will encounter a variety of learning tools, we should teach them by using a variety of teaching tools. By planning ahead for each topic, teachers can decide whether concepts should be taught with demonstrations, hands-on activities, inquiry-based activities, group activities, discussions, research, experiments, computer applications, or other means. Using such a variety of techniques requires flexibility by teachers, and it stimulates flexibility in our students.

Using a variety of learning techniques in school is not enough. Kids need to see the ways that each learning technique is useful. To help promote this understanding, teachers can begin new lessons by discussing the ways in which the learning strategy to be used is appropriate for the type of learning that will occur. This practice helps young minds see the best uses for various learning strategies. To practice making their own choices in learning strategies, students can be given the option of choosing how they wish to learn about a new topic. This develops the mental skill and habit of assessing learning goals and deciding which learning techniques are best suited to meet those goals.

We Should See Students Who ...	PEQs for Students
👁 Engage in a variety of learning methods, developing their skills in the use of many tools and strategies	❓ With which learning tools and strategies do I feel most comfortable?
👁 Assess and recognize which learning tools and strategies are best suited for their styles of thinking and learning	❓ With which learning tools and strategies do I best understand and retain new concepts?
👁 Assess which learning tools and strategies are best suited for various learning goals	❓ Different learning strategies and tools seem to be best suited for different learning goals. Which method is best suited for my current learning goal of _____?
	PESs for Students
	• I know which learning tools and strategies work best for me.
	• I recognize that learning different types of knowledge and skills might require that I use different types of learning tools and strategies.

Students who ask questions and make statements like these grow into adults who are capable of using a variety of learning techniques.

10 Taking the Time to Fully Process New Ideas

17 - Learning
How to Learn

When people are learning, they need to move at a pace that allows for reflection upon and mental digestion of new ideas. Teachers should stimulate young minds to move at an appropriate pace that allows their brains to fully process new information. This practice develops the lifelong habit of learning at a pace that allows for mental reflection.

When discussing new concepts, teachers need to *pause* for students to digest the new information. When we ask questions, we need to stop and allow everyone to think before we simply call on the first and quickest hand that pops into the air. We must allow learners time to process and create a lifelong habit of careful thinking.

Problem: Frantic Writing Leads to Clouded "Understanding" and Low Retention

In all my years of schooling, I noticed that many teachers asked students to simultaneously learn new ideas while scrambling to write down notes. Even when summarizing and writing only key pieces of information, this rushed pace made it difficult for me and others to learn the new information. We were trying so hard to write down the key ideas that we didn't have time to think, reflect, and digest what we were supposed to be "learning." Have you ever been in a situation where you scrambled to write down a bunch of information and when finished, you realized that you didn't have a firm grasp of what you wrote? Imagine how hard this would be for some of our struggling learners. (*A larger problem with the story above is that learning by simply listening and taking notes does not promote 21st century skills.*) I'm not saying we should never ask our kids to record information. Writing things down can reinforce and promote the retention of new learning.

Solution ... Use "Fill-it-in Notes" after a Learning Activity

I like to teach new concepts with a learning activity (with a 21st Century Challenge embedded). If I want students to record, discuss, and review what we learned after finishing the activity, I create a sheet that has a good deal of information already written, but I leave blank lines or sections for key ideas. Then, when the class fills out the "fill-it-in notes" sheet together, we can spend more time discussing, thinking, reflecting, and digesting new ideas and less time frantically writing. Amazingly, kids can do their "notes" in less time, but gain better understanding of concepts. They also develop the habit of taking the time to reflect as they learn. Fill-it-in notes are so much more efficient than traditional note-taking that I can introduce new concepts, processes, and words through learning activities (that reflect 21st century skills) and still have time to reinforce concepts with "notes" when needed.

Some educators might worry that students won't get the benefit of learning to summarize key ideas without traditional note-taking. To maintain the development of summarization, while cutting frantic writing through the use of fill-it-in notes, an additional step can be used. Students can be given an assignment to summarize the key ideas developed on fill-it-in notes. In this way, class time promotes deep understanding without frantic writing and the skill of summarization can be developed through a meaningful assignment that also promotes a review of the concepts. Because fill-it-in notes take less class time, the summarization activity can be done in class following the notes. Another option is to give the summarization activity as a meaningful homework assignment and use the extra time created by fill-it-in notes to engage students in classroom learning activities.

On a side note, fill-it-in notes can be used with the flipped classroom model. Kids can fill in the blanks on the note sheet as they watch video lessons, helping to focus their attention on key ideas. When they need more time to think as they note ideas, they can simply pause the video.

Another Solution … Record New Ideas *while* Engaging in Learning Activities
Many learning activities can include a guide sheet in which kids record observations as they progress through the activity. In these situations, no note-taking is needed to record new concepts, because the key words and concept summaries are recorded on the guide sheet as students perform the activity. (The guide sheet becomes the "notes" that can be referenced later.) The practice of introducing new concepts through learning activities (instead of through note taking) promotes the mental skill and habit of taking the time to reflect while learning.

We Should See Students Who ...	**PEQs for Students**
👁 Pause and reflect while learning 👁 Engage in learning activities that require reflection, rather than learning by frantically taking notes	❓ Stop. Do I understand this? ❓ What questions do I have? ❓ Am I moving at a reasonable pace for my brain to process this new information? **PES for Students** • I take time to reflect upon and digest new learning in order to maximize understanding.

Students who ask questions and make statements like these grow into adults who stop and reflect as they encounter new information.

11 Breaking Down New Terminology

Throughout life, people encounter new words on a regular basis. Our students will be more empowered to understand new words if we teach them the skill of breaking down and assessing the parts of words. Whatever the subject area and grade level, our youth are constantly exposed to new terminology. Thus, there are opportunities for all teachers to help students learn to analyze new terms.

For example, the words **"endotherm"** (warm-blooded creature) and **"ectotherm"** (cold-blooded creature) are commonly used in biology classes. Science teachers can stimulate our students to learn the root words that make them up.

- "therm" means "heat"
- "endo" means "inside"
- "ecto" means "outside"

Thus, an "ectotherm" is a living organism that creates *heat* on the *inside* and determines its own temperature (warm-blooded). An "ectotherm" is a living organism that relies on its outside environment to supply it with *heat* (cold-blooded).

When students learn these root words, they can be challenged to make connections to other terms that they know. They can discover that "therm" is in the word "thermos," which describes something meant to trap *heat*. "Therm" is in the word "thermometer," which describes a tool to measure *heat*. When young minds recognize these connections, they better understand and retain the meanings of words. Throughout the school year, a biology class will encounter other words with the root words "therm," "endo," and "ecto." Each time, they will have an idea of what the new terms mean before learning them (and an easier time remembering them after the learning occurs).

Whatever the age bracket or the subject taught, many new words can be broken apart to give insight into their meaning. This can make it much easier to remember what the words mean in the future. Also, students are more likely to accurately predict the meanings of unfamiliar terms in the future.

We Should See Students Who ...	PEQs for Students
👁 Break down and analyze new vocabulary words 👁 Connect new words to prior knowledge 👁 Predict the meanings of new words based on the parts of the new words	❓ What similarities does this new word have to those that I already know? ❓ Does this term have any root words that give insight into its meaning? ❓ What do I predict is the meaning of this word? ❓ Now that I understand the parts of this word, in what other words do these parts appear? **PES for Students** • By analyzing the parts of vocabulary terms, I can predict the meaning of new words and relate new words to those I already know (by comparing and contrasting).

Students who ask questions and make statements like these grow into adults who can better predict the meanings of new words that they encounter.

12   Learning New Ideas in an Easily Understood Context

Learning New Ideas in an Easily Understood Context

- **Using New Ideas in Context While Learning**
- **Understanding the Concept, Then Learning the Word**
- **Creating Definitions for New Words that Make Contextual Sense**

---

a) Using New Ideas in Context While Learning

Young minds need to develop the habit of framing new ideas in an understandable context when they learn. Assignments that ask students to simply look up new words or concepts and write definitions do not satisfy this need. These regurgitation-style assignments give no framework for understanding the meaning and use of the new words and concepts. Instead, students need to learn new words and concepts in such a way that their young minds immediately begin to make use of the ideas in context (through discussions or activities).

b) Understanding the Concept, Then Learning the Word

Some new words can be introduced after their meanings are introduced. A teacher can introduce new concepts and then follow up by saying, "Here's the word that goes with that." The new word immediately has meaning and context, and the class's understanding of the concept isn't clouded by an unfamiliar term. For example, a teacher can boil water and discuss what is happening and why. *Then*, the term "vaporization" can be introduced. For an English class, a teacher can make a few statements, such as, "Fish are smart because they enjoy being in schools" or "The students' math skills were multiplying quickly." The teacher can discuss the fact that each of these statements has more than one meaning and ask the students to create statements that follow the same rule. Afterward, the teacher can say, "You have just learned how to create puns." Thus, the students easily understand the concept of the word "pun" when they hear it, because they have already created some puns of their own.

c) Creating Definitions for New Words that Make Contextual Sense

The "official" wording of a definition for a word or concept does not have to be used. Teachers can often use definitions of words that make more sense to the minds of youngsters than the definitions that exist in textbooks or dictionaries. By using definitions that make better contextual sense to young minds, greater understanding is developed in students. In addition, kids recognize that they have the power to create definitions in their own words that will resonate better in their minds.

When teaching new terms and ideas, educators can often introduce them conversationally to help students develop understanding. Then, students can write down a definition. When recording it, the class can be asked to tell the teacher what should be used as a class definition. (Students enjoy this empowerment.) The classroom definition of the word or idea reflects how it has been used up to that point in conversation. From class to class or year to year, there might be variations in wording, but the essence of the definition will be exactly the same. Of course, teachers should make sure, with some guidance, that the definition that each class creates correctly reflects its meaning.

Overall Learning in Context

We Should See Students Who ...	PEQs for Students
👁 Use new words and concepts in context as they learn those new ideas	❓ How can I use this new word or concept in conversation?
👁 Develop definitions for words and concepts that make contextual sense in their own minds	❓ How can I define this idea in my own words?
	PES for Students
	• I can summarize new vocabulary and

	concepts in my own words and also use new vocabulary in context.

Students who ask questions and make statements like these grow into adults who can find meaningful contexts and uses for new words and concepts.

13 Staying Focused and Alert when Learning

If a person is not alert and focused on the task at hand, the chances of comprehending new concepts are seriously diminished. This makes it critical that a classroom runs in a fashion that promotes alertness and focus. By taking measures to promote alertness in students, we develop lifelong habits that will help our kids learn.

Staying Focused and Alert when Learning

- **Changing Up Learning Activities**
- **Stimulating the Senses**

a) Changing Up Learning Activities

When learning new ideas, people need to stay mentally fresh. When they grow into adults, our youth will need to be able to avoid repetitious learning activities that diminish focus and create boredom. In classrooms, we can show our students how learning can be kept fresh and engaging by changing up the styles of learning activities on a regular basis. For example, one activity might require inquiry and critical thinking. The next learning activity might promote interactive skills and speaking skills. The next might promote creativity. The next might ask students to develop an opinion based on what they've learned.

I have found that both high school students and adults have an attention span for one particular activity that lasts about twenty minutes. From leading children in classroom activities to leading adult teachers in professional development, the magic number of minutes for optimal focus seems to be about twenty. (In some activities, people have a little shorter attention span and in other activities, they have a little longer attention span.) After this amount of time, minds need to shift to a new activity or style of learning. Although I have not taught elementary school children, I would guess that they have a shorter time period (than for older students) in which focus on a task begins to deteriorate.

Sometimes, the type of learning at hand does not easily allow for a complete shift in activities. Thus, a small mental break needs to be taken. On these occasions in my classes, I might do a few different things like … stop an activity and ask a question to ponder, do something silly, tell a quick story from which they can learn something about life, have a student tell something about himself or herself, sing the school fight song, or ask about upcoming school events.

Sense the Mood

Of course, teachers need to be careful when purposefully interjecting something that is not related to the activity at hand. Sometimes, kids can be hard to redirect. Instructors need to have a good feeling for the mood of a class and know when a break is needed for focus and when a break would actually be a bad idea. This goes to show how the art of teaching is not a lock-step event, but is a flexible activity.

By keeping the style of learning fresh or by taking periodic mental breaks, alertness and focus are promoted. In addition, kids develop the understanding that learning can and should be something that is engaging and not repetitious.

b) Stimulating the Senses

Another way to keep things fresh is to stimulate multiple senses. Rather than only talking to their class, teachers can make use of visual, musical, tactile, and auditory stimuli in a variety of ways. Students can carry this habit into adulthood by seeking new learning through a variety of sensory inputs. Thus, students will be more likely to use learning tools in the future that stimulate their senses and focus their attention.

Overall Focus and Alertness in Learning

We Should See Students Who ...	PEQs for Students
👁 Periodically shift learning activities in order to stay alert and focused and to avoid repetition 👁 Take quick mental breaks when learning 👁 Stimulate their senses as they learn	❓ Am I staying focused on the task at hand? ❓ Should I shift my attention to another learning strategy for a while? ❓ Do I need a quick mental break? ❓ Would a break actually be worse for my focus right now? ❓ How can I stimulate my senses to maximize alertness while learning? **PES for Students** • I employ strategies to keep myself mentally alert and focused when learning.

Students who ask questions and makes statements like these grow into adults who take steps to maintain alert and focused learning.

14 ⭐ Retaining New Knowledge and Skills

The strategies for becoming an empowered learner, as discussed above, have an additional benefit. Because these strategies all help people develop a deeper understanding of new learning, the strategies also help people to better retain the new learning. In my experience, people understand *and remember* better when they develop understanding through inquiry, create connections to new learning, use new learning for real-world tasks, summarize and simplify new learning, break down new terminology, etc. In addition to the ideas discussed above, there are some other learning practices that can help children retain new learning.

Retaining New Knowledge and Skills

- Continuously Reviewing
- Using Memory Strategies
- Developing Sound Study Skills

---

a) Continuously Reviewing

A crucial requirement for promoting long-term memory is continuous review. The more exposure to an idea, the more engrained it will become in students' brains, because the exposure helps to move ideas toward long-term memory. Because of this, it's important that concepts are not simply presented and then left behind in the wake of new ideas that come in the following days.

A variety of methods can be used to promote continuous review. For instance, a teacher can introduce an idea through a learning activity, practice the use of the new concept or skill, and then make a record of it in a journal or notebook. A process like this continually exposes students to the new information. This is more effective for promoting lasting memory than a style of teaching in which information is presented, noted, and left behind … all at once … with no use and no reflection.

An important idea to remember with continuous review is that it is more effective when it occurs over a series of days. Each day that goes by without revisiting a new concept diminishes the brain's ability to remember it in the long term. Continuous review can take many forms: warm-up review questions at the beginning of a class, the use of a journal as a review tool, team activities, quick games, daily quizzes, or activities that use previous concepts in new ways.

Side Notes

Continuous Review … Without Being Boring
An important key in continuous review is to ***avoid doing it in a way that's boring!*** Repetition by its very nature has the potential to create boredom. It needs to be done in such a way that it activates long-term memory, but remains engaging and "new." This can be done by introducing new tasks and challenges that exercise a concept. While the same concept is repetitively addressed, the method of applying it is continuously changed, keeping it "fresh."

A Visual Record of Activities
My sister, a science teacher, takes digital pictures of some learning activities, like labs and investigations, and then uses them as a resource for continuous review in the days that follow. She can display them with a TV or projector and asks probing questions to enhance understanding and promote continuous review. Revisiting previous activities can activate memory by taking the brain back to the initial point of learning.

17 - Learning How to Learn

The more teachers encourage students to continuously revisit the concepts that are learned in school, the more the habit of continuous reflection becomes engrained in the minds of our students … helping them become more effective learners for life.

b) Using Memory Strategies

When teaching new concepts and ideas, I often ask the class what techniques can be used to improve retention of the new information. I call these "memory strategies." A variety of memory strategies can be used, including mnemonics, pictures, word associations, and rhymes. Here are some quick examples.

1. **HOMES** – The five Great Lakes are **H**uron, **O**ntario, **M**ichigan, **E**rie, and **S**uperior.

2. On a map of South America, Peru can be identified by looking for the country shape like a "P."

3. The **L**egislature makes **L**aws; the **J**udiciary has **J**udges.

4. In caves, STALAC**T**ITES form on the ceiling, and STALAG**M**ITES form on the floor.

5. **Pro**karyotic cells have **no** nucleus ... **PRO-NO**

An infinite number of memory strategies can be created. A teacher doesn't have to be good at thinking of memory strategies to have the class use them, and not all of the kids have to be great at creating memory strategies to make use of them. Students can share their memory strategy ideas with others in order to help everyone see new ways to make memory strategies. As students practice making memory strategies, they will get better.

Thinking of memory strategies is itself a memory strategy, because it does a couple of things. As young minds try to imagine a memory strategy, they are continuously reflecting on and connecting with a new concept. Also, the process causes some repetitive thought about a new concept … in a fun way.

c) Developing Sound Study Skills

To help students develop sound study skills, attitudes, and habits, we can discuss relevant factors, such as study time planning, study environment, diligence, consistency, and study strategies.

After promoting good habits, a teacher might need to contact parents to help stimulate student studying. Teachers can also send parents a checklist of sound study skills.

Because there are so many and varying study techniques that an educator can teach students, we will not go into depth on many strategies here. I would like to mention a couple very effective strategies, though.

Predict the Assessment

Many students benefit from predicting assessment tasks or questions that they think the teacher might use (and then perform the task or answer the question). This promotes retention as students are forced to reflect upon the concepts they have learned. When children make predictions about assessments and then find that some or many of their predictions were correct, they say, "Awesome! I thought that I might be asked that question." (This strategy also promotes student creativity.)

To stimulate kids to make assessment predictions, teachers can give a review assignment that requires students to anticipate and create assessment tasks, questions, problems to solve, etc.

Backtrack Review

Another study skill that I like to promote is a strategy for review. Let's say that a child takes home materials to review, including guide sheets for classroom learning activities, a note sheet, and a journal entry that he or she used to summarize classroom learning at the end of each day. (Among all the materials, there are four or five pages of new ideas.) If the student simply reads straight through all of the materials, he or she will likely find that he or she does not remember much of the information when finished. Here is the problem … by the time the student reaches the fifth page, the brain has forgotten the first page. There has been no repetition or time to reflect and let ideas sink in.

A better technique for the student (that matches how the brain retains information) is to start reviewing on the first page and go over it a couple times until he or she is in command of the material. Then, the student can move to the second page and go over it a couple times until the information is retained. Before moving to the third page, however, the student should backtrack and revisit the first page. There is a little more repetition and reflection, allowing the student to retain the information from the first page as he or she moves forward. This process of backtracking before moving forward can be done throughout the review of the materials. By the time the student gets to the last page, his or her brain will have had a chance to better retain the concepts. This strategy takes advantage of how the brain works. If our brains were like computers, we could simply read straight through materials and simply remember what we read. Because we are not androids, we have to use techniques to match our humanity and allow for repetition.

17 - Learning
How to Learn

Overall Knowledge and Skill Retention

We Should See Students Who …	PEQs for Students
👁 Assess and reflect upon recent learning	❓ What have I learned recently?
👁 Continuously review	❓ What should I remember from recent lessons?
👁 Use memory strategies to aid their memory of new ideas	❓ What can I do to review what I have learned?

👁 Plan for study time 👁 Create a distraction-free study environment 👁 Use effective study strategies that best meet the learning and thinking style of each student 👁 Study consistently 👁 Study diligently 👁 Predict how they will need to use new information 👁 Continuously backtrack as they review	❓ What word play, pun, picture, acronym, simile, metaphor, mnemonic device, or other memory strategy will help me remember this new word or idea? ❓ Which memory strategies seem to work best for me? ❓ When will I get my studying done? ❓ How can I make time to study a little of each topic each day, rather than waiting until later? ❓ How will I manage my time while studying? ❓ What elements create a positive learning environment for me? ❓ What strategies will help me study effectively? ❓ How can I stay on task while studying? ❓ What tasks will I possibly need to perform using my new knowledge or skills? (What questions might a teacher ask me?) ❓ Am I backtracking to review when I study so that I don't forget earlier concepts? **PESs for Students** • I employ the strategies that suit my needs for studying, remembering new concepts, and reviewing. • I find effective ways to remember new concepts in the short term and long term.

Students who ask questions and make statements like these will grow into adults who effectively review and retain their new learning.

15 Taking Personal Responsibility for Learning

For our youth to become adults who are effective in learning new skills and ideas, they must learn to take responsibility for acquiring the necessary skills for success. Our students need the attitude that they are in control of their own skill set. Anything that we can do in the classroom to promote this attitude of personal responsibility will greatly help our pupils.

We Should See Students Who ...	**PEQs for Students**
👁 Have an attitude of empowerment, control, and responsibility	❓ What are my personal responsibilities as a student, a worker, and a citizen? ❓ In what ways am I empowered to learn and grow? **PESs for Students** • I can and will learn.

| | • I take personal responsibility for doing what it takes to succeed.
• I have a great support network, but my actions are the biggest key to my success. |

Students who ask questions and make statements like these grow into adults who proactively take responsibility for seeking helpful work skills. They seek to empower themselves.

 16 Setting Goals and Monitoring One's Progress in Learning

We want our youth to grow into adults who proactively assess their own abilities and knowledge, determine what new knowledge and skills are necessary, assess which methods would be best for obtaining new knowledge and skills, and monitor their progress toward their learning goals. To instill this habit in our youth, teachers should stimulate kids to develop and reflect upon their short-term and long-term learning goals. Also, we should stimulate young minds to monitor their learning progress.

We Should See Students Who ...	PEQs for Students
👁 Assess their own skills to determine what new learning is necessary, beneficial, or empowering 👁 Set goals for learning 👁 Seek effective methods to learn needed or desired knowledge and skills 👁 Monitor their progress toward their learning goals and adjust their strategies as needed	❓ What are my current career and life goals? ❓ What are my strengths and weaknesses? ❓ What knowledge and skills do I need to be successful in current and future situations? ❓ What do I need to learn to stay on the cutting edge? ❓ What new knowledge and skills would make me indispensable as a worker? ❓ What are my learning goals? ❓ How, where, and with what resources will I learn? ❓ How am I progressing toward my learning goals? ❓ Is my current learning strategy the best for achieving my goals? **PES for Students** • I know what short-term and long-term goals I want to achieve, and I can see my progress in reaching these goals.

Students who ask questions and make statements like these grow into adults who set learning goals, find effective learning strategies, and assess their own learning progress. They seek to empower themselves.

 17 Engaging in a Mindset that Leads to Success

In learning and developing, people's mindsets are a critical element in their level of success. In her book, *Mindset: The New Psychology of Success*, Carol Dweck, Ph.D describes the idea that there are two major mindsets, the fixed mindset and the growth mindset. People who have a fixed mindset believe that "qualities are carved in stone," while people with a growth mindset believe that their intelligence, abilities, and qualities can be developed over time through effort.[26]

The results that come from these two mindsets are strikingly different. People with a growth mindset are more likely to display a passion for learning, work to improve their qualities, challenge themselves, work through difficult tasks and situations, try harder when faced with disappointments, remediate their deficiencies, look for relationships with people who challenge them to develop, and take the actions of bullies less personally. People with a fixed mindset are more likely to avoid learning opportunities, cope poorly with failure, see less value in effort, avoid challenges, fear not being smart, and take bullying more personally.[27] The differences that result from these two mindsets make it clear that educators should promote a growth mindset as an essential learning attitude. Dweck's book even points out that as students progress into older grades, a growth mindset improves grades.[28]

So, how can educators promote a growth mindset? They can teach children that people's minds can grow and are not simply fixed in ability. This idea can be reinforced by framing class activities as opportunities to develop and grow the mind:

- Challenges can be described as growth opportunities, in which success does not mean that students are always correct.
- Activities, assignments, and homework can be described as growth tools.
- Discussions can be described as cooperative growth sessions, in which ideas are developed and comments are the building blocks for growth.
- Assessments can be described as opportunities to demonstrate learning growth.

When teachers talk with kids, they can discuss how students' efforts, rather than their abilities and smarts, relate to their levels of success. This sends the message that success comes from growth through effort, rather than from fixed abilities.[29]

Educators can also teach parents about the benefits of a growth mindset and enlist them to promote it at home.

We Should See Students Who ...	PEQs for Students
👁 See their abilities as traits that can and should be developed over time 👁 Embrace challenges 👁 Do not fear setbacks, but see setbacks as learning opportunities 👁 Work to develop their weaknesses 👁 Are passionate about learning	❓ How can I grow and develop my abilities today? ❓ What exciting challenges can I tackle today? ❓ How can I learn from this setback? ❓ What are my strengths and weaknesses, and how can I improve my weaknesses? **PESs for Students**

---

[26] (Dweck, 2007, pages 6 and 7)
[27] (Dweck, 2007, pages 7, 8, 10, 16, 17, 36, 167)
[28] (Dweck, 2007, page 57)
[29] (Dweck, 2007, page 71 and 72)

	• Through effort, my abilities can be grown over time. • My mind develops with every challenge I embrace, even if I do not always succeed. • I will encounter setbacks, and I can use them to learn and grow.

Students who ask questions and make statements like these will carry a growth mindset into adulthood and be more likely to work to develop their abilities.

Learning to Learn: Wrap-up

Helping our students be capable of learning new things independently requires more than simply teaching skills and information in a traditional teacher-centered classroom. In the real world, our youth will need skills, abilities, and habits that empower them to learn whatever they need to know, whenever they need to know it. The topics in this chapter help our students develop this independence.

Thinking About It

- **In what ways do you promote the ability of students to become effective life-long learners?**
- **What new things can you do to empower students as independent learners?**

How Does This Chapter Support the Goals of This Book?

Let's take a moment to think about the ways in which the ideas of this chapter help us address the three main goals of this book by looking at the "Building Blocks of a 21st Century Education" on page 13 and the "Daily Thoughts for Educators" on page 18. We now have tools and strategies for empowering our youth by developing their ability to learn.

Make Note of Your Great Ideas!

If you haven't already, note your ideas for implementing the strategies in this chapter in your Teacher Empowerment Menu (for 21st Century Educators). In the future, you can easily reference usable ideas for your class.

In addition, consider the ways in which you can stimulate students to develop their learning skills by using the Personal Empowerment Menu (for 21st Century Students), which contains the relevant PEQs, PESs, and assessment rubric for this chapter.

17 - Learning
How to Learn

Leadership and Motivating Others

A Great Side Effect of Promoting Connections & a 21st Century Challenge

At first, I planned to write a chapter on leadership and motivating others. When I set out to write it, I realized that all of the qualities that make a good leader and motivator are already addressed in the chapters of this book. The skills and knowledge in these chapters simply need to be applied with the goal of leadership in mind. Let's look at the attributes of a good leader and note how those attributes have already been addressed:

Leadership and Motivational Skills	Addressed in Chapter
Building Connections that Increase Team Success	**Ch. 3-10　Building Connections** • Connections with Learning (Ch. 3) • Connections with the Future (Ch. 4) • Connections with Educators (Ch. 5) • Connections with the Team-Working Environment (Ch. 6) • Connections with Peers (Ch. 7) • Connections with the Spirit of the Team (Ch. 8) • Connections with Parents (Ch. 9) • Connections with the Community and the World (Ch. 10)
Assessing Teams, Performances, Systems, Processes, and Structures for Improvement	**Ch. 11　Critical Thinking and Assessment**
Taking Actions to Facilitate Effective Teams, Performances, Systems, Processes, and Structures	**Ch. 12　Moving from Critical Thinking to Action: Problem Solving and Other Real-World Actions**
Infusing Creativity into Leadership and Motivational Actions	**Ch. 13　Creativity in Action**
Effectively Interacting with and Motivating Others	**Ch. 14　Understanding and Interacting with Others** • Understanding What Makes People Tick - *wants, needs, and motivations* • Communicating and Displaying Social Skills - *speaking, listening, interpreting, and tact* • Collaborating Through Teamwork • Understanding Language and Culture • Explaining and Presenting Ideas • Competing

Effectively Using Personal Skills, Attitudes, and Habits to Lead and Motivate	Ch. 15 Personal Skills, Attitudes, and Habits • Setting Goals • Displaying Proper Work Ethic *with discipline, determination, proactivity, and responsibility* • Adapting, Changing, and being Versatile • Managing Stress • Being Organized and Efficient • Behaving Ethically • Assessing Risks • Being Financially Literate
Using Technology to Lead and Motivate	Ch. 16 Technological and Media Literacy
Continuously Learning New Strategies to Lead and Motivate	Ch. 17 Learning How to Learn

We have been addressing skills that leaders need throughout the chapters dealing with connections and a 21ˢᵗ Century Challenge. The key is that kids need to apply these skills, attitudes, and habits in *leadership situations*.

There should be opportunities in schools for youngsters to pool all of the skills of the 21ˢᵗ century together in leadership exercises. All students need opportunities to lead. You never know, a quiet student might grow to be a leader. We can promote this ability of leadership and motivation through Classroom Exercises, Teacher Stories / Modeling, Assessment by Students, and Curricular Examples. As always, an appropriate rubric can help kids think about the various aspects of this skill when assessing a classroom activity.

We Should See Student Leaders Who ...	Personal Empowerment Questions PEQs for Student Leaders
✆ Connect with what they learn about leadership (Ch. 3)	❓ What does my learning teach me about leadership?
✆ Connect with their future as potential leaders (Ch. 4)	❓ What leadership roles might I have in the future?
✆ Learn about leadership from connections with their teachers (Ch. 5) and parents (Ch. 9)	❓ How can I learn about leadership from mentors and leaders like my teachers and parents?
✆ Motivate and lead others by promoting connections with the team-working environment (Ch. 6), connections with their peers (Ch. 7), and connections with the spirit of the team (Ch. 8).	❓ How can I connect my team to our working environment in order to motivate them and maximize their work experience and effort?
✆ Motivate and lead through connections with the community and the world (Ch. 10)	❓ How can I promote peer connections in order to motivate my team, promote teamwork, and maximize their work experience and effort?
✆ Assess teams, performances, systems, processes, and structures for improvement (Ch. 11)	❓ How can I promote team spirit in order to motivate my team, promote teamwork, and maximize their work experience and effort?
✆ Take actions to facilitate effective teams, performances, systems, processes, and structures (Ch. 12)	❓ How can I develop motivating connections between my team and the

👁 Infuse creativity into leadership and motivational actions (Ch. 13)

👁 Effectively interact with and motivate others by …
- Understanding what makes people tick (wants, needs, and motivations)
- Demonstrating quality communication / social skills
- Collaborating through teamwork
- Understanding language and culture
- Explaining and presenting ideas
- Being able to compete (Ch. 14)

👁 Effectively use personal skills by …
- Setting goals
- Displaying proper work ethic (with discipline, determination, proactivity, and responsibility)
- Adapting, changing, and being versatile
- Managing stress
- Being organized and efficient
- Behaving ethically
- Assessing risks
- Being financially literate (Ch. 15)

👁 Use technology to lead and motivate (Ch. 16)

👁 Continuously seek and learn new strategies for leadership and motivation (Ch. 17)

community and world?

❓ How well is this team, performance, system, process, or structure working?

❓ What needs to be and can be improved?

❓ What level of motivation does my team have?

❓ How can I lead others in improving our team, performances, systems, processes, and structures?

❓ How can I motivate my team to take action?

❓ How can I infuse creativity into my leadership actions?

❓ How can I use my resources to do something new?

❓ What new methods can we use to accomplish our goals?

❓ What new goals can we set out to achieve?

❓ How can I motivate in a creative way?

❓ What are the needs, wants, and motivations of my teammates?

❓ How can I effectively communicate with my team?

❓ How can I improve collaboration among my team members?

❓ How can I motivate my team?

❓ How do other leaders motivate their teams, communicate effectively, and show charisma?

❓ How can I build connections among my teammates?

❓ How can I show respect for and confidence in my team?

❓ How can I make my teammates feel validated and appreciated?

❓ How can I prepare my team for competition?

❓ What goals can our team create?

❓ How do I use, display, and promote a quality work ethic, adaptability, a calm demeanor, organization, efficiency, a motivated attitude, ethical behavior, competent risk assessment, and financial literacy?

❓ What technologies and information will

	allow me to better lead?
	❔ How can technology help my team function better to accomplish its goals?
	❔ What information and technology will allow me to motivate my team?
	❔ What can I learn to improve as a leader and motivator?
	❔ What do my experiences as a leader teach me about handling future leadership situations?

Students who ask questions like these grow into adults who can implement their 21ˢᵗ century skills in leadership situations.

Wrapping up
Goals #1 and #2

Goal #1 - Foundation of Connections
Goal #2 - 21st Century Challenge

We have now finished the first two major goals of this book. On the following page, let's remind ourselves how a foundation of connections and a 21st Century Challenge can be assembled to empower students for the 21st century.

Empowering Your Students for the 21ˢᵗ Century:
Building Blocks of a 21ˢᵗ Century Education

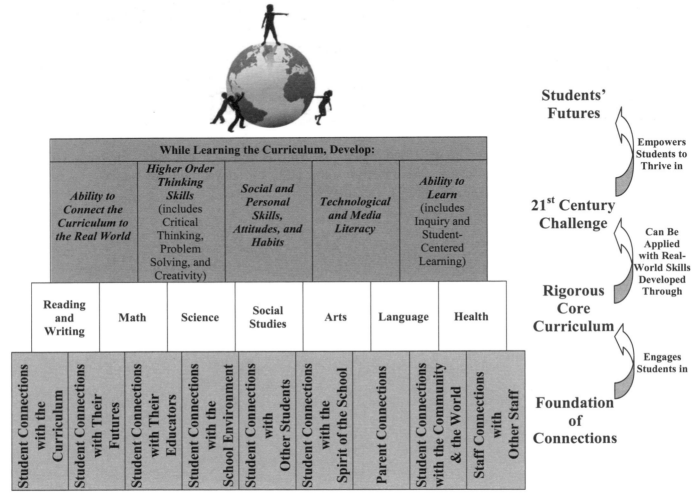

Reading from the foundation upward, we should see a 21ˢᵗ Century Education in which:

- **A foundation of connections engages students in a rigorous core curriculum.**
- **A rigorous core curriculum can be applied with real-world skills developed through a 21ˢᵗ Century Challenge.**
- **A 21ˢᵗ Century Challenge empowers students to thrive in their futures.**

Goal #3

Putting Together the Building Blocks of a 21ˢᵗ Century Education:
Using a System of Thoughtful Teaching Practices
(Ch. 18-21)

Beyond developing meaningful connections within the learning environment and providing a 21ˢᵗ Century Challenge for students, the third goal of this book is to develop an effective and systematic approach to teaching in modern schools so that all students develop short- and long-term understandings of new information and skills.

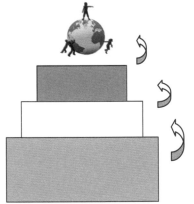

**Building Blocks of
21ˢᵗ Century Education
(Ch. 3-17)**

**Putting Together the
Building Blocks
(Ch. 18-21)**

It might seem overwhelming to embark on a voyage that goes beyond simply teaching the school curriculum to weaving in connections and new 21ˢᵗ Century Challenges … all while looking out for the success of all students. Because of this, we will look at how to effectively and realistically meet the demands of a 21st Century Education. This will include the development of appropriate planning, assessment, remediation, and knowledge / skill retention. These four actions will allow us to successfully put together the building blocks of a 21ˢᵗ Century Education.

> ### *Putting Together the Building Blocks of a 21st Century Education Using a System of Thoughtful Teaching Practices*
>
> - **Effectively Planning to Empower 21ˢᵗ Century Students -** Goal-oriented and long-term planning: ***Ch. 18***
> - **Using Assessments to Empower 21ˢᵗ Century Students -** Using assessment to promote learning: ***Ch. 19***
> - **Using Interventions / Remediation to Empower 21ˢᵗ Century Students -** Systematic proactive, immediate, short-term, and long-term interventions: ***Ch. 20***
> - **Promoting Knowledge and Skill Retention to Empower 21ˢᵗ Century Students -** Teaching to understand *and* remember: ***Ch. 21***

18 Effectively Planning to Empower 21st Century Students

Fitting a large curriculum into one school year is a common problem for teachers. This can make the idea of weaving connections and the skills, attitudes, and habits of the 21st century into our classrooms seem challenging. However, effective planning will allow these 21st century goals to be addressed within the teaching of the curriculum. Let's look at some things that educators can do to address planning.

> ## Effectively Planning to Empower 21st Century Students
>
> 1. **Goal-Oriented Planning**
> 2. **Long-Term Planning**

1 Goal-Oriented Planning

Curriculum and 21st Century Skills Should Guide Teaching; Textbooks Should Aid Teaching

When planning to meet the curriculum, teachers might look at their school / state benchmarks and think, "Chapter 1 of our textbook covers these benchmarks; chapter 2 covers those benchmarks; the project we do in the fall covers yet other benchmarks ...." When planning this way, teachers find it is very difficult to cover all of the chapters and projects that address all of the benchmarks. There is a fundamental problem for educators who plan this way. Textbooks and other resources for teaching generally contain more information than is necessary to address the required curricular benchmarks; so much more, in fact, that attempting to teach everything within these resources is often impossible. Am I saying that resources like textbooks shouldn't be used? No way! What I am saying is that educators need to filter out those portions of their resources that are helpful in teaching the curricular benchmarks. The only way to do this is to plan by focusing on the goals of student learning.

Educators commonly start their lesson planning by looking over their resources and developing lessons that cover the material within those resources. Then, they create an assessment or test to see how well the students have learned the material. Effectively, a textbook becomes the curriculum standards. Instead, we must start with our goals in mind.

First, we should look to see exactly what benchmark standards, knowledge, and skills are required (as well as consider which 21ˢᵗ century skills, attitudes, and habits can be promoted within the curriculum). Then, we should look over our available resources to decide which portions of each are helpful in teaching our benchmark standards and the skills of the 21ˢᵗ century. In this way, textbooks and other learning materials become *tools* for teaching the curriculum, rather than guides. When educators use their learning goals as a guide and their resources as tools for teaching, they focus their teaching in a time-saving manner; they are not trying to teach "everything."

The efficiency of this sort of planning is compounded when teachers begin to assess their lessons, activities, and projects in order to see how they address their learning goals. When teachers begin to do this, they realize that they may have multiple lessons that address a single benchmark or skill when one or two are actually enough for student comprehension. They may also find that some activities that they previously considered helpful actually do not address benchmarks or goals within the curriculum. When teachers focus on learning goals, they weed out unnecessary (and time-consuming) activities. This focus on goals also frees up a great deal of classroom time to enhance or redesign lessons that are more applicable to the real world and help to develop the skills discussed in this book. But 21ˢᵗ century skills aside, lessons created in the manner described above are better, because they actually focus on the *benchmarks* … rather than focusing on textbook chapters that "cover" the benchmarks. Focusing on goals allows teachers to avoid over- or under-emphasis of certain objectives, while completely removing unnecessary learning activities.

> **Planning:**   **Goals → Assessments → Lessons**

A large focus in many of my education courses in college was to take goal-oriented planning one step further to include assessment. The idea is as follows.

- Teachers start their planning by first looking at the benchmarks (as discussed above).
- Then, they determine which types of assessments students should be able to do if they understand the benchmarks.
- Finally, lessons are created that will help students meet the requirements of the assessments.

If you look carefully, this is the opposite order compared to how these things are commonly done. Therefore, it is referred to as "Backward Design." This curriculum design is described in *Understanding by Design* by Grant Wiggins and Jay McTighe.[30] Even though it is considered backward, the process is actually very logical. This strategy makes more sense than popping open a textbook (with the assumption that the textbook reflects the curriculum) and using it as a guide for teaching. By using this process and being more efficient, I believe that teachers can more easily create time to weave 21ˢᵗ century skills into their lessons. So, let's look at a solid plan for planning to teach a unit.

---

[30] (Wiggins, 2001, pages 8 and 9)

Planning to Teach a Unit

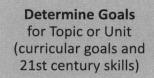

Notice that this order of planning leads to lessons that reflect the original curricular goals, thus, avoiding unnecessary activities that will squeeze a teacher for time later in the year. These lessons do not over- or under-emphasize any material.

If the backward method was applied to a soccer game, the coach would first focus on which rules and objectives are associated with winning a game (like benchmark goals). Then, the coach would determine which kicking, passing, and strategic tasks the players would need to be able to perform in a game (like a performance assessment) in order to win. Finally, he or she would determine how the players should learn and practice (lessons) in order to meet their performance tasks in a game. In this way, the team's practice activities prepare them for soccer game performance tasks that will eventually lead to game winning goals … pun intended. Notice that the planning process is considered "backward," because it is the reverse of how the tasks will be carried out.

Let's put goal-oriented planning together with teaching and assessments to create a "System of Thoughtful 21st Century Teaching Practices."

System of Thoughtful 21st Century Teaching Practices

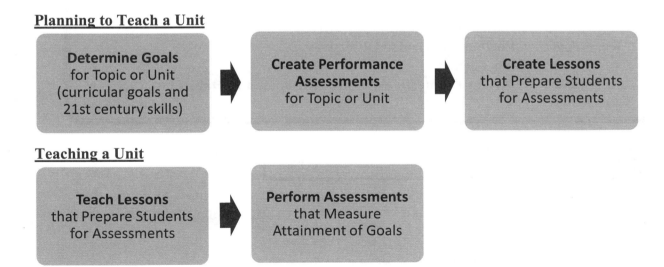

This reasonable style of planning and preparation helps teachers focus on what is important when creating lessons and makes it easier to incorporate 21st century skills.

Goal-Oriented Planning

We Should See Educators Who ...	Personal Empowerment Questions (PEQs) for Educators
👁 Focus on learning goals and desired outcomes when planning and determining the use of resources 👁 Follow a planning order of: Goals→Assessments→Lessons	❓ What are my curricular goals? ❓ What do I want my students to know and be able to do? ❓ How can I also address 21ˢᵗ century skills as part of my curricular goals? ❓ What assessments should students be able to do if they achieve my curricular goals? ❓ What lessons will allow the kids to learn the knowledge and skills that reflect my assessments and goals?

Educators who ask questions like these will plan to effectively teach both their curricula and 21ˢᵗ century skills in their schools and empower students to thrive in the new century.

⭐ 2 Long-Term Planning

Another essential facet of meeting all of the curricular objectives for a class is long-term planning. This involves developing a long-term plan for teaching the curriculum and the skills of the 21ˢᵗ century. Some goals for long-term planning are as follows.

> **Long-term planning allows teachers to …**
>
> - **Sequence the Teaching of Curricular Objectives**
> - **Merge Together Various Curricular Objectives**
> - **Create Overarching Themes**
> - **Interweave 21ˢᵗ Century Connections, Skills, Attitudes, and Habits into the Curriculum**

a) Sequence the Teaching of Curricular Objectives

When teachers start the school year by analyzing the curriculum as a whole, they might find that the order in which a textbook or other resource presents information can be modified for improvement.

b) Mesh Together Various Curricular Objectives

Reviewing the curriculum as a whole allows educators an opportunity to find different curricular objectives that can be taught together in the same lesson or assessed at the same time. Sometimes, learning activities can be tweaked or merged to reflect multiple learning goals, saving a lot of time. Objectives from different parts of the school year can be merged and some objectives from the same unit can be merged. This blending of objectives is highly unlikely without preplanning.

c) Create Overarching Themes

Another great reason for long-term planning is to help educators see the "big picture" of the curriculum. When teachers see how all of the concepts are interconnected, they can create and plan overarching themes and activities. These activities can add meaning to the curriculum as students make connections among the learning objectives. If teachers are not thinking about larger themes and the connections among topics, it is unlikely that they will find ways to convey the "big picture" and its connections to students.

d) Interweave 21ˢᵗ Century Connections, Skills, Attitudes, and Habits into the Curriculum

A final reason for long-term planning is based on the goals of this book. When educators look at their objectives for the school year, they can reflect on the best times to weave 21ˢᵗ century elements into the curriculum. With preplanning, teachers can identify opportunities for inquiry; critical thinking; creativity; connections; developing interactive skills; and other 21ˢᵗ century skills, attitudes, and habits.

Overall Long-Term Planning

We Should See Educators Who ...	PEQs for Educators
👁 Engage in both short-term and long-term planning	❓ What larger learning goals do I need to accomplish by the end of this year or semester?
👁 Rationally sequence learning activities through careful planning	❓ What short-term learning goals will lead me to accomplishing my long-term goals?
👁 Merge related parts of the curriculum to make connections and save time	❓ Am I over- or under-emphasizing any goals in my classroom?
👁 Use overarching themes that tie concepts together and help students see the big picture that unites smaller topics	❓ How does the sequence of major learning goals affect student understanding, and what is the best order of topics?
👁 Treat 21ˢᵗ century skills as curricular goals and seamlessly weave these skills into learning activities and assessments	❓ What goals can I merge together in order to create connections and save time?
	❓ What themes can draw connections between various ideas?
	❓ Will my classroom activities help my students go beyond simply learning curricular facts to developing 21ˢᵗ century skills?

Educators who ask questions like these think about their long-term learning goals and curriculum in order to thoughtfully plan to empower students.

Let's add long-term planning to the "System of Thoughtful 21st Century Teaching Practices." (New ideas are in red.)

System of Thoughtful 21st Century Teaching Practices

Beginning of the School Year

> **Make Long-Term Plan**
> for Teaching Major
> Topics and Skills

Planning to Teach a Unit

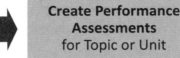

> **Determine Goals**
> for Topic or Unit
> (curricular goals and
> 21st century skills)

> **Create Performance Assessments**
> for Topic or Unit

> **Create Lessons**
> that Prepare Students
> for Assessments

Teaching a Unit

> **Teach Lessons**
> that Prepare Students
> for Assessments

> **Perform Assessments**
> that Measure
> Attainment of Goals

Planning: Wrap-up

The key idea to take from this chapter is the idea that the process of successful teaching begins with planning. This is not just any kind of planning, but a method that begins with a focus on the goals and desired outcomes that you want your students to meet. By starting our planning with the goals of our instruction in mind, we can more easily focus on the important things that we must achieve. We also are able to avoid an over-emphasis of some goals and an under-emphasis of others.

18 - Planning to Empower

Thinking About It

- **In what ways is long-term planning helpful in promoting curricular understanding and 21st century skill development?**
- **Which curricular and 21st century skills goals can you merge?**

How Does This Chapter Support the Goals of This Book?

Let's take a moment to think about the ways in which the ideas of this chapter help us address the three main goals of this book by looking at the "Building Blocks of a 21st Century Education" on page 13 and the "Daily Thoughts for Educators" on page 18. We now have guidelines for thoughtful planning, which help us put together the pieces of an empowering 21st century education.

Make Note of Your Great Ideas!

If you haven't already, note your ideas for implementing the practices in this chapter in your Teacher Empowerment Menu (for 21st Century Educators). In the future, you can easily reference these personalized ideas.

19 Using Assessments to Empower 21st Century Students

In order for 21st century teachers to empower students, we must go beyond using assessments as grading tools. Assessments should be used to promote the development of curricular understanding and the skills, attitudes, and habits required in the 21st century.

Using Assessments to Empower 21st Century Students

1. **Using Assessments as Formative Tools** (that provide feedback, identify misconceptions, guide interventions, stimulate student reflection, and drive further instruction)
2. **Using Data from Assessments to Improve Teaching Strategies**
3. **Using Proficiency-Based Assessments**
4. **Using Assessments to Develop Student Awareness of Learning Progression**
5. **Using Assessments to Reinforce the Real-World Value of the Curriculum**
6. **Using Assessments as Learning Activities**
7. **Challenging Students at All Levels of Understanding in Assessments**
8. **Using Range-Line Rubrics to Provide Empowering Feedback**

---

1 Using Assessments as Formative Tools

There are two major types of assessment in education: formative and summative. According to Susan Brookhart, author of *Grading*, "Formative assessment means information gathered and reported for use in the development of knowledge and skills, and summative assessment means information gathered and reported for use in judging the outcome of that development."[31]

How can these assessments be used by educators? Summative assessments, such as tests, exams, or culminating projects, can measure how much students have learned … often for the purpose of grading. Formative assessments, on the other hand, can measure and assess student

---

[31] (Brookhart, 2009, page 45)

understanding for the purpose of giving students feedback, which allows educators to address misconceptions and guide further instruction.

There are some potential pitfalls in assessing students. Sometimes, educators might treat what could be formative assessments as summative assessments. For example, when a test is given, it might be used as a measurement of what has been learned for the purpose of grading, rather than as a formative tool for identifying / addressing misconceptions and improving teaching. Similarly, assignments might be given a grade and not really used to provide feedback to students. Furthermore, educators might not take opportunities while students are working on assignments or activities in class to walk around and answer questions, address misconceptions, or ask questions. ***The bottom line is that tests and projects, along with informal classroom assessments, should be used in a more <u>formative</u> manner … meaning that they need to be used for identifying student difficulties and quickly remediating those difficulties with appropriate instructional techniques.***

The alternative to this is devastating. When assessments are continuously treated more as tools for grading than as tools for learning, students don't get the feedback they need to improve and succeed. Instead, they eventually end up in need of major remediation. This can be very challenging, because student misconceptions can build and build over time until they are numerous. To make a long story short, the best time to learn about and remediate misconceptions is now … before they compound and grow. It doesn't make much sense to wait until kids are days, weeks, or months behind to finally give them feedback and remediation.

I am not suggesting that assessments should not be used as summative tools for grading. I am suggesting that assessments can serve a dual role to both summarize learning achievement and to provide essential formative feedback for learning.

Formative Assessments Should be Used to …

> Provide Feedback

> Identify Misconceptions

> Guide Interventions

> Stimulate Students to Reflect on Their Level of Understanding

> Drive Further Instruction

How can we bring formative assessment into the classroom for the purposes above?

Bringing Formative Assessment into the Classroom

- Classroom Circulation
- Classroom Surveying
- Classroom Response Systems
- Discussion
- Writing
- Diagramming

- Using Authentic, Summative Assessments as Formative Assessments
- Correcting and Revising Summative Assessments
- Moving Beyond Giving Credit for Simple Completion

a) Classroom Circulation

When students work to accomplish the goals of formative assessment, they will be much better off if their formative learning needs are met quickly to keep misconceptions from growing and requiring major remediation later.

During all types of activities, educators can actively circulate around the classroom to assess student comprehension by glancing at answers, scanning work, answering questions, asking questions, and generally gauging understanding. (If classroom activities don't often lend themselves to this type of assessment, it might be because students are sitting, listening, and absorbing as opposed to developing their own knowledge and applying it to a task.) Teachers may be tempted to stay at their desk and use class time (when students are working on a task) to grade previous assessments. The problem with this practice is that the class time is not used to assess and remediate misconceptions on the current assignment. So, rather than immediately identifying students' challenges and addressing those challenges, misconceptions are building up in students' minds (which will require much more time and effort to address later).

The Case of "Mr. Z"

Let's imagine a teacher, Mr. Z, who grades papers or takes care of other things while kids are working on a task in class. He believes that he is being efficient by planning and grading papers while students work. He assumes that if students have questions, they will come to his desk … and some do.

The biggest improvement in Mr. Z's teaching comes when he tries something else; he stops sitting and begins walking around his room. While circulating, Mr. Z finds that he can give students instant feedback on problems and tasks. He can also identify misconceptions while the students are learning and intervene immediately. Before Mr. Z began the practice of circulating, students would not get immediate feedback. Instead, kids waited until Mr. Z had a chance to collect an assignment, grade it, and return it. Because he was not providing instant feedback for the concepts of each lesson, some students had trouble with the next day's concepts as well. Additionally, Mr. Z realizes that with his old system, many youngsters did not seek help, because they did not realize that they were doing something wrong. When walking around the room and scanning students' work and answers, he can immediately identify when students have misconceptions and remediate them. Mr. Z can also identify students who really understand a concept well and get them to help their neighbors.

Not only does the practice of circulating help Mr. Z *provide feedback, identify misconceptions, and intervene*, it also allows him to ask probing questions in order to *stimulate students to reflect* upon their learning. (Using probing questions not only allows him to help struggling students, but to stimulate advanced students with challenging questions and connections.) The educator also gets a better feel for what he should be doing the next day in class and how fast or slow he should go … *driving further instruction.*
At first, Mr. Z thinks that circulating, instead of grading papers, will make it harder for him to fit all of his work into one day. He finds, however, that as he moves around the room scanning student work, he has a chance to assess much, and sometimes all, of the students'

assignments during class … reducing the amount of assessment (grading) time needed outside of class. (He can mark student papers as he walks to remind himself later what he has already checked.)

Mr. Z finds that another very important reason to wander the classroom is that students are much more likely to stay focused and on task if they know a teacher will be cruising past their desk a few times during class.

One final and HUGE reason Mr. Z has for "walking" is that it provides opportunities for him to interact with students in such a way that connections are created. Through informal interactions, he can get to know his students in ways that are not possible from the front of the classroom.

Lessons that Allow Circulating

Because teacher-student interactions are very important for many formative assessments (and for creating connections), it is important that teachers create classroom activities that allow for "walking." Classrooms where our youth constantly sit, listen, and regurgitate information in favor of developing understanding through engaging activities and lessons will not allow for much meaningful interaction.

Circulating Students Past the Teacher

Another form of "walking" is to require students to periodically come to the teacher. I like to do this during some self-guided inquiry activities in which students are given a series of tasks that will facilitate the learning of new concepts and skills. I give them a guide sheet to fill in as they complete the tasks. Periodically, students will find a star on their guide sheet that says, "Check with teacher" next to it. This practice forces kids to think and develop understanding independently (21ˢᵗ century skill), yet periodically come to me for formative assessment purposes. I can use my observations to *provide feedback, identify misconceptions, guide interventions, stimulate student reflection, and drive further instruction.*

b) Classroom Surveying

When teaching a lesson or leading a discussion with a whole class, gauging the level of student understanding can be difficult. Teachers can ask questions during a discussion or lesson to get formative feedback. The only challenge is that the kids who understand tend to raise their hands, while those who do not understand tend to keep to themselves. There are some strategies to deal with this. One example is to provide students with cards with numbers (like 1, 2, 3, and 4) that signal to the teacher the level of comfort the students have for a concept. This can be used to *drive* the pacing and path of a lesson. Similarly, these cards can be used to signal answers to questions. This strategy allows a teacher to *identify misconceptions* during a lesson. Then, the teacher can determine the best way to *intervene* … rather than moving along with the assumption that everyone understands. Another similar idea is to provide cards to students with "true" and "false" written on the cards and then ask the class true-false questions.

The problem with the strategies listed above is that they do not allow teachers to ask open-ended (non-multiple choice or true-false) questions to glimpse into students' thought processes. A simple strategy to glimpse into thought processes is to provide students with small dry erase boards on which they can write words, draw pictures, or draw graphs in order to answer probing questions. The students can then hold up their boards for the teacher to scan for understanding and misconceptions.

c) Classroom Response Systems

As mentioned in a previous chapter on the topic of technology, Chapter 17, there is a useful surveying tool called a classroom response system. With this technology, students are provided with remote answer pads that send answers to a teacher computer. The teacher learns who understands and whether the class is ready to move forward. (While the teacher knows who is right and wrong on each question, the rest of the class does not.)

With free online tools, teachers can survey a class with text messages sent from student cell phones. Students can submit answers to both multiple choice and open-ended questions. The teacher can observe the answers on the website (and also display the answers for the class). When students submit text answers, teachers can assess the understanding of those students.

These surveying technologies are great tools for gathering information to help *provide feedback, identify misconceptions, guide interventions, stimulate student reflection, and drive further instruction.*

d) Discussion

Discussions are great for formative assessment, because students are required to describe their thoughts, allowing teachers to assess various individuals' levels of understanding. I like to give kids a couple of round plastic chips before a discussion or debate and require that everyone turn in their chips by making a comment. This forces everyone to participate. Teachers can learn about the level of student understanding in order to *provide feedback, identify misconceptions, guide interventions, stimulate student reflection, and drive further instruction.*

e) Writing

Writing allows teachers to assess every student with more extensive, open-ended questions (making it the "grand champion" of formative assessment). Writing allows educators to peek into the thinking and logic of students in a way that other techniques cannot. Formative writing assessments can be short essays, journals, or blogs (in class or at home). At the end of a lesson, day, or unit, children can write a short essay, journal entry, or blog entry about the key concepts and skills they learned. Kids can answer specific questions or generally summarize what they have learned. In addition, they can make a note of which concepts or practices exercised during a lesson were the easiest and the most difficult to comprehend. Going further, students can apply ideas learned in class to new concepts, new ideas, opinions, or real-world situations.

With consistent journal writing or other writing, teachers can probe into students' minds on a regular basis. Beyond that, this exercise can be very helpful to the students themselves. As they reflect upon their learning, they can assess their own needs for further instruction or their challenges with each lesson. Students can also review past journal entries and reflect upon their strengths and areas for improvement.

In all, writing provides an avenue that allows teachers to *provide feedback, identify misconceptions, guide interventions, stimulate student reflection, and drive further instruction.*

f) Diagramming

We cannot forget the use of concept mapping and diagram creation (such as Venn diagrams) for probing student understanding. Like writing, these diagrams allow us to see the logic and connections students are developing.

g) Using Authentic, Summative Assessments as Formative Assessments

Above, we talked about finding ways to look at students' thought processes (through formal assessments) on regular tasks. We should also find ways to allow summative assessments (meant for grading) to double as formative assessments (which allow us to see the thought patterns of our youth). The best way to make our summative assessments provide formative feedback is to use assessments that reflect authentic tasks.

Let's think about the reasons that authentic tasks allow for formative assessment in ways that more traditional summative tests do not. When students get questions wrong on a multiple choice test, we generally don't get to see where their understanding breaks down. All we know is that the kids picked the wrong answers. When authentic tasks are used to make summative assessments for grades, kids are allowed to create, design, solve problems, explain, write, or answer open-ended questions. These real-world assessments allow teachers to more easily dissect students' thinking processes. These assessments allow teachers to *provide feedback, identify misconceptions, guide interventions, stimulate student reflection, and drive further instruction.* When possible, these types of summative assessments should be used.

Some educators might fear that authentic assessment tasks such as these do not prepare children for high-stakes tests. The truth, however, is that these assessments challenge students to develop a deeper level of understanding that can translate into better performance on more traditional assessments (such as a multiple choice test).

Tasks like these are not only great for assessment, but are crucial for developing complex critical thinking, creativity, the ability to explain, and other skills necessary for a worker in the new 21st century economy.

h) Correcting and Revising Summative Assessments

When teachers return a summative assessment, such as an assignment, a project, or a test, to students, some students will simply look at their score and give no further thought to anything marked incorrect (or any feedback from a rubric that goes with a project). Kids should be stimulated to remediate and correct those things that they do incorrectly on assessments (through personal reflection or the aid of classmates and the teacher). I like to require that kids make corrections or revisions to anything that they did incorrectly on an assessment. (Students can be required to write down a sentence or two that proves that they understand each concept that they did incorrectly on an assessment, rather than simply writing down a correct answer without proving that they understand it.) Whatever the assessment task or the style used to relearn, correct, or revise, kids must address those things that they did incorrectly. How else will they learn and maximize their potential if we just give back assessments and simply move along? By stimulating students to reflect upon and remediate their deficiencies on assessment tasks, we can make summative assessments serve a formative purpose instead of simply being used to assign grades.

Be Willing to Back Up and Reteach

Side Note

In addition to requiring corrections or revisions, it can be useful to discuss specific topics or questions that many in the class had trouble tackling on an assessment. Sometimes, it might be clear that teachers need to back up and generate an activity that reteaches a difficult concept or concepts (or teachers who think long term might recognize that an activity that will come later could be tweaked in order to address a prior misconception).

i) Moving Beyond Giving Credit for Simple Completion

If students complete an activity or a homework assignment and then credit is awarded for simply completing the work, a formative opportunity is missed. An obvious way to assess understanding is to collect work, assess it, and return it later. This process, however, can create a problem, because there is a lag time between collecting the assignment and *providing feedback* to students. Often, teachers need to give immediate feedback to support the next lesson. So, teachers might decide to give points for completion of the task and then discuss the correct answers with the class. This creates a new problem. While kids are getting feedback, teachers are not able to easily *identify misconceptions* and *intervene*, because they do not get a chance to see how well the students did on the assignment (and many students might not point out that they didn't do well on the assignment in front of the whole class). There is also little incentive for the students to strive for understanding and accuracy as they complete tasks when those students expect to be rewarded for completion alone. If teachers want to more quickly *provide feedback, identify misconceptions, intervene, stimulate student reflection, and drive further instruction*, they can get creative. One idea is to give a very small warm-up activity or quiz on the key ideas or skills contained within an assignment at the time it is due and count this as a portion of the grade. Methods for doing this include the use of a classroom response system; note cards with A, B, C, or D written on them; or small dry erase boards that students hold up to show answers for a short "understanding quiz." Giving a short quiz not only helps teachers get and give quicker feedback, it allows them to stimulate the class to strive for understanding and accuracy on a task. (It also discourages students from simply writing down what their friends put on an assignment, because they need to understand the assignment in addition to finishing it.) It would be more productive and fair when using an "understanding quiz or assessment" for an assignment to allow students to ask questions and get feedback before beginning the assessment.

If educators get creative, they can find their own systems that allow them to quickly get feedback, give feedback, reward understanding (not simple completion), and stimulate conscious effort on tasks.

Overall Formative Assessment

We Should See Educators Who ...	Personal Empowerment Questions (PEQs) for Educators
👁 Use formative assessment 👁 Walk and interact with students 👁 Get into students' minds 👁 Provide feedback to students 👁 Identify student misconceptions 👁 Intervene and remediate 👁 Stimulate student reflection 👁 Use formative assessments to drive further instruction 👁 Create lessons that allow for formative assessment 👁 Generate creative methods to determine the level of student understanding 👁 Make use of writing for formative assessment when appropriate 👁 Stimulate students to assess and remediate misconceptions from summative assessments	❓ How can I craft my lessons so that I am able to monitor the progress of my students? ❓ If my lesson does not allow for moving among my students, how can I get into my students' minds to assess understanding? <u>Based on what I am finding through assessments …</u> ❓ How can I provide timely feedback to students? ❓ How can I identify student misconceptions? ❓ How can I intervene to remediate misconceptions? ❓ What do my students understand well and not so well? ❓ How can I stimulate students to reflect on their level of understanding? ❓ In what ways do I need to tweak or add further instruction on this topic? ❓ What can I do to improve students' remediation after an official summative assessment?

Educators who ask questions like these will be able to use assessments to provide feedback, identify misconceptions, guide interventions, stimulate student reflection, and drive further instruction.

⭐ 2 Using Data from Assessments to Improve Teaching Strategies

Whether we use short-term formative assessments or long-term summative assessments, educators can use assessments as tools for improving teaching. This requires that we constantly analyze our students' strengths and weaknesses to determine which educational processes and tools are working and which need to be replaced or improved.

On a short-term basis, we can make use of daily formative assessment data to determine which practices are most effective and to adjust lessons for future years. This type of data tends to be informal and based on observations of and interactions with students.

On a long-term basis, we can use data from large projects, authentic tasks, tests, and exams to get feedback on our teaching practices. This data can provide details about which curricular goals we are achieving and which goals are not being met (and require revised teaching strategies).

Long-term assessment data cannot simply replace short-term formative assessment data. Notice that when teachers continuously gather data in their minds through formative assessments during the process of teaching, they can easily pinpoint which specific activities and portions of activities are effective and which are not. For example, a teacher might say one small thing in a way that is difficult to understand and this moment creates confusion for students on a whole lesson. If the teacher is continuously taking in data through formative assessments, he or she will quickly identify moments when kids are not understanding concepts … allowing the teacher to learn about their miscues and adjust.

If, instead, teachers rely on summative assessment data gathered long after learning takes place, they will have a much more difficult time pinpointing exactly which activities and portions of activities are creating learning difficulties for students. Teachers can learn that the teaching of a topic did not go well, but they cannot identify which lessons or portions of lessons need improvement. Don't take this the wrong way. Long-term assessment data is valuable for identifying areas for improvement, but it is not a replacement for formative assessment data used while teaching.

Finding Time to Make Lesson Revisions for Future Teaching

Side Note

When teachers use data to think of ways to improve lessons, we can find it difficult to find time to stop and revise (or replace) a lesson that we won't teach again until the next year … because we need to focus our attention on the next lessons to be taught *this* year.

I like to keep all of my lessons and assessments in a binder. When I think of a way to improve a lesson after using it during one school year, but then don't have time to immediately make the change, I make notes to myself and attach the notes to the activities (so that I can rework the activities the next year).

Using Data from Assessments to Improve Teaching Strategies

We Should See Educators Who ...	PEQs for Educators
👁 Gather data on classroom activities using formative assessments, and gather data on overall outcomes using summative assessments	❓ What types of data can I obtain during classroom activities through formative assessment?
👁 Use data in order to continue using strategies that work and modify or replace those that do not	❓ How can I gather and assess data on overall outcomes using summative assessments?
👁 Consider curricular goals and 21st century skills when assessing the effectiveness of their teaching strategies	❓ What are my learning goals for my students (considering the curriculum and 21st century skills)?
👁 Are willing to change when things don't work as planned	❓ Are my strategies working as well as needed in order to achieve my goals for student success?
	❓ What things am I doing that should remain the same, and what things am I doing that need to change?

Educators who ask questions like these will be empowered to use assessments to drive further successful instruction.

3 Using Proficiency-Based Assessments

Often, I teach concepts that I know students must understand before they can understand later concepts. Because it is critical that they gain immediate understanding, I use a proficiency-based assessment that requires students to retry the assessment until they demonstrate acceptable proficiency. I got the idea from my college math classes at the University of Michigan. They used a system where students had to take and retake what was called a "Gateway" quiz until they met a minimum proficiency. (Even though I got the idea from a college math course, the model works for all grade levels and all subject areas.)

When teaching chemistry, I might give a short quiz on the key ideas of the structure of atoms (something that kids *must* understand to learn throughout the year). If students do not meet a minimum proficiency, they must obtain help from me or peers and try again (with a different version of the same quiz) … until they meet the minimum proficiency. I continued to call this proficiency-based assessment technique the "Gateway" assessment out of habit from college. Others in my science department have picked up the practice. It has also spread to other departments in my school from math to Language Arts.

I have seen the Gateway used in a Language Arts setting to stimulate proficiency in grammar. Gateways for various parts of speech were used to make sure that each and every student understood the concepts and was successful. This example of using the Gateway in an English setting made me realize that it can be used for almost any class or concept. For example, an English teacher can require that students revise a piece of writing until it meets a minimum proficiency. If you think about it, this really makes sense. If every single essay that a student writes is worthy of a "D" and they are never forced to learn and revise their work to meet a minimum proficiency, they will have never created something of higher quality. They will certainly not be prepared for the 21st century (or high stakes state and national testing).

The key idea with proficiency-based assessments is that students need to be pushed to meet their greatest potential and not simply be allowed to have sub-par knowledge and skills.

Valuable Aspects and Outcomes of Proficiency-Based Assessments

Proficiency-Based Assessments …
- Set the expectation that everyone can learn.
- Go beyond simple assessments by stimulating students to work toward remediation when needed … rather than simply moving forward to compound difficulties on newer concepts.
- Stimulate students to review and work toward mastery.
- Stimulate students to talk to instructors and peers to get help on concepts about which they are "shaky." (This is something that kids might not otherwise do.)

- Meet the needs of all students. Teachers can require students to meet a minimum proficiency, but allow / encourage them to shoot for more. While one child strives to meet the minimum proficiency, another is stimulated to shoot for 100 percent.
- Succeed in creating lasting long-term memory, because students seek a deeper level of initial concept understanding or skill performance.
- Improve student confidence.
- Might improve test scores on state and national assessments. (The outright focus of proficiency-based assessments might not be for improving performance on a state assessment test, but this might be the result.)

Proficiency-Based Assessments

We Should See Educators Who ...	PEQs for Educators
👁 Expect students to show proficiency 👁 Use assessments that promote proficiency and stimulate students to meet their highest potential 👁 Empower students to diagnose their level of understanding and improve 👁 Stimulate students to use resources (such as teachers, peers, classwork, and technology) to attain proficiency 👁 Stimulate student confidence through mastery 👁 Stimulate students to show a deeper, longer-lasting ability to understand concepts and perform tasks	❓ What must my students know or be able to do to be proficient in my class? ❓ What must my students know or be able to do to succeed with learning that is yet to come this year? ❓ With each topic, what do I consider to be an acceptable level of proficiency? ❓ How can I structure assessments to require students to demonstrate proficiency? ❓ How will my assessments empower students to diagnose their level of understanding? ❓ How will my assessments enable students to improve? (What resources will be at their disposal?) ❓ What mechanisms can I build into my assessments to stimulate students to take the activities seriously? (Will I correlate a grade with minimum proficiency? Give a reward for mastery?)

Educators who ask questions like these stimulate students to achieve their highest potential on proficiency-based assessments.

Using Assessments to Develop Student Awareness of Learning Progression

4

Students need to be aware of their learning goals to see the "big picture" of their learning and develop an awareness of their progression. Educators can convey learning goals in a variety of ways: verbally, topic questions related to the curriculum, rubrics, and outlines. Rubrics are especially important as they allow students to see where their strengths and areas for improvement lie.

It is not quite enough for students to simply know the learning goals. They also need to be aware of their progression in meeting those goals. This awareness can be accomplished with formal feedback, informal conversations during class, conferencing, etc.

Using Assessments to Develop Student Awareness of Learning Progression

We Should See Educators Who ...	PEQ for Educators
👁 Promote student awareness of curricular and 21ˢᵗ century learning goals and the value of those goals 👁 Use tools and strategies that help students see their progress in meeting the curricular goals	❓ How can I help my students develop an awareness of the curriculum and its value? ❓ In what ways can I help students develop an awareness of their progression in learning?

Educators who ask questions like these will help students develop an awareness of their progress toward valuable learning goals.

Using Assessments to Reinforce the Real-World Value of the Curriculum

Authentic, real-world assessment tasks provide opportunities for students to demonstrate 21ˢᵗ century skills as they show their understanding of curricular objectives and benchmarks. These types of tasks are also more engaging and promote the idea that curricular knowledge and skills have real uses in the real world ... as opposed to more traditional style multiple choice, true-false, or fill-in-the-blank tests.

Connect Benchmarks to the Real World

Side Note

At the end of a unit, I like to give my students real-world questions that can be answered only with an understanding of the concepts, skills, and language of the curriculum. In this way, children are forced to relate educational benchmarks and terms to the real world. This helps youngsters see the value of the curriculum and not ask, "Why do we need to know this?" I can see their level of understanding quite easily, because the students are writing. This provides insight into their thoughts in ways that a multiple choice test cannot.

Example - Various Content Areas

For writing content areas, students can write an authentic letter to a person or organization. In science, learners can design tests to figure out something about the real world. Social Studies students can generate debate points that reflect historical facts. Math students can design a structure like an engineer.

In all of these cases, kids do a real-world task that requires the use of relevant skills from the curriculum.

Real-World Assessments

We Should See Educators Who ...	PEQs for Educators
👁 Use authentic tasks that allow students to see the real-world value of their learning 👁 Use authentic tasks that allow for the	❓ How is this curricular content valuable in the real world? ❓ In what ways can students perform a real-

assessment of curricular understanding	world task in order to demonstrate an understanding of the curriculum?

Educators who ask questions like these will create and employ real-world assessments that are engaging and help students see the real-world value of the curriculum.

6   Using Assessments as Learning Activities

Assessments can be used to provide new learning opportunities, instead of simply being used to monitor what has been learned so far. This can be accomplished in two ways.

Using Assessments as Learning Activities

- Creating Assessments that Teach
- Assessing Other Student's Assessments

---

a) Creating Assessments that Teach

Assessment tasks can often be structured to help students develop a deeper understanding of the concepts and skills being assessed. I stumbled upon an example of this a few years ago when I decided to assess students' understanding of disease and the immune system in two ways: with a traditional test and with a creative cartoon activity. I first asked the kids to create a cartoon complete with characters in which a virus (such as a cold) was attempting to invade a person's body. In this activity, the kids had to demonstrate what the cold virus would attempt to do and what the human body would do in response. I created a checklist of key ideas that had to be rationally and creatively included. After doing this cartoon assessment, I gave a more traditional test and found that the students' scores were much higher than the previous year. Through informal conversations with various students, I learned that the cartoon *assessment* had actually been a great *learning tool*. In order to plan and complete the task, the students were forced to analyze and rationalize all of the components and processes involved in fighting off a virus.

Example - Can Be Applied to All Content Areas

After realizing the *learning* benefits of alternative assessments, I used cartoons with other topics, such as a person's digestive system. Then, I had students write creative stories about some scientific processes as we learned them in class. With each, kids learned from the thought process that went into completing the assessment task. Another nice benefit of these types of tasks is that they promote many of the skills emphasized in this book ... for example, critical thinking and creativity skills.

Beyond the alternative assessment example above, there are other opportunities for assessments to serve as learning tools. This is often the case for real-world, authentic task assessments. In these, students can develop a deeper sense of the real-world value and uses of knowledge and skills. Furthermore, with assessment tasks, teachers can ask students to apply some basic ideas learned in class to more advanced situations that they have not previously encountered, helping the class to move their understanding beyond a basic level.

Example - Various Content Areas

In a Social Studies class, kids might be challenged to predict how a modern situation might unfold considering what they have learned about similar historical situations.

In a language arts content area, kids can use lessons learned from characters to describe how some situation or process generally works in the real world.

In math, an authentic task can serve as an assessment of previous learning and help students develop an understanding of a new real-world application of a math skill.

In all these examples, young minds learn about something new as they work to demonstrate their understanding of a topic.

b) Assessing Other Student's Assessments

The mental process of assessing is not just for teachers. Having kids assess the work of others is very valuable. On one hand, young minds see and learn from the mental processes, styles, techniques, and creativity of others. On the other hand, they improve their ability to identify errors or areas for improvement. When assessing others, kids are forced to dissect and rationalize processes and procedures.

Some teachers are comfortable with the practice of having students grade or assess one another's work on an assignment, test, or other formal assessment. This process can force students to reflect upon the correct answers or the best ways of expressing ideas.

Some educators are *not* comfortable with students assessing one another's work. This is not a problem. A class can still reap the benefits of participating in assessment processes when a teacher provides an anonymous piece of work from another class or a previous year. Making an activity out of this type of assessment can be both engaging and beneficial.

Beyond peer assessment, self-assessment is critical. In the real world, students must become masters of identifying their own strengths (to promote them) and weaknesses (to improve them).

19 - Using Assessments to Empower

Using Assessments as Learning Activities

We Should See Educators Who ...	PEQs for Educators
👁 Create assessments that allow students to learn and expand their understanding, while demonstrating their understanding of a topic	❓ What assessments will allow my students to deepen or expand their knowledge as they demonstrate their understanding of what we have already learned?
👁 Present students with new situations that require previously learned skills	❓ How can I stimulate my students to use their knowledge and skills in new ways when being assessed?
👁 Ask students to assess the work of	

others 👁 Ask students to assess their own work	❓ How can I stimulate my students to assess their own work and the work of others in order to learn from the assessment process?

Educators who ask questions like these will find ways to expand their students' learning into areas that have not previously been utilized. They will find ways to develop new understanding at all times … even when young minds are being assessed on previous learning.

Challenging Students at All Levels of Understanding in Assessments

   With a variety of students in a classroom, assessments can be crafted to challenge all of their young minds. This can mean that assessments are differentiated so that there is more than one level of difficulty. Also, assessments can be open-ended so that students with various depths of understanding can all show what they know and can do. Whether it is an essay or a product, open-ended questions can challenge everyone to work toward their highest ability. Open-ended assessments that challenge students of all levels of understanding can be attractive for teachers who do not easily find time to create multiple assessments for multiple ability levels.

Example - Various Content Areas

   Teachers can use open-ended assessments to ask students to design a piece of music, develop an experiment to test a question or phenomenon, analyze a situation and develop an opinion, create a game that reflects an understanding of a topic, or create a plan to accomplish a task.
   In all of these situations, teachers can give students a rubric that outlines what must be shown in order to demonstrate various levels of understanding from basic understanding to mastery.

Challenging Students at All Levels of Understanding in Assessments

We Should See Educators Who ...	PEQs for Educators
👁 Create differentiated assessments 👁 Create open-ended assessments 👁 Provide assessment opportunities for children to maximize their potential 👁 Create assessments that allow feedback for improvement to be given to *all* students of all levels of understanding (If we test only for minimum competency, higher-level students will receive no feedback on how to grow.)	❓ How can my assessments be created to allow me to see the degree of understanding of all my students? ❓ How can I differentiate this assessment? ❓ How can I make this assessment more open-ended in order to allow kids of various levels of understanding to show their competency? ❓ Which assessment will give me insight into the thought processes of my kids?

Educators who ask questions like these will find ways to challenge *all* students to maximize their potential on assessments.

Using Range-Line Rubrics to Provide Empowering Feedback (Improving Upon the Traditional Rubric)

8

Traditional rubrics have been very useful in helping teachers set clear expectations and consistent guidelines for grading. Here is an example that represents a portion of a rubric for writing a five-paragraph essay. It is similar in style to rubrics used in education. Take a moment to determine what expectations the rubric outlines.

Traditional Rubric

Elements	4	3	2	1	Totals
Organization of Essay	Essay has a logical sequence with a clear introduction (including a thesis), at least three supporting points, and a clear conclusion.	Sequence does not flow well *or* essay is missing an introduction, missing a supporting point, or missing a conclusion.	Sequence does not flow well *and* missing an introduction, or missing a supporting point, or missing a conclusion.	Essay is difficult to follow and/or is missing multiple elements.	
Quality of Supporting Evidence	Supporting points are clearly stated, connected to the thesis, and supported by examples or research.	Most points are clearly stated, connected to the thesis, and supported by examples or research.	Two to three points are vague, unrelated to the thesis, or lack supporting examples or evidence.	Multiple points are poorly stated, related to the thesis, or lack supporting examples or evidence.	

Next, let's look another way to organize these requirements. The next rubric takes a different approach. First, it separates each element, such as "Organization of Essay," into sub-elements, like "Sequence of Essay," "Introduction," "Supporting Points," and "Conclusion. In addition, the rubric gives each sub-element a line with a range of feedback options. Thus, it is called a "range-line rubric."

Range-Line Rubric

Elements	Sub-Element Feedback			Totals
Organization of Essay	3 — Logical Order	2 — 1 item out of place	1 — Disorganized	
	Sequence of Essay			
	3 — Clear with thesis	2 — Unclear / no thesis	1 — No Introduction	
	Introduction			
	3 — 3 or more Present	2 — 2 Present	1 — 1 or none Present	
	Supporting Points			
	3 — Clear	2 — Vague	1 — Not Present	
	Conclusion			
Quality of Supporting Evidence	3 — All clear	2 — Some vague	1 — Difficult to Follow	
	Clarity of Supporting Points			
	3 — All	2 — 1 is not	1 — 2 or more are not	
	Connected to Thesis			
	3 — All	2 — 1 is not	1 — 2 or more are not	
	Examples or Research to Support Points			

What advantages does the range-line rubric provide?

- Teachers can use the rubric with ease. They can simply scan the range lines and circle the appropriate level of student performance. This contrasts with the traditional rubric in which teachers must slowly sift through each box of an element in order to find one that matches a student's performance. To see the difference, take a moment to compare the boxes of the traditional rubric with the range lines of the range-line rubric.
- With the use of range-line rubrics, students can clearly and easily see each expectation and the range of possible performances. The range-line rubric is simply less confusing.
- Students can have a much easier time interpreting their feedback and pinpointing areas for improvement with the easy-to-read range lines. Kids are not left wondering, "Where did I go wrong?"
- The range-line rubric provides more options for specific grading. For instance, a student can receive anywhere from 1-12 possible points for "Organization of Essay" on the range-line rubric above. On the traditional rubric, the teacher would be limited to 1,2,3, or 4. This allows the grading to better reflect the student performance.

Using Range-Line Rubrics

We Should See Educators Who ...	PEQs for Educators
👁 Create easily understood elements and sub-elements that reflect student expectations 👁 Create easily understood range-line rubrics (showing the possible levels of performance) for each sub-element to be assessed	❓ What elements do I want to assess? ❓ What sub-elements are important to each element? ❓ What range of performance is possible for each sub-element? ❓ Does the organization of my rubric allow me to quickly and easily use it? ❓ Does the organization of my rubric allow students to easily understand their expectations and easily interpret feedback?

Educators who ask questions like these will create rubrics that empower students with an understanding of their expectations and feedback for improvement.

Assessment: Wrap-up

A key idea to take from this chapter is that assessments serve a critical role in education when they are used to *provide feedback, identify misconceptions, guide intervention, stimulate student reflection, and drive further teaching.* Assessments and learning activities should work together in such a way that they are inseparable. Let's now add assessment to the "System of Thoughtful 21ˢᵗ Century Teaching Practices" graphic that we used in the last chapter. (New ideas are in red.)

System of Thoughtful 21ˢᵗ Century Teaching Practices

Beginning of the School Year

> **Make Long-Term Plan**
> for Teaching Major Topics and Skills

Planning to Teach a Unit

> **Determine Goals**
> for Topic or Unit (curricular goals and 21st century skills)

> **Create Performance Assessments**
> for Topic or Unit that challenge *all* students

> **Create Lessons**
> that Prepare Students for Assessments (interwoven with *formative assessments*)

Teaching a Unit

Teach Lessons that Prepare Students for Assessments (interwoven with formative assessments to help *provide feedback, identify misconceptions, guide interventions, stimulate student reflection, and drive further teaching*)

Perform Assessments that Measure Attainment of Goals (use *data* to improve methods; make students aware of progress)

Common Thread

   Think for a moment about some of the goals for assessments that are outlined in this chapter: formative assessments, connecting new skills to their real-world value, using assessments as learning tools, and challenging students of all ability levels. There is a common thread that weaves through these goals. The goals can all be achieved when children are performing assessments in which they create something, apply new skills and knowledge in some way, develop opinions, assess situations, work on open-ended tasks, or write. On the flip side, assessments that simply ask students to regurgitate facts on a "classic-style" test do not allow us to gain the wealth of benefits that *action-based* assessments generate.

   If we truly want to address the goals outlined in our unit on a 21st Century Challenge, we must make use of action-based assessments in which kids *do something* with the concepts and skills they learn.

Thinking About It

- **What are some ways that formative assessments do and can work well in your educational setting?**
- **What tools could make formative assessment easier for you?**
- **How can you use formative and summative data to shape your teaching practices?**
- **How can you develop an awareness of learning progress among your students?**
- **How can your assessments be shaped to reflect the real-world value of the curriculum?**
- **In what ways do your assessments teach new lessons as students demonstrate understanding?**
- **How can your assessments be constructed so that students of all levels of understanding can demonstrate their full understanding?**

How Does This Chapter Support the Goals of This Book?

   Let's take a moment to think about the ways in which the ideas of this chapter help us address the three main goals of this book by looking at the "Building Blocks of a 21st Century Education" on page 13 and the "Daily Thoughts for Educators" on page 18. We now have guidelines for thoughtful assessment, which help us to put together the pieces of an empowering 21ˢᵗ century education.

Make Note of Your Great Ideas!

If you haven't already, note your ideas for implementing the practices in this chapter in your Teacher Empowerment Menu (for 21ˢᵗ Century Educators). In the future, you can easily reference these personalized ideas.

> "When used correctly, assessment is the most important part of education."
> - Michelle Guthrie (my sister, a wise teacher)

20 | Using Interventions / Remediation to Empower 21st Century Students

In Chapter 18, we looked at planning. We discussed the idea that teachers need to 1) have learning goals for their students in mind, then 2) determine what performance assessments will measure the success in meeting these learning goals, and finally 3) determine what learning activities or lessons will allow students to meet the assessments. In the previous chapter, we looked at assessments. A large emphasis was placed on weaving formative assessments into our teaching as tools that can *provide feedback, identify misconceptions, guide intervention, stimulate reflection, and drive further teaching.* Now, let's get more specific about what it means to intervene. Interventions are critical for empowering students for the 21st century. After careful planning, teaching, and assessment, we must take action to remediate and correct learning challenges that occur. We will address four types of interventions:

Interventions / Remediation

1. **Immediate Interventions** (Performed as students learn)
2. **Short-Term Interventions** (Performed within the days and weeks following the intended learning)
3. **Long-Term Interventions** (Performed when students are months or more behind the intended pace of learning)
4. **Proactive Interventions** (Performed before the intended learning takes place)

---

1   Immediate Interventions

Don't Let Little Problems Grow into Big Problems

Rightly so, educators put a lot of energy into helping students who have misunderstood concepts during a unit and who have fallen behind. The problem is that teachers cannot afford to wait until young minds have fallen behind by a few days, a week, or a unit to begin remediation. The best technique to remediate student misconceptions and academic deficiencies is to keep them from growing in the first place. This means that while we are teaching, we put in place mechanisms to assess the level of student understanding and immediately intervene to promote understanding and extinguish misconceptions. *I cannot stress this point enough; the teachers who have the easiest time with remediation are those who teach in a way that promotes understanding and addresses misconceptions* **immediately**. The better that students understand what is happening today, the easier it will be for them to build upon that knowledge tomorrow. The alternative is to use a style of assessment that does not discover student misconceptions until after a couple days, a week, or a unit, which allows learning deficiencies to grow and compound. A monstrous challenge is created in which teachers must determine where things went wrong and reteach a whole week or unit of lessons. The challenge that is created is so huge that kids are very likely to get left behind. This is why the last chapter focused so greatly on making assessments formative in nature and using them to *provide feedback, identify misconceptions, guide intervention, stimulate student reflection, and drive further teaching…* **immediately**.

Intervention and Remediation Through Root Causes

So, how do we intervene when we find misconceptions? Let's say that an educator creates a lesson and uses some type of formative assessment that allows him or her to walk around the room and measure understanding. As the teacher is moving about, he or she discovers a student who is not able to perform the task. The teacher realizes that there is a need for immediate intervention. However, the educator can't simply take action. He or she first needs to assess the reason that the child is struggling. **If a teacher is to successfully intervene, he or she must diagnose the root cause of the challenge.**

Potential Root Causes for Misconceptions that Require *Immediate* Intervention

- **Academic Reason** - The student does not understand one or more aspects of the topic at hand.
- **Behavioral Reason** - The student is distracted from the task at hand.
- **Motivational Reason** - The student is not motivated to give his or her best effort.
- **Emotional Reason** - Something in the student's life is affecting his or her emotions in such a way that the focus on learning is affected.

Only after a teacher has identified the origin of a student's misconceptions can he or she work to take appropriate action. Thus, a teacher should progress in the following way.

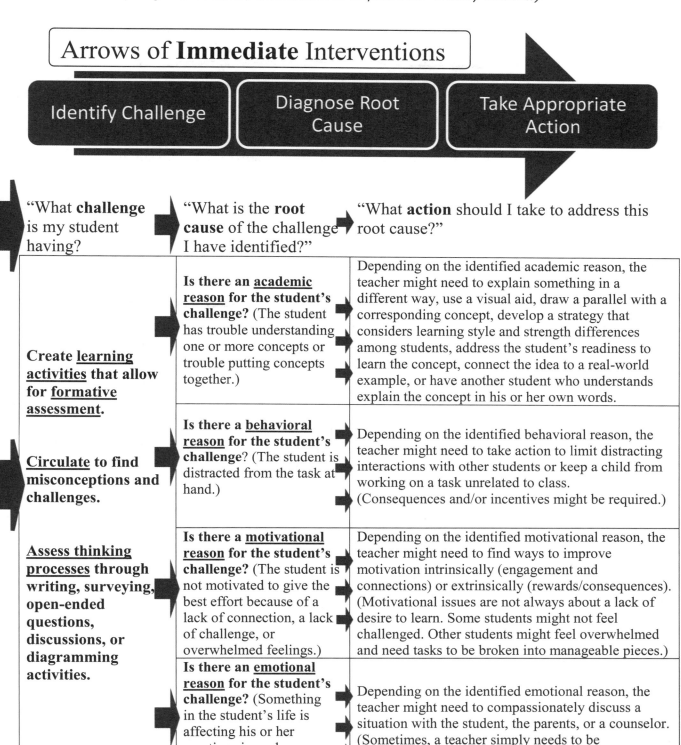

Connections and Flexibility Matter in Finding and Addressing Root Causes

Clearly, the more a teacher *understands and is connected* to his or her students, the easier it will be to determine the root cause of difficulties and then determine a course of action. In addition, a teacher needs to be *flexible* enough to recognize that students are different and to differentiate remediation techniques. What works with one youngster may or may not work with others. Kids come with different learning style strengths, prior knowledge, motivations, needs, wants, home lives, and social lives. We won't get into any specific courses of action for intervention, because there are so many possible root causes and possible plans to deal with them. The overarching key is that successful intervention requires successfully identifying the root cause of a misconception.

Why Worry so Much About Finding the Root Cause When Intervening?

Educators cannot simply make assumptions about the source of a child's challenges in class. For example, if a child is distracted by something, it doesn't matter how many different learning activities, explanations, or demonstrations a teacher uses. That child is not going to respond to these various strategies … because he or she is not focusing on the task. On the flip side, a child who *is* focusing will not benefit when the teacher simply tells him or her to try harder, rather than using an alternate method of explaining or demonstrating a concept.

When educators "intervene" without looking for the root cause of a child's misconception, it is like firing arrows (intervention solutions) without looking for the targets (root causes) … some arrows (intervention solutions) will hit their targets (root causes), but many will not.

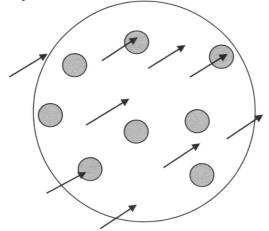

General Interventions
Using general interventions without addressing specific root causes is like firing many intervention arrows in the general direction of the challenges you face.

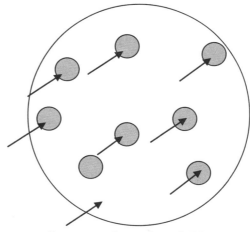

Interventions that Address Root Causes
Using interventions that address root causes is like firing specific intervention arrows at specific root causes that have been discovered. There are far fewer misses.

Involve Parents when Reasonable

If a student is having a little trouble one day in an isolated event, a teacher might decide that it is not significant enough to involve parents. However, *any solution (arrow) for <u>continuous difficulties</u> should involve the* **parents** whether the root cause of the issue is academic, behavioral, motivational, or emotional.

Also, some isolated events that require immediate interventions are serious enough that they require immediate parental involvement. When an educator notices something serious and out of the ordinary for a particular student, he or she must consider that parental involvement could be the key to making sure that the serious event is isolated and does not happen again.

Let's put things into perspective for a moment. We want to use immediate interventions as students are learning, so that misconceptions do not compound and become overwhelming. We can't do this if we do not create and use formative assessments that will allow us to see if learning goals are being achieved.

Immediate Interventions

We Should See Educators Who ...	PEQs for Educators
👁 Use assessments that allow them to immediately discover student challenges	❓ How will I discover challenges that my students are having?
👁 Identify root causes of student misconceptions and challenges	<u>Once a challenge is discovered …</u>
👁 Address challenges with targeted "arrows" of intervention solutions that address the root causes	❓ What is the root cause of my student's challenge?
👁 Immediately address challenges so that they do not grow and become more difficult to handle	❓ Is the root cause academic, behavioral, motivational, or emotional?
	❓ What solution will target this specific issue?
	❓ Will parental involvement help?

Educators who ask questions like these will address misconceptions and other concerns before they grow to be much larger ... as time goes by.

2 ★ **Short-Term Interventions** (for challenges that last days and weeks)

Don't Allow Small Problems to Grow into Huge Roadblocks to Learning

As stated in the last section, the best way to deal with remediation is to attack learning difficulties with immediate interventions. Even so, educators will encounter students with understanding deficiencies as a unit progresses or on culminating topic / unit assessments. Realistically, there will be kids who do not complete their homework. Realistically, there will be students who understand concepts as they are being learned, but don't translate that understanding into success on later assessments. Realistically, some learners might not review or study as they should. Realistically, some students will have grades that we do not consider a reflection of success.

While the best short-term intervention plan is to implement better immediate interventions, we need a plan for dealing with challenges that will inevitably occur over the course of days and weeks. We need a system of short-term interventions to deal with issues that we cannot simply address with an immediate classroom intervention.

Intervention and Remediation Through Root Causes

Guess what? Just as immediate interventions require finding the root cause, short-term interventions that address issues that last for days and weeks require that we find the root cause. **If a teacher is to successfully intervene, he or she must diagnose the root cause of the challenge.**

Potential Root Causes for Misconceptions that Require *Short-Term* Intervention

- **Academic Reason** - The student does not understand one or more aspects of the topic at hand.
- **Behavioral Reason** - The student is distracted from tasks on a regular basis.
- **Motivational Reason** - The student is not motivated to give his or her best effort on a regular basis.
- **Emotional Reason** - Something in the student's life is affecting his or her emotions in such a way that a focus on learning is affected on a regular basis.

Arrows of **Short-Term** (days / weeks) Interventions

Identify Challenge	Diagnose Root Cause	Take Appropriate Action

"What *short-term* **challenge** is my student having?"

"What is the **root cause** of the challenge I have identified?"

"What **action** should I take to address this root cause?"

Look for <u>overall performance on learning activities</u> over the course of a topic or unit. **Look for <u>difficulties on culminating assessments</u> for a topic or unit.** **Look for <u>missing classwork and homework</u>.** **<u>Survey students</u> to discover recurring challenges that they are having.**	**Is there an <u>academic reason</u> for the student's challenge?** (The student has continuous difficulty understanding concepts, trouble with an earlier concept on which others were built, difficulty retaining new learning, poor test-taking skills, trouble with the pace of activities, or a learning disability.)	Depending on the identified academic reason, the teacher might need to back up and reteach a topic, introduce a new teaching method to meet different styles of learning, help a student develop better study skills, work on strategies for improved memory, help a student with test taking strategies, differentiate to accommodate different learning needs, tutor a student outside of class time, or have extra time in class for help. (Involve parents)
	Is there a <u>behavioral reason</u> for the student's challenge? (The student is continuously distracted from tasks in class, is disorganized, or does not use time wisely.)	Depending on the identified behavioral reason, the teacher might need to take action to limit distracting interactions with other students, develop a behavior plan, or implement an organization plan. (Involve parents)
	Is there a <u>motivational reason</u> for the student's challenge? (The student is not motivated to give the best effort because of a lack of connection, a lack of challenge, or overwhelmed feelings.)	Depending on the identified motivational reason, the teacher might need to find ways to improve motivation intrinsically (engagement and connections) or extrinsically (rewards/consequences). Differentiation of instruction may be required to meet everyone's learning needs. (Involve parents)
	Is there an <u>emotional reason</u> for the student's challenge? (Something in the student's life is affecting his or her emotions in such a way that a focus on learning is affected.)	Depending on the identified emotional reason, the teacher might need to compassionately discuss a situation with the student, the parents, or a counselor. (Sometimes, a teacher simply needs to be understanding and listen.)

Notice that the arrows of short-term interventions follow the same format as those of immediate interventions. However, the identification of challenges, diagnoses of root causes, and appropriate actions take on new forms that reflect the fact that short-term interventions are for challenges that last for days and weeks.

Considering the vast variety of potential challenges, root causes, and plans of action with which educators deal, we must be careful to be systematic in our approach. We must not quickly jump to the conclusion that some blanket strategy will be a fix-all.

Involve Parents in Short-Term Interventions

When a student challenge occurs frequently enough to move it out of the realm of immediate interventions and into the realm of short-term interventions, parents should be involved. However, simply contacting parents and telling them that their child is not doing well does not go far enough. If the teacher knows the root cause of the issue, he or she needs to communicate that cause to the parents. If the teacher does not know the root cause, the parents should be enlisted in finding it. Then, involvement of the parents in dealing with the issue can be helpful … if not crucial. Creating a contract for the student, parents, and teacher that identifies each party's commitment to addressing the issue at hand may bring positive results. This practice helps all parties identify their responsibilities in the process and also creates a team approach to problem solving. (The three-legged stool concept, in which the educational hopes of a child are held up by the student, parents, and teachers, is reinforced.)

Keep Students Responsible

Another important principle in short-term interventions is that the interventions should not remove all responsibility for learning from the students involved. Instead, the interventions should work to promote and build student responsibility over time. Teachers and students can mutually create learning goals and plans.

Work as a Staff on Short-Term Interventions

The key thing for educators to recognize is that other teachers are probably struggling with similar issues that require short-term interventions. Colleagues can be a great source of ideas for discovering the root cause of an issue and taking steps to deal with it. To go further … when numerous teachers in one school deal with a similar issue, it can be helpful to create a school-wide system of short-term interventions. A school might collectively decide to implement strategies to deal with students who do not turn in assignments, have low motivation, have poor study skills, have poor organizational skills, or need extra help / tutoring.

Side Note

Short-Term Interventions

We Should See Educators Who ...	PEQs for Educators
👁 Actively look for student issues that might require a short-term intervention	❓ How will I discover difficulties that my students are having?
👁 Identify the root cause of a student's continuing difficulties	<u>Once a challenge is discovered …</u> ❓ What is the root cause of the student's difficulties?
👁 Address challenges with targeted "arrows" of intervention that address the	❓ Is the root cause academic, behavioral,

root cause 👁 Involve parents 👁 Continuously implement strategies (arrows) until an issue is resolved 👁 Implement potential blanket strategies as a school (without, of course, using these as substitutes for needed individual interventions) 👁 Promote student responsibility in overcoming challenges	motivational, or emotional? ❓ What solution will target this specific issue? ❓ How can I involve the parents in a solution? ❓ How can I stimulate the student to take on reasonable responsibility in addressing his or her challenge? ❓ Are other teachers encountering the same issue, and can we work together to find a small-scale or large-scale solution?

Educators who ask questions like these will take the necessary steps to discover the root causes of any student challenges and implement strategies that go to the hearts of the issues.

Long-Term Interventions (when kids are months behind schedule or are having huge difficulties that will take a long time to remediate)

Clearly, our goal should be to use immediate and short-term interventions to avoid situations where students are far behind in their academic progress. What do we do, though, when students are: a great deal behind in their academic progression, don't pass a class, don't meet minimum proficiency requirements for a class, or aren't on pace to graduate? In these instances, we again need to address the root cause of the problem. Some strategies for short-term intervention might be helpful. But realistically, students can sometimes be so far behind that they need a more aggressive long-term intervention.

Again, We Need Intervention through Root Causes ... but on a Larger Scale

Like immediate and short-term interventions, long-term challenges require that we seek out and discover the root cause of the issue at hand. Then, we can address the challenge appropriately. Long-term interventions are larger, longer lasting, and often more intensive.

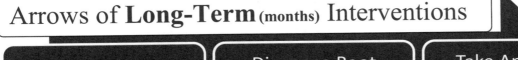

Arrows of **Long-Term** (months) Interventions

Identify Challenge   Diagnose Root Cause   Take Appropriate Action

Maybe some students need an afterschool tutoring program to help them catch up on the key ideas of a subject. Other kids might have poorer reading skills that are holding them back in all of their academics … perhaps they need additional time each day with help to improve their reading. Some students may need to enroll in summer school to catch up. In some schools, children might use virtual computer classes to recover. Some schools might hire paraprofessionals to help meet the needs of students who struggle to keep up in certain classes. A mentoring program might also be appropriate.

Because of the varying needs of students, resources, and philosophies in different school districts, long-term interventions will look different in different places. What different schools should have in common is a dedication to finding effective long-term interventions that address the root causes of challenges in order to get students up to acceptable levels of performance.

Long-Term Interventions

We Should See Educators Who ...	PEQs for Educators
👁 Actively identify student issues that might require long-term interventions	❓ How will I discover difficulties that my students are having?
👁 Identify the root cause of a student's long-term challenges	<u>Once a challenge is discovered …</u>
👁 Address challenges with targeted "arrows" of intervention that address the root cause	❓ What is the root cause of the student's difficulty?
👁 Involve parents	❓ Is the root cause academic, behavioral, motivational, or emotional?
👁 Continuously implement strategies (arrows) until an issue is resolved	❓ What solution will target the specific issue?
👁 Implement potential blanket strategies as a school	❓ How can I involve the parents in the solution?
👁 Promote student responsibility in overcoming challenges	❓ How can I stimulate the student to take on reasonable responsibility in addressing his or her challenge?
	❓ Are other teachers encountering the same issue, and can we work together to find a small-scale or large-scale solution?

Educators who ask questions like these will take the necessary steps to discover the root causes of any student challenges and implement strategies that go to the heart of the issues.

⭐ **4** **Proactive Interventions** (implemented before intervention is required)

Proactive, not Reactive

We've looked at immediate, short-term, and long-term interventions. All of these interventions are reactive in nature. Sometimes, there are situations in which we can be proactive, addressing an issue before it occurs. For example, educators might find that each and every year many students struggle with the same thing. This challenge might be an academic issue, such as study skills, writing skills, or learning skills. It might be a behavioral issue such as attendance. Whatever the challenge, if teachers know it is coming, they should create a strategy to proactively address the issue (before it arises).

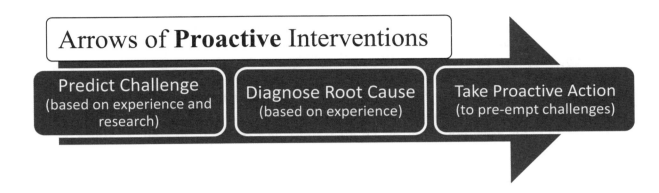

Blanket Strategies

Sometimes, teachers need blanket strategies when difficulties are widespread within a school. This is often the case for students making the transition from elementary school to middle school or middle school to high school. There are challenges and struggles that educators know these students will encounter. A set of proactive interventions should be enacted to create a smooth transition that allows students to be successful in their new environment. As with other types of intervention, proactive intervention requires that educators determine the root causes of issues and then address those causes.

Another example of a blanket strategy for proactive intervention is for teachers to recognize that, inevitably, there will be a variety of preferred learning styles within a group of students. With this in mind, teachers can set out to teach in such a way that the needs of all students will be met. For example, a teacher might start a lesson with an inquiry-based hands-on activity, move into an oral and visual discussion of the topic, and then wrap up by asking students to model the new skill or concept. In this way, the varying learning needs of the class are proactively addressed and the lesson is simply more engaging.

Individualized Proactive Interventions

a) Look to Previous Teachers

Beyond blanket strategies for proactive interventions, there are often times when we can be individually proactive with new students. How is this possible? How can we know the needs of our youngsters before we've interacted with them? The answer lies with former teachers. Former teachers have already discovered strategies that can best help each child. Why not tap into this resource? If an elementary school teacher finds a great method for helping a student with math or reading, there could be a system for the previous teacher to communicate that strategy to the next teacher. This is much better than waiting for the learner to encounter difficulties in math or reading the following year, leaving the student to struggle while his or her teacher works reactively to figure out what to do. Why not create an individualized transition mechanism that will work to support students and empower their new teachers?

Perhaps, there can be some sort of file that transfers from teacher to teacher or, maybe there can be a computer database of information that teachers can reference. I am not suggesting that this be a system for transferring negative information about children, but instead be a way to transmit helpful ideas and strategies that can give kids a leg up with their new teachers. It can include ideas about motivation, learning style, strengths, and student-specific best practices. Schools can create an individualized system that helps with not only the transitions from school to school, but from grade to grade within schools.

b) Early Diagnosis

Another idea for proactively determining the learning needs of students is to start a school year with diagnostic assessments and activities that can help teachers learn the students' prior knowledge and thinking styles. This information can then be used in effectively planning learning strategies during the year.

The bottom line is that there are many opportunities for us to be proactive rather than reactive. Often the best interventions are those that are proactive and don't wait for problems to arise.

Proactive Interventions

We Should See Educators Who ...	PEQs for Educators
👁 Proactively seek and predict student difficulties based on experience and research	❓ Which difficulties do I see each year, and what do I expect to see this year?
👁 Identify the potential root causes of potential challenges	Once a *potential* challenge is identified ...
	❓ What is the root cause of the student challenge I expect to see?
👁 Address challenges with targeted "arrows" of proactive intervention that address the root causes	❓ Is the root cause academic, behavioral, motivational, or emotional?
👁 Involve parents	❓ What solution will target this specific issue?
👁 Implement potential proactive blanket strategies as a school	❓ Who should I involve in the solution?
	❓ How can I make the student take on reasonable responsibility in proactively addressing his or her challenge?
	❓ Are other teachers encountering the same issue, and can we work together to find a small-scale or large-scale solution?

Educators who ask questions like these will take the necessary proactive steps to avoid or decrease many of the challenges that might otherwise occur.

Interventions / Remediation: Wrap-up

A successful system of interventions can be a major factor in student success. There are a few key ideas that must be considered.

- Long-term interventions are made easier by good short-term interventions; short-term interventions are made easier by good immediate interventions; immediate interventions are made easier with good proactive interventions.

- Successful interventions should address the root causes and needs of varying students.

- Educators need to be willing to continuously assess the understanding of individual students and shift strategies as needed in the immediate term, short term, and long term.

- The more connected teachers are to their students, the easier it will be to determine the root causes of issues that need to be addressed.

Thinking About It
- **Which methods and resources might be best suited for helping you find the root causes of student challenges that require intervention?**
- **What are the biggest obstacles in intervention, and how can you overcome them?**
- **How can a teacher consistently intervene as soon as possible in the process of learning?**

Let's add interventions / remediation to our "System of Thoughtful 21st Century Teaching Practices." (New ideas are in red.)

System of Thoughtful 21st Century Teaching Practices

Beginning of the School Year

Make Long-Term Plan for Teaching Major Topics and Skills

Determine Proactive Interventions and Plan for Timing of Implementation During Teaching

Planning to Teach a Unit

Determine Goals for Topic or Unit (curricular goals and 21st century skills)

Create Performance Assessments for Topic or Unit that challenge *all* students

Create Lessons that Prepare Students for Assessments (interwoven with formative assessments)

Teaching a Unit

Teach Lessons that Prepare Students for Assessments (interwoven with formative assessments to help *provide feedback, identify misconceptions, guide immediate interventions, stimulate student reflection, and drive further teaching*)

Perform Assessments that Measure Attainment of Goals (use data to improve methods; make students aware of progress)

To Be Done Continuously During the Year As Needed

Implement Short-Term Intervention Systems to deal with issues that go beyond quick and immediate classroom fixes (such as providing a tutor; providing a mentor; reteaching concepts; or promoting better study skills, better organization, improved assignment completion, and enhanced connections)

Implement Long-Term Interventions in order to deal with large and long-term student challenges that threaten overall educational success

How Does This Chapter Support the Goals of This Book?

Let's take a moment to think about the ways in which the ideas of this chapter help us address the three main goals of this book by looking at the "Building Blocks of a 21st Century Education" on page 13 and the "Daily Thoughts for Educators" on page 18. We now have guidelines for thoughtful intervention and remediation, which help us to put together the pieces of an empowering 21ˢᵗ century education.

Make Note of Your Great Ideas!

If you haven't already, note your ideas for implementing the practices in this chapter in your Teacher Empowerment Menu (for 21ˢᵗ Century Educators). In the future, you can easily reference these personalized ideas.

21 Promoting Knowledge and Skill Retention to Empower 21st Century Students

The Knowledge and Skill Retention Challenge

After educators pour their hearts into successful planning, instruction, assessment, and remediation to create student success in learning concepts and skills, wouldn't it be silly to allow kids to forget what they learn? Well … this seems to be a common occurrence. *There is not enough emphasis placed on retention of new knowledge and skills in education today.* In many instances, students and teachers put great effort into new learning, but then little goes into strategies for hanging on to new concepts and abilities. What are we doing to help students retain new ideas and empower them for the 21st century?

There are times when we can see evidence of the challenge of knowledge and skill retention. Let's say some sixth-grade students learn a certain curriculum in their English (Language Arts) class. The seventh-grade teacher who teaches the kids the next year might be surprised and even frustrated when his or her class doesn't seem to remember the concepts from the previous year. (This makes it harder to build upon those concepts without spending precious time reteaching). It's not that the kids didn't effectively learn the sixth-grade concepts or that the sixth-grade teacher did something wrong, it is the simple problem that the human brain slowly forgets.

Let's consider another example: A high school teacher might do all the right things throughout the course of the year and is excited about the prospect of student success on a final exam. Then, the teacher is deflated when he or she finds that the students seem to have forgotten the things that they definitely understood earlier in the year. The exam scores don't seem to reflect the learning that surely occurred. This isn't just discouraging for the teacher. Students who are attempting to study for the final exam can be frustrated when they realize how many concepts they have forgotten, even though they previously understood those concepts. This leaves young minds overwhelmed.

In a final example, a fourth grade teacher works on math skills during the school year and knows that the kids are prepared for a standardized test. Similar to the examples above, the kids might not perform as expected, simply because they forgot some skills that they had previously learned. Again, it's not that the educator was ineffective in teaching; the young minds have just slowly forgotten some concepts.

All of the examples above can give teachers headaches. The frustration comes from knowing that the curriculum and lessons reflect the skills that kids need in their futures and that once successful learning has occurred, the important concepts slowly fade away. So, here are the questions: *If educators are going to teach important things to our youth and are not also going to promote and improve memory retention, aren't teachers wasting a good deal of their efforts? Furthermore, isn't this a disservice to our youth's futures?* Clearly, teachers need to address the issue of retention of concepts and skills.

The Time Challenge

There is a potential educator reaction to the idea that we should focus on knowledge and skills retention. Some might say that they do not have time to focus on retention and review because of all the "stuff" that they have to teach in a year. Here are the key questions for this line of thinking.

Would we rather rush to get through everything in our curricula and have our kids remember very little, or would we rather get through 90-95 percent of the curricula (while taking time to review and retain) and have our kids remember most or all of it?

Furthermore, we do have time to both review and complete the curriculum. The key is that we must plan with our goals in mind as described in Chapter 18 (to maximize our available time). This is the best option.

Lasting Long-Term Memory

We have all had experiences like the following situation. Imagine that a person is told a new phone number, dials that number, and then doesn't think about that number again. He or she will likely forget it quickly, even in seconds. The information leaves the person's short-term memory. If instead, the person writes down the number, looks at it again, repeatedly says it out loud, and dials it many times, he or she is more likely to remember the number. The actions taken are shifting the number into the brain's long-term memory.

As teachers, we need to shift new information from our students' short-term memory to their long-term memory. It's not quite that easy, though. Many teachers have experienced situations in which their students learned new concepts and successfully demonstrated competence on an assessment task. It seemed that the new learning had been transferred into the long-term memory of the kids' brains. However, as months passed by, the children didn't seem to remember the new information or skills. The memories lasted only for a few days or weeks.

We need to move beyond creating memories that last for only a couple of weeks and then fade. We need to promote long-term memory that lasts for *months and years … or **lasting long-term memory**.*

There are two major categories of things that we can do to create lasting long-term memory. First, there are important things that we can do *in the process of student learning* that promote the movement of new ideas toward long-term memory. We have looked at these methods already in Chapter 17 - Learning How to Learn. Many of the strategies that improve our ability to learn also strengthen our memory of new concepts. Second, there are important things we can do *in the weeks and months after the learning occurs* to develop lasting long-term memory. This chapter will focus on the strategies that teachers should consider after the initial process of learning a topic occurs.

<u>Learning Skills from Chapter 17 that Promote the Development of Lasting Long-Term Memory *in the Process of Learning*</u>

1. **Learning Through Inquiry**
2. **Activating and Building on Prior Knowledge**
3. **Constructing the Learning of New Concepts Piece by Piece**
4. **Using New Learning for Real-World Tasks**
5. **Making Personal Connections with New Learning**
6. **Creating Depth of Understanding**
7. **Summarizing and Simplifying New Concepts**
8. **Comparing and Contrasting New Concepts**
9. **Using a Variety of Learning Methods**
10. **Taking the Time to Fully Process New Ideas**
11. **Breaking Down New Terminology**
12. **Learning New Ideas in an Easily Understood Context**
13. **Staying Focused and Alert when Learning**
14. **Retaining New Knowledge and Skills**
15. **Taking Personal Responsibility for Learning**
16. **Setting Goals and Monitoring One's Progress in Learning**
17. **Engaging in a Mindset that Leads to Success**

Take a moment and think about the ways in which the learning skills above (from Chapter 17) strengthen the ability of the human brain to retain new learning into the future. Next, move on to look at the ways that the following strategies (addressed in this chapter) can create lasting long-term memory *after* the learning occurs.

<u>Promoting Lasting Long-Term Memory *After the Learning Occurs*</u>

1. **Continuously Connecting Old Concepts to New Concepts**
2. **Continuously Using Review Activities Throughout a School Year**
3. **Using Proficiency-Based Long-Term Review Assessments**
4. **Using the Summer**

1 Continuously Connecting Old Concepts to New Concepts

After a new concept is learned in school, we cannot simply ignore it. Throughout the course of a school year, educators should work to connect new ideas to previously learned ideas. In some instances, the connections between new and old learning are obvious and easy to bring to the attention of students. In other instances, it takes more effort to find ways to revisit previously-taught ideas when addressing newer ideas. Educators need to make a conscious effort to do two things.

a) Look Forward and Plan to Connect

First, when a concept is learned in class, we need to ask ourselves if there will be a time later in the year when we can revisit this concept to review it. Then, we can make a note to ourselves in our long-term outline. (This reinforces the need for long-term planning.)

b) Look Backward and Reconnect

Second, we can look backward when teaching a concept. We can ask ourselves which previous ideas can be revisited and used to enhance new learning. The bottom line is that the more often we expose students' brains to the ideas within our curricula, the more likely young minds are to retain those ideas and create *lasting long-term memories*.

Side Note

Look Back to Previous Years
Not only can we revisit the knowledge and skills gained within the current school year, we can revisit those things attained in previous school years. If some middle school students learn about world history one year and United States history the next year, they can use lessons learned about world history to enhance lessons about our country's history. The connection reinforces memory retention. When I teach any science class, I often bring up examples from previous science classes that the students have taken. Again, the connection between the subjects deepens understanding and retention; the review of "old" ideas does the same.

Whether it is within one year or over the course of many years, continuously revisiting prior learning to connect that learning to new learning is a critical aspect of creating lasting long-term memory.

Connecting Old Concepts to New Concepts

We Should See Educators Who ...	Personal Empowerment Questions (PEQs) for Educators
👁 Look forward to plan for review opportunities later in the school year	❓ When in the future will I be able to review this concept with my students?
👁 Look back and think about previous concepts that can be reinforced when learning new concepts	❓ What previous concepts can I connect to new learning that is occurring now?
👁 Make connections to previous years' concepts	❓ What did the students learn in previous years that can be reinforced with new learning from this year?

Educators who ask questions like these help students continuously review by connecting old and new concepts.

2 Continuously Using Review Activities Throughout a School Year

Likely, the first thing that pops into many teachers' minds when they think of how to promote lasting long-term memory is to have students do activities specifically meant to review prior knowledge.

Review activities can take many forms, including games, journal reviews, writing review essays, simple question sheets, projects that tie together ideas, or review tests. One challenge is that educators might view these activities as activities that use valuable class time needed to learn newer concepts. Again, I have to ask the question: ***If no time is dedicated to creating lasting long-term memory, what good does it do to get through a bunch of stuff … when the students don't remember that stuff later. I specifically use the word "stuff" because when students forget what they have learned, their learning goes from being something that could empower them in their futures to being "stuff" that they temporarily knew.*** (In order to save class time, some review activities can be assigned as homework.)

Example

I have found a review technique that uses the following steps to be quite successful:
- I distribute a master review (MR) of everything students have learned. As the year moves along, I continue to add to the MR.
- Rather than allowing students to forget the items on the review, I give a very short (three minutes maximum) review quiz two-three times per week. Each short quiz focuses on a portion of the MR. This narrow focus allows students to give proper attention to each small portion of their MR without being overwhelmed.
- After quizzing on a few sections of the MR, students take a back-track quiz over the materials from the past few quizzes.
- Then we continue to quiz our way through the MR one section at a time, pausing to take a back-track quiz periodically.
- Sometimes, I'll give a mega backtrack quiz that goes all the way back to the beginning of the MR.

This whole review and backtrack process creates great results, including:
- Students review continuously so that they do not forget previously learned knowledge and skills.
- By taking very short quizzes a few times per week, a tiny amount of class time is shifted from new learning. (It actually saves time, because there is no eventual need to dedicate time to relearning forgotten concepts.)
- By focusing on small portions of material, student minds more effectively focus on each portion of review and remember it.
- By taking a periodic backtrack quiz on previously reviewed sections of the MR, kids do not let items slide out of their brains. Furthermore, periodic mega backtrack review quizzes (that go back to the beginning of all the review materials) help maintain knowledge and skills in the long run.
- When my students get to the end of the year, the concepts they understand and remember the best are the *oldest* concepts that they have reviewed the most! The continuous review makes kids *maintain and enhance* prior knowledge.

Using Review Activities

We Should See Educators Who ...	PEQs for Educators
👁 Engage students with meaningful review activities throughout the school year 👁 Assess the curriculum and plan for opportunities to review 👁 Recognize the importance of stimulating students to review and remember new concepts, rather than simply allowing students to forget new concepts	❓ What types of review activities can I ask students to perform during the year? ❓ When is the best time for me to stimulate students with review activities? ❓ Why is it important that I take the time to include review activities in my class?

Educators who ask questions like these stimulate students to review and retain new knowledge and skills. Students develop the habit of review.

3   Using Proficiency-Based Long-Term Review Assessments

Proficiency-Based Long-Term Review Assessments

There is a common problem with review activities. If a class does a review activity or review assessment, they get exposure to previously learned concepts. But exposure in itself is not good enough. We need to make sure that students actually regain ideas that they have forgotten and relearn ideas with which they originally struggled. Many review activities expose kids to past learning, but do not impose concept retention and relearning.

To deal with this issue, we can bring back the idea of proficiency-based assessments, discussed in Chapter 19 (Using Assessments to Empower 21ˢᵗ Century Students). In this case, we can require students to meet a minimum proficiency on long-term review tests. A few years ago, the science department at my school set out to do just this thing.

About every ten to twelve weeks, each science student performed the proficiency-based assessment for his or her science class. This assessment was cumulative and included all of the major concepts and skills addressed from the beginning of the year up to that point. We required that students redo the assessment until they met a minimum level of proficiency. Kids were given opportunities to redo portions (that addressed various topics) of the assessment to demonstrate a minimum level of overall understanding. Alternate versions of the assessment were created, so that kids couldn't simply memorize the original assessment … they actually had to relearn or review the concepts. Students who achieved minimum proficiency in their first attempt were also allowed to retry portions of the assessment in order to drive up their score. Thus, students of all ability levels were encouraged to review and achieve their highest potential. (Special needs students got modifications for the activity to meet their needs. Also, modifications to the assessment were made for those who struggled with the format, but understood the concepts.)

Valuable Aspects and Outcomes

Proficiency-Based Long-Term Review Assessments …

- Set the expectation that everyone can learn.

- Go beyond simple review activities in such a way that it expects students to remediate forgotten concepts or items on which they originally struggled.

- Stimulate students to review.

- Stimulate students to talk to instructors and peers to get help on concepts about which they are "shaky." (This is something that kids might not otherwise do.)

- Move beyond being a form of review to something that promotes remediation … a large focus of the previous chapter.

- Meet the needs of all students. While one child strives to meet the minimum proficiency, another is stimulated to shoot for 100 percent.

- Serve as a diagnostic tool. By breaking the assessment into sections, students can identify the topics about which they need review or remediation and then focus on those topics. When they retry the assessment, they focus on their own personal needs as a learner and retake the sections on which they personally need improvement.

- Succeed in creating a lasting long-term memory. Before the use of the proficiency-based activity, we gave a semester exam in January that covered the first half of the school year. Then, we gave a semester exam in June that covered the second half of the school year. Because the assessment activity helped our students continuously review, we were able to give a final exam in June that was a cumulative assessment of the whole year… and grades got *better*. Think about that. The grades on an assessment (given in June) that covered the learning goals of the *whole year* were better than the grades we previously got using an assessment (given in June) that covered the learning goals of just the second half of the year.

    When using the proficiency-based assessment, our students were in a completely different situation when they took their final exams. In the years before using the assessments, kids would try to remember and relearn all the concepts and skills that they addressed months before the final exams. These older topics were the hardest parts of their final exam. After using proficiency-based assessments, continuous review every eight weeks meant that the oldest concepts and skills were the *easiest* to remember. That was clearly a great situation for kids.

- Improve student confidence.

- Promote continuous review, making it easier to teach new concepts that rely on an understanding of older concepts.

- Promote mastery. I have heard about schools using periodic review tests, but their process simply stops at giving the test and assigning a score. While this will promote review before the assessment, it does not stimulate students to remediate, relearn, and review those items that they did not get correct. The proficiency-based review stimulates this very important extra step.

- Might improve test scores on state and national assessments. (The focus of proficiency-based assessments might not be for improving performance on a state assessment test, but this might be the result.)

Proficiency-Based Long-Term Review Assessments

We Should See Educators Who ...	PEQs for Educators
👁 Implement review activities that promote proficiency and stimulate students to meet their highest potential 👁 Empower students with a review activity structure that helps students diagnose their level of understanding and then improve 👁 Show confidence in students	❓ What types of review activities will stimulate students to become proficient and strive to meet their potential, rather than simply accepting results that are below their potential? ❓ How will my review activities empower students to diagnose their level of understanding? ❓ How will my review activities enable students to improve? (What resources will be at their disposal?) ❓ What mechanisms can I build into my assessments to stimulate students to take the activities seriously? (Will I correlate a grade with minimum proficiency? Give a reward for mastery?)

Educators who ask questions like these stimulate students to achieve their highest potential on review activities.

4 Using the Summer

Because maintaining knowledge and skills stored in our lasting long-term memory requires that we continuously revisit and review them, we must consider what happens in the summer. Our students can't afford the summer break to be a time when they slowly forget the concepts and skills that they have learned. This is especially true of elementary school students who are learning basic reading and math skills. At a very minimum, schools should send home review materials with students (that include fun games). Unfortunately, these resources can get lost or forgotten by students during the summer. To avoid this challenge, schools can periodically mail or email review activities or tips for review during the summer. Activities can also be posted on a website. Summer reading can be promoted in various ways, including the promise of prizes for the amount of reading done over the summer. Schools can offer summer programs (short or long, daily or weekly) to bridge the gap between school years. This would be useful not only for elementary students, but for students of all ages.

We shouldn't simply look at the summer as a time during which we need to maintain knowledge and skills. It can be a time to advance the skills of students, whether they need remediation or higher level skills. Any system or program that turns the summer into an advantage for students, rather than a disadvantage, is helpful. As always, the involvement of parents is very beneficial. Workshops can help parents learn strategies to help their children during the summer break.

Using the Summer

We Should See Educators Who ...	PEQs for Educators
👁 Stimulate students to review and learn in the summer	❓ What methods can I use to stimulate review and learning during the summer?
👁 Involve parents in summer review and learning	❓ How can I get parents involved in summer review and learning?

Educators who ask questions like these stimulate students to maintain and expand knowledge and skills in the summer.

⬅ Retention of Knowledge and Skills: Wrap-up ➡

As mentioned earlier in this chapter, promoting and maintaining lasting long-term memory is as important as the original learning of new ideas. If we don't stimulate young minds to remember what they learn, we are effectively wasting our efforts. We must help our students learn and retain the knowledge and skills that will make them successful and empower them in the future. This should happen continuously during and after our teaching of knowledge and skills.

Thinking About It
- **What are your strategies for helping kids retain new knowledge and skills?**
- **What new ideas would you like to try?**
- **What are the best ideas for long-term review and memory retention in your educational setting?**

Let's add retention of knowledge and skills to our "System of Thoughtful 21st Century Teaching Practices." (New ideas are in red.)

System of Thoughtful 21ˢᵗ Century Teaching Practices

Beginning of the School Year:

Make Long-Term Plan for Teaching Major Topics and Skills

Determine Proactive Interventions and Plan for Timing of Implementation During Teaching

Planning to Teach a Unit:

Determine Goals for Topic or Unit (curricular goals and 21st century skills)

Create Performance Assessments for Topic or Unit that challenge *all* students

Create Lessons that Prepare Students for Assessments (interwoven with formative assessments and methods for promoting retention)

Teaching a Unit:

Teach Lessons that Prepare Students for Assessments (interwoven with formative assessments to help *provide feedback, identify misconceptions, guide immediate interventions, stimulate student reflection, and drive further teaching* and are also interwoven with methods for promoting knowledge and skill retention)

Perform Assessments that Measure Attainment of Goals (use data to improve methods; make students aware of progress)

To Be Done Continuously During the Year As Needed:

Implement Short-Term Intervention Systems to deal with issues that go beyond quick and immediate classroom fixes (such as providing a tutor; providing a mentor; reteaching concepts; or promoting better study skills, better organization, improved assignment completion, and enhanced connections)

Implement Long-Term Interventions in order to deal with large and long-term student challenges that threaten overall educational success

Perform Periodic Review Activities to promote lasting long-term knowledge, skill retention, and proficiency

How Does This Chapter Support the Goals of This Book?

Let's take a moment to think about the ways in which the ideas of this chapter help us address the three main goals of this book by looking at the "Building Blocks of a 21st Century Education" on page 13 and the "Daily Thoughts for Educators" on page 18. We now have guidelines for thoughtfully promoting the retention of new learning which help us put together the pieces of an empowering 21st century education.

Make Note of Your Great Ideas!

If you haven't already, note your ideas for implementing the practices in this chapter in your Teacher Empowerment Menu (for 21st Century Educators). In the future, you can easily reference these personalized ideas.

22 | Avoiding and Overcoming Obstacles to Creating a 21st Century Education

It is very obvious that the old methods of education have to be overhauled. Our youth can no longer remain in classrooms where they sit, listen, and then regurgitate information. We need to get serious about creating connections, stimulating students to learn the curriculum with a 21st Century Challenge, and using thoughtful teaching practices to put these educational building blocks together. There are some potential hurdles to achieving an empowering 21st Century Education. Let's look at how to achieve our 21st century goals without stumbling on these challenges.

Avoiding and Overcoming Obstacles to Creating a 21st Century Education

1. **Creating a Vision with Goals**
2. **Creating Buy-In and Commitment**
3. **Being Consistent without "Kicks and Drops"**
4. **Feeling Empowered to Meet the Great Needs of a 21st Century Education**
5. **Embracing Teamwork**
6. **Using a Systematic Problem Solving Process**

1 Creating a Vision with Goals

If the school staff members set out to create positive change, they must begin by creating a vision for success. Creating mission statements, vision statements, or even acronyms to describe a general philosophy is good. The problem is that these statements can often sound lofty and give limited direction to the staff. For instance, the staff might create a school improvement vision statement that includes the statements "elevate student success" and "develop student skills that are relevant to a global economy." These statements sound great, but what do they mean to the school staff? Does "elevate student success" mean that the educators should try to improve the graduation rate? Student grades? Test scores? Does "develop student skills that are relevant in a global economy" mean that the school needs more focus on creativity?

Interpersonal skills? Critical thinking? Technology? All of these? In other words, what goals does the staff want to achieve with the vision?

A good vision statement is useful only if it is accompanied by specific and accomplishable goals that support the general vision. These goals give the teachers, administrators, and others something toward which they can work.

Side Note

Monitor Progress Toward Goals

Goals should be created so that their success can be monitored. Formal data can be tracked, such as monitoring statistics on graduation rates or collecting evidence of creativity through student project portfolios. Informal data can also be observed, such as teachers monitoring the general attitudes of students toward school spirit. If a staff has specific goals that are realistic and that staff can monitor their success with formal and informal data, their vision can become a reality rather than becoming a superficial pie in the sky.

Creating a Vision with Goals

We Should See Educators Who ...	Personal Empowerment Questions (PEQs) for Educators
👁 Create a vision for the types of knowledge, skills, attitudes, and habits that students will develop in the educators' school	❓ What knowledge, skills, attitudes, and habits will our students need in order to thrive in the 21ˢᵗ century?
👁 Create a vision that empowers students for the 21ˢᵗ century	❓ What empowering educational vision can we set out to achieve?
👁 Identify goals that need to be met to achieve the vision	❓ What goals do we need to meet in order to achieve our vision?
👁 Monitor progress toward the vision and goals	❓ How will we monitor our progress toward the vision and goals?

Educators who ask questions like these will dedicate themselves to helping their students thrive in the 21ˢᵗ century.

② Creating Buy-In and Commitment

In my years of interacting with educators from many different places, I have found that the success of a program or philosophy is profoundly affected by the level of buy-in generated among a staff. In order to be motivated to do something, a staff needs to be convinced that they are doing it for an important reason and that there are thoughtful strategies for implementation.

I set out to create buy-in among the readers of this book by beginning with a description of the 21ˢᵗ century circumstances that face our youth. Then, I detailed which skills, attitudes, and habits are necessary for success in the 21ˢᵗ century.

Similarly, we educators can create buy-in among our peers by educating them about the realities of the 21ˢᵗ century. We must work to get out the word. Educators need to know which skills, attitudes, and habits are required in the 21ˢᵗ century. Additionally, educators need to know how to promote these skills.

We must let our peers know that *a new 21st Century Education is incredibly important, and it is here to stay.* It is not simply the topic de jour in the educational community. *It is something that we can and must address.*

22 - Avoiding and Overcoming Obstacles

An Engaging Online Video is Available to Spread the Word

I have created and posted, on my website, a short online video which outlines the need for a 21st Century Education. When the website opens, this engaging video draws people in with dramatic and inspiring ideas, sounds, and sights. To spread the word of a new 21st Century Education, you can send others the link for the website, www.empoweringyourstudents.com.

Creating Buy-In and Commitment

We Should See Educators Who ...	PEQs for Educators
👁 Recognize the challenges of the 21st century that our youth face	❓ What challenges do our kids face in the 21st century?
👁 Recognize that they have the power to make positive change	❓ In what ways am I empowered to help my students thrive in this new world?
👁 Buy in and commit to promoting a 21st Century Education	❓ How will I commit to helping my students?
👁 Are willing to change old practices and continuously seek improvement	❓ Why is it important that I am willing to continuously improve the ways in which I empower my students?
👁 Stimulate other educators to act	❓ How will I educate other educators about the 21st century skills that our students need and stimulate these other educators to act?

Educators who ask questions like these will dedicate themselves to helping their students thrive in the 21st century.

3 Being Consistent without "Kicks and Drops"

As mentioned in Chapter 2, educators often experience a series of "kicks and drops" in schools and in the educational community at large. Each year seems to bring a new "kick" (or educational goal) into which a ton of energy is poured. Then, this kick seems to get "dropped" over time as new kicks come along and shift everyone's focus.

We must break this system of "kicks and drops." This would be true with or without new 21st century educational demands. In an attempt to break this cycle, this book offers a few ideas.

Avoiding "Kicks and Drops"

- Using a "Teacher Empowerment Menu"
- "Meshing" a 21st Century Challenge within Learning Activities
- Avoiding an Overemphasis on Various Goals
- Using "Daily Thoughts for Educators" to Keep Educators Thinking about All Goals, not Just "Kicks"

a) Using a "Teacher Empowerment Menu"

A Teacher Empowerment Menu (for 21ˢᵗ Century Educators) has been created that mirrors the key ideas of this book. This menu is extremely valuable, because it allows teachers to have an all-encompassing reference to which they can refer continuously. It helps break the cycle of "kicks and drops," because it creates a single place for new ideas and strategies as they are developed. This year's "kick" will not fade when next year comes, because the "kick" will be contained within the "Teacher Empowerment Menu," along with all of the school's previous "kicks." Now, instead of slowly forgetting about previous educational focuses, teachers can continuously build a master plan of educational focuses. By having a reference to the ideas that are important to education, teachers can think of ways to interweave various important goals, rather than cycling through them over the years. The "Teacher Empowerment Menu" promotes organization.

Continuous referral to the menu can remind a teacher to ask himself or herself a question like, "Have I recently connected with all of my students in some small or large way?" A teacher might then realize that he or she does not yet have a great connection with a particular student, stimulating him or her to chat with that child and seek out a connection. The Teacher Empowerment Menu might also make a teacher say, "Hey, the topic I am about to teach can include more critical thinking." Then, he or she is stimulated to tweak the lesson for the topic so that it stimulates kids to develop critical thinking skills.

b) "Meshing" a 21ˢᵗ Century Challenge within Learning Activities

When educators address a new educational goal by adding new activities to their regular curricular activities, time constraints arise. It becomes increasingly difficult to accommodate new ideas. So, as new focuses (or "kicks") arise over the years, teachers tend to let go of some older activities. How do we get around this challenge of time and consistency?

This book continuously reminds us that we must *interweave* or **"mesh"** our connections and 21ˢᵗ Century Challenge within the regular curriculum. This saves time and allows us to include many strategies (in our lessons) that are relevant to the 21ˢᵗ century without finding additional class time. This meshing technique keeps us from cycling through different focuses from year to year.

Not only does the embedding of 21ˢᵗ century skills within lessons allow us the time to meet our goals, but it does one other critical thing. When we design and redesign curricular lessons so that they *include* the elements of connections and a 21ˢᵗ Century Challenge, we won't drop these elements in the future … which we might do if the elements are tacked on as extra activities. Interweaving the goals of this book within our regular lessons, rather than adding them on top of our regular lessons, will help us consistently address our 21ˢᵗ century educational goals into the future.

c) Avoiding an Overemphasis on Various Goals

When educators get on "kicks," they generally try to address something that they perceive to be lacking in their school or classroom. The problem is that a huge emphasis on a "kick" will naturally draw attention away from other important goals. Then, years down the road, staff members will realize that while they are energetically focusing on newer goals (or "kicks"), they are neglecting older important goals. This creates the need to address the neglected goals with yet other new "kicks" … and the cycle continues.

In this book, we have focused on weaving *multiple* 21st century skills, attitudes, and habits into our lessons *at the same time*. There is no reason that one lesson cannot address many goals of this book, such as exercising critical thinking, social skills, and making connections. By doing this, we reduce the need for new "kicks" each year. Instead, we ask ourselves, "What are all of the possible skills and goals that can be supported in this unit, activity, or lesson?"

d) Using "Daily Thoughts for Educators" to Keep Educators Thinking about All Goals, not Just "Kicks"

By referencing the "Daily Thoughts for Educators" at the end of Chapter 2, teachers can focus on all the goals of a 21st Century Education, rather than getting on "kicks."

Overall Being Consistent Without "Kicks and Drops"

We Should See Educators Who ...	PEQs for Educators
👁 Use tools of organization, such as the "Teacher Empowerment Menu"	❓ What are the goals of a 21st Century Education?
👁 Focus on interweaving multiple skills, attitudes, and habits of the 21st century into their lessons, rather than jumping on a "kick" (and "dropping" other important goals)	❓ How can I interweave the skills, attitudes, and habits of the 21st century within the regular curriculum in such a way that I will be consistent in their emphasis?
👁 Use long-term planning, and reflect on past practices and potential future practices in order to avoid a "drop" of previously successful strategies	❓ How can I use an organizational tool like the "Teacher Empowerment Menu" in order to keep myself focused on my major educational goals and the strategies for achieving them?
👁 Consider a broad set of curricular and 21st century learning goals when planning	❓ What are all the 21st century teaching goals that I can accomplish within this lesson, activity, or unit?
👁 Engage in the "Daily Thoughts for Educators" to assess how well their lessons and practices will empower students for the 21st century	❓ Have I engaged in the "Daily Thoughts for Educators" (at the end of Ch. 2) today so that I am sure to empower my students?

Educators who ask questions like these will avoid the "kicks and drops" that shift the focus from one important goal to another, rather than integrating them together.

Feeling Empowered to Meet the Great Needs of a 21ˢᵗ Century Education
4

Educators might get discouraged when they consider the challenges our youth will face in the real world and the new 21ˢᵗ century economy. It might seem that the task of preparing our kids is too overwhelming.

This book was designed to make the task quite manageable. We have major goals broken into building blocks. These building blocks are addressed one at a time with specific smaller goals and strategies for implementation offered.

Quite often, society talks generally about the challenges we face without talking nearly as much about the solutions for overcoming them. This book avoids simply telling you about the challenge at hand and then leaving you with some very general or vague ideas for what to do; in your hands is a roadmap.

Feeling Empowered to Meet the Great Needs of a 21st Century Education

We Should See Educators Who ...	PEQs for Educators
👁 Use a systematic approach to address the challenge of empowering students for the 21ˢᵗ century (such as the approach presented in this book)	❓ How can we systematically prepare our kids for the 21ˢᵗ century?
👁 Achieve the larger goals of a 21ˢᵗ Century Education by addressing smaller building blocks with effective strategies	❓ What major goals must we achieve to empower our students?
	❓ What framework will we use to address these goals?
	❓ What are the building blocks of a new education that we must address, and what strategies will allow us to address these building blocks?

Educators who ask questions like these will systematically address the large and small goals necessary for empowering our youth.

Embracing Teamwork
5

A 21ˢᵗ Century Education can draw some educators out of their comfort zone. Because of this, we must support and motivate our peers. We must work with one another to find great ideas to implement the strategies that will support our students' futures. By working together, we are much more likely to boldly attack this task and stay consistent.

Working as a team boosts creativity by bringing together a diversity of ideas. I have encountered many situations in which a group has generated amazing ideas that would not have been generated without the collective knowledge and skills of the peers involved. Working as a team also creates more buy-in among the people who will carry out a plan. Everyone becomes invested.

For all of these reasons, we should make teamwork a focus in addressing the creation of a 21ˢᵗ Century Education.

Embracing Teamwork

We Should See Educators Who ...	PEQs for Educators
👁 Support one another as they work toward common goals 👁 Derive creativity from the collective ideas of a group 👁 Create buy-in as a result of mutual ownership of ideas among a group	❓ How can I support my colleagues in creating a 21st Century Education? ❓ In what ways can others help me? ❓ How can we use our collective ideas most effectively to empower our kids? ❓ How can we involve everyone in the development of new ideas, so that we motivate through mutual ownership of practices?

Educators who ask questions like these support one another to create successful strategies that empower students for the 21st century.

6   Using a Systematic Problem-Solving Process

In many different professions, there is a difficulty to overcome in group meetings: keeping the group focused on a particular goal. Educational professionals can encounter this same problem. Imagine a school improvement meeting where educators discuss some goals that the enthusiastic staff members have created. There is the potential for individuals to move from topic to topic without focusing on one goal long enough make any progress. Staff members might say a variety of things on a variety of topics, such as: "I have an idea for improving student motivation," "I believe that students are doing poorly on tests because of inadequate study skills," or "I think that we should have a staff party to create cohesion." A lot of important challenges, concerns, and solutions might be discussed on a variety of topics, but in the end ... it is possible that nothing comes of the meeting. The people involved may feel they have discussed a lot of important things, but they end up with no focused strategies for addressing their goals. The problem is that they did not focus on particular goals and did not follow any process for dissecting the goals and creating strategies. So what can they do?

They can use a problem-solving process similar to the Future Problem Solving process described in the Final Thoughts at the end of the Higher Order Thinking Skills Unit. Let's look at how the process can be utilized in school improvement.

Problem-Solving Process for School Improvement

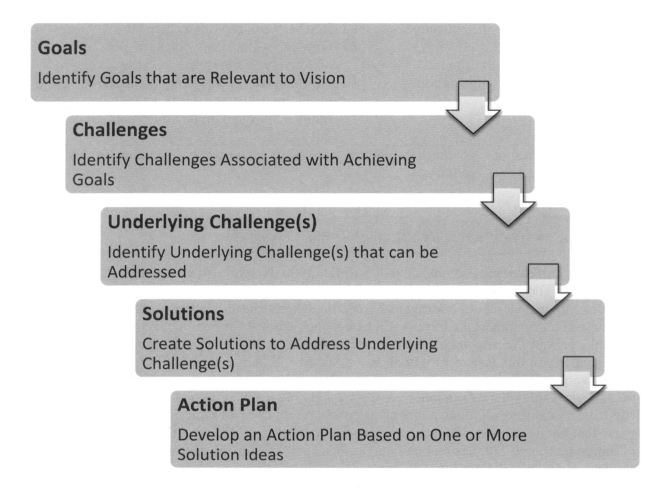

Goals

Identify Goals that are Relevant to Vision

Challenges

Identify Challenges Associated with Achieving Goals

Underlying Challenge(s)

Identify Underlying Challenge(s) that can be Addressed

Solutions

Create Solutions to Address Underlying Challenge(s)

Action Plan

Develop an Action Plan Based on One or More Solution Ideas

Let's look in depth at each step. To help us understand how this problem-solving process can be applied, we will follow an example.

Steps of Problem-Solving Process	Example of Each Step
1. **Goals** - Identify a specific goal for a meeting that will be discussed by the staff or a smaller group. Once the group picks *one* goal upon which to focus, they will stick to it and not stray to other unrelated topics during the problem-solving process. This strategy points everyone in the direction of coming out of the meeting with something specific accomplished, rather than scattering attention.	1. **Goal Examples** - Possible goals can be to improve grades, increase ACT/SAT scores, improve parent communication, or increase extra-curricular participation. (For the continuation of the following steps, we will imagine that a group of educators has chosen to focus on "improving student grades" in their school.)
2. **Challenges** - Discuss and identify the challenges that are associated with accomplishing the goal. This should involve extensive brainstorming with the group writing down all of their ideas. Everyone picks apart the issue until they are satisfied that they have noted all the relevant challenges.	2. **Challenge Examples** - As a group sets out to "improve student grades" in their school, let's imagine that they list the following challenges related to the topic. a) Students not turning in assignments b) Poor assessment scores c) Poor attendance d) Lack of long-term retention of knowledge e) Poor student focus in class
3. **Underlying Challenges (to address) -** Look at the various challenges identified in the previous step. Look for an underlying challenge that you would like to solve. The underlying challenge can be the most important problem or it can be the root cause of a variety of challenges you face in reaching your goal. Form a Question for the Underlying Challenge - After determining an underlying challenge, the group should formulate a question they can use to generate ideas to address their underlying challenge. The question should be phrased in the following way: *In what ways might we _____, so that _____?*	3. **Underlying Challenges (to address) Example** - The group looks over the challenges listed above and decides that their biggest concerns are late assignments, poor assessment scores, and poor long-term retention. The staff decides that the probable root cause of these challenges is an inadequate level of student studying and discipline outside the classroom. This is a core issue that they would like to improve. It underlies their major concerns. Form a Question for the Underlying Challenge - This question will allow the group to generate ideas to address the underlying challenge: *In what ways might we **improve the studying and work that our students do outside of the classroom,** so that **assignment and assessment scores improve?***

4. **Solutions** - Look at the underlying problem and brainstorm as many solution ideas as possible for addressing it. The group needs to stay focused on the underlying problem they have chosen to fix.

   The group can do research to see what other schools have tried. (When doing this, the group should be careful not to assume that something that works in one school will work in another.)

4. **Solution Examples** - The staff members create the following list of possible solutions:
   a) Teachers promote a study skill of the week in all classrooms.
   b) Students are required to keep a journal of which assignments they have due at school.
   c) Teachers communicate with the parents of students who need to be more disciplined outside the classroom.
   d) The staff works to make homework better connect with students to increase motivation.
   e) The staff has a study skills seminar for struggling students.
   f) The staff implements an intervention system of consequences and rewards in order to promote dedication outside the classroom.

5. **Action Plan** - After generating as many solution ideas as possible, the group generates a realistic action plan using the best of the ideas that were generated in the previous step.

   When deciding which solution(s) to use, the following criteria should be considered.
   - What is realistic?
   - What resources do we have for our action plan?
   - How can we create real, not superficial, change?
   - What can be done to get the staff to buy into the plan?
   - What can be done to involve and motivate those involved to get things done?
   - What data will be kept in order to monitor progress?
   - What will be done, if the plan works, to keep it going?
   - What are some back-up ideas if the plan does not work?

5. **Action Plan Example** - After considering the possible solutions and some criteria for assessing the solutions, the group decides to create an intervention system that uses rewards and consequences with parent communication involved.

   They also decide to work toward creating more engaging activities for homework that create connections between the students and the concepts of the activities.

   Teachers will keep data on the assessment averages and assignment scores before and after the action plan is enacted. The staff will later assess the system in order to see if the plan adequately addresses the underlying problem.

Sometimes a group might identify two or three underlying challenges that they would like to address individually. Each underlying challenge could be carried through the rest of the problem-solving process. In our example, the group identified "study behaviors" as their key issue to address. If a school also had a serious issue with attendance, then it would be appropriate to create a second underlying challenge, brainstorm solutions for it, and generate another action plan related to attendance.

Why is This Process so Useful?

a) Focus on One Goal at a Time

First of all, the process forces a group to identify a single goal and focus on it. They can worry about other goals later in the meeting or at other meetings. With this attention on one topic at a time, everyone is helping address the task at hand. Minds are not wandering and taking the group off task. (The more time spent off task, the less likely a group will develop a practical plan of action.)

b) Focus on One Step of the Process at a Time

Another huge reason that this process works so well is that it forces a group to think about the same step of the process at the same time. Everyone first focuses on the challenges associated with a goal and then everyone focuses on the underlying problem. This sequence of steps prevents a group from having a circular discussion in which some are talking about challenges, some are talking about solutions, and yet others are talking about how to create an action plan.

c) Sequential Dissection of Goal

This process also forces stepwise thinking and forces people to think about the core and underlying challenges before they start dreaming up solutions. Without this logical pattern, you may have a meeting at which group members are thinking about solutions before they have even identified what needs to be solved. An illogical pattern can often lead to groups creating plans of action that leave many people wondering, "Gee, how is this plan going to lead to anything truly productive?" This is avoided with systematic thinking.

d) Works with All Group Sizes

Another reason that this process is so useful is that it can be used in groups of all sizes from three people to fifty. A large staff can tackle one issue together or break into smaller groups and address different goals in each group.

e) Universal Process

This process is universal. It makes sense for problem solving in business, education, medicine, social life, or government. This is why educators should use this process in school improvement and teach this process in our classrooms.

Using a Systematic Problem-Solving Process

We Should See Educators Who ...	PEQs for Educators

👁 Use a systematic process for addressing school improvement goals
👁 Use the following problem-solving steps:
  • Create goals
  • Identify challenges to overcome in reaching the goals
  • Identify one or more underlying challenge(s) to solve
  • Create solutions for the underlying challenge(s)
  • Create an action plan that uses one or more of the solutions to address the underlying challenge
👁 Work as a team to solve problems
👁 Work through the problem-solving process in a stepwise fashion
	❓ What goal for our school would we like to address?
	❓ What challenges do we need to overcome to achieve our goal?
	❓ What underlying challenge(s) should we solve in order to achieve our goal?
	❓ Which solution(s) will work the best, be the most feasible, create real change, and make the best use of our available resources?
	❓ How can we create an action plan for our best solution(s) that will stimulate staff buy-in, motivate the people involved, measure results through data collection, use resources wisely, and have long-lasting effects?
	❓ How can we work as a team to address our school goals and solve problems?

Educators who ask questions like these will work as a team in an efficient and stepwise manner to solve the problems that stand in the way of achieving the goals of a school.

Avoiding and Overcoming Obstacles: Wrap-up

By being mindful of the potential roadblocks that can affect our quest to deliver a 21st Century Education, we can proactively work to avoid these obstacles. This is crucial if we wish to prepare our kids for the world that awaits them.

Thinking About It

- **How can the Teacher Empowerment Menu help you empower your students?**
- **How can you create a vision for your school with goals that will promote the vision?**
- **How can you create buy-in and dedication among your staff toward creating a 21st Century Education that empowers your students?**
- **How does a systematic problem-solving process improve the ability of a group to overcome challenges?**
- **What are some challenges that you would like to overcome using a systematic problem-solving process with your staff?**

Bibliography

Future Problem Solving Program International, Inc. - Home. Retrieved from Future Problem Solving Program International, Inc.: http://fpspi.org/index.html

Offshoring Tax Returns Preparation to India, ValueNotes. (2006, Nov). Retrieved from Research and Markets: http://www.researchandmarkets.com/reports/c46387

Understanding High School Graduation Rates. (2009, July). Retrieved from Alliance for Excellent Education: http://www.all4ed.org/publication_material/understanding_HSgradrates

The World Factbook - Country Comparison: Population. (2012, July est.). Retrieved from Central Intelligence Agency: https://www.cia.gov/library/publications/the-world-factbook/rankorder/2119rank.html

Anderson, L. & Krathwohl, D. (2001). *A Taxonomy for Learning, Teaching, and Assessing: A Revision of Bloom's Taxonomy of Educational Objectives*. New York: Addison Wesley Longman, Inc.

Bergin, C. & Bergin, D. (2009, June). Attachment in the Classroom. *Educational Psychology Review, 21*, 141-170. Retrieved from Springer: http://rd.springer.com/article/10.1007/s10648-009-9104-0#

Bergmann, J. & Sams, A. (2011). *How the Flipped Classroom Was Born*. Retrieved from The Daily Riff: How the Flipped Classroom is Radically Transforming Learning: http://www.thedailyriff.com/articles/how-the-flipped-classroom-is-radically-transforming-learning-536.php

Brookhart, S. (2009). *Grading*. Upper Saddle River, NJ: Pearson Education, Inc.

Casner-Lotto, J., Barrington, L., & Wright, M. (2006, Oct). *Are They Really Ready To Work: Employers' Perspectives on the Basic Knowledge and Applied Skills of New Entrants to the 21st Century U.S. Workforce*. Retrieved from The Partnership for 21st Century Skills: http://www.p21.org/storage/documents/FINAL_REPORT_PDF09-29-06.pdf

Dweck, C. (2007). *Mindset: The New Psychology of Success*. New York: Ballantine Books.

Eberle, B. (1996). *Scamper: Games for Imagination Development*. Waco, TX: Prufrock Press, Inc.

ETR Associates. *What is Service-Learning?* Retrieved from National Service-Learning Clearinghouse: http://www.servicelearning.org/what-service-learning

Friedman, T. (2005). *The World is Flat: A Brief History of the Twenty-first Century*. New York: Farrar, Straus and Giroux.

Huff, D. (1993). *How to Lie with Statistics*. New York: W. W. Norton & Company.

Wiggins, G. & McTighe, J. (2001). *Understanding by Design*. Upper Saddle River, NJ: Prentice-Hall, Inc.

As of the publication of this book in 2012, all webpage links were active.